Apache Camel Developer's Cookbook

Solve common integration tasks with over 100 easily accessible Apache Camel recipes

Scott Cranton

Jakub Korab

BIRMINGHAM - MUMBAI

Apache Camel Developer's Cookbook

First published: December 2013

Production Reference: 1181213

Published by Packt Publishing Ltd.
Livery Place
35 Livery Street
Birmingham B3 2PB, UK.

ISBN 978-1-78217-030-3

www.packtpub.com

Cover Image by
VisitRenoTahoe.com and Reno-Sparks Convention and Visitors Authority (RSCVA)

Credits

Authors

Scott Cranton

Jakub Korab

Reviewers

Bilgin Ibryam

Claus Ibsen

Christian Posta

Phil Wilkins

Acquisition Editors

Saleem Ahmed

Sam Wood

Lead Technical Editor

Ankita Shashi

Technical Editors

Dipika Gaonkar

Pramod Kumavat

Tarunveer Shetty

Project Coordinator

Anugya Khurana

Proofreaders

Simran Bhogal

Maria Gould

Indexers

Hemangini Bari

Tejal R. Soni

Graphics

Ronak Dhruv

Abhinash Sahu

Production Coordinator

Arvindkumar Gupta

Cover Work

Arvindkumar Gupta

About the Authors

Scott Cranton is an open source software contributor and evangelist. He has been working with Apache Camel since the release of version 1.5 almost 5 years ago, and has over 20 years of commercial experience in middleware software as a developer, architect, and consultant. During his time at FuseSource, and now Red Hat, he has worked closely with many core committers for Apache Camel, ActiveMQ, ServiceMix, Karaf, and CXF. He has also helped many companies successfully create and deploy large and complex integration and messaging systems using Camel and other open source projects.

He divides his professional time between hacking code, delivering webinars on using Camel and open source, and helping companies to learn how to use Camel to solve their integration problems.

I want to thank my amazing wife, Mary Elizabeth, for putting up with me these many years, and always answering the phone when I'd call late at night from the office while I've got a compile going. This book would not have been possible without her always being there for me no matter what. To my three wonderful children, Gilbert, Eliza, and Lucy, who always make me smile especially during crazy weekend writing sessions when they'd want me to take a break, "... but Dad, it's the weekend..." I love you all!

Jakub Korab is a consulting software engineer specializing in integration and messaging. With a formal background in software engineering and distributed systems, in the 14 years that he has worked in software across the telecoms, financial services, and banking industries, he naturally gravitated from web development towards systems integration. When he discovered Apache Camel, it became apparent to him how much time and effort it could have saved him in the past compared to writing bespoke integration code, and he has not looked back since.

Over the years, working as a consultant, he has helped dozens of clients build scalable, fault-tolerant, and performant systems integrations. He currently runs his own specialist consultancy, Ameliant, which focuses on systems integration and messaging using a stack of integration products from the Apache Software Foundation, of which Camel is a corner stone.

When not gluing systems together, you will find him spending time with his young family, and far too infrequently kitesurfing or skiing—neither of which he gets much chance to do in his adopted home, London.

The writing of this book has taken place against the background of starting a new company, a huge amount of work travel, a quickly growing baby, house move, and hundreds of little distractions that get in the way of sitting down in what is left of the day to put pen to paper. It could never have happened without the love, support, and understanding of my wife, Anne-Marie. It has been a team effort. Thank you.

Also to my little girl, Alex, for helping me keep it all in perspective.

Acknowledgments

We would like to thank the Apache Camel community for being so awesome. Very welcoming and vibrant, they have always been willing to answer questions and accept code contributions. Big thanks to the many, many Camel community members.

We would like to also thank all the reviewers, editors, and unseen people in the background. Getting a book out is a substantial project of which the writing is only one part, and it could not have happened without you.

Thanks to Rob Davies, Claus Ibsen, and the whole Fuse team for showing us how much fun open source is by always being there to answer questions, geek out about some new project, and drinking beer on those rare occasions when we could get together. It's been a real pleasure working with you all, and we hope it continues for a long time.

Special thanks to James Strachan for being so James; your infectious enthusiasm and love of writing code makes you truly inspirational to all those who meet you. We hope to keep playing with you on any and all of your latest new projects.

About the Reviewers

Bilgin Ibryam is a software engineer with master's degree in Computer Science and he currently works for Red Hat as Middleware Consultant. His passions include distributed applications, message-oriented middleware, and application integration. He is the author of a book about Apache Camel and Enterprise Integration Patterns called *Instant Apache Camel Message Routing*. He is also heavily involved with open source and is a committer to Apache OFBiz, and other Apache Camel projects. In his spare time, he enjoys contributing to open source projects and blogging at http://ofbizian.com. He can be contacted via his Twitter handle @bibryam.

Claus Ibsen has worked as a software engineer, architect, and consultant for more than 15 years. For the past five years he has been working full time as an open source developer at FuseSource and Red Hat in the middleware team, on the Fuse products. He has worked extensively on the Apache Camel project for over six years, being the top contributor, and has given talks at conferences about integration using Apache Camel.

He is author of *Camel in Action, Manning Publications*, 2011.

> I would like to congratulate Scott and Jakub for stepping up and writing this fantastic book. It is great to see the Camel community grow from strength to strength. This book will help new users to become more successful with "riding" Apache Camel, and experienced users can find valuable information from many of its recipes.

Christian Posta is based in Phoenix, AZ, and is a Principal Consultant and Architect. He specializes in messaging-based enterprise integrations with high scalability and throughput demands. He has been in development for over 10 years covering a wide range of domains; from embedded systems to UI and UX design and lots of integration in between. He's passionate about software development, loves solving tough technical problems, and enjoys learning new languages and programing paradigms. His favorite languages are Python and Scala, but he spends a lot of time writing Java too. He is a committer on Apache Camel, Apache ActiveMQ, and Apache Apollo projects as well as PMC on ActiveMQ. He blogs about Camel, ActiveMQ, and integration at `http://www.christianposta.com/blog` as well as tweets about interesting technology on his Twitter handle `@christianposta`.

Thanks to Scott and Jakub for asking me to review the book. I think this work is the ultimate complement to the other Camel book. The material cuts right to the chase and shows you how to accomplish otherwise challenging integrations using this wonderful library.

Phil Wilkins has spent nearly 25 years in the software industry working with both multinationals and software startups. He started out as a developer and has worked his way up through technical and development management roles. The last 12 years have been primarily in Java-based environments. He now works as an enterprise technical architect within the IT group for a global optical healthcare manufacturer and retailer.

Outside of his work commitments, he has contributed his technical capabilities to supporting others in a wide range of activities from the development of community websites to providing input and support to people authoring books, and developing software ideas and businesses.

When not immersed in work and technology, he spends his free time pursuing his passion for music and time with his wife and two boys.

I'd like to take this opportunity to thank my wife Catherine and our two sons Christopher and Aaron for their tolerance for the innumerable hours that I've spent in front of a computer contributing to both my employer and the many other IT related activities that I've supported over the years.

www.PacktPub.com

Support files, eBooks, discount offers and more

You might want to visit www.PacktPub.com for support files and downloads related to your book.

Did you know that Packt offers eBook versions of every book published, with PDF and ePub files available? You can upgrade to the eBook version at www.PacktPub.com and as a print book customer, you are entitled to a discount on the eBook copy. Get in touch with us at service@packtpub.com for more details.

At www.PacktPub.com, you can also read a collection of free technical articles, sign up for a range of free newsletters and receive exclusive discounts and offers on Packt books and eBooks.

http://PacktLib.PacktPub.com

Do you need instant solutions to your IT questions? PacktLib is Packt's online digital book library. Here, you can access, read and search across Packt's entire library of books.

Why Subscribe?

- ▶ Fully searchable across every book published by Packt
- ▶ Copy and paste, print and bookmark content
- ▶ On demand and accessible via web browser

Free Access for Packt account holders

If you have an account with Packt at www.PacktPub.com, you can use this to access PacktLib today and view nine entirely free books. Simply use your login credentials for immediate access.

Instant Updates on New Packt Books

Get notified! Find out when new books are published by following @PacktEnterprise on Twitter, or the *Packt Enterprise* Facebook page.

Table of Contents

Preface   1

Chapter 1: Structuring Routes   15
  Introduction   15
  Using Camel in a Java application   16
  Embedding Camel in a Spring application   20
  Using Camel components   24
  Reusing routing logic by connecting routes   27
  Asynchronously connecting routes   29
  Spanning Camel contexts within a single Java process   32
  Using external properties in Camel routes   34
  Reusing endpoints   37
  Reusing routing logic through template routes   38
  Controlling route startup and shutdown   42

Chapter 2: Message Routing   47
  Introduction   47
  Content Based Routing   48
  Filtering out unwanted messages   52
  Wire Tap – sending a copy of the message elsewhere   54
  Multicast – routing the same message to many endpoints   59
  Recipient List – routing a message to a list of endpoints   64
  Throttler – restricting the number of messages flowing to an endpoint   67
  Request-response route sending a one-way message   70
  One-way route waiting on a request-response endpoint   72
  Dynamic Routing – making routing decisions at runtime   74
  Load balancing across a number of endpoints   77
  Routing Slip – routing a message to a fixed list of endpoints   81

Chapter 3: Routing to Your Code	**85**
Introduction	85
Routing messages directly to a Java method	86
Sending messages directly to a Camel endpoint	88
Using a Java method as a Predicate	91
Writing a custom Camel Processor	93
Mapping the message to method parameters	97
Writing a custom data marshaller	100
Writing a custom data type converter	104
Chapter 4: Transformation	**109**
Introduction	109
Transforming using a Simple Expression	110
Transforming inline with XQuery	112
Transforming with XSLT	116
Transforming from Java to XML with JAXB	120
Transforming from Java to JSON	122
Transforming from XML to JSON	124
Parsing comma-separated values (CSV)	127
Enriching your content with some help from other endpoints	130
Normalizing messages into a common XML format	136
Chapter 5: Splitting and Aggregating	**143**
Introduction	143
Splitting a message into fragments	144
Splitting XML messages	146
Processing split messages in parallel	150
Aggregating related messages	152
Aggregating with timeouts	157
Aggregating with intervals	159
Processing aggregated messages in parallel	160
Splitting a message, and processing and gathering responses	163
Splitting messages and re-aggregating them using different criteria	166
Chapter 6: Parallel Processing	**171**
Introduction	171
Increasing message consumption through multiple endpoint consumers	172
Spreading the load within a route using a set of threads	175
Routing a request asynchronously	178
Using custom thread pools	181
Using thread pool profiles	184
Working with asynchronous APIs	186

Chapter 7: Error Handling and Compensation   191

Introduction   191
Logging errors   193
Dead Letter Channel – handling errors later   195
Retrying an operation   199
Conditional retry   202
Customizing each redelivery attempt   205
Catching exceptions   207
Marking exceptions as handled   210
Fine-grained error handling using doTry...doCatch   212
Defining completion actions   216
Defining completion actions dynamically   221

Chapter 8: Transactions and Idempotency   225

Introduction   225
Preventing duplicate invocation of routing logic   227
Transactional file consumption   234
Using transactions with a database   236
Limiting the scope of a transaction   241
Rolling back a transaction   245
Using transactions with messaging   248
Idempotency inside transactions   254
Setting up XA transactions over multiple transactional resources   260

Chapter 9: Testing   271

Introduction   271
Testing routes defined in Java   272
Using mock endpoints to verify routing logic   278
Replying from mock endpoints   281
Testing routes defined in Spring   283
Testing routes defined in OSGi Blueprint   290
Auto-mocking of endpoints   295
Validating route behavior under heavy load   297
Unit testing processors and Bean Bindings   302
Testing routes with fixed endpoints using AOP   304
Testing routes with fixed endpoints using conditional events   307

Chapter 10: Monitoring and Debugging   313

Introduction   313
Logging meaningful steps within your route   315
Debugging using logging   318
Throughput logging   320
Enabling step-by-step tracing in code   322

Disabling JMX   **326**

Configuring JMX   **328**

Naming your routes to make it easier to monitor   **331**

Adding JMX attributes and operations   **334**

Monitoring other systems using the Camel JMX Component   **337**

Setting breakpoints in your routes   **341**

Chapter 11: Security   **347**

Introduction   **347**

Encrypting configuration properties   **348**

Digitally signing and verifying messages   **352**

Encrypting and decrypting a message   **358**

Encrypting all or parts of an XML message   **363**

Authentication and authorization using Spring Security   **370**

Chapter 12: Web Services   **377**

Introduction   **377**

Generating the service stubs from a WSDL   **378**

Invoking a remote web service from Camel   **382**

Implementing a web service with a Camel route   **385**

Providing multiple web service operations within a single route   **389**

Handling web service faults   **392**

Web service proxying   **395**

Index   **399**

Preface

Apache Camel is a Java framework for building system integrations.

Why, you may well ask, does anyone need such a framework? System integration is pretty much a solved problem. After all, we have been connecting various frontends to web services, message brokers, and databases for years! Surely this is a well-understood domain that requires no further abstractions.

Not quite.

Apache Camel, since its release in 2007, has disrupted the integration market much like the Spring Framework disrupted the Java EE market back in 2003. Camel enables a new way of doing, and thinking about, system integrations that results in much cleaner, easier to understand code, which in turn results in less work, less bugs, and easier maintenance. These are big claims, and to validate them you only need to look at the large and active Apache Camel community, the growing number of commercial integration products based on Camel, and the talks on Camel that appear at most middleware developer conferences to feel that there is a good buzz around Camel, and for very good reason.

This book is targeted at readers who already have some familiarity with Camel, and are looking for tips on how Camel may be able to better help them solve more complex integration challenges. This book is structured as a series of over 100 how-to recipes, including step-by-step instructions on using Camel to solve common integration tasks. Each recipe includes a brief explanation of what Camel is doing internally, and references on where to find more information for those who want to dig deeper.

This book may not be a good introduction/beginner book about Camel, though if you have familiarity with other integration technologies, and learn well by doing, you may find this book's recipe approach helpful. This book does not spend a lot of time explaining Camel concepts in great depth.

For readers looking for more conceptual coverage of Camel (with lots of code examples), we would recommend reading the excellent book *Camel in Action* by Claus Ibsen and Jonathan Anstey, published by Manning. For a more introductory guide, look at *Instant Apache Camel Message Routing* by Bilgin Ibryam, published by Packt Publishing. The Apache Camel website (`http://camel.apache.org`) is the authoritative site on Camel, with a long list of articles and documentation that will help you on your journey of using Camel.

What is Camel?

This section provides a quick overview of what Camel is, and why it was created. Its goal is to help remind the reader of the core concepts used within Camel, and to help the reader understand how the authors define those concepts. It is not intended as a comprehensive introduction to Camel. Hopefully, it will act as a quick reference for Camel concepts as you use the various recipes contained within this book.

Integrating systems is hard work. It is hard because the developers doing the integration work must understand and how the endpoint systems expose themselves to external systems, how to transform and route the data records (messages) from each of the systems. They must also have a working knowledge of the ever growing number of technologies used in transporting, routing, and manipulating those messages. What makes it more challenging is that the systems you are integrating with were probably written by different teams of developers, at different times, and are probably still changing even while you are trying to integrate them. This is equivalent to connecting two cars while they are driving down the highway.

Traditional system integrations, in the way that we have built them in the past decades, require a lot of code to be created that has *absolutely nothing* to do with the higher-level integration problem trying to be solved. The vast majority of this is boilerplate code dealing with common, repetitive tasks of setting up and tearing down libraries for the messaging transports and processing technologies such as filesystems, SOAP, JMS, JDBC, socket-level I/O, XSLT, templating libraries, among others. These mechanical concerns are repeated over and over again in every single integration project's code base.

In early 2000, there were many people researching and cataloging software patterns within many of these projects, and this resulted in the excellent book *Enterprise Integration Patterns: Designing, Building, and Deploying Messaging Solutions* by Gregor Hohpe and Bobby Woolf, published by Addison Wesley. This catalog of integration patterns, EIPs for short, can be viewed at `http://www.enterpriseintegrationpatterns.com`. These patterns include classics such as the Content Based Router, Splitter, and Filter. The EIP book also introduces a model of how data moves from one system to another that is independent of the technology doing the work. These named concepts have become a common language for all integration architects and developers making it easier to express what an integration should do without getting lost in how to implement that integration.

Camel embraces these EIP concepts as core constructs within its framework, providing an executable version of those concepts that are independent of the mechanics of the underlying technology actually doing the work. Camel adds in abstractions such as **Endpoint URIs** (Uniform Resource Identifier) that work with **Components** (Endpoint factories), which allows developers to specify the desired technology to be used in connecting to an endpoint system without getting lost in the boilerplate code required to use that technology. Camel provides an integration, **domain-specific language** (**DSL**) for defining integration logic that is adapted to many programming languages (Java, Groovy, Scala, and so on) and frameworks (Spring, OSGi Blueprint, and so on), so that the developer can write code that is an English-like expression of the integration using EIP concepts. For example:

```
consume from some endpoint,
split the messages
  based on an expression, and
  send those split messages to some other endpoint
```

Let us look at a concrete example to show you how to use Camel.

Imagine that your boss comes to you, asking you to solve an integration problem for your project. You are asked to: poll a specific directory for new XML files every minute, split those XML files that contain many repeating elements into individual records/messages (think line items), and send each of those individual records to a JMS queue for processing by another system. Oh, and make sure that the code can retry if it hits any issues. Also, it is likely the systems will change shortly, so make sure the code is flexible enough to handle changes, but we do not know what those changes might look like. Sound familiar?

Before Camel, you would be looking at writing hundreds of lines of code, searching the Internet for code snippets of how best to do reliable directory polling, parsing XML, using XPath libraries to help you split those XML files, setting up a JMS connection, and so forth. Camel hides all of that routine complexity into well-tested components so you just need to specify your integration problem as per the following example using the Spring XML DSL:

```
<route>
  <from uri="file://someDirectory?delay=60000"/>
  <split>
    <xpath>/xpath/to/record</xpath>
    <to uri="jms:queue:myProcessingQueue"/>
  </split>
</route>
```

Wow! We still remember when we first saw some Camel code, and were taken aback by how such a small amount of code could be so incredibly expressive.

This Camel example shows a **Route**, a definition (recipe) of a graph of channels to message processors, that says: consume files *from* `someDirectory` every 60,000 milliseconds; *split* that data based on an XPath *expression*; and send the resulting messages *to* a JMS queue named `myProcessingQueue`. That is exactly the problem we were asked to solve, and the Camel code effectively says just that. This not only makes it easy to create integration code, it makes it easy for others (including your future self) to look at this code and understand what it is doing.

What is not obvious in this example is that this code also has default behaviors for handling errors (including retrying the processing of files), data type transformation such as File object to XML Document object, and connecting and packaging data to be sent on a JMS queue.

But what about when we need to use different endpoint technologies? How does Camel handle that? Very well, thank you very much. If our boss told us that now we need to pick up the files from a remote FTP server instead of a directory, we can make a simple change from the File Component to the FTP Component, and leave the rest of the integration logic alone:

```
<route>
  <from uri="ftp://scott@remotehost/someDirectory?delay=60000"/>
  <split>
    <xpath>/xpath/to/record</xpath>
    <to uri="jms:queue:myProcessingQueue"/>
  </split>
</route>
```

This simple change from `file:` to `ftp:` tells Camel to switch from using the hundreds of lines of well-tested code doing local directory polling to the hundreds of lines of well-tested FTP directory polling code. Plus, your core record-processing logic to split and forward on to a JMS queue remains unchanged.

At the time of writing, there are over 160 components within the Camel community dealing with everything; from files, FTP, and JMS, to distributed registries such as Apache Zookeeper, low-level wire formats such as FIX and HL7, monitoring systems such as Nagios, and higher-level system abstractions that include Facebook, Twitter, SAP, and Salesforce. Many of these components were written by the team that created the technology you are trying to use, so they generally reflect best practices on using that technology. Camel allows you to leverage the best practices of hundreds of the best integration technologists in the world, all in an easy to use, open source framework.

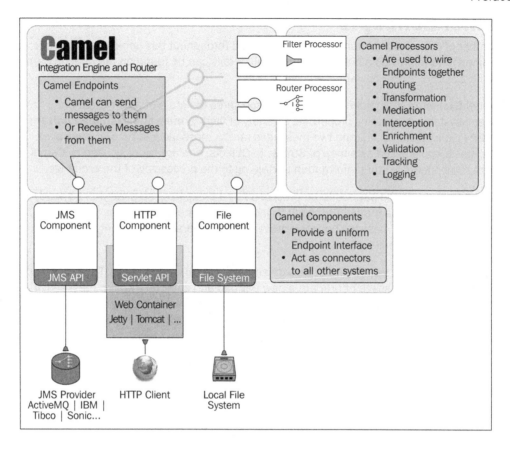

Another big innovation with Camel is that it does not require the messages flowing through its processing channels (routes) to be of any fixed/canonical data type. Instead, Camel tracks the current data type of the message, and includes an extensible data type conversation capability that allows Camel to try to convert the message to the data type required by the next step in the processing chain. This also helps Camel in providing seamless integration with your existing Java libraries, as Camel can type convert to and from your Java methods that you call as part of your Camel route. This all combines into an extremely flexible mechanism where you can quickly and easily extend almost any part of Camel with some highly focused Java code.

There is so much more to Camel than what can be covered in this very brief overview.

Camel Concepts

A number of Camel architectural concepts are used throughout this book and are briefly explained here to provide a quick reference. Full details can be found on the Apache Camel website at `http://camel.apache.org`.

A Camel **Exchange** is a holder object that encapsulates the state of a conversation between systems. It contains properties, a variety of flags, a **message exchange pattern** or **MEP** (`InOnly` or `InOut`), and two messages (an In message and an `Out` message). Properties are expressed as a map of Strings to Objects, and are typically used by Camel and its components to store information pertaining to the processing of the exchange.

A **message** contains the payload to be processed by a processing step, as well as headers that are expressed as a map of Strings to Objects. You use headers to pass additional information about the message between processors. Headers are commonly used to override endpoint defaults.

An `In` message is always present on an exchange as it enters a processor. The processor may modify the `In` message or prepare a new payload and set it on the `Out` message. If a processor sets the `Out` message, the Camel context will move it to the `In` message of the exchange before handing it to the next processor. For more, see `http://camel.apache.org/exchange.html` and `http://camel.apache.org/message.html`.

A Camel **Processor** is the base interface for all message-processing steps. Processors include predefined EIPs such as a Splitter, calls to endpoints, or custom processors that you have created implementing the `org.apache.camel.Processor` interface. For more, see `http://camel.apache.org/processor.html`.

A Camel **Route** is a series of message processing steps defined using Camel's DSL. A Route always starts with one consumer endpoint within a `from()` statement, and contains one or more processor steps. The processing steps within a route are loosely coupled, and do not invoke each other, relying on the Camel context instead to pass messages between them. For more, see `http://camel.apache.org/routes.html`.

The Camel **Context** is the engine that processes exchanges along the steps defined through routes. Messages are fed into a route based on a threading model appropriate to the component technologies being consumed from. Subsequent threading depends on the processors defined on the route.

A Camel **Component** is a library that encapsulates the communication with a transport or technology behind a common set of Camel interfaces. Camel uses these components to produce messages to or consume messages from those technologies. For a full list of components, see `http://camel.apache.org/components.html`.

A Camel **Endpoint** is an address that is interpreted by a component to identify a target resource, such as a directory, message queue, or database table that the component will consume messages from or send messages to. An endpoint used in a `from()` block is known as a Consumer endpoint, while an endpoint used in a `to()` block is known as a Producer endpoint. Endpoints are expressed as URIs, whose attributes are specific to their corresponding component. For more, see `http://camel.apache.org/endpoint.html`.

A Camel **Expression** is a way to script up Route in-line code that will operate on the message. For example, you can use the Groovy Expression Language to write inline Groovy code that can be evaluated on the in-flight message. Expressions are used within many EIPs to provide data to influence the routing of messages, such as providing the list of endpoints to route a message to as part of a Routing Slip EIP. For more, see `http://camel.apache.org/expression.html`.

The Camel DSL

All integration routes are defined in Camel through its own domain-specific language (DSL). This book presents the two main DSL flavors when discussing routing, the Java DSL, and the Spring XML DSL. OSGi Blueprint XML DSL is modeled after Spring, and is touched on lightly in this book. The Spring and OSGi Blueprint XML DSLs are collectively referred to as the XML DSL). There are other DSL variants available for defining Camel routes, including Groovy and Scala. For details on these see the following links:

- Groovy DSL: `http://camel.apache.org/groovy-dsl.html`
- Scala DSL: `http://camel.apache.org/scala-dsl.html`

Here is an example of a classic Content Based Router configured in Camel using both the XML and Java DSLs. You can find out more details on this in the Content Based Router recipe in *Chapter 2, Message Routing*.

In the XML DSL, you would write the routing logic as:

```
<route>
  <from uri="direct:start"/>
  <choice>
    <when>
      <simple>${body} contains 'Camel'</simple>
      <log message="Camel ${body}"/>
    </when>
    <otherwise>
      <log message="Other ${body}"/>
    </otherwise>
  </choice>
  <log message="Message ${body}"/>
</route>
```

In the Java DSL, the same route is expressed as:

```
from("direct:start")
  .choice()
    .when().simple("${body} contains 'Camel'")
      .log("Camel ${body}")
    .otherwise()
      .log("Other ${body}")
  .end()
  .log("Message ${body}");
```

The decision of which flavor of DSL to use is largely a personal one, and using one does not rule out using another alongside it. There are pros and cons to each, though none are functional. All of the DSL variants allow you to fully use Camel's features.

DSL	Pros		Cons
Java	▸ Routes can be defined in a very flexible manner (for example, the definition of a route can be conditional depending on the environment) ▸ `RouteBuilder` objects can be instantiated multiple times with different processors and endpoints, allowing route templating ▸ Routes tend to be shorter in terms of lines of code than the corresponding XML ▸ Each `RouteBuilder` can be tested independently without requiring the startup of every route in the whole Camel context		▸ Route definitions can sometimes get too clever in their use of advanced Java language features, such as large anonymous inner classes code blocks for in-lined processor steps, obscuring the intent of the route, and making future code maintenance more difficult ▸ As routes are defined using the builder pattern, automatic code reformatting in an IDE will mess up your indentation ▸ It may not always be obvious where a block of processing steps within an EIP ends ▸ It is sometimes necessary to break up the use of some EIPs within other EIPs to their own sub-routes due into limitations of using Java as a language for writing DSLs

DSL	Pros	Cons
XML	► Easily formatted automatically	► Verbose ("death by angle bracket")
	► Easier to read by non-Java programmers	► Not as easy to test as standalone Java routes; any Spring bean dependencies within routes pointing to external resources need to be mocked or stubbed in test Spring configurations
	► Supported by round-trip engineering tools such as the Fuse IDE and hawtio	
	► Easier to use for environments where it may be difficult to deploy Java code, for example, alongside ActiveMQ configurations	

What this book covers

Chapter 1, Structuring Routes, introduces you to the fundamentals of structuring Camel integrations; getting the framework running inside Java and Spring applications, using Camel components, and breaking down and reusing routing logic.

Chapter 2, Message Routing, details the use of the main EIPs used to route messages within Camel integrations; everything from if-else style content-based routing to more complex, dynamic options.

Chapter 3, Routing to Your Code, describes how to interact with a Camel runtime from your Java code, and how your Java code can be used from within Camel routes.

Chapter 4, Transformation, provides some off-the-shelf strategies for converting between and manipulating common message formats such as Java objects, XML, JSON, and CSV.

Chapter 5, Splitting and Aggregating, takes a deep dive into the related Splitter and Aggregator EIPs. It details the impacts of completion conditions, parallel processing options, and using the EIPs in combination with each other.

Chapter 6, Parallel Processing, outlines Camel's support for scaling out processing through the use of thread pools, profiles, and asynchronous processors.

Chapter 7, Error Handling and Compensation, details the mechanisms provided by the Camel DSLs for dealing with failure, including capabilities for triggering compensating routing steps for non-transactional interactions that have already completed.

Chapter 8, Transactions and Idempotency, presents a number of variations for dealing with transactional resources (JDBC and JMS). It additionally details the handling of non-transactional resources (such as web services) in such a way that they will only ever be invoked once in the event of message replay or duplicates.

Chapter 9, Testing, outlines Camel's test support that allows you to verify your routes' behavior without the need for backend systems. It also presents ways to manipulate routes with additional steps for testing purposes, without altering the code used at runtime.

Chapter 10, Monitoring and Debugging, describes Camel's support for logging, tracing, and debugging. Monitoring is examined through Camel's support for JMX, which includes the ability to define your own attributes and operations.

Chapter 11, Security, covers encrypting communication between systems, hiding sensitive configuration information, non-repudiation using certificates, and applying authentication and authorization to your routes.

Chapter 12, Web Services, shows you how to use Camel to invoke, act as a backend to, and proxy SOAP web services.

What you need for this book

This book is best used in conjunction with the example sources found at `http://github.com/CamelCookbook/camel-cookbook-examples`. You can also get a copy of the code through your account at `http://www.packtpub.com`.

> From the start we set out with the goal that working code should back up every single recipe. As a result the supporting code base supports multiple variants of each example, all backed up by working unit tests. In fact, if you printed out all of the source code, you would end up with a book nearly four times as thick as the one you are holding!

All of the examples are driven through JUnit tests, and are collectively structured as a set of Apache Maven projects. To execute them, you will need a copy of the Java 6 or 7 JDK (`http://www.oracle.com/technetwork/java/javase/downloads/index.html`) and an Apache Maven 3 installation (`http://maven.apache.org/`). Maven will download all of the appropriate project dependencies.

Maven has become the build tool of choice over the last few years within the broader Java community for a number of reasons, including:

> ▸ Standard way of laying out projects, leading to a quicker comprehension of a project layout by new developers.
>
> ▸ A set of standard, customizable build plugins that allow the developer to declare what build steps need to be performed at various stages of the build, without worrying about explaining the details.
>
> ▸ A mechanism for working with library dependencies. This has been Maven's largest success, and has become the gold standard approach for dependency management, being reused by numerous other build systems, such as Ant (via the Ivy dependency management extension), Groovy's Gradle, Scala's SBT, and others.

A full coverage of Maven is beyond the scope of this book, but interested readers should take a look at *Better Builds with Maven* by MaestroDev (http://www.maestrodev.com/better-builds-with-maven/about-this-guide/) for an excellent walkthrough.

Who this book is for

This book is for programmers working with Apache Camel who just want to get things done, without learning the entire framework up front. Those who are new to Camel and need a starting point will find it particularly useful in building up momentum with the framework.

We intended this book to be read as a set of individual *how-to* recipes to be accessed when needed. It is possible to read the book from cover to cover, but you should feel free to jump around between recipes; most are entirely self-contained, and those that are not reference the required prerequisites. Each recipe contains links to in-depth background reading, and pointers to other recipes that may come in handy when building system integrations using the techniques being discussed.

Conventions

In this book, you will find a number of styles of text that distinguish between different kinds of information. Here are some examples of these styles, and an explanation of their meaning.

Code words in text, Camel endpoint URIs, folder names, filenames, file extensions, pathnames, and dummy URLs are shown as follows: "In both cases `${spring-version}` is a property that you define in the `properties` section of your POM that states which version of Spring you are using."

A block of code is set as follows:

```
from("direct:processXml")
  .choice()
    .when()
      .xpath("/order[@units > 100]")
      .to("direct:priorityXmlOrder")
    .otherwise()
      .to("direct:normalXmlOrder")
  .end();
```

When we wish to draw your attention to a particular part of a code block, the relevant lines or items are set in bold:

```
from("direct:processXml")
  .choice()
    .when()
      .xpath("/order[@units > 100]")
      .to("direct:priorityXmlOrder")
    .otherwise()
      .to("direct:normalXmlOrder")
  .end();
```

Any command-line input or output is written as follows:

```
# java -jar camel-jasypt-2.12.2.jar -c encrypt
-p encryptionPassword -i myDatabasePassword
```

New terms and **important words** are shown in bold.

Warnings or important notes appear in a box like this.

Tips and tricks appear like this.

Reader feedback

Feedback from our readers is always welcome. Let us know what you think about this book—what you liked or may have disliked. Reader feedback is important for us to develop titles that you really get the most out of.

To send us general feedback, simply send an e-mail to feedback@packtpub.com, and mention the book title via the subject of your message.

If there is a topic that you have expertise in and you are interested in either writing or contributing to a book, see our author guide on www.packtpub.com/authors.

Customer support

Now that you are the proud owner of a Packt book, we have a number of things to help you to get the most from your purchase.

Downloading the example code

The latest version of the example code for this book can be found at http://github.com/CamelCookbook/camel-cookbook-examples.

You can also download the example code files for all Packt books you have purchased from your account at http://www.packtpub.com. If you purchased this book elsewhere, you can visit http://www.packtpub.com/support and register to have the files e-mailed directly to you.

Errata

Although we have taken every care to ensure the accuracy of our content, mistakes do happen. If you find a mistake in one of our books—maybe a mistake in the text or the code—we would be grateful if you would report this to us. By doing so, you can save other readers from frustration and help us improve subsequent versions of this book. If you find any errata, please report them by visiting http://www.packtpub.com/submit-errata, selecting your book, clicking on the **errata submission form** link, and entering the details of your errata. Once your errata are verified, your submission will be accepted and the errata will be uploaded on our website, or added to any list of existing errata, under the Errata section of that title. Any existing errata can be viewed by selecting your title from http://www.packtpub.com/support.

Piracy

Piracy of copyright material on the Internet is an ongoing problem across all media. At Packt, we take the protection of our copyright and licenses very seriously. If you come across any illegal copies of our works, in any form, on the Internet, please provide us with the location address or website name immediately so that we can pursue a remedy.

Please contact us at `copyright@packtpub.com` with a link to the suspected pirated material.

We appreciate your help in protecting our authors, and our ability to bring you valuable content.

Questions

You can contact us at `questions@packtpub.com` if you are having a problem with any aspect of the book, and we will do our best to address it.

1
Structuring Routes

In this chapter, we will cover the following recipes:

- ▶ Using Camel in a Java application
- ▶ Embedding Camel in a Spring application
- ▶ Using Camel components
- ▶ Reusing routing logic by connecting routes
- ▶ Asynchronously connecting routes
- ▶ Spanning Camel contexts within a single Java process
- ▶ Using external properties in Camel routes
- ▶ Reusing endpoints
- ▶ Reusing routing logic through template routes
- ▶ Controlling route startup and shutdown

Introduction

This chapter will introduce you to the fundamentals of running Apache Camel inside your applications. You will learn how to make use of Camel's rich set of components, and how to structure routes in such a way that common integration logic is able to be reused without duplication. These topics will provide you with the foundation for developing integrations using the framework.

Downloading the example code

Complete examples for each of the code snippets are located at `http://github.com/CamelCookbook/camel-cookbook-examples`, and through your account on the Packt Publishing's website at `http://www.packtpub.com`. If you purchased this book elsewhere, you can visit `http://www.packtpub.com/support` and register to have the files e-mailed directly to you.

To try these examples for yourself, obtain the example code, and build it using Apache Maven 3.0 or newer (`http://maven.apache.org`). Use the following command from the top-level directory of the project. Complete instructions are also provided in the included `README` file.

```
# mvn clean install
```

The code for this chapter is contained within the `camel-cookbook-structuring-routes` module of the examples.

Using Camel in a Java application

Camel is a framework that is composed of a set of JARs, much as any other library that lives alongside your code. If you wanted to run Camel from the command line, you would define the libraries used within as a list of JARs to be considered by the `java` and `javac` command-line tools.

The supporting code for this book uses Camel within the context of Maven projects that build standalone JARs. The JARs are not meant to be executed themselves, rather the Maven project structure is used as a convenient harness for driving JUnit tests that demonstrate the behavior being described.

The Camel libraries are broken up into two categories:

▸ Core set of artifacts containing the runtime, test support classes, and build tools.

▸ Optional libraries that abstract away the details of dealing with a given technology (for example, messaging via JMS or SOAP services via CXF). At the time of writing, Camel integrates with over 140 technologies (`http://camel.apache.org/components.html`), and each is encapsulated within its own library with its own dependencies.

This recipe will show you the basic steps to start and stop Camel routes from within your Java application.

Getting ready

The minimal set of libraries typically required to use Camel within a Maven build are:

```
<dependency>
  <groupId>org.apache.camel</groupId>
  <artifactId>camel-core</artifactId>
  <version>${camel-version}</version>
</dependency>
<dependency>
  <groupId>org.apache.camel</groupId>
  <artifactId>camel-test</artifactId>
  <version>${camel-version}</version>
  <scope>test</scope>
</dependency>
```

The Camel version is usually defined in a `properties` block within the Maven POM file once, as follows, so as to not need to be repeated over and over:

```
<properties>
  <camel-version>2.12.2</camel-version>
</properties>
```

A note on versions

Camel is a very mature framework that can be considered as being "core-complete". It has become the core library for integration in a number of commercial ESBs, and at this stage the underlying architecture is very stable and unlikely to be radically changed.

This book has been written against what will most certainly be an outdated version by the time you read this. Any changes made to Camel since the time of writing are likely to have been additive. There will be more components, and more options around the various integration patterns as further use cases require them. For the very latest detailed documentation, refer to the Camel website.

The Java code for this recipe is located in the `org.camelcookbook.structuringroutes.simple` package.

How to do it...

1. Define a route using the Camel Java DSL, by extending the `org.apache.camel.builder.RouteBuilder` abstract class:

    ```
    public class LogMessageOnTimerEventRouteBuilder
        extends RouteBuilder {
    ```

```
      @Override
      public void configure() throws Exception {
        from("timer:logMessageTimer?period=1s")
          .log("Event triggered by ${property.CamelTimerName}"
            + " at ${header.CamelTimerFiredTime}");
      }
    };
```

2. The following steps occur in your application's `main` method. See `SimpleCamelApplication` from this example. Create a `CamelContext` implementation:

```
CamelContext context = new DefaultCamelContext();
```

3. Add the route definition to the context; this can be invoked as many times as you have routes:

```
context.addRoutes(
    new LogMessageOnTimerEventRouteBuilder());
```

4. Start the context. This loads the route definitions that you have added, and processes messages through them in the background:

```
context.start();
```

 The `CamelContext.start` method is non-blocking. It will start up associated Components on internal threads, and return to the caller.

5. When the Camel application is ready to be shut down, call:

```
context.stop();
```

How it works...

The `CamelContext` interface is the heart of the Camel framework. It is responsible for processing messages along routes.

The `from(...)` statement at the start of a route defines an endpoint, or a technology-specific location, that the Camel routing engine uses to fetch messages. Endpoints are defined using URIs, such as in the preceding example, `timer:logMessageTimer`. The first part of the URI specifies the component that is being used to consume the message, and the remaining is a set of instructions for that specific component. See the *Using Camel components* recipe in this chapter for more details.

The Camel routing engine consumes exchanges from these endpoints and processes them sequentially through each of the steps defined in the route. The engine is responsible for threading, transactions, error handling, copying messages where required, and many other details.

The Camel context is a *long-running* object; it is intended to live for as long as the application does, and therefore its initialization and shutdown is usually tied to the lifecycle of the application. Typical deployments of Camel define the context within:

- The `main()` method of a standalone command-line application; here it waits indefinitely until the user terminates the process
- As an instance variable within a `javax.servlet.ServletContextListener` in a web app, starting up and shutting down along with the application
- An object tied to an OSGi bundle's lifecycle
- An object within a Spring or OSGi Blueprint context that is itself tied to the application's lifecycle

Routes, which are definitions of the steps that messages should be processed through, are typically added to the newly created context, though they can be added, removed, and modified at runtime. Route definitions can only be added to a context before the context is started, though they can be stopped and restarted while the context is running.

Extending the `RouteBuilder` abstract class gives access to Camel's Java route definition DSL, or simply the **Java DSL**. What this means in practice is that within the mandatory `configure()` method, after typing the first `from(...)` statement that defines the start of a route, you get context-specific code completion of whichever integration patterns you might be using.

A `RouteBuilder` implementation may implement one or many routes. That is, within the `configure()` method, you can specify multiple `from(...)` statement that Camel will translate into multiple runtime route instances, one per `from(...)` statement.

There's more...

Camel is a highly configurable framework, in which most behaviors can be customized through **service provider interfaces** (**SPIs**). An SPI encapsulates a single behavior, such as a route naming strategy (Camel gives your routes sensible names if you do not do so explicitly). To override the default behavior, you provide your own implementation of the SPI class and set it on the `CamelContext` object. The context allows you to define the following, amongst others:

- Listeners that are notified of Camel lifecycle events
- Naming strategies for routes, route nodes, and JMX
- Strategies for shutting down the application gracefully
- Mechanisms for managing thread pools

It is therefore worthwhile getting familiar with the options that this class gives you by going over the Javadocs.

The `CamelContext` interface makes use of an internal object registry that allows it to look up objects by name. When using a `DefaultCamelContext`, a JNDI-aware registry is used.

This feature is used extensively throughout the framework for finding components, thread pools, named processor beans, data formats, and the like.

Occasionally, it is necessary to add objects directly to the registry, as in the case of beans that you want to execute, as one of the processing steps in a route. To do this, instantiate an implementation of org.apache.camel.spi.Repository, usually org.apache.camel.impl.SimpleRegistry, and pass it into the constructor of the DefaultCamelContext:

```
SimpleRegistry registry = new SimpleRegistry();
registry.put("payloadTransformer", new MyPayloadTransformer());
CamelContext context = new DefaultCamelContext(registry);
```

The CamelContext interface defines type-safe utility methods for setting certain object types, such as components, that allow you to set them without worrying about the registry internals.

Consider the following manual step:

```
registry.put("mylogger", new LogComponent());
```

This can be written in a type-safe way as follows:

```
context.addComponent("mylogger", new LogComponent());
```

The Registry in Camel can hold any named Java instance, and these instances can be referenced by name from the Camel DSL. The addComponent method of the CamelContext is specifically used for registering Camel components by name. Both approaches do effectively the same thing, though there are some subtle differences, and we would recommend using the addComponent method for components, and adding all your POJOs and custom processors into the registry.

See also

- ▸ Camel Context: http://camel.apache.org/camelcontext.html
- ▸ Route Builder: http://camel.apache.org/routebuilder.html
- ▸ Camel Registry: http://camel.apache.org/registry.html

Embedding Camel in a Spring application

This recipe will show you how to integrate Camel into a Spring application.

Getting ready

When using Camel within a Spring application, it is necessary to add the following dependencies to the minimal set defined in the *Using Camel in a Java application* recipe in this chapter:

```xml
<dependency>
  <groupId>org.apache.camel</groupId>
  <artifactId>camel-spring</artifactId>
  <version>${camel-version}</version>
</dependency>
<dependency>
  <groupId>org.apache.camel</groupId>
  <artifactId>camel-test-spring</artifactId>
  <version>${camel-version}</version>
  <scope>test</scope>
</dependency>
```

The `${camel-version}` property is defined once in the Maven POM.

The Java code for this recipe is located in the `org.camelcookbook.structuringroutes.simplespring` package. The Spring XML files are located under `src/main/resources/META-INF/spring` and prefixed with `simplespring`.

How to do it...

In order to embed Camel into a Spring application, perform the following steps:

1. In the XML namespace declaration, define the Camel schema alongside any Spring schemas in use:

```xml
<beans
  xmlns="http://www.springframework.org/schema/beans"
  xmlns:camel="http://camel.apache.org/schema/spring"
  xmlns:xsi="http://www.w3.org/2001/XMLSchema-instance"
  xsi:schemaLocation="
    http://www.springframework.org/schema/beans
    http://www.springframework.org/schema/beans/spring-beans.xsd
    http://camel.apache.org/schema/spring
    http://camel.apache.org/schema/spring/camel-spring.xsd">
```

2. The `camelContext` element should be defined once within the Spring configuration, and it should use the Camel Spring namespace. This signifies that everything within it will be considered Camel configuration as opposed to Spring.

```
<camelContext
    xmlns="http://camel.apache.org/schema/spring">
  <!-- routing logic goes here -->
</camelContext>
```

3. Routes can then be defined within the `camelContext` element using the **XML DSL**:

```
<route>
  <from uri="timer:logMessageTimer?period=1s"/>
  <to uri="mylogger:insideTheRoute?showHeaders=true"/>
  <log
      message="Event triggered by
              ${property.CamelTimerName} at
              ${header.CamelTimerFiredTime}"/>
</route>
```

How it works...

Camel was designed to be closely integrated with Spring from its inception. The `camelContext` element results in a `SpringCamelContext` object being created, initialized with any routes defined within it, and started when the Spring context starts up. The `camelContext` element is itself a Spring managed object that can optionally be given an ID and treated like any other bean.

The preceding example shows Camel's XML DSL being used. One of the nice things about the DSL is that an XML schema is used to define it. This means that it is possible for your IDE to provide you with code completion.

```
<camelContext xmlns="http://camel.apache.org/schema/spring">
  <route>
    <from uri="timer:logMessageTimer?period=1s"/>
    <to uri="mylogger:insideTheRoute?showHeaders=true"/>
    <|
```

< > camel:aggregate	**Element : aggregate**
< > camel:aop	**Content Model :** ((description?),
< > camel:bean	(correlationExpression, completionPredicate?,
< > camel:choice	completionTimeout?, completionSize?, (aop |
< > camel:convertBodyTo	aggregate | bean | doCatch | when | choice |
< > camel:delay	otherwise | convertBodyTo | delay | dynamicRouter |
< > camel:description	enrich | filter | doFinally | idempotentConsumer |
< > camel:doCatch	inOnly | inOut | intercept | interceptFrom |
< > camel:doFinally	interceptToEndpoint | loadBalance | log | loop |
< > camel:doTry	marshal | multicast | onCompletion | onException |
< > camel:dynamicRouter	pipeline | policy | pollEnrich | process | recipientList |
	removeHeader | removeHeaders | removeProperty |

It is not mandatory to use the XML DSL with Spring. It is possible to use the Java DSL instead, or alongside routes defined through the XML DSL.

To plug in the route defined in the `LogMessageOnTimerEventRouteBuilder` class that we used in the previous recipe, we first instantiate it as a bean:

```
<!-- package name has been abbreviated -->
<bean id="logMessageOnTimerEvent"
      class="org.camelcookbook.structuringroutes.simple
             .LogMessageOnTimerEventRouteBuilder"/>
```

Then we add it to the `camelContext` element using the `routeBuilder` tag:

```
<camelContext xmlns="http://camel.apache.org/schema/spring">
  <routeBuilder ref="logMessageOnTimerEvent"/>
</camelContext>
```

Multiple `routeBuilder` elements can be used within a `camelContext`.

There's more...

If you define a number of `RouteBuilder`s in the same package, it is possible for Camel to scan that package and instantiate all of the routes that it finds:

```
<camelContext xmlns="http://camel.apache.org/schema/spring">
  <packageScan>
    <package>org.camelcookbook.structuringroutes</package>
  </packageScan>
</camelContext>
```

You can add multiple `package` elements within the `packageScan` element, and also use wildcards to include or exclude `RouteBuilder`s by name, using the `excludes` and `includes` elements.

Spring provides an alternative feature called **component scanning**. When enabled, the Spring application context recursively scans a package, and instantiates any class within that is annotated with `org.springframework.stereotype.Component`. Any properties annotated with `@Autowired`, or the CDI equivalent `@Inject`, have their dependencies injected. Camel can be configured to pick up any `RouteBuilder`s wired through this process. The `RouteBuilder`s must first be marked as components:

```
@Component
public class LogMessageOnTimerEventRouteBuilder
    extends RouteBuilder {
  //...
};
```

To enable the wiring, turn on component scanning in Spring:

```
<component-scan
  base-package="org.camelcookbook.structuringroutes"
  xmlns="http://www.springframework.org/schema/context"/>
```

Then add the appropriate feature to the Camel context to tie it all together:

```
<camelContext xmlns="http://camel.apache.org/schema/spring">
  <component-scan/>
</camelContext>
```

See also

- ▶ Context scanning: `http://static.springsource.org/spring/docs/current/spring-framework-reference/html/beans.html#beans-classpath-scanning`

- ▶ Camel Spring: `https://camel.apache.org/spring.html`

- ▶ Groovy DSL: `http://camel.apache.org/groovy-dsl.html`

- ▶ Scala DSL: `http://camel.apache.org/scala-dsl.html`

Using Camel components

When writing integration code, you will inevitably have to work directly with libraries that deal with the technology being integrated. The details of invoking web services, consuming or sending files to FTP servers, or messaging over JMS often take up a substantial proportion of development time on a project. Camel abstracts away the repeated details of consuming from or producing to these "transports", by encapsulating this interaction within a Component.

Camel provides a rich set of components, which abstract away this plumbing code from you. These allow you to focus your energies on the business logic of your integration without worrying about the finer details of the transport.

This recipe will show you the basic steps of associating a Camel Component for a given technology with your integration routing logic.

Getting ready

To make use of a component, you will need to make sure that the component's library is included in your project. The `camel-core` library provides a set of fundamental components to get you started underneath the `org.apache.camel.component` package.

For integration with any other technologies, your first stop should be the component listing on the Camel website (`http://camel.apache.org/components.html`). Once you have found the technology that you are looking for, add the JAR dependency to your project, ensuring that the version matches that of the `camel-core` library you are using. For example, to use the Camel FTP component within your Camel route, you need to add the `camel-ftp` dependency to your POM:

```
<dependency>
   <groupId>org.apache.camel</groupId>
   <artifactId>camel-ftp</artifactId>
   <version>${camel-version}</version>
</dependency>
```

The `${camel-version}` property is defined once in the Maven POM.

The Java code for this recipe is located in the `org.camelcookbook.structuringroutes.simple` package. The Spring XML files are located under `src/main/resources/META-INF/spring` and prefixed with `simplespring`.

How to do it...

In order to use a Camel component you need to instantiate and register the component, and then reference it from your Camel route as per the following steps:

1. If working within a Spring application, you use a Component by instantiating it as a `bean` and give it a meaningful name (`id`); the Component is automatically visible to Camel:

   ```
   <bean id="mylogger"
         class="org.apache.camel.component.LogComponent"/>
   ```

   Alternatively, in a non-Spring Java application, you register a Component by instantiating it and then adding it to the `CamelContext` before starting it:

   ```
   CamelContext context = new DefaultCamelContext();
   camelContext.addComponent("mylogger", new LogComponent());
   // add routes here
   context.start();
   ```

2. To use the component as an endpoint in a `to(...)` or `from(...)` statement, refer to the name that you assigned it within the scheme part of the endpoint URI:

   ```
   .to("mylogger:insideTheRoute?showHeaders=true")
   ```

How it works...

To understand exactly what happens when we use an endpoint URI, it is easiest to take a brief look under the covers at the classes that Camel uses within its component framework.

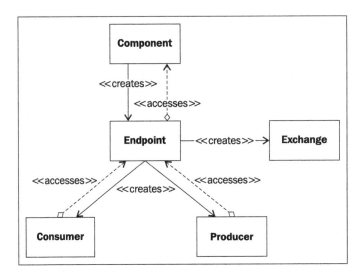

A Component is a factory for creating Endpoints that can act as message Consumers, or Producers, or both. An implementation will typically have bean properties on it that will apply to the transport as a whole. For example, the JMS Component requires that a ConnectionFactory be set on it, in order to make use of the same message broker for all JMS communication:

```
<bean id="myFavouriteMQ"
      class="org.apache.camel.component.jms.JmsComponent">
  <property name="connectionFactory"
            ref="myConnectionFactory"/>
</bean>
```

All Components implement a method used to parse the endpoint URI:

```
Endpoint createEndpoint(String uri) throws Exception;
```

An Endpoint can be thought of as an address that is specific to the component technology–it is instantiated from the URI by the framework when the route using it is started. The scheme portion of the URI, the part before the first colon (:), identifies the component implementation being used.

Continuing the JMS example, given that the Component already knows where a message broker is, the Endpoint itself describes which queues or topics a message should be sent to or received from, and how:

```
myFavouriteMQ:someQueue?concurrentConsumers=5
```

The portion of the URI after the scheme is specific to the endpoint technology. The URI properties themselves, such as `concurrentConsumers`, correspond to bean properties on the endpoint implementation for that technology, and are set using introspection. If you were to take a look inside the JMS Component library, you would see a `JmsEndpoint` object with a `setConcurrentConsumers(int consumers)` method.

You should always refer back to the applicable Camel component page for a full list of properties that can be used.

The Endpoint is also a factory. Camel uses it for creating Producers and Consumers, depending on the context of where the URI is used. The following factory methods are defined on the interface:

```
Producer createProducer() throws Exception;
Consumer createConsumer(Processor processor) throws Exception;
```

These classes handle the heavy lifting of talking to the underlying technology.

If the endpoint URI is used in a `from(...)` statement, Camel will create a `Consumer`. If it is used in a `to(...)` block, will create a `Producer`.

There's more...

The same component can be instantiated multiple times with different IDs. For example, two JMS components might be used when writing routing logic to bridge message brokers from different vendors.

See also

  ▸   Camel Components: `http://camel.apache.org/components.html`

Reusing routing logic by connecting routes

It is frequently necessary to execute the same processing steps within multiple routes. Camel provides you with a mechanism to call routing steps in a shared route. You can then reuse that route in a similar fashion to a method in a regular Java program.

This recipe will show you a strategy for developing your routes so that common routing tasks can be defined within a shared route called from other routes.

Getting ready

Determine the routing logic that you would like to reuse, and move it to a route that consumes from a `direct:` URI.

The Java code for this recipe is located in the `org.camelcookbook.structuringroutes.direct` package. The Spring XML files are located under `src/main/resources/META-INF/spring` and prefixed with `direct`.

How to do it...

Create a route with the `from` URI using the `direct:` endpoint, and then in another route, call the shared route using the same `direct:` endpoint.

1. The `direct:` endpoint name, which is an arbitrary alphanumeric string, follows the colon in the URI, must be unique within the containing Camel context:

   In the XML DSL, it is used as follows:

   ```
   <route>
     <from uri="direct:prefixBodyWithHello"/>
     <transform>
       <simple>Hello, ${body}</simple>
     </transform>
     <log message="Prefixed message: ${body}"/>
   </route>
   ```

   In the Java DSL, the same thing is expressed as:

   ```
   from("direct:prefixBodyWithHello")
       .transform(simple("Hello, ${body}"))
       .log("Prefixed message: ${body}");
   ```

2. Invoke the shared route from within the top-level route that needs to make use of this logic by using the same `direct:` URI:

   In the XML DSL, this is written as follows:

   ```
   <route>
     <from uri="..."/>
     <to uri="direct:prefixBodyWithHello"/>
   </route>
   ```

   In the Java DSL, this appears as:

   ```
   from(...).to("direct:prefixBodyWithHello");
   ```

How it works...

Each `direct:` endpoint may only be consumed (used within the `from(...)` block) by one route in a Camel context. However, multiple routes may produce, or send, messages to that URI. This allows you to compose your routing logic in easily understandable blocks, much as you would when using methods in a regular Java program.

The shared route can be considered as a part of the top-level route. It operates on the same Exchange object, and participates in any transactions that the top-level route has initiated.

Regardless of whether the message exchange pattern on the exchange is `InOnly` or `InOut`, the behavior of invoking a `direct:` endpoint is the same; that is, the exchange will flow through all of the processing steps defined in the shared route and will be returned to the calling route on completion where it will proceed to the next processing step.

There's more...

It is possible to invoke the shared route, and merge the returned exchange with the exchange containing the original state before the route was invoked. See the *Enriching your content with some help from other endpoints* recipe in *Chapter 4*, *Transformation*, for more details.

See also

> ▶ Direct Component: `http://camel.apache.org/direct.html`

Asynchronously connecting routes

It is not uncommon to have a portion of route take a long time to process. Rather than tying up a thread that might otherwise be servicing requests from a consumer endpoint, it may be preferable to split out the time consuming step into a separate route, and let that stage of processing be handled by a dedicated pool of threads.

This recipe will show you how to call a route from another, such that the calling route does not block waiting for the response from the called route.

Getting ready

Split out the long running steps into their own shared routes, and assign them with a `seda:` endpoint with a name that is unique to the Camel context.

The Java code for this recipe is located in the `org.camelcookbook.structuringroutes.seda` package. The Spring XML files are located under `src/main/resources/META-INF/spring` and prefixed with `seda`.

How to do it...

Create a shared route using the `seda:` endpoint, and then call it from other routes using the same named `seda:` endpoint.

1. Create a route consuming (`from`) using a `seda:` endpoint. Optionally, define the number of threads that will consume from this endpoint using the `concurrentConsumers` attribute.

   In the XML DSL, this is written as:

   ```
   <route>
     <from
       uri="seda:longRunningPhase?concurrentConsumers=15"/>
     <process ref="longRunningProcessor"/>
     <to uri="..."/>
   </route>
   ```

   In the Java DSL, the same thing appears as:

   ```
   from("seda:longRunningPhase?concurrentConsumers=15")
     .process(new LongRunningProcessor())
     .to(...); // remainder of route
   ```

2. In the calling route, pass the current exchange to the shared route by invoking the `seda:` endpoint by name.

   In the XML DSL, this is done as follows:

   ```
   <route>
     <from uri="timer:ping?period=200"/>
     <to uri="seda:longRunningPhase"/>
   </route>
   ```

   In the Java DSL, this same thing is written as:

   ```
   from("timer:ping?period=200")
     .to("seda:longRunningPhase");
   ```

How it works...

In the preceding example, a `timer:` endpoint is used to trigger messages on a regular basis, every 200 ms. The Timer Component uses one thread per timer name (`ping`). An event can only be raised 200 ms later if the thread is not processing the previous exchange.

As part of our integration, we want to trigger events regularly, and yet have a long-running processor as part of the route. Camel allows us to deal with this scenario by splitting the long-running part into a shared route, and linking the two routes with a `seda:` endpoint.

SEDA is an acronym that stands for **Staged Event-Driven Architecture**. It is designed as a mechanism to regulate the flow between different phases of message processing. The idea is to smooth out the frequency of message output from an overall process so that it matches the input.

In practical terms, it allows an endpoint's consumer threads to offload the work of long-running operations into the background, thereby freeing them up to consume messages from the transport.

When an exchange is passed to a `seda:` endpoint, it is placed into a `BlockingQueue`. The list exists within the Camel context, which means that only those routes that are within the same context can be joined by this type of endpoint. The queue is unbounded by default, although that can be changed by setting the `size` attribute on the URI of the consumer.

By default, a single thread assigned to the endpoint reads exchanges off the list and processes them through the route. As seen in the preceding example, it is possible to increase the number of `concurrentConsumers` to ensure that exchanges are getting processed from that list in a timely fashion.

Assuming our slow processor takes 3,000 ms to complete, we would need to use a number of threads equal to *the processing time/the timer frequency* to ensure that the triggered events are processed in a timely fashion. Therefore, plugging in the numbers, 3,000 ms / 200 ms, we arrive at 15 threads.

There's more...

It is possible to define multiple routes that consume from the same logical name, unlike a `direct:` endpoint. To enable this, both routes should set `multipleConsumers=true` on the `seda:` URI:

```
from("seda:timerEvents?multipleConsumers=true")
  // define one set of routing logic here

from("seda:timerEvents?multipleConsumers=true")
  // another here
```

The effect will be that each route gets its own copy of the exchange, making it a sort of simple in-memory publish-subscribe system. It is often much cleaner to handle this type of requirement using the Multicast pattern. See the *Multicast – routing the same message to many endpoints* recipe in *Chapter 2, Message Routing*, for more details.

The SEDA pattern is best suited to processing the `InOnly` messages, where one route finishes processing and hands off to another to deal with the next phase. It is possible to ask for a response from a `seda:` endpoint by calling it when the message exchange pattern is `InOut`.

In this instance, the endpoint will act much like a synchronous `direct:` endpoint, only with a timeout if the task runs for longer than expected. The default timeout is 30 seconds, but this can be overridden in the producer URI using the `timeout` attribute.

It is important to note that when using `seda:`, the shared route does not take part in any transactions started by the top-level route, as transactions are bound to a thread and the `seda:` route is using its own thread. If the system unexpectedly halts for whatever reason (for example, a power outage), any messages that are being processed within that route will be lost.

If you would like to get the benefits of a SEDA, but have the messages persisted to disk instead of in-memory, and be processed within a transaction, use the JMS or ActiveMQ endpoints with a message broker instead. This also gives you the ability to share the work across Camel contexts and JVMs.

See also

▸ SEDA Component: `http://camel.apache.org/seda.html`

▸ Timer Component: `http://camel.apache.org/timer.html`

To trigger a background job to run based on the current exchange while your main route continues processing, refer to the Wire Tap EIP. See *Wire Tap – sending a copy of the message elsewhere* recipe in *Chapter 2, Message Routing*, for more details.

Spanning Camel contexts within a single Java process

Sometimes it is convenient to share routing logic between integrations hosted in the same container, for example, as web apps or OSGi bundles. Camel provides two components that allow you to do this, synchronously through a Direct VM Component, or asynchronously through a VM Component.

This recipe will show you how a Camel route can call another route running in a different Camel context.

Getting ready

In order for messages to be passed between routes using the `vm:` or `direct-vm:` transports, the *exact same instance* of the `camel-core` library must be available within the classloader hierarchy of both applications.

In an application server such as Apache Tomcat, this means placing the `camel-core.jar` file in the `/ext` directory of the server. Applications deployed onto the server should not contain `camel-core` within their WAR files.

When using an OSGi container such as Apache Karaf or Apache ServiceMix, it is simply a case of ensuring that the `camel-core` bundle is installed and running.

No additional work is necessary to use these transports if you intend to communicate between Camel contexts in the same application.

The Java code for this recipe is located in the `org.camelcookbook.structuringroutes.vm` package. The Spring XML files are located under `src/main/resources/META-INF/spring` and prefixed with `vm`.

How to do it...

Create a route to be shared consuming (`from`) with the `vm:` endpoint, and reference it from other routes using the same endpoint name.

1. Split out the integration logic that you want to share into a route and select a VM Component to consume from that best suits your threading requirements. If your route should handle requests using the same thread as the caller, choose `direct-vm:`, otherwise if you want the exchange to be processed asynchronously by a different thread, choose `vm:`. Give the endpoint a name that will be unique across the JVM.

   In the XML DSL, this is written as follows:

   ```
   <route>
     <from uri="vm:logMessageToBackendSystem"/>
     <to uri="..."/>
   </route>
   ```

   In the Java DSL, you express the same thing as:

   ```
   from("vm:logMessageToBackendSystem").to(...);
   ```

2. Invoke the shared route from within the top-level route that needs to make use of this logic by using the same URI prefix.

   In the XML DSL, write the following:

   ```
   <route>
     <from uri="..."/>
     <to uri="vm:logMessageToBackendSystem"/>
   </route>
   ```

   In the Java DSL, this is written as:

   ```
   from(...).to("vm:logMessageToBackendSystem");
   ```

How it works...

The VM Component is equivalent in functionality to SEDA, but works across applications within the same JVM. All of the same configuration options for a `seda:` endpoint also apply to the `vm:` endpoint. As in `seda:` endpoints, care should be taken that the endpoint name used in the top-level route matches that of the shared route. Otherwise, the exchange is placed onto a named in-memory queue that will never be consumed from.

Aside from working across applications, `direct-vm:` is functionally equivalent to `direct:`. The endpoint uses the same thread between the two applications, meaning that it can participate in the same transactions. This should be tested thoroughly to ensure that applications have been correctly configured. For this to work, both applications should make use of the same transactional resources (for example, JDBC `DataSource` or JMS `ConnectionFactory`) with the same transaction manager.

When using `direct-vm:` you should pay particular attention to the order in which the applications or contexts are started up. You can use the `block=true` option on `direct-vm:` so that it will block until there is an active consumer associated with it. If the top-level route starts sending messages to the shared route before it is available, an exception similar to the following will be thrown by the Camel runtime:

```
org.apache.camel.CamelExchangeException : No
consumers available on endpoint: Endpoint[direct-
vm://someMissingEndpoint]
```

See also

- ▸ VM Component: `http://camel.apache.org/vm.html`
- ▸ Direct-VM Component: `http://camel.apache.org/direct-vm.html`

Using external properties in Camel routes

One of the many nice features in Spring is the ability to use property placeholders such as `${database.url}` to externalize information outside the application in a properties file. This allows your application's deployable artifacts to be built once and move through environments such as development, system test, UAT, and production, each time changing their behavior based on those external values. Camel provides a corresponding mechanism that you can use to externalize values used within routes.

This recipe will show you an approach for externalizing values, such as host name and port number, such that those values can be changed independent of the routing code.

Getting ready

Define a `propertyPlaceholder` tag inside the `camelContext` element:

```
<camelContext xmlns="http://camel.apache.org/schema/spring">
  <propertyPlaceholder
      id="properties"
      location="classpath:placeholder.properties"/>
  <!-- other code here -->
</camelContext>
```

Properties contained in the file `placeholder.properties` can then be used directly inside your Camel route using placeholders.

 The `id` value "`properties`" is mandatory.

The Java code for this recipe is located in the `org.camelcookbook.structuringroutes.propertyplaceholder` package. Spring XML files are located under `src/main/resources/META-INF/spring` and prefixed with `propertyPlaceholder`.

How to do it...

The placeholder syntax is different from the usual Spring `${..}` format, in that properties are delimited by `{{` to start and `}}` to end.

```
<route>
  <from uri="{{start.endpoint}}"/>
  <transform>
    <simple>{{transform.message}}: ${body}</simple>
  </transform>
  <to uri="{{end.endpoint}}"/>
</route>
```

Consider the following properties file content:

```
start.endpoint=direct:in
transform.message=I hear you
end.endpoint=mock:out
```

Configured with these, the preceding route will consume a message from an in-memory endpoint, prefix the body with `I hear you` and send the result to a mock endpoint for testing.

How it works...

This bridging functionality is necessary since Spring has some limitations in terms of allowing third-party libraries to use its property placeholder mechanism.

The location URI scheme can take the following forms:

`ref:`	Uses a named `java.util.Properties` object defined in the context
`file:`	Refers to a fixed path on the filesystem
`classpath:`	Refers to a file within the current application

Location URIs can themselves contain placeholders for JVM system properties and environment variables:

```
file:${karaf.home}/etc/application.properties
file:${env:CATALINA_HOME}/etc/application.properties
```

Instead of using a `property-placeholder` tag, you can also define a `PropertiesComponent` object in the Spring context with `id` as "`properties`", and it will be integrated as expected:

```
<bean id="properties"
      class="org.apache.camel.component.properties
             .PropertiesComponent">
  <property name="location"
            value="classpath:placeholder.properties"/>
</bean>
```

This also works when using Camel directly from a Java application without Spring:

```
PropertiesComponent properties = new PropertiesComponent();
properties.setLocation("classpath:placeholder.properties");
camelContext.addComponent(properties);
```

The placeholder mechanism just shown also works when defining routes in Java. The following route works as expected inside a Camel context that has a properties placeholder configured:

```
from("{{start.endpoint}}")
  .transform().simple("{{transform.message}}: ${body}")
  .log("Set message to ${body}")
  .to("{{end.endpoint}}");
```

There's more...

Camel provides a drop-in replacement for a Spring `PropertyPlaceholderConfigurer`, that enables Spring beans to be initialized with ${...} configuration while allowing Camel logic to make use of {{...}} placeholders, with the one piece of configuration.

```
<bean id="bridgePropertyPlaceholder"
      class="org.apache.camel.spring.spi
            .BridgePropertyPlaceholderConfigurer">
  <property name="location"
            value="classpath:placeholder.properties"/>
</bean>
```

See also

▶ Using Property Placeholder: http://camel.apache.org/using-propertyplaceholder.html

Reusing endpoints

When an endpoint is going to be used multiple times in a Camel context it is preferable to define it at a single place so that it is used consistently. This recipe will show you a way to do that.

Getting ready

Define your desired routing logic as described in either the *Using Camel in a Java application* recipe, or the *Embedding Camel in a Spring application* recipe.

How to do it...

In the XML DSL, define an `<endpoint/>` element with an `id` attribute and an `uri` attribute setting that is set to the URI value you wish to share:

```
<camelContext xmlns="...">
  <endpoint id="restfulOrdersService"
            uri="jetty:http://localhost:8080/orders"/>
  <route>
    <from ref="restfulOrdersService"/>
    <!-- ... -->
  </route>
</camelContext>
```

If using the Java DSL, simply define the URI as a String within `RouteBuilder configure()` method:

```
String restfulOrdersService =
    "jetty:http://localhost:8080/orders";

from(restfulOrdersService) //...
```

Reusing routing logic through template routes

One of the key advantages of using Java for defining routes is the ability to define the same, or similar, routing logic multiple times in your integrations, while changing key elements.

Consider the case of a route that:

▸ Consumes bulk order data from CSV files in an input directory

▸ Splits it into individual orders

▸ Extracts the date of each order, formatted specific to the country, and converts it to a universal one

▸ Places an order confirmation into another directory

Now consider that you may have orders from dozens of different countries, with different order and confirmation directories, and different date formats.

You could write similar routes dozens of times, but that is going to create a maintenance problem. Alternatively, using Camel's Java DSL, you can write the common routing logic once, and then use dependency injection to vary the values that are different when you instantiate the route.

This recipe will show you a strategy for creating Camel routes that can be created with different values at runtime, parameterizing your common routing logic.

Getting ready

Define your route within a `RouteBuilder` as usual, only this time make the start and end URIs, as well as any beans involved in the processing, properties of the `RouteBuilder` class:

```
public class OrderProcessingRouteBuilder extends RouteBuilder {
    String inputUri;
    String outputUri;
    private OrderFileNameProcessor orderFileNameProcessor;

    @Override
```

```
public void configure() throws Exception {
  from(inputUri)
    // split into individual lines
    .split(body(String.class).tokenize("\n"))
      .process(orderFileNameProcessor)
      .log("Writing file: ${header.CamelFileName}")
      .to(outputUri)
    .end();
  }
}
```

> Note that the URI variables are defined as package scoped.
> This will help us to test the class later.

The Java code for this recipe is located in the `org.camelcookbook.structuringroutes.` `templating` package. The Spring XML files are located under `src/main/resources/` `META-INF/spring` and prefixed with `templating`.

How to do it...

Use property setters on your `RouteBuilder` implementation to instantiate multiple instances of the route with different property values injected.

1. Add setters for the properties:

```
public void setInputDirectory(String inputDirectory) {
  inputUri = "file://" + inputDirectory;
}
public void setOutputDirectory(String outputDirectory) {
  outputUri = "file://" + outputDirectory;
}
public void setOrderFileNameProcessor(
    OrderFileNameProcessor orderFileNameProcessor) {
  this.orderFileNameProcessor = orderFileNameProcessor;
}
```

> A useful trick is to construct the endpoint URIs within the setters.
> This way, when instantiating the `RouteBuilder`, you only have to
> worry about which directories to use, not about the various additional
> attributes that you want to repeat for the file component each time.

2. Validate that the mandatory bean properties were set. The following code uses the `org.apache.commons.lang.Validate` class to check for nulls and empty Strings:

```
@PostConstruct
public void checkMandatoryProperties() {
    Validate.notEmpty(inputUri, "inputUri is empty");
    Validate.notEmpty(outputUri, "outputUri is empty");
    Validate.notNull(orderFileNameProcessor,
                    "orderFileNameProcessor is null");
}
```

 If you are using the `RouteBuilder` from Spring, add a `@PostConstruct` method to check that all of the properties have been set. This way, if all of the fields have not been initialized correctly, the application will refuse to start up.

3. To complete the integration we need to add a `Processor` that parses dates from a line of CSV text, changes the date to a universal format, and sets a header with the output filename. We encapsulate this logic in a class whose instances vary by a date format that is injected. The source for this class is available in the example code under: `org.camelcookbook.structuringroutes.templating.OrderFileNameProcessor`.

4. In your Spring XML file, you can now create multiple instances of this class:

```
<bean id="dateFirstOrderFileNameProcessor"
        class="org.camelcookbook.structuringroutes.templating
                .OrderFileNameProcessor">
    <property name="countryDateFormat" value="dd-MM-yyyy"/>
</bean>

<bean id="monthFirstOrderFileNameProcessor"
        class="org.camelcookbook.structuringroutes.templating
                .OrderFileNameProcessor">
    <property name="countryDateFormat" value="MM-dd-yyyy"/>
</bean>
```

5. We now have all of the pieces in place to perform the same integration for a number of countries that use different input and output directories, and date formats, within their order files. We can now go ahead and instantiate the `RouteBuilders` and inject them into the Camel context:

```
<bean id="ukOrdersRouteBuilder"
        class="org.camelcookbook.structuringroutes.templating
                .OrderProcessingRouteBuilder">
    <property name="inputDirectory"
            value="/orders/in/UK"/>
```

```
        <property name="outputDirectory"
                value="/orders/out/UK"/>
      <property name="orderFileNameProcessor"
                ref="dateFirstOrderFileNameProcessor"/>
   </bean>

   <bean id="usOrdersRouteBuilder"
        class="org.camelcookbook.structuringroutes.templating
              .OrderProcessingRouteBuilder">
   <property name="inputDirectory"
            value="/orders/in/US"/>
      <property name="outputDirectory"
                value="/orders/out/US"/>
      <property name="orderFileNameProcessor"
                ref="monthFirstOrderFileNameProcessor"/>
   </bean>

   <camelContext
        xmlns="http://camel.apache.org/schema/spring">
     <routeBuilder ref="ukOrdersRouteBuilder"/>
     <routeBuilder ref="usOrdersRouteBuilder"/>
   </camelContext>
```

How it works...

By treating our `RouteBuilder` implementation as just another bean to use in a Spring context, we were able to instantiate it multiple times, introducing varying behavior by changing the injected values. In the future, if we were to change the routing logic, perhaps by adding more logging, it would all be done in one place in the code.

When we defined our URI properties in the `RouteBuilder`, we set them as package scoped. This is a handy strategy that allows us to inject endpoint types from within the same package that are not `file:` endpoints, which are set when our public setter methods are used. Since test classes are typically co-located in the same package, this allows us to initialize our `RouteBuilder` with more easily testable endpoints:

```
OrderFileNameProcessor processor = new OrderFileNameProcessor();
processor.setCountryDateFormat("dd-MM-yyyy");

OrderProcessingRouteBuilder routeBuilder =
    new OrderProcessingRouteBuilder();
routeBuilder.inputUri = "direct:in";
routeBuilder.outputUri = "mock:out";
routeBuilder.setOrderFileNameProcessor(processor);
```

See *Chapter 9*, *Testing*, for more details on testing.

See also

▶   File Component: `https://camel.apache.org/file2.html`

Controlling route startup and shutdown

When integration logic is composed of routes depending on other routes via `direct:`, it is important that they start up in such a way that dependencies are available before exchanges start flowing. If not, you are likely to see this sort of exception being thrown:

```
org.apache.camel.CamelExchangeException: No consumers available on
endpoint: Endpoint[direct://someMissingEndpoint]
```

Conversely, on application shutdown, messages should complete processing gracefully rather than fail because a dependent route is no longer available. Camel provides a mechanism to define an order for startup and shutdown that addresses both of these issues at the same time.

This recipe will show you how to control the startup and shutdown order of your routes.

Getting ready

Define your desired routing logic as described in either the *Using Camel in a Java application* recipe, or the *Embedding Camel in a Spring application* recipe.

The Java code for this recipe is located in the `org.camelcookbook.structuringroutes.routecontrol` package.

How to do it...

Set the `startupOrder` property associated with the route.

In the XML DSL, add a `startupOrder` attribute to the `route` element:

```xml
<route startupOrder="20">
  <from uri="jms:queue:orders"/>
  <to uri="direct:processOrder"/>
</route>

<route startupOrder="10">
  <from uri="direct:processOrder"/>
  <process ref="orderProcessor"/>
</route>
```

In the Java DSL, call the `startupOrder(..)` method after the `from` statement:

```
from("jms:queue:orders").startupOrder(20)
  .to("direct:processOrder");

from("direct:processOrder").startupOrder(10)
  .process(new OrderProcessor());
```

How it works...

Routes are started in *ascending* `startupOrder`. In the preceding examples, the `direct:` route will be started before the main entry point to the integration, which consumes from JMS.

You can assign any integer greater than `0` and less than `1,000` to the `startupOrder`. You cannot assign the same value more than once in a Camel context, otherwise it will refuse to start up. Camel will automatically assign values greater than 1,000 to any routes that do not specifically have one defined.

> Drawing inspiration from BASIC programming (for those old enough to remember it), it is useful to assign `startupOrder` values in increments of 10. As your integration grows and you find yourself breaking routes down for reuse, it pays to have numbers available so that you do not have to renumber every route.

When you shut down the application, Camel will turn off the routes in the *reverse order* to that in which it started them. Routes are turned off in *descending* order.

When a route shuts down, the endpoint consumer is first turned off, and any messages that are flowing through the route ("in-flight") are allowed to complete before the route itself is shut down. Any messages that remain in-flight will be discarded after a timeout of 300 seconds. The timeout is configurable on the Camel context's associated `ShutdownStrategy`.

There's more...

Routes can be started and shut down programmatically through the `CamelContext` `startRoute()` and `stopRoute()` methods. Since the context is accessible through an `Exchange` it is possible to perform custom route control logic. Take, as an example, the following class that stops a route whose name is specified by the body of the exchange:

```
public class RouteStoppingProcessor implements Processor {
  @Override
  public void process(Exchange exchange) throws Exception {
    final String routeName =
        exchange.getIn().getBody(String.class);
    final CamelContext context = exchange.getContext();
```

```
      new Thread(new Runnable() {
        @Override
        public void run() {
          try {
            context.stopRoute(routeName);
          } catch (Exception e) {
            throw new RuntimeException(e);
          }
        }
      }).start();
    }
  }
```

It is best practice to manually shut down routes in Camel in a separate thread than in the one that is processing the exchange. The reason behind this is that Camel waits for all exchanges that are flowing through a route to complete before it stops the route. If a thread processing an exchange attempts to shut down the route through which that exchange is flowing, this results in a deadlock.

See the following for more details: http://camel.apache.org/how-can-i-stop-a-route-from-a-route.html.

Routes can also be stopped and started through the use of a Control Bus endpoint:

```
from("direct:in").id("mainRoute")
  .log("Stopping route")
  .to("controlbus:route?routeId=mainRoute&action=stop
      &async=true")
  .log("Signalled to stop route")
  .to("mock:out");
```

Note the use of async=true to shut down the route in a background thread and thereby prevent a deadlock.

Manual route control does not take into account the startupOrder, so you must take care when performing it that any routes that you start up or shut down are controlled in an orderly manner.

Routes can be turned off at startup by setting the autoStartup attribute to false.

In the XML DSL, add an `autoStartup` attribute to the `route` element:

```
<route autoStartup="false">
  <from uri="jms:queue:orders"/>
  <!-- ... -->
</route>
```

In the Java DSL, call the `autoStartup(..)` method after the `from` statement:

```
from("jms:queue:orders").autoStartup(false)...
```

You would use this feature if you want to control route availability manually, or through a **route policy**.

A `RoutePolicy` is an interface that you can build upon to determine whether routes should be running or not. Camel provides route policies out of the box for throttling routes (`ThrottlingInflightRoutePolicy`), defining uptime through a timer (`SimpleScheduledRoutePolicy`), and `cron` expressions (`CronScheduledRoutePolicy`).

See also

- Configuring route startup ordering and auto startup: `http://camel.apache.org/configuring-route-startup-ordering-and-autostartup.html`

- Graceful shutdown: `http://camel.apache.org/graceful-shutdown.html`

- Route Policy: `http://camel.apache.org/routepolicy.html`

- Camel Control Bus: `http://camel.apache.org/controlbus.html`

2
Message Routing

In this chapter, we will cover the following recipes:

- ► Content Based Routing
- ► Filtering out unwanted messages
- ► Wire Tap – sending a copy of the message elsewhere
- ► Multicast – routing the same message to many endpoints
- ► Recipient List – routing a message to a list of endpoints
- ► Throttler – restricting the number of messages flowing to an endpoint
- ► Request-response route sending a one-way message
- ► One-way route waiting on a request-response endpoint
- ► Dynamic Routing – making routing decisions at runtime
- ► Load balancing across a number of endpoints
- ► Routing Slip – routing a message to a fixed list of endpoints

Introduction

This chapter explains how to make use of Camel's built-in EIPs (Enterprise Integration Patterns) to write typical integration logic. Once a message is consumed from an endpoint, you will want to make decisions about what steps should be taken to process it (such as routing), and these EIPs provide you with many different message routing options. The EIPs are used within routes defined by the Camel DSLs (Domain Specific Language).

The EIPs are first class constructs within the DSL. As such, your integration logic will be able to more clearly express how the message is being routed–that is, which EIP is being used. The more you can use these EIP DSL statements within your Camel code, versus doing a lot of routing within custom Java processors, the easier it will be for you and others to understand what the Camel route is doing for future maintenance. This is a key value of Camel, so take full advantage of it within your code, and you will find that you have gained more flexibility and clarity in even the most complex integration scenarios than you ever had with your past custom code efforts.

A number of Camel architectural concepts are used throughout this chapter. There is a broader overview of Camel concepts in the *Preface*. Full details can be found on the Apache Camel website at `http://camel.apache.org`.

The code for this chapter is contained within the `camel-cookbook-routing` module of the examples.

Content Based Routing

When you need to route messages based on the content of the message, and/or based on the headers or properties associated with the message, using Camel's Content Based Router EIP is a great way to do that.

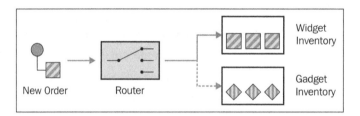

Content Based Routing and Filtering are very similar. A Content Based Router has multiple predicates, and the contained steps are performed on the *first* predicate that the message matches, or the optional `otherwise` statement if none matches (similar to an `if () {..}` `else if () {..} else {..}` statement in Java).

Camel's Filter EIP tests against a single predicate, executing the contained processing steps only if the message matches that predicate. The equivalent of a Filter in Java would be a single `if` statement.

In this recipe, we will see how to use a Content Based Router to route a message to one of the several destinations based on the content (the body) of the message.

Getting ready

The Java code for this recipe is located in the `org.camelcookbook.routing.contentbasedrouter` package. The Spring XML files are located under `src/main/resources/META-INF/spring` and prefixed with `contentBasedRouter`.

How to do it...

You need to use the `choice` DSL statement with one or more `when` statements, with their associated predicate tests, to see if the message should be routed down their path, and an *optional* `otherwise` statement that will catch all the messages that do not match any other `when` predicates.

1. Within your route, create a `choice` statement with at least one `when` statement. Each `when` statement must start with a predicate statement followed by one or more processor steps (for example, `<to uri="..."/>`).

   In the XML DSL, this is written as:

   ```
   <choice>
     <when>
       <simple>${body} contains 'Camel'</simple>
       <to uri="mock:camel"/>
       <log message="Camel ${body}"/>
     </when>
     <!-- ... -->
   </choice>
   ```

   In the Java DSL, this is expressed as:

   ```
   .choice()
     .when()
       .simple("${body} contains 'Camel'")
       .to("mock:camel")
       .log("Camel ${body}")
       //...
   .end()
   ```

In the Java DSL, you need to end the `choice` statement explicitly with a call to `end()` if you want to have further steps run after the Content Based Router is complete. The `end()` statement is like the closing `}` of a Java `if` statement–it lets the routing engine know that you are done with the Content Based Router instructions.

2. Add an `otherwise` statement to handle all of the messages that do not match any of your `when` predicates. An `otherwise` statement includes one or more steps:

In the XML DSL, this is written as:

```
<choice>
  <!-- ... -->
  <otherwise>
    <to uri="mock:other"/>
    <log message="Other ${body}"/>
  </otherwise>
</choice>
```

In the Java DSL, the same thing is written as follows:

```
.choice()
  //...
  .otherwise()
    .to("mock:other")
    .log("Other ${body}")
.end()
```

How it works...

A Content Based Router depends on Camel's Predicate capabilities. The preceding example uses Camel's *Simple* Expression Language. The Simple Expression Language provides a robust set of operators that can work on all of the data contained within the exchange (message, headers, and properties). Each `when` element requires one predicate, which can be any one of the many built-in Camel Expression Languages, including any one of the POJO (Plain Old Java Object) methods that returns a `boolean` value.

The message is routed to the *first* `when` predicate that matches, in other words, returns `true`. The message will then be routed to the one or more processor steps specified after the `when` predicate's expression, by default executing multiple processors as a **Pipeline**, that is, in sequence. If the message does not match any of the `when` predicates, it will be routed to the `otherwise` block, if specified.

After routing the message to the first matching `when` predicate, or the `otherwise` statement if there are no matches, it will route to the next processor specified (if any) after the `choice` statement.

There's more...

If you want to nest a Content Based Router within another Content Based Router, the inner `choice` statement should be defined in its own route to help with code clarity:

```
from("direct:start")
```

```
    .choice()
      .when()
        .simple("${body} contains '<xml>'")
        .to("direct:processXml")
      .otherwise()
        .to("direct:processPlainText")
    .end();

from("direct:processXml")
  .choice()
    .when()
      .xpath("/order[@units > 100]")
      .to("direct:priorityXmlOrder")
    .otherwise()
      .to("direct:normalXmlOrder")
  .end();
```

If you are routing within the when or otherwise statements to other EIP patterns, such as Load Balancer or Splitter that specify a Pipeline (sequence) of processors and finish their list of steps with an end() statement, the list of steps should instead be terminated with endChoice() statement. This works around the Java language's inability to maintain the nested context properly, and explicitly returns control from the nested EIP back to the containing choice statement:

```
.choice()
  .when().simple("${body} contains 'Camel'")
    .to("mock:camel")
    .loadBalance()
      .to("mock:a")
      .to("mock:b")
    .endChoice()
    .log("Camel ${body}")
  .otherwise()
    .to("mock:other")
    .log("Other ${body}")
.end()
```

See also

▶ Content Based Router: http://camel.apache.org/content-based-router. html

▶ Predicate: http://camel.apache.org/predicate.html

▶ endChoice: http://camel.apache.org/why-can-i-not-use-when-or-otherwise-in-a-java-camel-route.html

Filtering out unwanted messages

When you need to perform a sequence of steps only when a message matches a certain condition (Predicate), then a Filter is a good option.

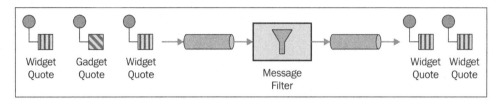

Content Based Routing and Filtering are very similar. Filtering processes a message only if it matches the single predicate provided (much like a single `if` statement).

A Content Based Router routes a message based on the *first* of the multiple predicates, or the optional `otherwise` statement if none of the provided predicates matched (similar to an `if () {..} else if () {..} else {..}` statement in Java).

This recipe will show you how to perform message processing steps only on those messages that match a specified predicate.

Getting ready

The Java code for this recipe is located in the `org.camelcookbook.routing.filtering` package. The Spring XML files are located under `src/main/resources/META-INF/spring` and prefixed with `filtering`.

How to do it...

Create a `filter` statement followed by a predicate using any of the Camel Expression Languages. After the predicate, specify one or more processor steps (multiple processor steps are executed in sequence, by default).

In the XML DSL, this routing logic is written as follows:

```
<filter>
  <simple>${body} regex '^C.*'</simple>
  <to uri="mock:C"/>
</filter>
```

In the Java DSL, the same thing is written as:

```
.filter()
  .simple("${body} regex '^C.*'")
  .to("mock:C")
.end()
```

 In the Java DSL, it's a good practice to put an `end()` statement after the last processor statement you want executed on a predicate match.

How it works...

Camel's Filtering depends on Camel's Predicate capabilities. The preceding example uses Camel's *Simple* Expression Language. The Simple Expression Language provides a robust set of operators that can work on all of the data contained within the Camel exchange (message, headers, and properties). Each `filter` element requires one predicate, which can be any one of the many built-in Camel Expression Languages, including any one of the POJO (Plain Old Java Object) methods that returns a `boolean` value. The message will be routed to the one or more processor steps specified after the predicate expression of `when`, by default executing multiple steps as a **Pipeline**, that is, in sequence.

There's more...

Camel will set a `boolean` property on the exchange named `CamelFilterMatched` (defined as a constant, `Exchange.FILTER_MATCHED`). It will be set to `true` if the message matched the previous Filter's predicate. Be careful if you have multiple Filter statements, as the `FilterMatched` property will be set to `true` or `false` by each Filter's predicate, meaning it will represent the value of the *last* Filter's predicate that processed the message.

See also

- Filter: `http://camel.apache.org/message-filter.html`
- Predicate: `http://camel.apache.org/predicate.html`

Wire Tap – sending a copy of the message elsewhere

When you want to process the current message in the background (concurrently) to the main route, without requiring a response, the Wire Tap EIP can help. A typical use case for this is logging the message to a backend system. The main thread of execution will continue to process the message through the current route as usual, while Wire Tap allows additional messaging processing to occur outside of the main route.

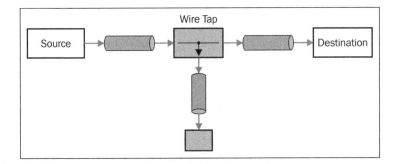

This recipe will show you how to send a copy of the message to a different endpoint.

Getting ready

The Java code for this recipe is located in the `org.camelcookbook.routing.wiretap` package. The Spring XML files are located under `src/main/resources/META-INF/spring` and prefixed with `wireTap`.

How to do it...

Use the `wireTap` statement and specify the endpoint URI of where to send a copy of the message.

In the XML DSL, this is written as follows:

```
<route>
  <from uri="direct:start"/>
  <wireTap uri="mock:tapped"/>
  <to uri="mock:out"/>
</route>
```

In the Java DSL, the same route is expressed as:

```
from("direct:start")
  .wireTap("mock:tapped")
  .to("mock:out");
```

How it works...

The Wire Tap processor, by default, makes a shallow copy of the Camel Exchange instance, and then processes it on a thread from a pool managed by the Camel routing engine. The copy of the exchange is sent to the endpoint specified in the `wireTap` DSL statement.

In the preceding example, this thread simply dispatches it to a `mock:` endpoint.

A typical use case for the Wire Tap is to log the current message to a backend system. An implementation of this would pass the current message to another route via a `direct:` reference. The second route would be responsible for formatting a message based on the payload before invoking the backend system.

When the message is copied, the headers and a direct reference to the original message are copied into a new Exchange object. This allows the route that processes the wire-tapped message to make changes to the message without affecting the original message flowing through the main route.

The **Message Exchange Pattern** (**MEP**) on the wire-tapped message is set to `InOnly`, indicating that the main route expects no response from the side route.

The body of the wire tapped message is the same object as that in the original message, as Camel performs a shallow copy of the exchange. It is therefore possible that two routes executing on the wire-tapped message object may change the internal state of that object, thereby leaking information into each other. See the following *Deep copying of the exchange* section for details on doing a deep copy of the exchange.

We are going to pass an instance of a `Cheese` class into a route:

```
public class Cheese {
    private int age; // getters and setters omitted
}
```

Within the route, we want the message to be processed concurrently by the following code:

```
public class CheeseRipener {
  public static void ripen(Cheese cheese) {
    cheese.setAge(cheese.getAge() + 1);
  }
}
```

Here is the route that we will call, starting with a call to the `direct:start` endpoint, logging the current age of `Cheese`, asynchronously passing the message to another route `direct:processInBackground`, delaying by 1,000 ms, and then passing the message to an endpoint `mock:out`:

```
from("direct:start")
   .log("Cheese is ${body.age} months old")
   .wireTap("direct:processInBackground")
   .delay(constant(1000))
   .to("mock:out");

from("direct:processInBackground")
   .bean(CheeseRipener.class, "ripen")
   .to("mock:tapped");
```

The result of passing `Cheese` with an age of 1 into `direct:start` will be that `mock:out` will see the age changed to 2, even though the modification to the `Cheese` state happened in the wire tapped route.

Deep copying of the exchange

Whenever possible, this sort of state leakage can be avoided by making messages immutable by setting state through constructors only. When this is not possible, and the tapping route modifies the state, the Wire Tap EIP provides us with a mechanism to perform a "deep" copy of the message.

To exercise this functionality, we add a deep cloning method to our model `Cheese`:

```
public Cheese clone() {
   Cheese cheese = new Cheese();
   cheese.setAge(this.getAge());
   return cheese;
}
```

Implement a `Processor` class to perform the cloning step:

```
public class CheeseCloningProcessor implements Processor {
   public void process(Exchange exchange) throws Exception {
      Message in = exchange.getIn();
      Cheese cheese = in.getBody(Cheese.class);
      if (cheese != null) {
         in.setBody(cheese.clone());
      }
   }
}
```

Finally, modify the original route by setting the `onPrepare` attribute with our custom processor:

```
.wireTap("direct:processInBackground")
  .onPrepare(new CheeseCloningProcessor())
```

In the XML DSL, we need to define an instance of the implementation as a bean in the surrounding context:

```
<bean id="cheeseCloningProcessor"
      class="org.camelcookbook.routing.CheeseCloningProcessor"/>
```

We then refer to the bean instance from within the route definition:

```
<route>
  <from uri="direct:start"/>
  <wireTap uri="direct:processInBackground"
           onPrepareRef="cheeseCloningProcessor"/>
  <to uri="mock:out"/>
</route>
```

There's more...

Camel sets up a default thread pool, which is usually adequate enough that you would not need to customize it.

> The default thread pool starts with 10 threads, and grows to 20 when necessary, shutting down threads after 60 seconds of inactivity (see `org.apache.camel.impl.DefaultExecutorServiceManager`).

It is possible to set up a custom thread pool that is more suited to your particular use case, and to refer to it directly from within the EIP. The following code sets up a pool with a single thread that will process the wire-tapped messages in sequence, and record the name of the thread in the exchange:

```
<threadPool id="oneThreadOnly"
            threadName="JustMeDoingTheTapping"
            poolSize="1"
            maxPoolSize="1"
            maxQueueSize="100"/>

<route>
  <from uri="direct:start"/>
  <wireTap uri="direct:tapped"
           executorServiceRef="oneThreadOnly"/>
  <to uri="mock:out"/>
```

```
    </route>

    <route>
      <from uri="direct:tapped"/>
      <setHeader headerName="threadName">
        <simple>${threadName}</simple>
      </setHeader>
      <to uri="mock:tapped"/>
    </route>
```

An abridged Java equivalent would be:

```
ThreadPoolBuilder builder = new ThreadPoolBuilder(getContext());
ExecutorService oneThreadOnly =
    builder.poolSize(1).maxPoolSize(1)
      .maxQueueSize(100).build("JustMeDoingTheTapping");

from("direct:start")
  .wireTap("direct:tapped").executorService(oneThreadOnly)
  .to("mock:out");

from("direct:tapped")
  .setHeader("threadName").simple("${threadName}")
  .to("mock:tapped");
```

See also

- Wire Tap: http://camel.apache.org/wire-tap.html
- SEDA for asynchronous processing by another route: http://camel.apache.org/seda.html
- Multicast for processing by multiple processors: http://camel.apache.org/multicast.html
- Content Enricher EIP for calling out to a side route, and merging the response with the original message: https://camel.apache.org/content-enricher.html
- Thread pools and thread pool profiles: http://camel.apache.org/threading-model.html

Multicast – routing the same message to many endpoints

When you want to route the same message to a number of endpoints and have them process the message in different ways, the Multicast EIP is a good choice.

This recipe will show you the default, sequential way to use Camel's Multicast EIP. *Chapter 6, Parallel Processing*, contains a recipe for using Multicast with concurrency (threads).

Getting ready

The Java code for this recipe is located in the `org.camelcookbook.routing.multicast` package. The Spring XML files are located under `src/main/resources/META-INF/spring` and prefixed with `multicast`.

How to do it...

Use the `multicast` DSL statement, and list the endpoints and processing steps within it.

In the XML DSL, this routing logic is written as:

```
<route>
  <from uri="direct:start"/>
  <multicast>
    <to uri="mock:first"/>
    <to uri="mock:second"/>
    <to uri="mock:third"/>
  </multicast>
</route>
```

In the Java DSL, the same thing is written as follows:

```
from("direct:start")
  .multicast()
    .to("mock:first")
    .to("mock:second")
    .to("mock:third")
  .end();
```

How it works...

The example has each of the specified steps called in sequence on the same thread. We will talk about how to do this with multiple threads in *Chapter 6, Parallel Processing*.

When a message hits the Multicast EIP, a shallow copy of the message (see the *Wire Tap – sending a copy of the message elsewhere* recipe for an explanation) is made for each step specified in the EIP definition. The thread currently processing the message triggers each of the specified steps one by one with a unique copy of the message. Any changes made to these copied messages will not be visible in the original message that continues flowing down the main route once the Multicast is complete.

It is, however, possible for mutable state to leak information between messages when the body of a message is modified (see the *Wire Tap – sending a copy of the message elsewhere* recipe for an explanation).

A Multicast is quite different from merely invoking a number of steps in sequence:

```
from("direct:start")
  .to("direct:first")
  .to("direct:second")
  .to("direct:third");
```

In this route, each of the endpoints operates on the *same* message object; in a Multicast, each receives a *copy* of the original. In the preceding example, any changes made to the exchange within the route referenced by direct:first such as the setting of header values will be visible in the exchange when processing direct:second and direct:third.

In a Multicast, the MEP (Message Exchange Pattern) of the copied messages will be set to InOnly by *default* regardless of the MEP of the original message. This means that the original route will not receive a response. In this respect, the default behavior of a Multicast is similar to a Wire Tap with multiple steps; only the thread executing through the main route is responsible for processing the message copies through the steps. You can change this behavior, as described in the next section.

There's more...

Sometimes you may want to receive responses from the processor that you invoke in a Multicast, and modify the original message with the response. In order to do this, you need to provide an implementation of the AggregationStrategy interface to the Multicast EIP. This interface defines a single method:

```
public Exchange aggregate(Exchange oldExchange,
                          Exchange newExchange)
```

The `newExchange` parameter is the current Multicast response being processed, and `oldExchange` parameter is the merged result so far. Note that the first time the `aggregate()` method is called, `oldExchange` will be `null` (see the Aggregator EIP for more details).

The following is a simple `AggregationStrategy` to concatenate String responses:

```
public class ConcatenatingAggregationStrategy
    implements AggregationStrategy {
  @Override
  public Exchange aggregate(Exchange oldExchange,
                            Exchange newExchange) {
    if (oldExchange == null) {
      return newExchange;
    } else {
      String oldBody =
          oldExchange.getIn().getBody(String.class);
      String newBody =
          newExchange.getIn().getBody(String.class);
      String merged = (oldBody == null) ? newBody
          : oldBody + "," + newBody;
      oldExchange.getIn().setBody(merged);
      return oldExchange;
    }
  }
}
```

Defining an aggregation repository on the EIP will result in the MEP on the messages sent to the Multicast steps to be set to `InOut`.

To enable this as part of the Multicast:

```
from("direct:start")
  .multicast().aggregationStrategy(
      new ConcatenatingAggregationStrategy())
  // list one or more endpoints here
  .end();
```

In the XML DSL, we need to define an instance of the implementation as a bean in the surrounding context:

```
<bean id="concatenatingStrategy"
      class="ConcatenatingAggregationStrategy"/>
```

We then refer to the bean instance from within the route definition.

In the XML DSL, we need to define an instance of the implementation as a bean in the surrounding context:

```
<route>
  <from uri="direct:start"/>
  <multicast aggregationStrategyRef="concatenatingStrategy">
    <!-- list one or more endpoints here -->
  </multicast>
</route>
```

The aggregation strategy defined here will only aggregate responses with each other, not the original message. If you want to merge the responses with the request, you should use Multicast in combination with the Content Enricher EIP using the same `AggregationStrategy` instance for both EIPs:

```
AggregationStrategy concatenationStrategy =
    new ConcatenatingAggregationStrategy();

from("direct:start")
  .enrich("direct:performMulticast", concatenationStrategy)
  // copy the In message to the Out message;
  // this will become the route response
  .transform(body());

from("direct:performMulticast")
  .multicast().aggregationStrategy(concatenationStrategy)
    .to("direct:first")
    .to("direct:second")
  .end();
```

There are two ways to deal with an exception in a Multicast:

▶   Use the `multicast().stopOnException()` flag. This will stop any further endpoints from being called and immediately terminate the processing of the message through the current route.

▶   Handle the exception within an `AggregationStrategy` implementation. This can be performed by checking the value of `newExchange.isFailed()` and taking appropriate action.

The following will result in a `org.apache.camel.CamelExecutionException` being thrown by the Camel runtime in a Multicast. This exception cannot be caught.

- Failure to handle the exception in the sub-route, when not using an `AggregationStrategy` implementation.

- Throwing exceptions from an `AggregationStrategy` implementation. To gracefully handle an exception within `AggregationStrategy`, check the value of `newExchange.isFailed()`.

It is possible to invoke each step in the Multicast in parallel rather than sequentially. To enable this, the `parallelProcessing` statement should be used within the EIP:

```
from("direct:start")
    .multicast().parallelProcessing()
        .to("mock:first")
        .to("mock:second")
    .end();
```

The default thread pool behavior may be modified as per the Wire Tap EIP, by further referring to a custom thread pool.

An Exchange instance maintains a `UnitOfWork` object. This encapsulates the details of any transaction that the message is participating in, and provides the Camel routing engine with hooks to commit or rollback any transactional resources that have been used within a route.

Each of the steps within the Multicast receives a copy of the original message, which, by default, does not include the original `UnitOfWork`. In a Multicast, each step will see a different `UnitOfWork` object. Setting the `shareUnitOfWork` attribute of the EIP to `true` can modify this behavior so that all routing is performed in the context of the same transaction.

Sharing the `UnitOfWork` object is usually a bad idea when used in conjunction with `parallelProcessing`. Transactional resources such as JMS `Session` objects and JDBC `Connection` objects are intended for use by a single thread at a time.

See also

- Take a look at *Chapter 8, Transactions and Idempotency*, for a description of the `UnitOfWork` object, and how it may not work as expected when shared across thread boundaries

- Multicast: `http://camel.apache.org/multicast.html`

Recipient List – routing a message to a list of endpoints

When you want to dynamically (at runtime) decide a list of endpoints that an individual message should be sent to, use the Recipient List EIP. This EIP is made up of two phases: deciding where to route the message, and subsequently invoking those route steps. It can be thought of as a dynamic Multicast, and behaves in much the same way.

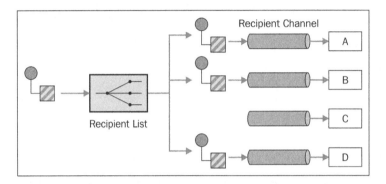

This recipe will show you how to route a message to a number of dynamically specified endpoints.

Getting ready

The Java code for this recipe is located in the `org.camelcookbook.routing.recipientlist` package. The Spring XML files are located under `src/main/resources/META-INF/spring` and prefixed with `recipientList`.

How to do it...

Use the `recipientList` DSL statement, which includes an Expression that tells it where to get, the list of endpoints for routing the message at runtime.

In the XML DSL, this routing logic is written as:

```
<route>
  <from uri="direct:start"/>
  <setHeader headerName="endpointsToBeTriggered">
    <method ref="messageRouter"
            method="getDestinationsFromMessage"/>
  </setHeader>
  <recipientList>
    <header>endpointsToBeTriggered</header>
  </recipientList>
</route>
```

In the Java DSL, the same thing is expressed as:

```
from("direct:start")
  .setHeader("endpointsToBeTriggered")
    // you implement the method below
    .method(MessageRouter.class,
           "getDestinationsFromMessage")
  .recipientList(header("endpointsToBeTriggered"));
```

How it works...

The first phase of the process, deciding which steps to route to, could be as follows:

1. An explicit step that you decide via a custom piece of logic based on the message contents.
2. Skipped, as the list of endpoint URIs is already contained somewhere in the message.

The second phase triggers the EIP implementation with an Expression telling it where the endpoint addresses to route to are found in the message.

In the preceding example, we set a header on the message with a list of endpoint URIs as a string delimited with a comma (,) symbol.

```
public class MessageRouter {
  public String getDestinationsFromMessage (Exchange exchange) {
    String orderType = exchange.getIn()
        .getHeader("orderType", String.class);
    if (orderType == null) {
      return "direct:unrecognized";
    } else if (orderType.equals("priority")) {
      return "direct:order.priority,direct:billing";
    } else {
      return "direct:order.normal,direct:billing";
    }
  }
}
```

You can change the character used to delimit the list of endpoints in the String through the `delimiter` attribute.

You do not have to use a header, the Recipient List DSL statement can use any Expression to determine the list of endpoint URIs to send to.

The `recipientList` statement can also process any `iterable` type, so you could just as well return an array, a `java.util.Collection`, `java.util.Iterator`, or `org.w3c.dom.NodeList`. By default, the EIP will iterate over the endpoint URIs in order, and invoke them with a copy of the original exchange one after the other in the same thread.

There's more...

If one of the endpoint URIs named by your Expression is unrecognized, Camel will throw an `org.apache.camel.ResolveEndpointFailedException`. "Unrecognized" in this context means that one of the endpoint URIs that was returned by the Recipient List Expression referred to an endpoint that could not be resolved by Camel. The body of the exception might look as follows:

```
Failed to resolve endpoint: randommq://cheese due to: No component
found with scheme: randommq
```

This is a type of exception that cannot be handled by the route. It indicates a serious problem with the routing logic that is not detected until runtime. You can, however, relax this constraint by using the `ignoreInvalidEndpoints` attribute:

```
from("direct:start")
  .setHeader("multicastTo")
    .constant("direct:first,direct:second,randommq:cheese")
  .recipientList()
    .header("multicastTo").ignoreInvalidEndpoints();
```

The Recipient List and Multicast EIPs share a lot of functionality. In fact, the only real difference is that the list of endpoints is worked out through an Expression. With both EIPs it is possible to:

- Execute each endpoint using a different thread via `parallelProcessing`
- Aggregate responses from the endpoints together using a custom `AggregationStrategy`
- Avoid calling any uncalled endpoints via `stopOnException`
- Share the transactional context via `shareUnitOfWork`
- Perform deep cloning of the exchange using `onPrepareRef`

See also

- The *Multicast – routing the same message to many endpoints* recipe
- Recipient List: `http://camel.apache.org/recipient-list.html`

Throttler – restricting the number of messages flowing to an endpoint

When you need to limit the number of messages flowing through a route during a specified time period, the Throttler EIP can help. For example, if you have a downstream system that can only handle 10 requests per second, using a Throttler EIP within your route can ensure that you do not exceed that rate.

This recipe will show you how to restrict the number of messages routed to a set of endpoints during a specified time period.

Getting ready

The Java code for this recipe is located in the `org.camelcookbook.routing.throttler` package. The Spring XML files are located under `src/main/resources/META-INF/spring` and prefixed with `throttler`.

How to do it...

In order to use the Throttler, perform the following steps:

1. You must specify the maximum number of messages to be allowed per time period (defaults to 1,000 ms).

   In the XML DSL, this is specified as an Expression to allow for the maximum rate to be changed at runtime. In this example, we are using the Constant Expression Language to set the maximum number of messages to 5.

   ```
   <route>
     <from uri="direct:start"/>
     <throttle>
       <constant>5</constant>
       <to uri="mock:throttled"/>
     </throttle>
   </route>
   ```

   In the Java DSL, you can provide either `java.lang.Long`, which will be interpreted like the results of a Constant Expression Language expression, or you can provide an Expression that will be evaluated for each message to determine the current maximum number of messages per time period.

You need to specify `.end()` statement after the steps you want constrained by the Throttler if you have additional steps afterwards.

```
from("direct:start")
  .throttle(5)
    .to("mock:throttled")
  .end()
  .to("mock:after");
```

2. Optionally, explicitly specify the time period over which throttling is performed in your route. This is the time period for which the Throttler will only allow the maximum number of messages you specified in the previous step. This example sets the time period to 2,000 ms or 2 seconds, so every 2 seconds the Throttler will allow up to 5 messages to be processed.

   In the XML DSL, this is written as:

   ```
   <route>
     <from uri="direct:start"/>
     <throttle timePeriodMillis="2000">
       <constant>5</constant>
       <to uri="mock:throttled"/>
     </throttle>
   </route>
   ```

   In the Java DSL, the same route is expressed as:

   ```
   from("direct:start")
     .throttle(5).timePeriodMillis(2000)
       .to("mock:throttled")
     .end()
     .to("mock:after");
   ```

How it works...

The Throttler evaluates the `maximumRequestsPerPeriod` Expression for each message being processed. The processing of this message is delayed if it exceeds the specified rate. The use of an Expression allows for the throttling rate to be changed at runtime through aspects of the current message, or calls to an external Java object (using the Bean Expression Language). By default, the Throttler will block the route's thread of execution until the throttle rate drops below the specified maximum.

An example of using a message header, `ThrottleRate`, to set the throttle rate is as follows. In this example, the header name can be anything, you just need to provide the name of the header whose value will be evaluated as `java.lang.Long` and used as the `maximumRequestsPerPeriod`.

```
<throttle timePeriodMillis="10000">
  <header>ThrottleRate</header>
  <to uri="mock:throttled"/>
</throttle>
```

There's more...

The Throttler provides an `asyncDelayed` option that will take messages that would exceed the throttle rate, and schedule future execution for them, releasing the route's current thread for other uses. An alternative thread pool can be provided through the `executorServiceRef` option. Here's an example in the XML DSL:

```
<camelContext xmlns="http://camel.apache.org/schema/spring">
  <threadPoolProfile id="myThrottler"
                     poolSize="5"
                     maxPoolSize="20"
                     maxQueueSize="1000"
                     rejectedPolicy="CallerRuns"/>

  <route>
    <from uri="direct:start"/>
    <to uri="mock:unthrottled"/>
    <throttle timePeriodMillis="10000"
              asyncDelayed="true"
              executorServiceRef="myThrottler">
      <constant>5</constant>
      <to uri="mock:throttled"/>
    </throttle>
    <to uri="mock:after"/>
  </route>
</camelContext>
```

If your needs are less exacting, you can use `org.apache.camel.impl.ThrottlingInflightRoutePolicy` class instead of the Throttler. The `ThrottlingInflightRoutePolicy` is less accurate than the Throttler, but can be more easily applied to one or more routes within a Camel context.

See also

▶ Throttler: `http://camel.apache.org/throttler.html`

▶ Expression: `http://camel.apache.org/expression.html`

▶ `ThrottlingInflightRoutePolicy`: `http://camel.apache.org/`
`routepolicy.html#RoutePolicy-ThrottlingInflightRoutePolicy`

Request-response route sending a one-way message

When processing a message in a Request-Response (`InOut`) route, you sometimes need to send the message to an endpoint, but do not want to receive a response. This recipe shows you how to invoke such an endpoint using the `InOnly` MEP.

The MEP used can radically alter the behavior of an endpoint. For example, if you invoke a JMS endpoint within a request-response (`InOut`) route, it will send a message to a queue and set up a listener on a temporary destination waiting for a response; this is known as request-response over messaging. If the consumer of the message on the other side of the queue has not been written to send a response message, your route will wait indefinitely (or as long as the configurable timeout of the component).

This recipe shows how you can alter the MEP temporarily in order to send messages one way in a request-response route.

Getting ready

The Java code for this recipe is located in the `org.camelcookbook.routing.` `changingmep` package. The Spring XML files are located under `src/main/resources/` `META-INF/spring` and prefixed with `changingMep`.

How to do it...

Use the `inOnly` DSL statement to explicitly route a message to that endpoint with that specific MEP:

In the XML DSL, this is written as:

```
<route>
  <from uri="direct:start"/>
  <inOnly uri="direct:oneWay"/>
  <transform>
    <constant>Done</constant>
  </transform>
</route>
```

The Endpoint invocation could also be written as:

```
<to uri="direct:oneWay" pattern="InOnly"/>
```

In the Java DSL, the same thing is expressed as:

```
from("direct:start")
  .inOnly("direct:oneWay")
  .transform().constant("Done");
```

The Endpoint invocation could also be written as:

```
to(ExchangePattern.InOnly, "direct:oneWay")
```

How it works...

When the message reaches the stage in the route that sends to the InOnly endpoint, the MEP associated with the exchange is temporarily changed to InOnly for the call to the specified endpoint and restored on completion of that call.

There is no need to copy the message as this DSL statement is just like a normal to statement sending the message to an endpoint; it just temporarily changes the MEP such that it does not wait for a response from that endpoint.

There's more...

The thread that processes the exchange through the main route is also used to process it through the producer endpoint (direct:oneWay). This makes this pattern very different to a Wire Tap, where we hand over the processing of the message to another thread.

See also

- The *Wire Tap – sending a copy of the message elsewhere* recipe
- Wire Tap: http://camel.apache.org/wire-tap.html
- Multicast: http://camel.apache.org/multicast.html

One-way route waiting on a request-response endpoint

Assume that you have a route that uses the InOnly Message Exchange Pattern (MEP). The consumer that fed a message into the route expects no response. Any endpoint listed in the route will, as a consequence, be invoked with the InOnly MEP.

This recipe shows how you can alter the MEP temporarily to InOut in order to request a response from an endpoint used in a one-way route.

Getting ready

The Java code for this recipe is located in the org.camelcookbook.routing. changingmep package. The Spring XML files are located under src/main/resources/META-INF/spring and prefixed with changingMep.

How to do it...

Use the inOut DSL statement to explicitly route a message to that endpoint with that specific MEP.

In the XML DSL, this logic is written as follows:

```
<route>
  <from uri="direct:in"/>
  <inOut uri="direct:modifyMessage"/>
  <to uri="mock:afterMessageModified"/>
</route>
```

The Endpoint invocation could also be written as:
```
<to uri="direct:modifyMessage" pattern="InOut"/>
```

In the Java DSL, the same thing is expressed as:

```
from("direct:start")
  .inOut("direct:modifyMessage")
  .to("mock:afterMessageModified");
```

> The Endpoint invocation could also be written as:
>
> ```
> .to(ExchangePattern.InOut, "direct:modifyMessage")
> ```

How it works...

When the message is passed to the `modifyMessage` endpoint in the example, the MEP on the exchange is temporarily changed from `InOnly` to `InOut`. The same thread that processed the message down the main route will process the message through the `InOut` endpoint. The message continues to take part in any transactions defined in the main route.

When a response is returned, and the message resumes its flow down the main route, the MEP will be restored to that of the original exchange's MEP, as in the preceding example, `InOnly`.

If you want to permanently switch the MEP to `InOut` for the remainder of the route use the `setExchangePattern` DSL statement. This will not affect the behavior of the route's consumer (`from`) endpoint.

In the XML DSL, this is written as:

```
<setExchangePattern pattern="InOut"/>
```

In the Java DSL, the same thing is expressed as:

```
.setExchangePattern(ExchangePattern.InOut)
```

There's more...

This recipe is frequently seen in integrations that use JMS messaging as a source. Here, a route consumes messages from a JMS queue, and invokes another queue with the `InOut` pattern; the intent being to perform a request-response operation over messaging over the second queue.

```
from("jms:inbound")
  .inOut("jms:serviceRequest")
  .log("Service responded with: ${body}");
```

See also

▸ SEDA Component: `https://camel.apache.org/seda.html`

Dynamic Routing – making routing decisions at runtime

When you need to route to a sequence of endpoints, and that list may change based on the response from any of those endpoints, a Dynamic Router can be a good solution. Similar to a Routing Slip, where a list of endpoints to route to is created and executed, the Dynamic Router can alter the next endpoint to route to, based on the results of previous endpoints via a feedback loop.

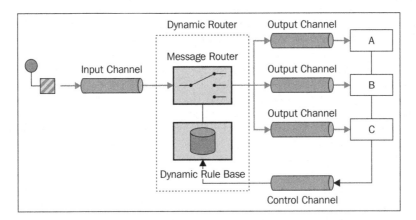

This recipe will show you how to efficiently route a message to endpoints by calling your code to make the routing decisions at runtime.

Getting ready

The Java code for this recipe is located in the `org.camelcookbook.routing.dynamicrouter` package. The Spring XML files are located under `src/main/resources/META-INF/spring` and prefixed with `dynamicRouter`.

How to do it...

There are two steps for a Dynamic Router: create a route consumer and optionally transform the message in preparation for dynamic routing, and call the Dynamic Router Expression (most commonly a Java method through the Method Expression Language).

1. Create a route and optionally transform the message in preparation for the initial call to the Dynamic Router Expression. The `dynamicRouter` takes an Expression that will most often be a call to a Java method. It must return `null` to indicate that routing is finished.

   In the XML DSL, this logic is written as:

   ```
   <route>
     <from uri="direct:start"/>
     <dynamicRouter>
       <method ref="myDynamicRouter"
               method="routeMe"/>
     </dynamicRouter>
   </route>
   ```

   In the Java DSL, the same thing is expressed as:

   ```
   from("direct:start")
     .dynamicRouter(method(MyDynamicRouter.class,
                           "routeMe"));
   ```

2. Create the Dynamic Router. In this example, we're calling a Java method, and we're using Camel's Bean Injection capabilities to pass parts of the exchange to the Java method versus the entire exchange for cleaner code.

   ```
   public String routeMe(String body,
     @Properties Map<String, Object> properties) {
     // store a property with the message exchange
     // this will drive the routing decisions of this
     // Dynamic Router implementation
     int invoked = 0;

     // property will be null on first call
     Object current = properties.get("invoked");
     if (current != null) {
       invoked = Integer.valueOf(current.toString());
     }
     invoked++;
     properties.put("invoked", invoked);

     if (invoked == 1) {
       return "mock:a";
   ```

```
      } else if (invoked == 2) {
        return "mock:b,mock:c";
      } else if (invoked == 3) {
        return "direct:other";
      } else if (invoked == 4) {
        return "mock:result";
      }

      // no more, so return null
      return null;
    }
```

How it works...

The Dynamic Router uses an Expression to do the routing. This Expression will be called repeatedly, once after Camel calls the endpoint URIs returned from the last Expression invocation. When routing is finished, the Expression must return `null`.

In the Dynamic Router EIP, this Expression keeps getting called until this condition is met, so it is very important to test that your Expression ultimately returns `null`, otherwise your route will loop infinitely.

If the Expression returns a list of endpoint URIs, these will be called in sequence. The Expression may separate the URIs with a delimiter, which, by default, is a comma (`,`). The separator can be changed using the `uriDelimiter` attribute of the `dynamicRouter` DSL statement.

There's more...

As it is so common for the Dynamic Router to be a Java method, we can use Camel's Bean Injection capabilities to put everything into the Java class using Java Annotations. The `@DynamicRouter` annotation provides the same information to Camel as the `dynamicRouter` statement within a Camel route. See *Chapter 3, Routing to Your Code*, for more details on Camel's strong integration with your Java code.

The `@Consume` annotation tells Camel to create a new route consuming on the provided endpoint URI; there is no need to provide a separate route definition.

You need to instantiate your annotated bean within a Camel supported dependency injection framework, like Spring or OSGi Blueprint, with a defined Camel context for this to work.

```
@Consume(uri = "direct:dynamicRouteAnnotated")
@DynamicRouter(delimiter = ",")
public String routeMe(String body,
    @Properties Map<String, Object> properties) {
  // ...
}
```

See also

▸ Dynamic Router: `http://camel.apache.org/dynamic-router.html`

▸ Bean Injection: `http://camel.apache.org/bean-integration.html`

▸ Bean Binding: `http://camel.apache.org/bean-binding.html`

▸ Expression: `http://camel.apache.org/expression.html`

Load balancing across a number of endpoints

When you need the ability to distribute a sequence of messages between a predefined set of endpoints, the Load Balancer EIP is a good choice. This is useful for tasks such as web service load balancing at the application level, when a hardware load balancer is not available for use. This EIP allows you to plug in a number of strategies to define how the messages should be distributed amongst the endpoints.

This recipe will show you how to load balance (route) a message across a set of endpoints using a specified policy (for example, round robin).

Getting ready

The Java code for this recipe is located in the `org.camelcookbook.routing.loadbalancer` package. The Spring XML files are located under `src/main/resources/META-INF/spring` and prefixed with `loadBalancer`.

How to do it...

The following demonstrates how you might distribute messages using a **round-robin** strategy.

In the XML DSL, this routing logic is written as follows:

```
<route>
  <from uri="direct:start"/>
  <loadBalance>
    <roundRobin/>
    <to uri="mock:first"/>
    <to uri="mock:second"/>
    <to uri="mock:third"/>
  </loadBalance>
  <to uri="mock:out"/>
</route>
```

In the Java DSL, the same thing is expressed as:

```
from("direct:start")
  .loadBalance().roundRobin()
    .to("mock:first")
    .to("mock:second")
    .to("mock:third")
  .end()
  .to("mock:out");
```

How it works...

The Load Balancer EIP can be thought of as a processing phase that has a number of producer endpoints to choose from when a message is fed into it. It decides which endpoint should get the next message based on the provided *load-balancing strategy*.

The preceding example uses the simplest of the pre-defined strategies, **round-robin**. The first message goes to the first endpoint, the second to the second endpoint, the third to the third endpoint, the fourth back to the first endpoint, and so on. In that respect, it can be thought of as a stateful switch.

There are a number of other strategies that can be used out of the box.

The **random** strategy is the most straightforward. It behaves as the name would suggest. In the XML DSL, it is used as follows:

```
.loadBalance().random()
```

The same thing written in the Java DSL appears as:

```
<loadBalance>
  <random/>
  <!-- ... -->
</loadBalance>
```

The **sticky** load-balancing strategy works similar to a round-robin in that it distributes messages evenly between endpoints; however, all messages that share the same result for a provided Expression will be routed to the same endpoint. You might use this strategy to ensure that the same server handles all processing requests for a given customer.

The following demonstrates its use in the Java DSL:

```
.loadBalance().sticky(header("customerId"))
```

In the XML DSL, it is expressed slightly differently:

```
<loadBalance>
  <sticky>
    <correlationExpression>
      <header>customerId</header>
    </correlationExpression>
  </sticky>
  <!-- ... -->
</loadBalance>
```

The sticky load balancer uses the correlation Expression to get a data value that is used to create a hash key that is used to bucket messages to the same load balanced endpoints.

The **failover** strategy allows you to define a set of steps that will be tried in sequence until one of them succeeds, or the maximum number of retries is reached. The default behavior is that the steps are attempted in a top-down order, but you can set it so the pattern otherwise acts like a round-robin.

In the Java DSL, this is written as:

```
.loadBalance()
  .failover(-1,     // max retry attempts
            false,  // whether the current route's error handler
                    // should come into play
            true)   // round-robin
  .to("direct:first")
  .to("direct:second")
.end()
```

The XML DSL version is a lot simpler to read:

```
<loadBalance>
  <failover roundRobin="true"/>
  <to uri="direct:first"/>
  <to uri="direct:second"/>
</loadBalance>
```

It is also possible to configure the failover to happen only on certain exceptions and otherwise revert back to the route's exception handling.

In the Java DSL, you express this as follows:

```
.failover(IllegalStateException.class)
```

In the XML DSL, this is written as:

```
<failover>
  <exception>java.lang.IllegalStateException</exception>
</failover>
```

It is also possible to use **weighted** load balancing strategies to favor certain steps over others. You may want to do this if you have a set of servers that are being integrated, some of which are more capable than others. The general idea is to provide a list of weightings that are used as a ratio.

In the XML DSL, this strategy is used as follows:

```
<loadBalance>
  <weighted roundRobin="true" distributionRatio="4,2,1"/>
  <to uri="mock:first"/>
  <to uri="mock:second"/>
  <to uri="mock:third"/>
</loadBalance>
```

In the Java DSL, the same thing is written as:

```
.loadBalance().weighted(true, // true = round-robin,
                        // false = random
              "4,2,1") // distribution ratio
  .to("mock:first")
  .to("mock:second")
  .to("mock:third")
```

A **topic** strategy also exists, which behaves in a similar manner to the Multicast EIP, but without the full options of that pattern.

There's more...

If one of the pre-defined strategies does not suit your use case, it is possible to define your own **custom** load balancing strategy and use it within this EIP. To do this, you would extend the abstract `org.apache.camel.processor.loadbalancer.LoadBalancerSupport` class (see the Camel implementations for details), and provide it to the Load Balancer EIP.

In the XML DSL, the `ref` attribute refers to a bean defined in your Camel context:

```
<loadBalance>
  <custom ref="myCustomLoadBalancingStrategy"/>
  <!-- ... -->
</loadBalance>
```

In the Java DSL, you can pass the instance directly into the `custom` statement:

```
.loadBalance().custom(new MyCustomLoadBalancingStrategy())
```

See also

- ▸ Load Balancer: `http://camel.apache.org/load-balancer.html`
- ▸ The *Multicast – routing the same message to many endpoints* recipe.

Routing Slip – routing a message to a fixed list of endpoints

When you need to dynamically compute the list of endpoints to route a message to at runtime, a Routing Slip EIP can help. The Routing Slip can use a message, an external source, or typically a message header (generated from a previous route step) to determine the list of endpoints to route the message to.

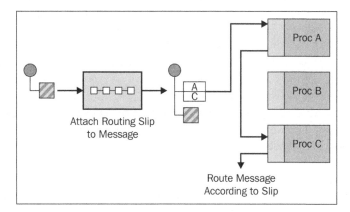

The Routing Slip is different from the Dynamic Router in that the Routing Slip Expression is only called once to determine the list of endpoints, whereas the Dynamic Router Expression is called multiple times until it decides it is time to stop routing (returns `null`).

This recipe will show you how to specify an Expression that will determine how to route each individual message to a runtime provided with a list of endpoints.

Getting ready

The Java code for this recipe is located in the `org.camelcookbook.routing.routingslip` package. The Spring XML files are located under `src/main/resources/META-INF/spring` and are prefixed with `routingSlip`.

How to do it...

Create a route with a `routingSlip` statement. The Expression within that statement must return a String or list of Strings, where each String identifies an endpoint URI to route the message to in sequence.

In these examples, the Routing Slip uses the contents of the message header `myRoutingSlipHeader`, which could either have been set with the original message or set by the previous route steps:

In the XML DSL, this logic is written as:

```
<route>
  <from uri="direct:start"/>
  <routingSlip>
    <header>myRoutingSlipHeader</header>
  </routingSlip>
</route>
```

In the Java DSL, the same thing is expressed as:

```
from("direct:start")
  .routingSlip(header("myRoutingSlipHeader"));
```

How it works...

The Routing Slip uses a Camel Expression to determine the list of endpoints to route to. This Expression is evaluated only once, and the message is routed in sequence to one or more endpoints specified in that list.

If the intent of the Expression is to return a list of endpoint URIs that will be called in sequence, the Expression may separate the URIs with a delimiter which by default is a comma (,). The separator can be changed using the `uriDelimiter` attribute of the `routingSlip` element.

If you find that you are trying to route to an endpoint that does not currently exist, and do not want this condition to be considered an error, you can configure the `ignoreInvalidEndpoints` option to `true` (defaults to `false`) to tell Camel to ignore the `ResolveEndpointFailedException` that would normally be thrown.

There's more...

We can use Camel's Bean Injection capabilities to put everything into the Java class using Java Annotations. The `@RoutingSlip` annotation provides the same information to Camel as the `routingSlip` element within a route. The `@Consume` annotation tells Camel to create a new route consuming on the provided endpoint URI no need to provide a separate route definition.

 You need to instantiate your annotated bean within a Camel supported dependency injection framework, like Spring or OSGi Blueprint, with a defined Camel context for this to work.

```
@Consume(uri = "direct:routingSlipAnnotated")
@RoutingSlip(delimiter = ",")
public List<String> routeMe(String body,
    @Headers Map<String, Object> headers) {
  //...
}
```

This pattern can also be considered a variation on the Recipient List EIP. In the Recipient List, an Expression is also used to determine a list of endpoint URIs; however, in that pattern each endpoint receives its own copy of the original message.

See also

▶ Routing Slip: `http://camel.apache.org/routing-slip.html`

▶ Dynamic Router: `http://camel.apache.org/dynamic-router.html`

▶ Recipient List: `http://camel.apache.org/recipient-list.html`

▶ Bean Injection: `http://camel.apache.org/bean-integration.html`

▶ Expression: `http://camel.apache.org/expression.html`

3
Routing to Your Code

In this chapter, we will cover the following recipes:

- ▸ Routing messages directly to a Java method
- ▸ Sending messages directly to a Camel endpoint
- ▸ Using a Java method as a Predicate
- ▸ Writing a custom Camel Processor
- ▸ Mapping the message to method parameters
- ▸ Writing a custom data marshaller
- ▸ Writing a custom data type converter

Introduction

In this chapter, we will be looking at a number of ways of extending Camel with your own Java code, and invoking Camel routes from your Java code.

Camel was designed to make it very easy to work with existing Java code, and to make it straightforward to invoke Camel through your code without a lot of boilerplate code typically involved in using the underlying technologies such as JDBC, JMS, and others commonly used in integration.

This chapter will explore how your Java code can send and receive message data in the form of Java parameters and return types. It will discuss how your code can be reused to inform Camel routing decisions and message processing. We will cover how to go about creating re-useable Camel abstractions that make it even easier for your team to perform common message translations, and data type conversions, that are repeated throughout your integrations.

A number of Camel architectural concepts are used throughout this chapter. There is a broader overview of Camel concepts in the *Preface*. Full details can be found on the Apache Camel web site at `http://camel.apache.org`.

The code for this chapter is contained within the `camel-cookbook-extend` module of the examples.

Routing messages directly to a Java method

When you just want to send the message received from an endpoint directly to one of your Java methods, Camel provides a Bean Integration capability called **POJO Consuming**. POJO Consuming allows you to annotate a Java method with the Camel URI for the endpoint that you want to receive messages from. Messages will be passed directly to that Java method.

Through an example, this recipe will demonstrate to you how to annotate a Java method to act as a JMS (or WS, or TCP/IP, or any other Camel consuming endpoint) listener, in the same way as a Java EE Message Driven Bean (MDB). It will also provide you with the ability to run the code inside an environment as simple as a standalone Java process, with no extra container required.

This recipe will show you how to annotate your Java code so that it will be called with messages received from any specified Camel endpoint.

Getting ready

The Java code for this recipe is located in the `org.camelcookbook.extend.consume` package. The Spring XML files are located under `src/main/resources/META-INF/spring` and prefixed with `consume`.

The included example uses an embedded (in-process) ActiveMQ instance to act as a JMS provider for its simple JMS message consuming method. In practice, you would normally connect Camel to an external messaging infrastructure.

How to do it...

Camel's POJO Consuming requires use of the `@Consume` annotation with the URI of the Camel endpoint you want to consume messages from. This example shows the creation of a JMS request/response message consumer. Camel will send the response returned from the `onMyMessage(..)` Java method as a message into the JMS queue that is specified in the `JMSReplyTo` header of the request message; Camel handles all of this for you.

```
import org.apache.camel.Consume;

public class ConsumeMdb {
    @Consume(uri="activemq:queue:sayhello")
```

```
  public String onMyMessage(String message) {
    return "Hello " + message;
  }
}
```

In order to use the `ConsumeMdb` class in Camel, it must be defined as a bean in the same Spring application context as the Camel context.

```
<beans xmlns="http://www.springframework.org/schema/beans" ...>
  <bean id="activemq"
        class="org.apache.activemq.camel.component
               .ActiveMQComponent">
    <property name="brokerURL"
              value="vm://myBroker?create=false"/>
  </bean>

  <bean class="org.camelcookbook.extend.consume
               .ConsumeMdb"/>

  <camelContext xmlns="http://camel.apache.org/schema/spring"/>
</beans>
```

How it works...

Camel's POJO Consuming uses an `@Consume` annotation on a method for letting Camel know it needs to create an endpoint consumer using the specified endpoint URI.

```
public class MyBean {
  @Consume(uri="someEndpoint")
  public String myMethod(String message) {
    //...
  }
}
```

At runtime, this is effectively equivalent to having explicitly created the following route in the Java DSL:

```
from("someEndpoint")
  .bean(MyBean.class, "myMethod");
```

Any exceptions thrown from your Java method will be handled in the same way as an exception thrown from any endpoint or processor; the route specified error handlers and exception handers would catch it. See *Chapter 7, Error Handling and Compensation,* for more details.

There's more...

Camel will handle the result of the method call in a similar fashion regardless of whether the method was called through POJO Consuming, or via using the Bean DSL statement as shown in the preceding equivalent route. If the method returns `void`, then it is equivalent to having called an `InOnly` processor. If the method returns something, then it is equivalent to having called an `InOut` processor, and the return value will be used as the new message body.

Camel uses its data type converters to automatically convert the message body to the type specified in the parameters of the method. A method parameter can also be of type `Exchange`, in which case the method would have full access to all of the data within the Camel exchange. See Camel's documentation on Bean Binding for more details.

See also

- ▸ POJO Consuming: `http://camel.apache.org/pojo-consuming.html`
- ▸ Bean Component: `http://camel.apache.org/bean.html`
- ▸ Bean Binding: `http://camel.apache.org/bean-binding.html`

Sending messages directly to a Camel endpoint

You can utilize Camel's endpoints directly from your Java code, making it easy to, for example, send a JMS message without any of the boilerplate code that is normally required. Camel makes it easy to send (one-way) or request (request-response) data from any Camel component or route. Camel calls this **POJO Producing**.

This recipe will show you how you can send data to a Camel endpoint, including a Camel route, from within your Java code.

Getting ready

The Java code for this recipe is located in the `org.camelcookbook.extend.produce` package. The Spring XML files are located under `src/main/resources/META-INF/spring` and prefixed with `produce`.

The included example uses an embedded (in-process) ActiveMQ instance to act as a JMS provider for its simple JMS message consuming method. In practice, you would normally connect Camel to an external messaging infrastructure.

How to do it...

Camel's POJO Producing makes use of the Camel's `ProducerTemplate` class to send or request data from an endpoint. To get a handle to a `ProducerTemplate` instance, define it as an variable of your class, and annotate it with `@Produce`. Refer to the following code:

```
import org.apache.camel.Produce;
import org.apache.camel.ProducerTemplate;

public class ProducePojo {
  @Produce
  private ProducerTemplate template;

  public String sayHello(String name) {
    return template.requestBody("activemq:queue:sayhello",
                                name, String.class);
  }
}
```

In order to have the `ProducerTemplate` injected into the `ProducePojo` class, it must be defined as a bean in the same Spring application context as the Camel context.

```
<beans xmlns="http://www.springframework.org/schema/beans" ...>
  <bean id="activemq"
        class="org.apache.activemq.camel.component
               .ActiveMQComponent">
    <property name="brokerURL"
              value="tcp://localhost:61616"/>
  </bean>

  <bean id="producer"
        class="org.camelcookbook.extend.produce
               .ProducePojo"/>

  <camelContext xmlns="http://camel.apache.org/schema/spring"/>
</beans>
```

How it works...

Camel's POJO Producing uses the `@Produce` annotation to inject a `ProducerTemplate` at runtime. The `ProducerTemplate` provides a large number of methods to `send..()` (InOnly/one-way) or `request..()` (InOut/request-response) data with or without additional message headers and properties. There are also asynchronous variants that allow you to get a callback when your send is complete or your requested data is available.

The `ProducerTemplate` can interact with any Camel endpoint such as the ActiveMQ Component, or it can call a full Camel route listening `from` an in-memory endpoint such as `direct:` or `seda:`. This allows you to easily call out to different transports and integration routes directly from your code with minimal disruption to your core logic.

There's more...

Camel's `@Produce` annotation can also be used to automatically create a proxy based on a Java interface provided by you. In this instance, Camel will, at runtime, wrap the call to `ProducerTemplate` handling the data type conversion for you. This provides more separation in your code, hiding Camel behind your Java interface.

For example, we can do the same thing as the preceding example with the following code:

```
public interface ProxyPojo {
   String sayHello(String name);
}

public class ProxyProduce {
   @Produce(uri = "activemq:queue:sayhello")
   ProxyPojo myProxy;

   public String doSomething(String name) {
      return myProxy.sayHello(name);
   }
}
```

In this code example, use of the `@Produce` annotation results in the creation and injection of a proxy object by the Camel context so that your code interacts just with your interface, and the only visible Camel code is the `@Produce` annotation. The `name` parameter will contain the body of the message, and the return value will become the Camel exchange message seen by the next processor in the route. The fact that the method returns a value implies that this should be treated as an `InOut` operation.

Camel uses its data type converters to automatically convert the message body to the type specified in the parameters of the method. A method parameter can also be of the type `Exchange`, in which case the method would have full access to all of the data within the Camel exchange. See Camel's documentation on Bean Binding for more details.

See also

▸ POJO Producing: `http://camel.apache.org/pojo-producing.html`
▸ POJO Producing FAQ: `http://camel.apache.org/why-does-camel-use-too-many-threads-with-producertemplate.html`

- ▸ Bean Binding: `http://camel.apache.org/bean-binding.html`
- ▸ Spring Remoting: `http://camel.apache.org/spring-remoting.html`

Using a Java method as a Predicate

Camel makes it very easy to call out to some existing Java code to act as a predicate when you are using an Enterprise Integration Pattern (EIP) such as Content Based Router or Filter. Any EIPs that require a Camel Predicate can use the Bean Expression Language to call any Java method that evaluates to a `boolean` value. Remember that a Camel Predicate is any Camel Expression that evaluates to a `boolean` value (`true` or `false`). This allows you to integrate complex decision making from your existing Java code into your routing logic.

This recipe shows you how to use any of your Java methods that returns a `boolean` value wherever Camel expects a predicate.

Getting ready

The Java code for this recipe is located in the `org.camelcookbook.extend.predicate` package. The Spring XML files are located under `src/main/resources/META-INF/spring` and prefixed with `predicate`.

How to do it...

Given an existing Java method that evaluates to a `boolean` value, such as:

```
public class MyPredicate {
  public boolean isWhatIWant(String body) {
    // evaluate message body and return true or false
  }
}
```

This method can be evaluated for use by any EIP that requires a predicate:

In the XML DSL, this is written as:

```
<beans xmlns="http://www.springframework.org/schema/beans"... >
  <bean id="myPredicate"
        class="org.camelcookbook.extend.predicate.MyPredicate"/>

  <camelContext xmlns="http://camel.apache.org/schema/spring">
    <route>
      <from uri="direct:start"/>
        <filter>
          <method ref="myPredicate"
```

```
            method="isWhatIWant"/>
        <to uri="mock:boston"/>
      </filter>
    </route>
  </camelContext>
</beans>
```

In the Java DSL, the same route is expressed as:

```
public class MyPredicateRouteBuilder extends RouteBuilder {
  @Override
  public void configure() throws Exception {
    MyPredicate predicate = new MyPredicate();

    from("direct:start")
      .filter().method(predicate, "isWhatIWant")
      .to("mock:boston");
    }
  }
}
```

How it works...

Behind the scenes, Camel uses a class called `PredicateBuilder` to convert any expression, in our case a Bean Expression Language expression bound using the `method` statement, into a predicate that will pass the contents of an exchange (message, headers, and properties) into a method returning a `boolean` value.

Camel uses a very sophisticated algorithm known as Bean Binding to perform the following steps:

1. Select which method on an object to call, if not explicitly specified or if there are overloaded methods.
2. Map the exchange contents into one or more of the method parameters.
3. Convert the result data type to a `boolean` value.

There are a number of Java annotations you can use to influence how Camel interacts with your Java objects. For example, if you wanted the first parameter to be mapped to a header, and the second parameter to the body of the message, you could perform the following:

```
public void doSomething(
    @Header("JMSCorrelationID") String correlationID,
    @Body String body)
{
    // process the message here
}
```

More details can be found in the Camel documentation on Parameter Binding Annotations (`http://camel.apache.org/parameter-binding-annotations.html`).

The preceding `method` statement is an Expression variant of the `bean` statement and the Bean Component, all of which allow you to call a Java method on the referenced Java class instance that is a POJO. The `method` statement requires a reference to an existing bean instance contained in the Camel context's Registry, and a method name. The `bean` statement takes either a reference name or a Java type (Camel will instantiate a singleton instance of that type), and an optional method name (Camel will use its Bean Binding algorithm to determine which method to call if none is provided). The Bean Component lets you specify a reference anywhere you can specify an endpoint URI, that is `.to("bean:myBean?method=foo")`.

There's more...

Camel supports the ability to combine one or more expressions into a compound predicate. This allows you to logically combine (`and`, `or`, `not`) multiple expressions together, even if they are in multiple expression languages. For example, you could create a compound predicate that first evaluates an XPath expression, and then evaluates a Java method.

```
import static org.apache.camel.builder.PredicateBuilder.and;

from("direct:start")
  .filter(and(xpath("/someXml/city = 'Boston'"),
            method(predicate, "isWhatIWant")))
    .to("mock:boston");
```

See also

▶ Camel Predicates: `http://camel.apache.org/predicate.html`

▶ Bean Binding: `http://camel.apache.org/bean-binding.html`

▶ Parameter Binding Annotations: `http://camel.apache.org/parameter-binding-annotations.html`

Writing a custom Camel Processor

A custom Camel Processor is very easy to write and use within a route, and gives you full access to all parts of the exchange being processed. This is the ultimate functional element within Camel as you can create, and reuse, custom message processors that can do anything you can imagine doing with Java.

This recipe will show you how to create you own Camel Processor implementation that can be used, and shared, within your Camel integration routes.

Getting ready

The Java code for this recipe is located in the `org.camelcookbook.extend.processor` package. The Spring XML files are located under `src/main/resources/META-INF/spring` and prefixed with `processor`.

How to do it...

In order to use a custom processor within your route, perform the following steps:

1. Create your processor class that implements the `org.apache.camel.Processor` interface:

```
import org.apache.camel.Exchange;
import org.apache.camel.Message;
import org.apache.camel.Processor;

public class MyProcessor implements Processor {
  @Override
  public void process(Exchange exchange) throws Exception {
    //...
  }
}
```

2. Implement the process method. The incoming message is contained within `exchange.getIn()`. If your processor needs to modify the message, most often you should just modify the `in` message directly (see the *How it works...* section of this recipe for more discussion):

```
public void process(Exchange exchange) throws Exception {
    String result = "Unknown language";

    final Message inMessage = exchange.getIn();
    final String body = inMessage.getBody(String.class);
    final String language =
        inMessage.getHeader("language", String.class);

    if ("en".equals(language)) {
      result = "Hello " + body;
    } else if ("fr".equals(language)) {
      result = "Bonjour " + body;
    }

    inMessage.setBody(result);
}
```

3. Reference your custom processor in your route:

In the XML DSL, this is written as:

```
<beans
    xmlns="http://www.springframework.org/schema/beans"...>
  <bean id="myProcessor"
        class="org.camelcookbook.extend.processor
                .MyProcessor"/>

  <camelContext
      xmlns="http://camel.apache.org/schema/spring">
    <route>
      <from uri="direct:start"/>
      <process ref="myProcessor"/>
      <to uri="mock:result"/>
    </route>
  </camelContext>
</beans>
```

In the Java DSL, the same thing is expressed as:

```
import org.apache.camel.builder.RouteBuilder;

public class MyProcessorRouteBuilder extends RouteBuilder {
  @Override
  public void configure() throws Exception {
    from("direct:start")
      .process(new MyProcessor())
      .to("mock:result");
    }
  }
}
```

Typically you will use the process directive when referencing custom Processors. You can also use the to directive to reference your custom processor like a bean if you've registered it in the Camel Registry. For example:

```
<to uri="bean:myProcessor?method=process"/>
```

How it works...

The Camel Processor is a fundamental building block within Camel, and provides complete access to all of the data associated within the message being processed, including the message body, any headers, and any properties associated with the message.

Your custom processor has the ability to modify the message, and add or modify headers and properties associated with the message. It is typically used whenever you want to perform multiple operations in one routing step, such as setting multiple related message headers as well as modifying the message body.

In the preceding example, your custom processor is being accessed as a singleton meaning that multiple messages (threads) are calling it concurrently. So you need to think about thread safety in the coding of your process method.

 Even though the Java DSL variant had a `new MyProcessor()` for when your processor is referenced, that code within the `configure()` method is only called once when your route is first added to the Camel context. As such, it is still a singleton. The fact that `configure()` is only called once, versus for each message, is a common source of confusion.

Generally processors just modify the `in` message. There is an `out` message on the exchange that makes it possible to return both the original message (request) and processed message (response). If setting the `out` message you need to be very careful to preserve all appropriate headers and properties associated with the message.

In the following code snippet, the `copyFrom` method copies the body, headers, and properties from the source message. The `ExchangeHelper.isOutCapable()` checks the message exchange pattern of the provided `exchange`, and returns `true` if it is `InOut`, which indicates that the calling route expects a response to be returned. In practice, it is rare that you should do more than just modify the `in` message. See the Camel Processor FAQ for more discussion on modifying the `in` versus `out` message:

```
if (ExchangeHelper.isOutCapable(exchange)) {
  exchange.getOut().copyFrom(exchange.getIn());
  exchange.getOut().setBody("<modified body>");
} else {
  exchange.getIn().setBody("<modified body>");
}
```

 The use of the `out` message was more common in earlier versions of Camel. In newer versions of Camel, you can always just use the `in` message and you will be fine.

There's more...

Within the Java DSL, you can inline your processor as an anonymous inner class as part of the route definition. In general, you would only want to do this if the body of your `process()` method is short.

If your processor involves a lot of code, you are much better off putting it into a separate class that you can test independently, and that does not distract the reader from the overall integration route flow.

```java
public class MyProcessorInlineRouteBuilder
    extends RouteBuilder {
  @Override
  public void configure() throws Exception {
    from("direct:start")
      .process(new Processor() {
        @Override
        public void process(Exchange exchange)
            throws Exception {
          // Some quick Java code
        }
      })
      .to("mock:result");
  }
}
```

See also

▶ Camel Processor: `http://camel.apache.org/processor.html`

▶ Camel Processor FAQ: `http://camel.apache.org/using-getin-or-getout-methods-on-exchange.html`

Mapping the message to method parameters

Camel provides a capability called **Parameter Binding**, which allows your route to explicitly map parts of the message to your method parameters when Camel invokes a Java method. This can be used anywhere you can use the Bean or Method Expression Languages, such as in a predicate, processor step, or expression.

This recipe will show you how to specify the mapping of the exchange values to your method parameters right within the DSL.

Getting ready

The Java code for this recipe is located in the `org.camelcookbook.extend.binding` package. The Spring XML files are located under `src/main/resources/META-INF/spring` and prefixed with `binding`.

This recipe assumes the existence of a Java class with the following definition, though the techniques explained in this recipe can be applied to any Java method call:

```
public class MyBean {
  public String sayHello(String name, boolean hipster) {
    return (hipster) ? ("Yo " + name) : ("Hello " + name);
  }
}
```

How to do it...

Within your Bean Expression Language calls, you can specify the parameter value mapping to use when calling out to a Java method using either literals or the Simple Expression Language.

In the XML DSL, this is written as:

```
<route>
  <from uri="direct:hipster"/>
  <bean ref="myBean"
        method="sayHello(${body}, true)"/>
</route>
<route>
  <from uri="direct:undecided"/>
  <bean ref="myBean"
        method="sayHello(${body}, ${header.hipster})"/>
</route>
```

In the Java DSL, the same routing logic is expressed as:

```
from("direct:hipster")
  .bean(MyBean.class, "sayHello(${body}, true)");

from("direct:undecided")
  .bean(MyBean.class, "sayHello(${body}, ${header.hipster})");
```

How it works...

Camel has a well-documented algorithm for how it maps exchange and Camel context data to the method parameters when calling out to a Java object (see `http://camel.apache.org/bean-binding#BeanBinding-Parameterbinding`).

In summary, it assumes that the first parameter is the message body, and automatically attempts to convert the body to the data type of that parameter, unless the first parameter is of the type `org.apache.camel.Exchange`, in which case it is bound directly. Parameter Binding allows the developer to specify how to map literals and message parts to the method parameters from within the Camel DSL.

Camel Parameter Binding allows you to specify literals (`true` or `false`, numbers, Strings, and `null`) as well as Simple Expressions as part of the binding string. You can also specify a wildcard asterisk(`*`) that tells Camel to use its normal parameter binding algorithm for that portion of the parameters.

For example, if you have a Java method that takes a `String` value and a `boolean` value:

```
public String myMethod(String name, boolean doDifferent)
```

You could call that from a Camel route in various ways, such as if you wanted to hard-code a value for the `boolean` parameter and use the default parameter mapping to pass the message body as a `String` for the first parameter:

```
.bean(MyBean.class, "myMethod(*, true)");
```

Alternatively, if you wanted to map a header value to the first parameter using a Simple Expression:

```
.bean(MyBean.class, "myMethod(${header.username}, false)");
```

This will also work within a `.to()` block, as part of a `bean:` endpoint URI:

```
.to("bean:myBean?method=myMethod(${header.username}, false)");
```

There's more...

Camel also provides a way for you to use annotations to tell it how to map the message to parameters. This approach allows the method creator to specify the mapping as opposed to the use of Parameter Binding, which is specified by the route developer:

```
public String myMethod(@Header("JMSCorrelationID") String id,
                       @Body String message) {
    //...
}
```

Parameter Binding Annotations also allow you to use other Expression Languages to provide more sophisticated mappings, such as using an XPath expression to map a value from the message to a parameter as follows:

```
public String myMethod(@XPath("/myData/people/@id") String id,
                        @Body String message) {
    //...
}
```

See also

► Camel Bean Binding: `http://camel.apache.org/bean-binding`
► Camel Parameter Binding Annotations: `http://camel.apache.org/parameter-binding-annotations.html`

Writing a custom data marshaller

Camel supports a pluggable ability to translate messages to and from binary and text formats through a feature called **Data Formats**. Data Formats are an implementation of the **Message Translator Enterprise Integration Pattern**.

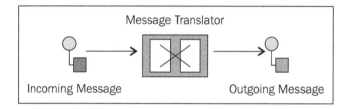

Camel's libraries include a number of Data Formats, such as JAXB, JSON, CSV, HL7, Base64, Crypto, Gzip, and so on. This recipe describes how to write your own Data Format for instances when you need more than what Camel provides out of the box.

This recipe will show you how to create your own Data Format implementation that can be easily shared across your Camel routes.

Getting ready

The Java code for this recipe is located in the `org.camelcookbook.extend.dataformat` package. The Spring XML files are located under `src/main/resources/META-INF/spring` and prefixed with `dataformat`.

How to do it...

There are two main steps for creating and using a custom Data Format. First, you need to create a Java class that implements the `DataFormat` interface, and second, you need to provide a reference to it within your route.

1. Creating a custom Data Format primarily consists of creating a Java class that implements the `org.apache.camel.spi.DataFormat` interface, which has two methods: `marshal` and `unmarshal`. Typically, you **marshal** from Java to a lower-level data representation, and **unmarshal** from that representation up to Java. This is true in most cases, but may vary depending on what the intent of your Data Format is, such as in this recipe's example where we are converting a String from one character set to a different character set.

    The following example converts between EBCDIC and Java Strings (UTF-8), which may be useful for performing Mainframe integrations. It marshals from a `String` to EBCDIC, and unmarshals from EBCDIC to a `String`.

```java
public class EbcdicDataFormat implements DataFormat {
  // US EBCDIC 037 code page
  private String codepage = "CP037";

  public EbcdicDataFormat() {}

  public EbcdicDataFormat(String codepage) {
    this.codepage = codepage;
  }

  @Override
  public void marshal(Exchange exchange,
                      Object graph, OutputStream stream)
      throws Exception {
    final String str =
      ExchangeHelper.convertToMandatoryType(exchange,
          String.class, graph);
    stream.write(str.getBytes(codepage));
  }

  @Override
  public Object unmarshal(Exchange exchange,
      InputStream stream) throws Exception {
    final byte[] bytes =
      ExchangeHelper.convertToMandatoryType(exchange,
          byte[].class, stream);
    return new String(bytes, codepage);
  }
}
```

2. You then need to reference your custom Data Format within your routes using the `marshal` and `unmarshal` statements.

   In the XML DSL, use the `custom` element within the `marshal` and `unmarshal` blocks to reference the bean ID for your custom Data Format:

```xml
<beans xmlns="http://www.springframework.org/schema/beans" ...>
  <bean id="ebcdic"
        class="org.camelcookbook.extend.dataformat
               .EbcdicDataFormat">
    <constructor-arg value="CP037"/>
  </bean>

  <camelContext
      xmlns="http://camel.apache.org/schema/spring">
    <route>
      <from uri="direct:marshal"/>
      <marshal>
        <custom ref="ebcdic"/>
      </marshal>
    </route>
    <route>
      <from uri="direct:unmarshal"/>
      <unmarshal>
        <custom ref="ebcdic"/>
      </unmarshal>
    </route>
  </camelContext>
</beans>
```

In the Java DSL, you refer to an instance of the data format:

```java
public class EbcdicDataFormatRouteBuilder
    extends RouteBuilder {
  @Override
  public void configure() throws Exception {
    EbcdicDataFormat dataFormat =
        new EbcdicDataFormat("CP037");

    from("direct:marshal").marshal(dataFormat);

    from("direct:unmarshal").unmarshal(dataFormat);
  }
}
```

How it works...

The Data Format's `marshal` and `unmarshal` methods will be called from the route with the current message body. Your implementation will be expected to convert the message to or from your format.

In your `marshal` implementation, the message body is passed in the second parameter `Object graph`, converted to your custom Data Format, and the results streamed into the third parameter `OutputStream stream`.

The `ExchangeHelper` utility class provides a number of helpful methods, such as `convertToMandatoryType`, which will use Camel's data type converters to convert the current message body to the data type you specify, and throws an exception if that fails. The mechanism for the actual data translation performed by your custom Data Format is up to you.

The `unmarshal` implementation is similar. You obtain the current message body from the provided `InputStream`, and either return the result of the translation from your method, or place it on the exchange through `exchange.getIn().setBody()`.

 It is worth noting that the functionality of `EbcdicDataFormat` shown in the preceding example can be achieved using Camel's built-in `StringDataFormat`. You would instantiate this built-in format with the String encoding you want to translate Java Strings (UTF-8) to and from, such as `"CP037"`, which indicates the US/Latin-1 EBCDIC Code Page 000037. See the `StringDataFormat` documentation for more details (`http://camel.apache.org/string.html`).

There's more...

Camel supports streaming data so that large data messages can flow through the integration route using less memory and greater speed. When possible, the data is streamed (incrementally pulled) from the consuming endpoint, through the processor steps defined in the route, and then streamed to a producer endpoint. If your data translation logic supports working on incremental parts or streams of data, you should apply it to your custom Data Format in order to work well with streaming.

For example, here is how the GZip Data Format implements streaming. Notice how in the `marshal` method the input message body is converted to an `InputStream`.

```
public class GzipDataFormat implements DataFormat {
   public void marshal(Exchange exchange, Object graph,
                    OutputStream stream) throws Exception {
     InputStream is =
        exchange.getContext().getTypeConverter()
         .mandatoryConvertTo(InputStream.class,
```

```
                                    exchange, graph);

     GZIPOutputStream zipOutput = new GZIPOutputStream(stream);
     try {
       IOHelper.copy(is, zipOutput);
     } finally {
       // must close all input streams
       IOHelper.close(is, zipOutput);
     }
   }
   //...
 }
```

See also

- ▸ Camel Data Format: `http://camel.apache.org/data-format.html`
- ▸ Camel Custom Data Format: `http://camel.apache.org/custom-dataformat.html`

Writing a custom data type converter

If you find that you have written one or more processors that are just casting or converting from one data type to another, then writing a custom Camel Type Converter will help you reduce that boilerplate code. Camel attempts to automatically convert from one data type to another within a route, and allows you to extend its type converter registry with converters between known types.

The Type Converters are like cast operations in Java. If you want to do a more complex data format change, say from XML to JSON, then you should look at *Chapter 4*, *Transformation*, Camel's built in Data Format Marshallers (`http://camel.apache.org/data-format.html`), and the *Writing a Custom Data Marshaller* recipe.

This recipe will show you how to create and register a custom Type Converter that Camel will use to automatically convert those specified data types.

Getting ready

The Java code for this recipe is located in the `org.camelcookbook.extend.typeconverter` package. The Spring XML files are located under `src/main/resources/META-INF/spring` and prefixed with `typeconverter`.

This recipe assumes a custom Java class, MyPerson, and a custom bean processor, MyPersonGreeter. The sayHello() method on MyPersonGreeter assumes that the message body is of the type MyPerson. For the purpose of our example integration, we will assume that we need to deal with String message bodies.

This String to MyPerson conversation is quite common in our fictitious integration scenario, so we are going to write a custom Type Converter, and that way Camel can do the conversation automatically for us; without the need to have an explicit step defined within our routes.

MyPerson is a simple data class with a couple of fields:

```
public class MyPerson {
   private String firstName;
   private String lastName;
   // getters, setters, and equals excluded for brevity
}
```

MyPersonGreeter is a Java class that takes a MyPerson object as a parameter and performs some processing on it:

```
public class MyPersonGreeter {
   public String sayHello(MyPerson person) {
      return "Hello " + person.getFirstName()
          + " " + person.getLastName();
   }
}
```

How to do it...

There are two main steps to creating and using a custom Type Converter. First, you need to create it, and second, you need to register it with Camel.

1. Create a Java class with a method whose first parameter is of the type you want to convert from, and the return type is of the type you want to convert to. The name of the method is not important. Mark both the class and the conversion method(s) with the @Converter annotation. The second conversion method parameter can optionally be Camel's Exchange if you require additional information to correctly perform the conversion, such as through a header or property.

    Your converter can be static or an instance method. Static methods require less instance caching on Camel's part, so are preferred. Instances, being objects that are configured through Spring, allow you to later inject field settings on a case-by-case basis to influence how the converter works.

    ```
    import org.apache.camel.Converter;

    @Converter
    ```

```
public final class MyPersonTypeConverter {
    // Utility classes should not have a public constructor
    private MyPersonTypeConverter() {}

    /**
     * Converts a String in the format of
     * "firstName|lastName" to a {@link MyPerson}.
     */
    @Converter
    public static MyPerson convertStringToMyPerson(
        String str) {
      final int index = str.indexOf("|");
      if (index > 0) {
        final MyPerson person = new MyPerson();
        person.setFirstName(str.substring(0, index));
        person.setLastName(str.substring(index + 1));
        return person;
      }

      throw new IllegalArgumentException("String must be in"
          + " format of '<firstName>|<lastName>'");
    }
}
```

2. Register your new Type Converter with Camel. To do this, include the file `META-INF/services/org/apache/camel/TypeConverter` within your Jar. This `TypeConverter` file contains a common separated list of either:

   - The fully qualified class names of your type converters (for example, `org.cookbook.extend.typeconverter.MyPersonTypeConverter`)
   - Java packages to be scanned for classes marked with the `@Converter` annotation (for example, **org.cookbook.extend.typeconverter**)

   In this example, the `TypeConverter` file only contains a single entry:

   `org.camelcookbook.extend.typeconverter.MyPersonTypeConverter`

Using fully qualified names is the recommended approach as it eliminates the need for Camel to scan all the Jars in the classpath for matches, and as some containers do not work as you would expect with package scanning.

Also note that the file is literally named `TypeConverter` with no file extension.

How it works...

Camel has a `TypeConverterRegistry` associated with each Camel context that maintains a list of all `TypeConverters`. Whenever Camel needs to convert data from one type to another, it uses this registry to find methods that take the source data type as a parameter, and returns the target data type.

There is no need to explicitly tell Camel to convert data; it does it automatically. There is a DSL operation called `convertBodyTo`, which allows you to explicitly convert data from one type to another. Generally, you do not need to do this unless, for example, your conversion is slow, and you would like to control when that conversion happens during your integration flow, or if the converter selection is potentially ambiguous.

You can also register your custom type converter at runtime using the following code, for example, to convert from a `String` to an instance of `MyOrder`:

```
context.getTypeConverterRegistry()
    .addTypeConverter(MyOrder.class, String.class,
                    new MyOrderTypeConverter());
```

There's more...

You can use Camel's type conversation capabilities within your own code as long as you have a reference to a Camel context (or an exchange, which knows its Camel context). The following code will convert a `String` type into `MyPerson`:

```
MyPerson person = context.getTypeConverter()
    .convertTo(MyPerson.class, "Scott|Cranton");
```

There is also an `org.apache.camel.util.ExchangeHelper` utility class that provides a number of static helper methods such as `convertTo`, `convertToMandatoryType`, and `getMandatoryInBody`. This helper class makes it easier, given an exchange, to perform operations with some internal `null` checking:

```
String str = ExchangeHelper.convertToMandatoryType(exchange,
    String.class, value);
```

See also

▶ Camel Type Converter: `http://camel.apache.org/type-converter.html`

4

Transformation

In this chapter, we will cover:

- ▸ Transforming using a Simple Expression
- ▸ Transforming inline with XQuery
- ▸ Transforming with XSLT
- ▸ Transforming from Java to XML with JAXB
- ▸ Transforming from Java to JSON
- ▸ Transforming from XML to JSON
- ▸ Parsing comma-separated values (CSV)
- ▸ Enriching your content with some help from other endpoints
- ▸ Normalizing messages into a common XML format

Introduction

In this chapter, we will be looking at a few of the ways that Camel allows you to transform or change the content of messages being processed. The book *Enterprise Integration Patterns* by Gregor Hohpe and Bobby Woolf defines the responsibility of translating data from one format to another within the Message Translator pattern (http://www.enterpriseintegrationpatterns.com/MessageTranslator.html). This is what Camel has based its transformation capabilities on.

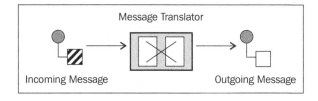

In this chapter we will explore a number of ways in which Camel performs message content transformation:

- Using the `transform` statement. This allows you to reference Camel Expression Language code within the route to do message transformations.

- Calling a templating component, such as Camel's XSLT or Velocity template style components. This will typically reference an external template resource that is used in transforming your message.

- Calling a Java method (for example, `beanref`), defined by you, within a Camel route to perform the transformation. This is a special case processor that can invoke any referenced Java object method.

- Camel's **Type Converter** capability that can automatically cast data from one type to another transparently within your Camel route. This capability is extensible, so you can add your own Type Converters.

- Camel's **Data Format** capability that allows us to use built-in, or add our own, higher order message format converters. A Camel Data Format goes beyond simple data type converters, which handle simple data type translations such as `String` to `int`, or `File` to `String`. Data Formats are used to translate between a low-level representation (XML) and a high-level one (Java objects). Other examples include encrypting/decrypting data, and compressing/decompressing data. For more, see `http://camel.apache.org/data-format.html`.

A number of Camel architectural concepts are used throughout this chapter. There is a broader overview of Camel concepts in the *Preface*. Full details can be found at the Apache Camel website at `http://camel.apache.org`.

The code for this chapter is contained within the `camel-cookbook-transformation` module of the examples.

Transforming using a Simple Expression

When you want to transform a message in a relatively straightforward way, you use Camel's `transform` statement along with one of the Expression Languages provided by the framework. For example, Camel's **Simple Expression Language** provides you with a quick, inline mechanism for straightforward transformations.

This recipe will show you how to use Camel's Simple Expression Language to transform the message body.

Getting ready

The Java code for this recipe is located in the `org.camelcookbook.transformation.` `simple` package. Spring XML files are located under `src/main/resources/META-INF/` `spring` and are prefixed with `simple`.

How to do it...

In a Camel route, use a `transform` DSL statement containing the Expression Language code to do your transformation.

In the XML DSL, this is written as follows:

```
<route>
  <from uri="direct:start"/>
  <transform>
    <simple>Hello ${body}</simple>
  </transform>
</route>
```

In the Java DSL, the same route is expressed as:

```
from("direct:start")
  .transform(simple("Hello ${body}"));
```

In this example, the message transformation prefixes the incoming message with the phrase `Hello` using the Simple Expression Language.

The processing step after the `transform` statement will see the transformed message content in the body of the exchange.

How it works...

Camel's Simple Expression Language is quite good at manipulating the `String` content through its access to all aspects of the message being processed, through its rich `String` and logical operators.

The result of your Simple Expression becomes the new message body after the `transform` step. This includes predicates such as using Simple's logical operators, to evaluate a `true` or `false` condition; the results of that Boolean operation become the new message body containing a String: `"true"` or `"false"`.

The advantage of using a distinct `transform` step within a route, as opposed to embedding it within a processor, is that the logic is clearly visible to other programmers. Ensure that the expression embedded within your route is kept simple so as to not distract the next developer from the overall purpose of the integration. It is best to move more complex (or just lengthy) transformation logic into its own subroute, and invoke it using `direct:` or `seda:`. See the *Reusing routing logic by connecting routes* recipe in *Chapter 1, Structuring Routes* for more details.

There's more...

The `transform` statement will work with any Expression Language available in Camel, so if you need more powerful message processing capabilities you can leverage scripting languages such as Groovy or JavaScript (among many others) as well. The *Transforming inline with XQuery* recipe will show you how to use the XQuery Expression Language to do transformations on XML messages.

See also

▸ Message Translator: `http://camel.apache.org/message-translator.html`

▸ Camel Expression capabilities: `http://camel.apache.org/expression.html`

▸ Camel Simple Expression Language: `http://camel.apache.org/simple.html`

▸ Languages supported by Camel: `http://camel.apache.org/languages.html`

▸ The *Reusing routing logic by connecting routes* recipe in *Chapter 1, Structuring Routes*

▸ The *Transforming inline with XQuery* recipe

Transforming inline with XQuery

Camel supports the use of Camel's XQuery Expression Language along with the `transform` statement as a quick and easy way to transform an XML message within a route.

This recipe will show you how to use an XQuery Expression to do in-route XML transformation.

Getting ready

The Java code for this recipe is located in the `org.camelcookbook.transformation.xquery` package. Spring XML files are located under `src/main/resources/META-INF/spring` and prefixed with `xquery`.

To use the XQuery Expression Language, you need to add a `dependency` element for the `camel-saxon` library, which provides the implementation for the XQuery Expression Language.

Add the following to the `dependencies` section of your Maven POM:

```
<dependency>
  <groupId>org.apache.camel</groupId>
  <artifactId>camel-saxon</artifactId>
  <version>${camel-version}</version>
</dependency>
```

How to do it...

In the Camel route, specify a `transform` statement followed by the XQuery Expression Language code to do your transformation.

In the XML DSL, this is written as:

```
<route>
  <from uri="direct:start"/>
  <transform>
    <xquery>
      &lt;books&gt;{
        for $x in /bookstore/book
        where $x/price>30
        order by $x/title
        return $x/title
      }&lt;/books&gt;
    </xquery>
  </transform>
</route>
```

 When using the XML DSL, remember to XML encode the XQuery embedded XML elements. Therefore, < becomes `&lt;` and > becomes `&gt;`.

In the Java DSL, the same route is expressed as:

```
from("direct:start")
  .transform(xquery("<books>{ for $x in /bookstore/book "
          + "where $x/price>30 order by $x/title "
          + "return $x/title }</books>"));
```

Feed the following input XML message through the transformation:

```
<bookstore>
  <book category="COOKING">
    <title lang="en">Everyday Italian</title>
    <author>Giada De Laurentiis</author>
    <year>2005</year>
    <price>30.00</price>
  </book>
  <book category="CHILDREN">
    <title lang="en">Harry Potter</title>
    <author>J K. Rowling</author>
    <year>2005</year>
    <price>29.99</price>
  </book>
  <book category="PROGRAMMING">
    <title lang="en">Apache Camel Developer's Cookbook</title>
    <author>Scott Cranton</author>
    <author>Jakub Korab</author>
    <year>2013</year>
    <price>49.99</price>
  </book>
  <book category="WEB">
    <title lang="en">Learning XML</title>
    <author>Erik T. Ray</author>
    <year>2003</year>
    <price>39.95</price>
  </book>
</bookstore>
```

The resulting message will be:

```
<books>
  <title lang="en">Apache Camel Developer's Cookbook</title>
  <title lang="en">Learning XML</title>
</books>
```

The processing step after the `transform` statement will see the transformed message content in the body of the exchange.

How it works...

Camel's XQuery Expression Language is a good way to inline XML transformation code within your route. The result of the XQuery Expression becomes the new message body after the `transform` step.

All of the message's body, headers, and properties are made available to the XQuery Processor, so you can reference them directly within your XQuery statement. This provides you with a powerful mechanism for transforming XML messages. If you are more comfortable with XSLT, take a look at the *Transforming with XSLT* recipe.

> In-lining the transformation within your integration route can sometimes be an advantage as you can clearly see what is being changed. However, when the transformation expression becomes so complex that it starts to overwhelm the integration route, you may want to consider moving the transformation expression outside of the route.
>
> See the *Transforming using a Simple Expression* recipe for another inline transformation example, and see the *Transforming with XSLT* recipe for an example of externalizing your transformation.

You can fetch the XQuery Expression from an external file using Camel's resource reference syntax. To reference an XQuery file on the classpath you can specify:

```
<transform>
  <xquery>resource:classpath:/path/to/myxquery.xml</xquery>
</transform>
```

This is equivalent to using XQuery as an endpoint:

```
<to uri="xquery:classpath:/path/to/myxquery.xml"/>
```

There's more...

The XQuery Expression Language allows you to pass in headers associated with the message. These will show up as XQuery variables that can be referenced within your XQuery statements. Consider, from the previous example, to allow the value of the books that are filtered to be passed in with the message body, that is, parameterize the XQuery, you can modify the XQuery statement as follows:

```
<transform>
  <xquery>
    declare variable $in.headers.myParamValue as
      xs:integer external;
    &lt;books value='{$in.headers.myParamValue}'&gt;{
      for $x in /bookstore/book
      where $x/price>$in.headers.myParamValue
      order by $x/title
      return $x/title
    }&lt;/books&gt;
  </xquery>
</transform>
```

Message headers will be associated with an XQuery variable called `in.headers.<name of header>`. To use this in your XQuery, you need to explicitly declare an external variable of the same name and XML Schema (`xs:`) type as the value of the message header.

The `transform` statement will work with any Expression Language enabled within Camel, so if you need more powerful message processing capabilities you can leverage scripting languages such as Groovy or JavaScript (among many others) as well. The *Transforming using a Simple Expression* recipe will show you how to use the Simple Expression Language to do transformations on `String` messages.

See also

- Message Translator: `http://camel.apache.org/message-translator.html`
- Camel Expression capabilities: `http://camel.apache.org/expression.html`
- Camel XQuery Expression Language: `http://camel.apache.org/xquery.html`
- XQuery language: `http://www.w3.org/XML/Query/`
- Languages supported by Camel: `http://camel.apache.org/languages.html`
- The *Transforming with XSLT* recipe
- The *Transforming using a Simple Expression* recipe
- The *Reusing routing logic by connecting routes* recipe in *Chapter 1, Structuring Routes*

Transforming with XSLT

When you want to transform an XML message using XSLT, use Camel's XSLT Component. This is similar to the *Transforming inline with XQuery* recipe except that there is no XSLT Expression Language, so it can only be used as an endpoint.

This recipe will show you how to transform a message using an external XSLT resource.

Getting ready

The Java code for this recipe is located in the `org.camelcookbook.transformation.xslt` package. Spring XML files are located under `src/main/resources/META-INF/spring` and prefixed with `xslt`.

How to do it...

In a Camel route, add the `xslt` processor step into the route at the point where you want the XSLT transformation to occur. The XSLT file must be referenced as an external resource, and depending on where the file is located, prefixed with either `classpath:` (default if not using a prefix), `file:`, or `http:`.

In the XML DSL, this is written as:

```
<route>
  <from uri="direct:start"/>
  <to uri="xslt:book.xslt"/>
</route>
```

In the Java DSL, the same route is expressed as:

```
from("direct:start")
  .to("xslt:book.xslt");
```

The next processing step in the route will see the transformed message content in the body of the exchange.

How it works...

The following example shows how the preceding steps will process an XML file.

Consider the following input XML message:

```
<bookstore>
  <book category="COOKING">
    <title lang="en">Everyday Italian</title>
    <author>Giada De Laurentiis</author>
    <year>2005</year>
    <price>30.00</price>
  </book>
  <book category="CHILDREN">
    <title lang="en">Harry Potter</title>
    <author>J K. Rowling</author>
    <year>2005</year>
    <price>29.99</price>
  </book>
  <book category="PROGRAMMING">
    <title lang="en">Apache Camel Developer's Cookbook</title>
    <author>Scott Cranton</author>
    <author>Jakub Korab</author>
    <year>2013</year>
    <price>49.99</price>
  </book>
  <book category="WEB">
    <title lang="en">Learning XML</title>
    <author>Erik T. Ray</author>
    <year>2003</year>
    <price>39.95</price>
  </book>
</bookstore>
```

Process this with the following XSLT contained in `books.xslt`:

```
<?xml version="1.0" encoding="UTF-8"?>
<xsl:stylesheet
    version="1.0"
    xmlns:xsl="http://www.w3.org/1999/XSL/Transform">
  <xsl:output omit-xml-declaration="yes"/>

  <xsl:template match="/">
    <books>
      <xsl:apply-templates
          select="/bookstore/book/title[../price>30]">
        <xsl:sort select="."/>
      </xsl:apply-templates>
    </books>
  </xsl:template>

  <xsl:template match="node()|@*">
    <xsl:copy>
      <xsl:apply-templates select="node()|@*"/>
    </xsl:copy>
  </xsl:template>
</xsl:stylesheet>
```

The result will appear as follows:

```
<books>
  <title lang="en">Apache Camel Developer's Cookbook</title>
  <title lang="en">Learning XML</title>
</books>
```

The Camel XSLT Processor internally runs the message body through a registered Java XML transformer using the XSLT file referenced by the endpoint. This processor uses Camel's Type Converter capabilities to convert the input message body type to one of the supported XML source models in the following order of priority:

- ▶ StAXSource (off by default; this can be enabled by setting `allowStAX=true` on the endpoint URI)
- ▶ SAXSource
- ▶ StreamSource
- ▶ DOMSource

Camel's Type Converter can convert from most input types (`String`, `File`, `byte[]`, and so on) to one of the XML source types for most XML content loaded through other Camel endpoints with no extra work on your part. The output data type for the message is, by default, a `String`, and is configurable using the `output` parameter on the `xslt` endpoint URI.

There's more...

The XSLT Processor passes in headers, properties, and parameters associated with the message. These will show up as XSLT parameters that can be referenced within your XSLT statements.

You can pass in the names of the books as parameters to the XSLT template; to do so, modify the previous XLST as follows:

```
<xsl:param name="myParamValue"/>

<xsl:template match="/">
  <books>
    <xsl:attribute name="value">
      <xsl:value-of select="$myParamValue"/>
    </xsl:attribute>
    <xsl:apply-templates
        select="/bookstore/book/title[../price>$myParamValue]">
      <xsl:sort select="."/>
    </xsl:apply-templates>
  </books>
</xsl:template>
```

The Exchange instance will be associated with a parameter called `exchange`; the IN message with a parameter called `in`; and the message headers, properties, and parameters will be associated XSLT parameters with the same name. To use these in your XSLT, you need to explicitly declare a parameter of the same name in your XSLT file. In the previous example, it is possible to use either a message header or exchange property called `myParamValue`.

See also

▶ Message Translator: `http://camel.apache.org/message-translator.html`

▶ Camel XSLT Component: `http://camel.apache.org/xslt`

▶ Camel Type Converter: `http://camel.apache.org/type-converter.html`

▶ XSL working group: `http://www.w3.org/Style/XSL/`

▶ The *Transforming inline with XQuery* recipe

Transforming from Java to XML with JAXB

Camel's JAXB Component is one of a number of components that can be used to convert your XML data back and forth from Java objects. It provides a Camel Data Format that allows you to use JAXB annotated Java classes, and then marshal (Java to XML) or unmarshal (XML to Java) your data.

JAXB is a Java standard for translating between XML data and Java that is used by creating annotated Java classes that bind, or map, to your XML data schema. The framework takes care of the rest.

This recipe will show you how to use the JAXB Camel Data Format to convert back and forth from Java to XML.

Getting ready

The Java code for this recipe is located in the `org.camelcookbook.transformation.jaxb` package. The Spring XML files are located under `src/main/resources/META-INF/spring` and prefixed with `jaxb`.

To use Camel's JAXB Component, you need to add a `dependency` element for the `camel-jaxb` library, which provides the implementation for the JAXB Data Format.

Add the following to the `dependencies` section of your Maven POM:

```xml
<dependency>
  <groupId>org.apache.camel</groupId>
  <artifactId>camel-jaxb</artifactId>
  <version>${camel-version}</version>
</dependency>
```

How to do it...

The main steps for converting between Java and XML are as follows:

1. Given a JAXB annotated model, reference that model within a named Camel Data Format.

2. Use that named Data Format within your Camel route using the `marshal` and `unmarshal` DSL statements.

3. Create an annotated Java model using standard JAXB annotations. There are a number of external tools that can automate this creation from existing XML or XSD (XML Schema) files:

```
@XmlAccessorType(XmlAccessType.FIELD)
@XmlType(name = "",
```

```
            propOrder = {
              "title",
              "author",
              "year",
              "price"
            }
  )
  @XmlRootElement(name = "book")
  public class Book {
    @XmlElement(required = true)
    protected Book.Title title;

    @XmlElement(required = true)
    protected List<String> author;

    protected int year;
    protected double price;

    // getters and setters
  }
```

4. Instantiate a JAXB Data Format within your Camel route that refers to the Java package(s) containing your JAXB annotated classes.

    In the XML DSL, this is written as:

```
<camelContext
    xmlns="http://camel.apache.org/schema/spring">
  <dataFormats>
    <jaxb id="myJaxb"
        contextPath="org.camelcookbook
                    .transformation.myschema"/>
  </dataFormats>

  <!-- route definitions here -->
</camelContext>
```

    In the Java DSL, the Data Format is defined as:

```
public class JaxbRouteBuilder extends RouteBuilder {
  @Override
  public void configure() throws Exception {
    DataFormat myJaxb =
      new JaxbDataFormat(
        "org.camelcookbook.transformation.myschema");

    // route definitions here
  }
}
```

5. Reference the Data Format within your route, choosing `marshal` (Java to XML) or `unmarshal` (XML to Java) as appropriate.

In the XML DSL, this routing logic is written as:

```
<route>
  <from uri="direct:unmarshal"/>
  <unmarshal ref="myJaxb"/>
</route>
```

In the Java DSL, this is expressed as:

```
from("direct:unmarshal").unmarshal(myJaxb);
```

How it works...

Using Camel JAXB to translate your XML data back and forth to Java makes it much easier for the Java processors defined later on in your route to do custom message processing. This is useful when the built-in XML translators (for example, XSLT or XQuery) are not enough, or you just want to call existing Java code.

Camel JAXB eliminates the boilerplate code from your integration flows by providing a wrapper around the standard JAXB mechanisms for instantiating the Java binding for the XML data.

There's more...

Camel JAXB works just fine with existing JAXB tooling like the `maven-jaxb2-plugin` plugin, which can automatically create JAXB-annotated Java classes from an XML Schema (XSD).

See also

- ▸ Camel JAXB: http://camel.apache.org/jaxb.html
- ▸ Available Data Formats: http://camel.apache.org/data-format.html
- ▸ JAXB Specification: http://jcp.org/en/jsr/detail?id=222

Transforming from Java to JSON

Camel's JSON Component is used when you need to convert your JSON data back and forth from Java. It provides a Camel Data Format that, without any requirement for an annotated Java class, allows you to marshal (Java to JSON) or unmarshal (JSON to Java) your data.

There is only one step to using Camel JSON to marshal and unmarshal XML data. Within your Camel route, insert the `marshal` (Java to JSON), or `unmarshal` (JSON to Java) statement, and configure it to use the JSON Data Format.

This recipe will show you how to use the `camel-xstream` library to convert from Java to JSON, and back.

Getting ready

The Java code for this recipe is located in the `org.camelcookbook.transformation.json` package. The Spring XML files are located under `src/main/resources/META-INF/spring` and prefixed with `json`.

To use Camel's JSON Component, you need to add a `dependency` element for the `camel-xstream` library, which provides an implementation for the JSON Data Format using the XStream library.

Add the following to the `dependencies` section of your Maven POM:

```
<dependency>
  <groupId>org.apache.camel</groupId>
  <artifactId>camel-xstream</artifactId>
  <version>${camel-version}</version>
</dependency>
```

How to do it...

Reference the Data Format within your route, choosing the `marshal` (Java to JSON), or `unmarshal` (JSON to Java) statement, as appropriate:

In the XML DSL, this is written as follows:

```
<route>
  <from uri="direct:marshal"/>
  <marshal>
    <json/>
  </marshal>
  <to uri="mock:marshalResult"/>
</route>
```

In the Java DSL, this same route is expressed as:

```
from("direct:marshal")
  .marshal().json()
  .to("mock:marshalResult");
```

How it works...

Using Camel JSON simplifies translating your data between JSON and Java. This is convenient when you are dealing with REST endpoints and need Java processors in Camel to do custom message processing later on in the route.

Camel JSON provides a wrapper around the JSON libraries for instantiating the Java binding for the JSON data, eliminating more boilerplate code from your integration flows.

There's more...

Camel JSON works with the XStream library by default, and can be configured to use other JSON libraries, such as Jackson or GSon. These other libraries provide additional features, more customization, and more flexibility that can be leveraged by Camel. To use them, include their respective Camel components, for example, `camel-jackson`, and specify the library within the `json` element:

```
<dataFormats>
  <json id="myJson" library="Jackson"/>
</dataFormats>
```

See also

▸   Camel JSON: `http://camel.apache.org/json.html`
▸   Available Data Formats: `http://camel.apache.org/data-format.html`

Transforming from XML to JSON

Camel provides an XML JSON Component that converts your data back and forth between XML and JSON in a single step, without an intermediate Java object representation. It provides a Camel Data Format that allows you to marshal (XML to JSON), or unmarshal (JSON to XML) your data.

This recipe will show you how to use the XML JSON Component to convert from XML to JSON, and back.

Getting ready

Java code for this recipe is located in the `org.camelcookbook.transformation.xmljson` package. Spring XML files are located under `src/main/resources/META-INF/spring` and prefixed with `xmljson`.

To use Camel's XML JSON Component, you need to add a `dependency` element for the `camel-xmljson` library, which provides an implementation for the XML JSON Data Format.

Add the following to the `dependencies` section of your Maven POM:

```
<dependency>
  <groupId>org.apache.camel</groupId>
  <artifactId>camel-xmljson</artifactId>
  <version>${camel-version}</version>
</dependency>
```

How to do it...

Reference the `xmljson` Data Format within your route, choosing the `marshal` (XML to JSON), or `unmarshal` (JSON to XML) statement, as appropriate:

In the XML DSL, this is written as follows:

```
<route>
  <from uri="direct:marshal"/>
  <marshal>
    <xmljson/>
  </marshal>
  <to uri="mock:marshalResult"/>
</route>
```

In the Java DSL, this same route is expressed as:

```
from("direct:marshal")
  .marshal().xmljson()
  .to("mock:marshalResult");
```

How it works...

Using the Camel XML JSON Component simplifies translating your data between XML and JSON, making it convenient to use when you are dealing with REST endpoints. The XML JSON Data Format wraps around the `Json-lib` library, which provides the core translation capabilities, eliminating more boilerplate code from your integration flows.

There's more...

You may need to configure XML JSON if you want to fine-tune the output of your transformation. For example, consider the following JSON:

```
[{"@category":"PROGRAMMING","title":{"@lang":"en","#text":
  "Apache Camel Developer's Cookbook"},"author":[
    "Scott Cranton","Jakub Korab"],"year":"2013","price":"49.99"}]
```

This will be converted as follows, by default, which may not be exactly what you want (notice the `<a>` and `<e>` elements):

```
<?xml version="1.0" encoding="UTF-8"?>
<a>
  <e category="PROGRAMMING">
    <author>
      <e>Scott Cranton</e>
      <e>Jakub Korab</e>
    </author>
    <price>49.99</price>
    <title lang="en">Apache Camel Developer's Cookbook</title>
    <year>2013</year>
  </e>
</a>
```

To configure XML JSON to use `<bookstore>` as the root element instead of `<a>`, use `<book>` for the individual elements instead of `<e>`, and expand the multiple author values to use a sequence of `<author>` elements, you would need to tune the configuration of the Data Format before referencing it in your route.

In the XML DSL, the definition of the Data Format and the route that uses it is written as follows:

```
<dataFormats>
  <xmljson id="myXmlJson"
           rootName="bookstore"
           elementName="book"
           expandableProperties="author author"/>
</dataFormats>

<route>
  <from uri="direct:unmarshalBookstore"/>
  <unmarshal ref="myXmlJson"/>
  <to uri="mock:unmarshalResult"/>
</route>
```

In the Java DSL, the same thing is expressed as:

```
XmlJsonDataFormat xmlJsonFormat = new XmlJsonDataFormat();
xmlJsonFormat.setRootName("bookstore");
xmlJsonFormat.setElementName("book");
xmlJsonFormat.setExpandableProperties(
    Arrays.asList("author", "author"));

from("direct:unmarshalBookstore")
  .unmarshal(xmlJsonFormat)
  .to("mock:unmarshalBookstoreResult");
```

This will result in the previous JSON being unmarshalled as follows:

```
<?xml version="1.0" encoding="UTF-8"?>
<bookstore>
  <book category="PROGRAMMING">
    <author>Scott Cranton</author>
    <author>Jakub Korab</author>
    <price>49.99</price>
    <title lang="en">Apache Camel Developer's Cookbook</title>
    <year>2013</year>
  </book>
</bookstore>
```

See also

  ▸ Camel XML JSON: `http://camel.apache.org/xmljson.html`

  ▸ Available Data Formats: `http://camel.apache.org/data-format.html`

  ▸ Json-lib: `http://json-lib.sourceforge.net`

Parsing comma-separated values (CSV)

The Camel Bindy Component is used to easily handle delimited data, such as comma-separated values (CSV). It provides a Camel Data Format that allows you to create a Java model, annotate it with the desired bindings to appropriate data fields, and then marshal (Java to delimited data), or unmarshal (delimited data to Java) your data.

The Bindy Component allows you to use your own Java classes annotated with processing instructions as a model for the Java representation of your field-based data. These annotations instruct Bindy on the following:

  ▸ What the separator character is (for example, ' , ')

  ▸ Field names, positions, and data types

  ▸ Special field handlers that define Date formats or instructions such as whether String contents should be trimmed

In addition, Bindy provides you with the ability to map a (limited) graph of objects to single row-delimited record.

This recipe will show you how to use the Bindy Component to convert CSV-formatted data.

Getting ready

The Java code for this recipe is located in the `org.camelcookbook.transformation.`
`csv` package. The Spring XML files are located under `src/main/resources/META-INF/`
`spring` and prefixed with `csv`.

To use Camel's Bindy Component, you need to add a `dependency` for the `camel-bindy`
library, which provides the implementation for the Bindy Data Format.

In your Maven's `pom.xml`, add the following to your `dependencies` section:

```
<dependency>
  <groupId>org.apache.camel</groupId>
  <artifactId>camel-bindy</artifactId>
  <version>${camel-version}</version>
</dependency>
```

How to do it...

There are three steps for using Camel Bindy to marshal and unmarshal CSV data:

1. Create an annotated Java model:

    ```
    @CsvRecord(separator = ",", crlf = "UNIX")
    public class BookModel {
      @DataField(pos = 1)
      private String category;

      @DataField(pos = 2)
      private String title;

      @DataField(pos = 3, defaultValue = "en")
      private String titleLanguage;

      @DataField(pos = 4)
      private String author1;

      @DataField(pos = 5)
      private String author2;

      @DataField(pos = 6, pattern = "MMM-yyyy")
      private Date publishDate;

      @DataField(pos = 7, precision = 2)
    ```

```
    private BigDecimal price;

    // getters and setters
}
```

2. Instantiate a Bindy Data Format within your Camel route, providing a reference to the Java package(s) containing your Bindy annotated Java classes:

   In the XML DSL, this is written as:

```
<camelContext
    xmlns="http://camel.apache.org/schema/spring">
  <dataFormats>
    <bindy id="bookModel"
           type="Csv"
           packages=
             "org.camelcookbook.transformation.csv.model"/>
  </dataFormats>

  <!-- route definitions here -->
</camelContext>
```

   In the Java DSL, the same thing is expressed as:

```
public class CsvRouteBuilder extends RouteBuilder {
  @Override
  public void configure() throws Exception {
    DataFormat bindy =
      new BindyCsvDataFormat(
        "org.camelcookbook.transformation.csv.model");

    // route definitions here
  }
}
```

3. Reference the Data Format within your route, choosing the `marshal` (Java to CSV), or `unmarshal` (CSV to Java) statement, as appropriate:

   In the XML DSL, this is written as:

```
<route>
  <from uri="direct:unmarshal"/>
  <unmarshal ref="bookModel"/>
</route>
```

   In the Java DSL, the same thing is expressed as:

```
from("direct:unmarshal").unmarshal(bindy);
```

How it works...

A very common pattern for integrations is to pick up delimited files from a directory or FTP server, parse them, convert them to a common canonical format, and forward them on to other message processors. The reverse of this flow, to generate delimited files is also commonplace. This allows for integration with batch file based systems, and where files are used to pass data between business partners.

This recipe helps with the first part of this flow – parsing and converting to a canonical format. Once you have the basic Camel routing steps in place for marshaling and unmarshaling the data, you will spend most of your time tweaking the model annotations to match changes to the delimited data format. See the *Normalizing messages into a common XML format* recipe for more details on creating a message normalizer.

There's more...

Bindy has support for handling fixed-length files (field positions defined as number of bytes or characters to read; with no delimiter such as a comma), and for multi-line records like those used in the FIX financial format and mainframe COBOL copybook format.

There are other Camel components that can help you with structured file handling, including: BeanIO, CSV, EDI, and Flatpack. Check out the Camel Data Format page for more options (`http://camel.apache.org/data-format.html`).

See also

- ▶ Camel Bindy: `http://camel.apache.org/bindy.html`
- ▶ Available Data Formats: `http://camel.apache.org/data-format.html`
- ▶ The *Normalizing messages into a common XML format* recipe

Enriching your content with some help from other endpoints

The Content Enricher EIP is used when you need to call out to some other endpoint (for example, a web service or Java method) to get *additional* content based on all, or parts, of your message. This recipe focuses on the most common scenario—when you want to modify the contents of your original message (including its body, headers, or properties) with the contents of the returned message.

When using the Enricher EIP, it is a common requirement to include a processing step before the `enrich` call to set up the message body to an appropriate request format for the enriching endpoint. It is also likely that you will need to define an additional processing step to merge the results of the endpoint invocation with your original exchange. This recipe will show you, through a simple example, how to perform these setup and enrichment steps when using the Enricher EIP.

Getting ready

The Java code for this recipe is located in the `org.camelcookbook.transformation. enrich` package. The Spring XML files are located under `src/main/resources/META-INF/spring` and prefixed with `enrich`.

This recipe will call out to an example Java method that will expand a US state's abbreviation into its full name. This recipe's approach would work equally well with any Camel endpoint, such as a SOAP web service or a database lookup.

The code for the `AbbreviationExpander` class is as follows:

```
public class AbbreviationExpander {
  public String expand(String abbreviation) {
    if ("MA".equalsIgnoreCase(abbreviation)) {
      return "Massachusetts";
    }

    if ("CA".equalsIgnoreCase(abbreviation)) {
      return "California";
    }

    throw new IllegalArgumentException(
      "Unknown abbreviation '" + abbreviation + ";");
  }
}
```

This Expander code is called from a wrapper Camel route, `direct:expander`, that will be called by the Enricher EIP:

```
from("direct:expander")
  .bean(AbbreviationExpander.class, "expand");
```

How to do it...

In order to enrich your exchange with the results of another route you will need to create:

- ▸ An `AggregationStrategy` to combine the results of your original message, and the response from the enrichment endpoint
- ▸ Code to setup the call to the enrichment endpoint
- ▸ A Camel route to tie them all together

These steps are performed as follows:

1. Create an `AggregationStrategy` implementation and associated setup code. This code combines the enrichment endpoint setup code with the `AggregationStrategy` code that will merge the results with the original message, as they are dependent on each other:

```
public class MergeInReplacementText
    implements AggregationStrategy {
  public static final String ENRICH_EXAMPLE_ORIGINAL_BODY =
      "EnrichExample.originalBody";
  public static final String
    ENRICH_EXAMPLE_REPLACEMENT_STRING =
      "EnrichExample.replacementString";

  /**
   * When using this AggregationStrategy, this
   * method must be called <b>before</b> the enrich call
   * as this method sets up the message body, and adds some
   * properties needed by the aggregate method.
   */
  public void setup(Exchange exchange) {
    final String originalBody =
        exchange.getIn().getBody(String.class);

    exchange.setProperty(ENRICH_EXAMPLE_ORIGINAL_BODY,
                         originalBody);

    final String enrichParameter =
        originalBody.substring(
          originalBody.lastIndexOf(" ") + 1);

    exchange.setProperty(ENRICH_EXAMPLE_REPLACEMENT_STRING,
                         enrichParameter);

    exchange.getIn().setBody(enrichParameter);
```

```
    }

    @Override
    public Exchange aggregate(Exchange original,
                             Exchange enrichResponse) {
        // The original.In.Body was changed to the replacement
        // string, so need to retrieve property with original
        // body
        final String originalBody =
            original.getProperty(ENRICH_EXAMPLE_ORIGINAL_BODY,
                                 String.class);
        Validate.notEmpty(originalBody,
            "The property '" + ENRICH_EXAMPLE_ORIGINAL_BODY
            + "' must be set with the original message body.");

        final String replacementString =
            original.getProperty(
                ENRICH_EXAMPLE_REPLACEMENT_STRING, String.class);
        Validate.notEmpty(replacementString,
            "The property '"
            + ENRICH_EXAMPLE_REPLACEMENT_STRING
            + "' must be set with the value to be replaced.");

        final String replacementValue =
            enrichResponse.getIn().getBody(String.class);

        // Use regular expression to replace the last
        // occurrence of the replacement string
        final String mergeResult =
            originalBody.replaceAll(replacementString + "$",
                                    replacementValue);

        original.getIn().setBody(mergeResult);

        return original;
    }
}
```

2. Within the Camel route, set up the call to the enrichment endpoint. This example involves calling another Camel route, but using any of Camel's endpoints will also work.

   In the XML DSL, define a `bean` and use it in a route as follows:

```
<beans xmlns="http://www.springframework.org/schema/beans"
       xmlns:xsi=
          "http://www.w3.org/2001/XMLSchema-instance"
```

```
       xsi:schemaLocation= "
         http://www.springframework.org/schema/beans
         http://www.springframework.org/schema/beans/
             spring-beans.xsd
         http://camel.apache.org/schema/spring
         http://camel.apache.org/schema/spring/camel-spring.xsd
       ">

  <bean id="myMerger"
        class="org.camelcookbook.transformation.enrich
              .MergeInReplacementText"/>

  <camelContext
      xmlns="http://camel.apache.org/schema/spring">
    <route>
      <from uri="direct:start"/>
      <bean ref="myMerger" method="setup"/>
      <enrich uri="direct:expander"
              strategyRef="myMerger"/>
    </route>
  </camelContext>
</beans>
```

In the Java DSL, the same idea is expressed as follows:

```
public class EnrichWithAggregatorRouteBuilder
        extends RouteBuilder {
    private MergeInReplacementText myMerger;

    @Override
    public void configure() throws Exception {
        from("direct:start")
            .bean(myMerger, "setup")
            .enrich("direct:expander", myMerger);
    }

    // Getters and Setters
}
```

3. Use the `enrich` DSL statement to call your enrichment endpoint, and reference your `AggregationStrategy` to process the results.

    In the XML DSL, this is written as follows:

```
<route>
  <from uri="direct:start"/>
```

```
        <bean ref="myMerger" method="setup"/>
        <enrich uri="direct:expander"
                strategyRef="myMerger"/>
    </route>
```

In the Java DSL, the same thing is expressed as:

```
from("direct:start")
    .bean(myMerger, "setup")
    .enrich("direct:expander", myMerger);
```

> The Java DSL version of enrich expects a reference to an
> AggregationStrategy instance; in this example this instance
> is injected into the RouteBuilder.

How it works...

The enrich EIP calls the referenced endpoint as Request-Response (MEP InOut), and merges the response with the original message through an AggregationStrategy implementation. If no AggregationStrategy reference is provided, the enricher will replace the original message body with the response from the enrichment endpoint call.

Camel will send the current message to the reference enrichment endpoint, so most of the time you will need to alter (set up) the message to be appropriate to call the external endpoint. In the provided example code for this recipe, the enrichment endpoint expects a US state abbreviation such as "MA", but if the original message is "Hello MA", then the Camel route alters the message to be just the state abbreviation "MA".

The associated Aggregator merges the results with the original message, so for this example it would replace the abbreviation "MA" with "Massachusetts" within the original source message: "Hello MA". The AggregationStrategy receives two Camel exchanges: the first parameter is the original exchange before the enrichment endpoint is called, and the second parameter is the exchange returned from the enrichment endpoint (that is, its response).

The Aggregator needs the original message, since it needs to replace the state abbreviation with the long version. In the setup method we store the original message and the abbreviated state value to be replaced in the Camel exchange as properties. This allows the aggregate method, called after the enrich callout, to merge in the endpoint's response ("Massachusetts") with the original message ("Hello MA"), and give us the desired end result ("Hello Massachusetts").

There's more...

There is a variant of enrich called pollEnrich that is used with endpoints that are Polling Consumers, such as file or database. For example, if you want to append data from a file in a directory that you expect to be created externally as part of an integration, you should use pollEnrich to fetch its contents:

```
from("direct:start")
  .pollEnrich("file:/path/to/data", myAppender);
```

> When using pollEnrich, it is a good idea to set its timeout option, which controls how many milliseconds it will wait for data. By default, the timeout is set to -1 meaning that it will wait forever for enrichment data. We recommend always setting this to some meaningful value for your integration so that your integrations do not appear to get stuck (hang).

See also

▸ Camel Enricher: http://camel.apache.org/content-enricher.html

▸ Polling Consumer: http://camel.apache.org/polling-consumer.html

Normalizing messages into a common XML format

This recipe will show you a strategy for normalizing input that arrives in many different data formats (CSV, JSON, and XML) into a single canonical XML format. The strategy shown here also allows you to handle unknown input formats.

This strategy uses the Normalizer EIP, which is a Content Based Router EIP (see the *Content Based Routing* recipe in *Chapter 2, Message Routing*) combined with Data Format translators. It detects the incoming message format, and performs one or more steps needed to transform the message to the canonical format. After the Content Based Router, all processing steps can now operate assuming the message is in canonical format.

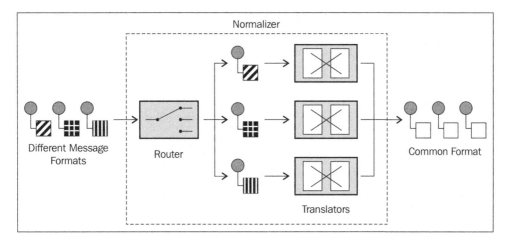

 It the following example, a subtle point to note is that we are transforming the message into an object graph of JAXB objects—a parsed version of the XML message. See the *Transforming from Java to XML with JAXB* recipe for more details.

Getting ready

The Java code for this recipe is located in the `org.camelcookbook.transformation.normalizer` package. Spring XML files are located under `src/main/resources/META-INF/spring` and prefixed with `normalizer`.

How to do it...

The main idea behind normalizing messages is to use a Content Based Router (see the *Content Based Routing* recipe in *Chapter 2, Message Routing*) whose `when` statements identify and transform each of the different formats to be normalized:

1. Lay out the Content Based Router, followed by processing steps that expect the canonical message format.

   In the XML DSL, this is written as:

   ```
   <route>
     <from uri="direct:start"/>
     <choice>
       <!-- normalize each input format here -->
     </choice>
     <to uri="mock:normalized"/>
   </route>
   ```

In the Java DSL, the same thing is expressed as:

```
public void configure() throws Exception {
  // setup Data Formats here

  from("direct:start")
    .choice()
      // normalize each input format here
    .end()
    .to("mock:normalized");
}
```

The `mock:normalized` endpoint should only receive messages as a graph of JAXB objects regardless of the format of the input message to this route.

2. Handle CSV input messages, and convert them to our canonical model. See the *Parsing comma-separated values (CSV)* recipe for more details on the Bindy Data Format.

In the XML DSL, this routing logic is written as:

```
<choice>
  <when>
    <simple>
      ${header.CamelFileName} regex '.*\.csv$'
    </simple>
    <unmarshal>
      <bindy type="Csv"
             packages="org.camelcookbook.transformation
                       .csv.model"/>
    </unmarshal>
    <bean ref="myNormalizer" method="bookModelToJaxb"/>
    <to uri="mock:csv"/>
  </when>
  <!-- normalize other formats -->
</choice>
```

In that Java DSL, the same thing is written as follows:

```
.choice()
  .when(header(Exchange.FILE_NAME).endsWith(".csv"))
    .unmarshal(bindy)
    .bean(MyNormalizer.class, "bookModelToJaxb")
    .to("mock:csv")
  // normalize other formats
.end()
```

The `MyNormalizer` Java call-out is to code that translates from the CSV Java model to JAXB.

Note that the XML DSL uses the Simple Expression Language's regular expression operator (regex) to detect the filename extension, while the Java DSL uses the Header Expression with a value builder predicate. It felt more natural in the Java DSL to use a Java-like expression (endsWith) versus a regular expression. There is no "best" approach in situations like this; use whichever you feel best matches your needs.

3. Handle JSON input messages, and convert them to our canonical model. See the *Transforming from Java to JSON* recipe for more details on the JSON Data Format.

   In the XML DSL, this is written as:

```
<choice>
  <when>
    <simple>
      ${header.CamelFileName} regex '.*\.json$'
    </simple>
    <unmarshal>
      <xmljson rootName="bookstore"
               elementName="book"
               expandableProperties="author author"/>
    </unmarshal>
    <to uri="mock:json"/>
  </when>
  <!-- normalize other formats -->
</choice>
```

   In that Java DSL, this is written as follows:

```
.choice()
  .when(header(Exchange.FILE_NAME).endsWith(".json"))
    .unmarshal(xmlJsonFormat)
    .to("mock:json")
  // normalize other formats
.end()
```

4. Handle XML input messages, and convert them to our canonical model. In this example, this means parsing the XML into Java using JAXB. See the *Transforming from Java to XML with JAXB* recipe for more details on the JAXB Data Format.

   In the XML DSL, this logic is written as:

```
<choice>
  <when>
    <simple>
      ${header.CamelFileName} regex '.*\.xml$'
    </simple>
    <unmarshal>
```

```
          <jaxb contextPath="org.camelcookbook.transformation
                             .myschema"/>
      </unmarshal>
      <to uri="mock:xml"/>
   </when>
   <!-- normalize other formats -->
</choice>
```

In that Java DSL, this is written as follows:

```
.choice()
  .when(header(Exchange.FILE_NAME).endsWith(".xml"))
    .unmarshal(jaxb)
    .to("mock:xml")
  // normalize other formats
.end()
```

5. Handle other unknown input messages by forwarding the message to some endpoint, such as a dead letter queue, and then using the `stop` statement to discontinue processing of this message within this route.

   In the XML DSL, this step is written as:

```
<choice>
   <!-- normalize input formats -->
   <otherwise>
     <to uri="mock:unknown"/>
     <stop/>
   </otherwise>
</choice>
```

   In that Java DSL, the same thing is expressed as:

```
.choice()
  // normalize input formats
  .otherwise()
    .to("mock:unknown")
    .stop()
.end()
```

How it works...

The main part of this recipe uses the Content Based Routing EIP to detect each incoming input message format, and performs the steps required to normalize that message to the desired canonical format.

A number of different types of expressions can be used to detect the incoming message format. The preceding example uses the `CamelFileName` header that is set by the File and FTP Components, to detect the input format based on the suffix of the filename. For a scenario with different XML inputs, using an XPath Expression and inspecting Namespaces might be a better way to normalize different versions of XML requests, followed by translations using XSLT or XQuery into the common XML format.

The `otherwise` portion of the Content Based Router is used in the example to catch other unknown input message formats that are not handled by the `when` statement's expressions. It is common in such cases to log or send the message to some external route or processor for later handling by a person or automated error-handling portion of your application. The route could also throw an exception, such as an `IllegalArgumentException`, if you want the caller to handle the issue. The Camel `stop` statement in this example tells Camel to stop processing, that is, to execute no more processing steps with this message within this route.

There's more...

In this example, within the processor steps for normalizing incoming CSV format messages, we see the usage of a Java callout to translate one Java object model to another. If this Java model conversation is common across your Camel routes, you could create and register a Camel Data Type Converter to allow Camel to automatically do the type conversation for you when needed. In this example, the Java callout to `MyNormalizer` could be replaced with the use of the Camel directive `convertBodyTo(org.camelcookbook.transformation.myschema.Bookstore)`, which arguably is clearer as to what's happening within the route. See the *Writing a custom data type converter* recipe in *Chapter 3, Routing to Your Code* for more details.

See also

- Camel Normalizer: http://camel.apache.org/normalizer.html
- Camel Content Based Router: http://camel.apache.org/content-based-router.html
- The *Transforming from Java to XML with JAXB* recipe
- The *Parsing comma-separated values (CSV)* recipe
- The *Transforming from Java to JSON* recipe
- The *Content Based Routing* recipe in *Chapter 2, Message Routing*
- The *Writing a custom data type converter* recipe in *Chapter 3, Routing to Your Code*

5
Splitting and Aggregating

In this chapter, we will cover:

- ▶ Splitting a message into fragments
- ▶ Splitting XML messages
- ▶ Processing split messages in parallel
- ▶ Aggregating related messages
- ▶ Aggregating with timeouts
- ▶ Aggregating with intervals
- ▶ Processing aggregated messages in parallel
- ▶ Splitting a message, and processing and gathering responses
- ▶ Splitting messages and re-aggregating them using different criteria

Introduction

This chapter will describe how to split exchanges into smaller fragments and process them individually. It will also explain how you can aggregate (join) multiple exchanges by grouping them according to arbitrary expressions. Finally, it will discuss how to split messages into fragments, process them individually, and re-aggregate the results; either back into the original exchange, or into a new combination of exchanges.

None of these operations are as straightforward as might be considered at first glance. The combination of options that you select alters behaviors such as error handling and threading quite substantially. The following recipes will explain some of these edge cases.

A number of Camel architectural concepts are used throughout this chapter. There is a broader overview of Camel concepts in the *Preface*. Full details can be found on the Apache Camel website at `http://camel.apache.org`.

The code for this chapter is contained within the `camel-cookbook-split-join` module of the examples.

Splitting a message into fragments

The **Splitter** EIP provides you with a versatile mechanism for breaking a message down into smaller fragments and processing them individually.

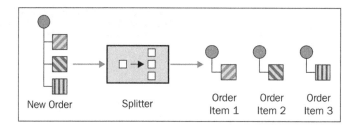

| New Order | Splitter | Order Item 1 | Order Item 2 | Order Item 3 |

This recipe will show you how to use the Splitter EIP, along with Camel's built-in Expression Languages, to easily slice up your messages.

Getting ready

The Java code for this recipe is located in the `org.camelcookbook.splitjoin.split` package. The Spring XML files are located under `src/main/resources/META-INF/spring` and prefixed with `split`.

How to do it...

Inside your route, create a `split` statement, whose first line is the split expression. The following code splits a message *naturally*, meaning that any message that is an array, `Collection`, or `Iterator` will have each element processed individually through the statements in the block, as through a loop:

```
<from uri="direct:in"/>
<split>
  <simple>${body}</simple>
  <to uri="mock:split"/>
</split>
```

Here, `${body}` is a Simple Expression Language that identifies the node in the object graph to be split.

In Java, the corresponding block could be written as follows:

```
from("direct:in")
  .split(body())
    .to("mock:split")
  .end();
```

Here the `body()` expression is used for convenience instead of writing `simple("${body}")`. The `end()` method designates the end of the `split()` block.

> It is not strictly necessary to use the `end()` statement unless you are going to have any further statements outside of the block. It is however a good habit to get into, as it makes the processing logic clearer, and therefore easier to reason about.

How it works...

The Splitter EIP evaluates the expression to obtain a collection of elements to process. Each element is processed individually through the statements within the `split` block, in the order evaluated by the expression.

The expression can be anything that uniquely identifies a collection of things that the EIP can split, or returns a collection of values. Consider the following class, which represents the body of an exchange flowing through the route:

```
public class ListWrapper {
    // getters and setters omitted
    private List<String> wrapped;
}
```

In order to process each of the `String`s individually, all we need to do is to modify the expression used within the Splitter to the following:

```
from("direct:in")
  .split(simple("${body.wrapped}"))
    .to("mock:out")
  .end();
```

The same thread that originally entered the block will process each of the split steps individually. When the thread exits the block, the body of the exchange will contain the original content. The reason behind this is that the Splitter has the option of aggregating the processed message fragments using `AggregationStrategy` (see the *Splitting a message, and processing and gathering responses* recipe). The default `AggregationStrategy` used always returns the original unsplit exchange.

When a message is split, a new exchange is created for each message fragment as it is processed through the route. This exchange contains a copy of the headers and properties of the original. In addition, the following message properties are set:

- `CamelSplitIndex`: A 0-based index of the message
- `CamelSplitSize`: The total number of fragments split from the original exchange body
- `CamelSplitComplete`: A `Boolean` that indicates whether this exchange contains the last fragment

There's more...

When an exception is thrown within your `split()` block, Camel will trigger the route's error handler for the exchange containing the split fragment. Beyond this, the default behavior is not what you would expect, in that the splitting process will not be interrupted like a traditional Java loop. Instead, the remainder of the split items will continue to be processed one by one. However, processing will be suspended at the completion of the `split()`, and then the exception will be thrown back to the consuming endpoint.

You can modify this behavior to what you might otherwise expect, by setting the `stopOnException` attribute to `true`:

In the XML DSL, this is written as:

```
<split stopOnException="true">
```

In the Java DSL, the same thing is expressed as:

```
.split(body()).stopOnException()
```

This will prevent the splitting process from processing any further fragments when an exception occurs.

See also

- Splitter: `http://camel.apache.org/splitter.html`
- Simple Expression Language: `http://camel.apache.org/simple.html`

Splitting XML messages

XML is one of the most frequently split payload types. This recipe will show how you can use Camel's support for implicit type conversion, and XPath support, to process XML fragments individually.

Getting ready

The Java code for this recipe is located in the `org.camelcookbook.splitjoin.splitxml` package. The Spring XML files are located under `src/main/resources/META-INF/spring` and prefixed with `splitXml`.

How to do it...

Consider the following XML file:

```
<books>
  <book category="Tech"
        title="Apache Camel Developer's Cookbook">
    <authors>
      <author>Scott Cranton</author>
      <author>Jakub Korab</author>
    </authors>
  </book>
  <book category="Cooking" title="Camel Cookbook">
    <authors>
      <author>Heston Ramsey</author>
      <author>Gordon Blumenthal</author>
    </authors>
  </book>
</books>
```

To extract the authors of a particular book category, you use an XPath Expression within the `split` DSL statement to isolate the nodes that you are interested in.

In the XML DSL, this is written as:

```
<from uri="direct:in"/>
<split>
  <xpath>//book[@category='Tech']/authors/author/text()</xpath>
  <to uri="mock:out"/>
</split>
```

In the Java DSL, the same route is expressed as:

```
from("direct:in")
  .split(xpath("//book[@category='Tech']/authors/author/text()"))
    .to("mock:out")
  .end();
```

As a result, two messages will be sent to the `mock:out` endpoint:

- ▸ `Scott Cranton`
- ▸ `Jakub Korab`

How it works...

The XPath Expression is used to uniquely identify XML DOM nodes that should be isolated for splitting. The Splitter processes each of the identified nodes, and any child nodes, through the steps defined within the `split` statement.

There's more...

The preceding example assumes an XML document without any namespaces. Using XML namespaces with XPath involves only a little bit of extra configuration.

Assume that the document being passed through the route varies from the previous example only in the definition of a namespace:

```
<books xmlns="http://camelcookbook.org/schema/books">
  <!-- remainder as per example above -->
</books>
```

In order for our XPath Expression to match, we will need to refer to the namespace through a prefix (`c:`):

```
//c:book[@category='Tech']/c:authors/c:author/text()
```

What remains is to define the association between the full namespace URI and that prefix.

In the XML DSL, the namespace definition is provided on some parent XML element such as the `camelContext`:

```
<camelContext
    xmlns="http://camel.apache.org/schema/spring"
    xmlns:c="http://camelcookbook.org/schema/books">
  <route>
    <from uri="direct:in"/>
    <split>
      <xpath>
        //c:book[@category='Tech']/c:authors/c:author/text()
      </xpath>
      <to uri="mock:out"/>
    </split>
  </route>
</camelContext>
```

When using the Java DSL, you can append a namespace to the `xpath()` expression:

```
from("direct:in")
  .split(
    xpath(
      "//c:book[@category='Tech']/c:authors/c:author/text()"
    ).namespace("c", "http://camelcookbook.org/schema/books")
  )
    .to("mock:out")
  .end();
```

Once again, two messages will be sent to the `mock:out` endpoint:

▸ Scott Cranton

▸ Jakub Korab

Multiple namespaces can be defined through chaining as follows:

```
.namespace("c", "http://camelcookbook.org/schema/books")
.namespace("se", "http://camelcookbook.org/schema/somethingElse")
```

If you are going to be using the same namespaces in multiple places throughout your routes, you can make use of the `org.apache.camel.builder.xml.Namespaces` builder to avoid repeating that definition:

```
Namespaces ns =
    new Namespaces("c", "http://camelcookbook.org/schema/books")
        .add("se", "http://camelcookbook.org/schema/somethingElse");

from("direct:in")
  .split(
    ns.xpath(
      "//c:book[@category='Tech']/c:authors/c:author/text()"
    )
  )
    .to("mock:out")
  .end();
```

> When splitting via an XPath Expression, Camel loads the entire XML document into memory. This may not be desirable for very large messages. See the Splitter documentation on the Camel website for details on using the Tokenizer Expression Language along with streaming to address this. You can also use the Camel StAX Component for this purpose.

See also

- ▶ Splitter: `http://camel.apache.org/splitter.html`
- ▶ XPath Expression Language: `http://camel.apache.org/xpath.html`
- ▶ Camel StAX: `http://camel.apache.org/stax.html`

Processing split messages in parallel

When building integrations, it is often necessary to increase the throughput of a route. Short of speeding up the individual steps, which may not always be possible, one of the most convenient ways to do this is to process portions of the route in parallel. This recipe will show how you can use the Splitter EIP's parallel processing option to hand off message fragments to a pool of threads for concurrent processing.

Getting ready

Java code for this recipe is located in the `org.camelcookbook.splitjoin.split` package. Spring XML files are located under `src/main/resources/META-INF/spring` and prefixed with `splitParallel` and `splitExecutorService`.

How to do it...

To process split messages through the route in parallel, set the `parallelProcessing` attribute to `true` on the `split` statement:

In the XML DSL, this is written as:

```
<from uri="direct:in"/>
<split parallelProcessing="true">
  <simple>${body}</simple>
  <log message="Processing message[${property.CamelSplitIndex}]"/>
  <to uri="mock:split"/>
</split>
```

In the Java DSL, the same this is expressed as:

```
from("direct:in")
  .split(body()).parallelProcessing()
    .log("Processing message[${property.CamelSplitIndex}]")
    .to("mock:split")
  .end()
```

How it works...

When `parallelProcessing` is set to `true`, Camel internally creates a thread pool that is used to service each of the split message fragments through the route, each on a thread from that pool. When `parallelProcessing` is set to `false`, all of the split messages are processed on the original thread from the route.

 Because of the non-determinism of the threading, it is highly possible that the split message marked as the last fragment (that is a message with the property `CamelSplitComplete` set to `true`) may not be the last one actually processed.

There's more...

Because the split messages are handed over to a thread pool, error handling is a little different from the normal case described in the *Splitting a message into fragments* recipe. As with the regular splitting process, when an exception is thrown, any split message fragments that are in-flight will continue to be processed through the route.

Things change somewhat if you specify that you would like to stop processing by setting the `stopOnException` attribute to `true`—the Splitter will be informed not to send any more message fragments to the thread pool. The end result may be that many more fragments are processed in the Splitter after an exception has been thrown. This option should therefore be used with care.

It is possible to include a `timeout` option with the maximum period in milliseconds that the processing of the full set of fragments should not exceed.

In the XML DSL, this is written as:

```
<split parallelProcessing="true" timeout="5000">
```

In the Java DSL, the same thing is expressed as:

```
.split(body()).parallelProcessing().timeout(5000)
```

When the timeout is reached, any fragments that have yet to be picked up by the thread pool for processing will be discarded, and fragments currently in flight through the route will be allowed to complete.

It is possible to customize the details of the thread pool used for `parallelProcessing` by referring to a `threadPool` instance defined within the Camel context by its `id`:

```
<camelContext xmlns="http://camel.apache.org/schema/spring">
  <threadPool id="customPool" poolSize="20" threadName="pool"/>

  <route>
    <from uri="direct:in"/>
    <split executorServiceRef="customPool">
      <!-- ... -->
    </split>
  </route>
</camelContext>
```

 Use of the `executorService` attribute implies `parallelProcessing`, so you do not need to define them together. You may, however, still set the `parallelProcessing` option to `true` to make the intent of your routing logic explicit.

The Java DSL contains an equivalent option by which you can refer to a thread pool in Camel's registry:

```
.split(body())
    .executorServiceRef("customPool")
```

See also

▶ Splitter: `http://camel.apache.org/splitter.html`

Aggregating related messages

Aggregation of related messages is a frequent use case in integration. It is also one of the more complicated cases to write by hand, since it involves state, which can be lost if you are not careful, as well as considerations like timing. Camel's implementation of the **Aggregator** EIP abstracts away the complexity of this task, leaving you to define the following:

▶ How two exchanges ought to be aggregated into one. This is done by providing an implementation of an `AggregationStrategy`, which is an interface used to merge multiple exchanges together.

▶ Which exchanges are to be aggregated with each other. This is defined by an expression that determines the grouping value from the exchange.

▶ When an aggregation is considered complete. For this, we use one of a number of completion conditions defined through the DSL that allow us to make this decision by: an aggregated exchange count; a predicate against the aggregated, or incoming, exchange; interval since last message; or a timeout.

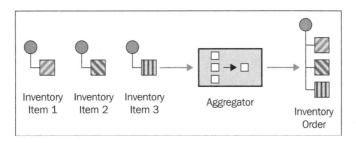

This recipe will show you how to use the Aggregator pattern to merge related exchanges into one using an aggregated exchange count, or completion size.

Getting ready

The Java code for this recipe is located in the `org.camelcookbook.splitjoin.aggregate` package. The Spring XML files are located under `src/main/resources/META-INF/spring` and prefixed with `aggregate`.

How to do it...

To aggregate related exchanges use the `aggregate` DSL statement with an associated `AggregationStrategy` implementation. The EIP implementation will use this class to do the actual combining of the exchanges:

1. Implement an `AggregationStrategy`. The following strategy aggregates `String` messages into a `Set`:

```
public class SetAggregationStrategy
    implements AggregationStrategy{
  @Override
  public Exchange aggregate(Exchange oldExchange,
                            Exchange newExchange) {
    String body =
        newExchange.getIn().getBody(String.class);
    if (oldExchange == null) {
      Set<String> set = new HashSet<String>();
      set.add(body);
      newExchange.getIn().setBody(set);
      return newExchange;
    } else {
```

```
          Set<String> set =
              oldExchange.getIn().getBody(Set.class);
          set.add(body);
          return oldExchange;
        }
      }
    }
```

The `AggregationStrategy` interface defines a single method:

```
Exchange aggregate(Exchange oldExchange, Exchange newExchange);
```

It receives two Exchange objects as parameters, and returns a single Exchange object that represents the merged result.

When it is called for the first time, the `AggregationStrategy` will receive a `null` for the `oldExchange` parameter, and, as such, needs to be able to deal with this condition. On subsequent invocations, the `oldExchange` parameter will contain the previously aggregated exchange.

If using the XML DSL, you will also need to instantiate your aggregation strategy implementation inside your Spring configuration:

```
<bean id="setAggregationStrategy"
      class="org.camelcookbook,splitjoin.aggregate
             .SetAggregationStrategy"/>
```

2. In your route, define an `aggregate` statement with a reference to the aggregation strategy bean you created in the `strategyRef` attribute. You will then need to set some other options on the `aggregate` statement to refine its behavior.

    The `completionSize` attribute is used to define the number of messages that will be aggregated before the resulting message is processed through the remainder of the `aggregate` block.

    Within the block, the `correlationExpression` element is used to define the value that will be used to aggregate messages. Exchanges that evaluate to the same expression result will be aggregated. The correlation expression appears as a nested element within the `aggregate` block.

    In the XML DSL, this is written as:

```
<route>
  <from uri="direct:in"/>
  <aggregate strategyRef="setAggregationStrategy"
             completionSize="5">
    <correlationExpression>
      <simple>${headers.group}</simple>
    </correlationExpression>
    <to uri="mock:out"/>
  </aggregate>
</route>
```

In the Java DSL, the `aggregate` block looks quite different. Here the correlation expression, which is always required, is passed directly in to the `aggregate()` statement. The `completionSize` option (which is one of two possible completion options—the other option being `completionTimeout`) follows on using the DSL's builder pattern:

```
from("direct:in")
  .aggregate(header("group"), new SetAggregationStrategy())
     .completionSize(5)
    .to("mock:out")
  .end();
```

The `end()` method designates the end of the `aggregate()` block.

How it works...

When a message is processed through the route, and reaches the `aggregate` block, the Aggregator's correlation expression is evaluated against that message. The resulting value is used to identify the group of related (correlated) messages that the current message belongs to.

The associated `AggregationStrategy` is invoked with the current Exchange instance in the `newExchange` argument.

If this message is the first message in that group, no `oldExchange` value is provided—a `null` value is passed in instead. In this case, the strategy will set the body of `newExchange` to an initial aggregated state. In the preceding example, this is a `Set` with a single value—the original body of the message. The `newExchange` value is then returned as the aggregated exchange.

Subsequent invocations of the strategy for this group will receive this aggregated Exchange instance as the `oldExchange` argument. It will then be augmented with the incoming message body before being returned.

Once a message has been aggregated, the completion condition is evaluated. If the condition is satisfied, the aggregated message is processed through the steps defined in the `aggregate` block.

If the completion condition is not satisfied, the aggregated exchange is saved away in an **Aggregation Repository**—the default behavior uses an in-memory implementation. The thread then finishes processing the exchange through that route.

 Aggregated messages will reside in an aggregation repository until this completion size is reached, which could be a very long time. To ensure that they do not reside there indefinitely you usually use an additional `completionTimeout` as per the *Aggregating with timeouts* recipe.

There's more...

Aggregations can be completed based on the number of messages aggregated according to `completionSize`, or by a completion predicate using any of Camel's Expression Languages. The predicate is evaluated against the aggregated message.

The following example shows the use of a completion predicate that examines the aggregated `Set` from our example above to determine whether or not to complete the aggregation.

In the XML DSL, this is written as:

```
<aggregate strategyRef="setAggregationRepository">
  <correlationExpression>
    <simple>${headers.group}</simple>
  </correlationExpression>
  <completionPredicate>
    <simple>${body.size} == 5</simple>
  </completionPredicate>
  <!-- ... -->
</aggregate>
```

In the Java DSL, the same thing is expressed as:

```
.aggregate(header("group"), new SetAggregationStrategy())
    .completionPredicate(simple("${body.size} == 5"))
```

The `completionSize` option can also be dynamically set using an expression. Unlike the `completionPredicate` statement, however, it is checked against the incoming exchange versus the the aggregated exchange.

In the XML DSL, this is written as:

```
<aggregate strategyRef="setAggregationRepository">
  <correlationExpression>
    <simple>${headers.group}</simple>
  </correlationExpression>
  <completionSize>
    <simple>${header[batchSize]}</simple>
  </completionSize>
  <!-- ... -->
</aggregate>
```

In the Java DSL, the same thing is expressed as:

```
.aggregate(header("group"), new SetAggregationStrategy())
    .completionSize(header("batchSize"))
```

Any aggregated state needs to be stored externally to the application if it is to survive the application shutting down. This is especially important if you are consuming high-value messages that cannot be replayed. Alternative `AggregationRepository` implementations that persist this state can be plugged into the aggregator through the use of the `aggregationRepository` attribute.

For example, the `JdbcAggregationRepository`, provided within the Camel SQL Component, is an excellent candidate for external storage of aggregated messages. Each time an aggregated state is saved, it is serialized through standard Java serialization, and stored inside a table as a BLOB associated with the aggregation's correlation expression. When a new message arrives to be aggregated, the stored state is read from the database, deserialized back into an exchange, and passed into the `AggregationStrategy`.

The processing of the aggregated message is fully transactional.

Since the serialized exchanges are constantly being written into, and read from the database, you need to keep in mind that the total aggregated message size is growing linearly. There comes a point when the cost of this I/O activity impacts the performance of the aggregation, especially when dealing with large message bodies. After all, a disk can only spin so fast. It is therefore worth doing some performance testing to ensure that the throughput meets your requirements. See the *Validating route behavior under heavy load* recipe in *Chapter 9, Testing*, for further details on how to do this.

You may also like to consider alternative `AggregationRepository` implementations, such as that provided by Camel HawtDB and Camel LevelDB Components, which allow you to trade off performance against reliability through background disk syncs.

See also

 ▶ Aggregator: `http://camel.apache.org/aggregator2.html`
 ▶ Camel SQL: `http://camel.apache.org/sql-component.html`
 ▶ Camel HawtDB: `http://camel.apache.org/hawtdb.html`
 ▶ Camel LevelDB: `http://camel.apache.org/leveldb.html`

Aggregating with timeouts

Aggregation according to size or predicate as described in the *Aggregating related messages* recipe is an excellent foundation for batching messages together. This recipe will describe how to use timeouts to release an aggregated message if no additional exchanges have been received for aggregation in a while.

Getting ready

The Java code for this recipe is located in the `org.camelcookbook.splitjoin.` `aggregatetimeouts` package. The Spring XML example is located in `src/main/` `resources/META-INF/spring/aggregateCompletionTimeout-context.xml`.

How to do it...

Inside your Aggregator definition, add a `completionTimeout` attribute containing a timeout in milliseconds. The attribute can be used as the sole aggregation condition, or in combination with others.

In the XML DSL, this is written as:

```
<from uri="direct:in"/>
<aggregate strategyRef="setAggregationStrategy"
           completionSize="10"
           completionTimeout="1000">
  <correlationExpression>
      <simple>${headers.group}</simple>
  </correlationExpression>
  <to uri="mock:out"/>
</aggregate>
```

In the Java DSL, the same route is expressed as:

```
from("direct:in")
  .aggregate(header("group"), new SetAggregationStrategy())
      .completionSize(10).completionTimeout(1000)
    .to("mock:out")
  .end();
```

How it works...

The Aggregator initializes a background thread that is responsible for keeping track of how long it has been since the *last* exchange was received for aggregation. When the Aggregator times out, the timeout thread processes the aggregated exchanges through the steps defined within the `aggregate` code block.

While the timeout thread is busy processing the aggregated message, no other messages are timed out. These will be processed when the thread has completed processing its exchange. If timing is critical, a thread pool can be used for processing messages—see the *Processing aggregated messages in parallel* recipe.

The `completionTimeout` attribute works in conjunction with any completion conditions defined on the Aggregator other than a `completionInterval` attribute (see the *Aggregating with intervals* recipe). In the preceding example, an aggregated message will be processed once for every 10 Exchange objects that have been aggregated, or if fewer have been aggregated and no further matching messages have been received within 1000 milliseconds.

See also

- ▶ Aggregator: `http://camel.apache.org/aggregator2.html`
- ▶ The *Aggregating related messages* recipe
- ▶ The *Processing aggregated messages in parallel* recipe

Aggregating with intervals

Aggregation according to size or predicate as described in the *Aggregating related messages* recipe is an excellent foundation for batching messages together. This recipe will describe how to use intervals to release an aggregated message per specified period.

Getting ready

The Java code for this recipe is located in the `org.camelcookbook.splitjoin.` `aggregateinterval` package. The Spring XML example is located in `src/main/` `resources/META-INF/spring/aggregateCompletionInterval-context.xml`.

How to do it...

Inside your Aggregator definition, define a `completionInterval` attribute containing a period in milliseconds. The attribute can be used as the sole aggregation condition, or in combination with others.

In the XML DSL, this is written as:

```
<from uri="direct:in"/>
<aggregate strategyRef="setAggregationStrategy"
           completionSize="10"
           completionInterval="400">
  <correlationExpression>
      <simple>${headers.group}</simple>
  </correlationExpression>
  <to uri="mock:out"/>
</aggregate>
```

In the Java DSL, the same route is expressed as:

```
from("direct:in")
  .aggregate(header("group"), new SetAggregationStrategy())
      .completionSize(10).completionInterval(400)
    .to("mock:out")
  .end();
```

How it works...

The Aggregator initializes a thread pool that is responsible for keeping track of how long it has been since the *first* exchange matching the aggregation expression was received for aggregation. Once the specified period passes, a thread processes it through the steps defined within the `aggregate` code block.

While the aggregation thread is busy processing the aggregated message, other threads are busy keeping track of the intervals and servicing of the other aggregated messages.

The `completionInterval` attribute works in conjunction with any completion conditions defined on the Aggregator other than a `completionTimeout` attribute (see the *Aggregating with timeouts* recipe). In the preceding example, an aggregated message will be processed once for every 10 Exchange objects that have been aggregated, or if fewer have been aggregated in the 400 milliseconds since the first message corresponding to the completion was received.

See also

▶ Aggregator: `http://camel.apache.org/aggregator2.html`

▶ The *Aggregating related messages* recipe

Processing aggregated messages in parallel

The default behavior of an Aggregator is to process the aggregated exchange through the steps defined within the `aggregate` block using a single thread. This is either the thread that pushes the last message into the block that triggers the completion condition, or the timer thread described in the *Aggregating with timeouts* recipe. This recipe will describe how to modify the Aggregator so that the aggregated messages can be processed in parallel.

Getting ready

The Java code for this recipe is located in the `org.camelcookbook.splitjoin.aggregateparallel` package. The Spring XML example is located in `src/main/resources/META-INF/spring/aggregateParallelProcessing-context.xml`.

How to do it...

Inside your `aggregate` statement, define a `parallelProcessing` attribute set to `true`. The attribute can be used alongside any aggregation condition.

In the XML DSL, this is written as:

```
<from uri="direct:in"/>
<aggregate strategyRef="setAggregationStrategy"
           completionSize="10"
           completionTimeout="400"
           parallelProcessing="true">
  <correlationExpression>
    <simple>${headers.group}</simple>
  </correlationExpression>
  <delay>
    <constant>500</constant>
  </delay>
  <log message="${threadName} - processing output"/>
  <to uri="mock:out"/>
</aggregate>
```

In the Java DSL, use the `parallelProcessing()` builder method with the `aggregate` statement:

```
from("direct:in")
    .aggregate(header("group"), new SetAggregationStrategy())
        .completionSize(10).completionTimeout(400)
        .parallelProcessing()
    .log("${threadName} - procesessing output")
    .delay(500)
    .to("mock:out")
    .end();
```

How it works...

The Aggregator initializes a thread pool that is responsible for processing the aggregated messages. When processing messages through the routes defined, you will see the logging output confirming that different threads are executing the work:

```
[#1 - Aggregator] INFO  route1 - Camel (camel-1) thread #1 -
Aggregator - processing output
[#2 - Aggregator] INFO  route1 - Camel (camel-1) thread #2 -
Aggregator - processing output
```

This is a useful strategy for Aggregators that work under a heavy load of incoming messages, and where the processing of the aggregated messages is time consuming.

There's more...

The default strategy for pooling in Camel is to instantiate a pool of 10 threads to service the aggregated messages. You can customize this by referring to a `threadPool` instance defined within the Camel context by its `id`.

In the XML DSL, this is written as:

```
<camelContext xmlns="http://camel.apache.org/schema/spring">
  <threadPool id="customPool" poolSize="20" threadName="pool"/>

  <route>
    <from uri="direct:in"/>
    <aggregate strategyRef="setAggregationStrategy"
               completionSize="10"
               completionTimeout="400"
               executorServiceRef="customPool">
      <!-- ... -->
    </aggregate>
  </route>
</camelContext>
```

 Use of the `executorService` attribute implies `parallelProcessing`, so you do not need to define them together.

The Java DSL contains an equivalent option where you can refer to a thread pool in Camel's registry:

```
.aggregate(header("group"), new SetAggregationStrategy())
    .completionSize(10).completionTimeout(400)
    .executorServiceRef("customPool")
```

It also allows you to define an `executorService` attribute inline:

```
.aggregate(header("group"), new SetAggregationStrategy())
    .completionSize(10).completionTimeout(400)
    .executorService(Executors.newFixedThreadPool(20))
```

See also

▸ The *Aggregating related messages* recipe

Splitting a message, and processing and gathering responses

This recipe will show you how you how to split a message into individual fragments, process each fragment individually, and re-aggregate the processed exchanges back into a single exchange. In EIP terms, this is known as a **Composed Message Processor**, and is made up of a combination of a Splitter and an Aggregator.

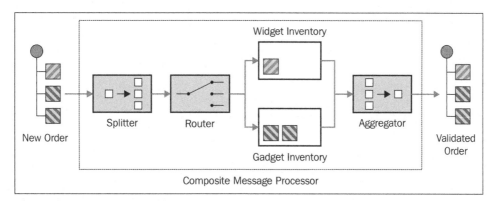

New Order — Splitter — Router — Widget Inventory / Gadget Inventory — Aggregator — Validated Order

Composite Message Processor

Getting ready

Java code for this recipe is located in the `org.camelcookbook.splitjoin.splitaggregate` package. The Spring XML examples are located under `src/main/resources/META-INF/spring` and prefixed with `splitAggregate`.

How to do it...

In order to split and aggregate (join) a message, combine a `split` DSL statement with an associated `AggregationStrategy` as follows:

1. Define an `AggregationStrategy` instance as described in the *Aggregating related messages* recipe. For this example, we will reuse the `SetAggregationStrategy` implementation from that recipe:

```
<bean id="setAggregationRepository"
      class="org.camelcookbook,splitjoin.aggregate
          .SetAggregationStrategy"/>
```

2. Define a regular `split` block as per the *Splitting a message into fragments* recipe, breaking up the payload as you see fit through the use of an expression. Reference the `AggregationStrategy` instance through the `strategyRef` attribute in the `split` element:

```
<from uri="direct:in"/>
<split strategyRef="setAggregationStrategy">
  <simple>${body}</simple>
  <inOut uri="direct:someBackEnd"/>
</split>
<to uri="mock:out"/>
```

In the Java DSL, refer to the `AggregationStrategy` instance as the second parameter to the `split()` statement:

```
from("direct:in")
  .split(body(), new SetAggregationStrategy())
    .inOut("direct:someBackEnd")
  .end()
  .to("mock:out");
```

How it works...

When an exchange reaches the `split` statement, it is broken up into individual fragments as expected, each of which is processed through the steps defined within the block. When each split fragment's exchange reaches the end of the `split` block, it is passed into the `AggregationStrategy` for aggregation.

When all of the fragments have been processed, the final aggregated message proceeds down the route from the `split` block. This is different from the normal Splitter behavior, which forwards the original message to that statement after the `split` statement.

 By default, all processing is performed by a single thread. You can parallelize the processing of each message fragment by using the `parallelProcessing` option as described in the *Processing split messages in parallel* recipe.

There's more...

Exception handling is different compared to that of the regular Splitter when using an `AggregationStrategy`. When an exception is thrown during the processing of the fragment, the exchange will be immediately passed to `AggregationStrategy`. It is then up to the strategy to decide what to do with this information.

The following strategy removes the exception from the message, effectively handling it, and modifies the body indicating the failure:

```java
public class ExceptionHandlingSetAggregationStrategy
    implements AggregationStrategy {
  @Override
  public Exchange aggregate(Exchange oldExchange,
                            Exchange newExchange) {
    String body = newExchange.getIn().getBody(String.class);
    Exception exception = newExchange.getException();
    if (exception != null) { // something went wrong
      newExchange.setException(null); // remove the exception
      body = "Failed: " + body;
    }
    if (oldExchange == null) {
      Set<String> set = new HashSet<String>();
      set.add(body);
      newExchange.getIn().setBody(set);
      return newExchange;
    } else {
      Set<String> set = oldExchange.getIn().getBody(Set.class);
      set.add(body);
      return oldExchange;
    }
  }
}
```

You may choose to handle the exception, or return the exchange with the Exception object intact. In the latter case, the default exception handling behavior of the Splitter will come into play, as defined in the *Splitting a message into fragments* and *Processing split messages in parallel* recipes if using `parallelProcessing`.

See also

▸ Composed Message Processor: `http://camel.apache.org/composed-message-processor.html`

Splitting messages and re-aggregating them using different criteria

The process described in the *Splitting a message, and processing and gathering responses* recipe broke up a message into fragments and aggregated those same processed fragments back into a result message that flowed out of a `split` block.

This recipe, which is a variant of the Composed Message Processor EIP, will describe how a message can be split up and aggregated, using criteria other than the original message ID. The aggregation phase may yield one or more aggregated messages.

In this example, we are going to accept, as input, XML messages that list books with titles and categories:

```
<books>
  <book category="Tech"
        title="Apache Camel Developer's Cookbook"/>
  <book category="Cooking"
        title="Camel Cookbook"/>
  <book category="Cooking"
        title="Double decadence with extra cream"/>
  <book category="Cooking"
        title="Cooking with Butter"/>
</books>
```

We are going to extract the book titles, and aggregate them into sets, by book category, before sending them to some destination endpoint. Based on the preceding input message, we want the target endpoint to receive two messages: one containing a set of `Tech` titles, and another containing `Cooking` titles.

Getting ready

The Java code for this recipe is located in the `org.camelcookbook.splitjoin.` `splitreaggregate` package. The Spring XML example is located in `src/main/` `resources/META-INF/spring/splitReaggregate-context.xml`.

How to do it...

In order to split a message up and re-aggregate its fragments using a criterion other than the original message ID, perform the following 2-step process:

1. Define a route that will split the message. Make sure the last step of the `split` block calls the route containing the aggregation that you will define in step 2:

   In the XML DSL, this is written as:

```
<from uri="direct:in"/>
<split>
  <xpath>/books/book</xpath>
  <setHeader headerName="category">
    <xpath resultType="String">/book/@category</xpath>
  </setHeader>
  <transform>
    <xpath resultType="String">/book/@title</xpath>
  </transform>
  <to uri="direct:groupByCategory"/>
</split>
```

   In the Java DSL, the same route is expressed as:

```
from("direct:in")
  .split(xpath("/books/book"))
    .setHeader("category",
        xpath("/book/@category").stringResult())
    .transform(xpath("/book/@title").stringResult())
    .to("direct:groupByCategory")
  .end();
```

2. Define another route that will accept the split fragments and aggregate them:

```
<from uri="direct:groupByCategory"/>
<aggregate strategyRef="setAggregationStrategy"
          completionTimeout="500">
  <correlationExpression>
    <simple>${header[category]}</simple>
  </correlationExpression>
  <to uri="mock:out"/>
</aggregate>
```

The `setAggregationStrategy` is the same strategy that we first defined in the *Aggregating related messages* recipe, and is defined in the Spring context as a bean.

In the Java DSL, this is written as:

```
from("direct:groupByCategory")
  .aggregate(header("category"),
      new SetAggregationStrategy()).completionTimeout(500)
    .to("mock:out")
  .end();
```

How it works...

This example combines the independent Splitter and Aggregator mechanisms that we have already seen in this chapter.

Within the example, the payload is first split by an XPath Expression that yields XML fragments. The category of each book is extracted through another expression, and set on the `category` message header. The message body is then replaced with the book's title, and the exchange is passed to another route containing the aggregation phase.

The Aggregator joins together fragments, grouping them according to the value of their category headers. In the preceding example, the aggregated exchanges are released for further processing, once no new messages have arrived in 500 milliseconds.

There's more...

It is not strictly necessary to divide up the split and aggregate phases in different routes like this, but it makes it much easier to read, and reason about, the routing logic's correctness. This is especially true when using the Java DSL where its easy to flatten out a route definition by omitting `end()` and `endParent()` statement. For comparison, this is the Java equivalent with everything in the one route:

```
from("direct:combined")
  .split(xpath("/books/book"))
    .setHeader("category",
        xpath("/book/@category").stringResult())
    .transform(xpath("/book/@title").stringResult())
    .aggregate(header("category"), new SetAggregationStrategy())
        .completionTimeout(500)
      .to("mock:out")
    .endParent()
  .end();
```

Even though the Aggregator will merge fragments from across multiple books' payloads, this is not immediately obvious, and will likely lead to headaches for anyone who has to maintain the code.

See also

▸ The *Splitting XML messages recipe*

▸ The *Aggregating related messages recipe*

▸ Composed Message Processor: `http://camel.apache.org/composed-message-processor.html`

6
Parallel Processing

In this chapter, we will cover:

- ▶ Increasing message consumption through multiple endpoint consumers
- ▶ Spreading the load within a route using a set of threads
- ▶ Routing a request asynchronously
- ▶ Using custom thread pools
- ▶ Using thread pool profiles
- ▶ Working with asynchronous APIs

Introduction

In this chapter, we will take a deeper look at using Camel's support for increasing throughput inside a single JVM by processing exchanges in parallel.

So far we have seen parallel processing mentioned in the context of a number of EIPs including Multicast, Splitter, and Aggregator. This chapter will introduce you to the ability to easily define processing phases in an ad hoc manner, in order to scale out your integrations as required.

Parallel processing is a useful tool as it allows you to do more work in a shorter space of time by distributing work across a set of worker threads.

Imagine that you have 100 messages, each requiring 0.1 seconds to execute. Using only one thread, this load should be processed in about 10 seconds. However, if you get 10 threads to work on this batch of messages, you might reasonably expect to process it in 1 second. That is the promise of parallelism.

Parallelism is not a silver bullet for performance problems. It will not scale infinitely; it is unlikely that your JVM will be able to run thousands of threads productively at the same time. You will inevitably hit a limit somewhere along the line at that point adding more worker threads will decrease your throughput, as the demands of servicing a large pool of threads cuts into the useful processing cycles of your CPU. You may also encounter contention problems as threads compete with each other for limited resources. What you do with each thread is as important, if not more so, as the number of threads in use.

Camel gives you a set of tools to scale out your processing where needed. It is up to you to use those mechanisms to tune your application. Performance tuning is often seen as a dark art, but it does not need to be. The general process is:

1. Test your application's performance by applying a message load to it through your favorite load-testing tool and measuring how long your application takes to process it.

2. Make a single change that you hope will improve performance and test again. If it improved things, keep going. If it made things worse go back to what you had.

When tuning your application for performance, you should keep in mind what else might be going on inside your JVM in a production setting. Five different integrations, that are perfectly tuned individually, might suffer from poor performance when executed at the same time. This can be due to contention around the CPU, memory, I/O, or other external resources.

 Always try to test an application as a whole after individual tunings to ensure that you have not introduced a problem.

A number of Camel architectural concepts are used throughout this chapter. There is a broader overview of Camel concepts in the *Preface*. Full details can be found on the Apache Camel website at `http://camel.apache.org`.

The code for this chapter is contained within the `camel-cookbook-parallel-processing` module of the examples.

Increasing message consumption through multiple endpoint consumers

One of the simplest ways of increasing throughput is to raise the number of threads that are consuming from an endpoint.

This recipe assumes that you are starting with a route that is asynchronous, for example using `seda:` as the consumer endpoint (using the `from` DSL statement). SEDA is a mechanism included in Camel Core for connecting routes to each other asynchronously by passing Exchange objects over an in-memory queue—see the *Asynchronously connecting routes* recipe in *Chapter 1, Structuring Routes*.

This is important as an endpoint such as `direct:` always uses the calling thread for executing the processing steps, so you need to use different techniques to switch processing to a different thread, or thread pool. This is discussed in the *Spreading the load within a route using a set of threads* recipe.

This recipe will show you how to increase the number of consumer threads for asynchronous consuming endpoints such as `seda:`.

Getting ready

The Java code for this recipe is located in the `org.camelcookbook.parallelprocessing.endpointconsumers` package. The Spring XML files are located under `src/main/resources/META-INF/spring` and prefixed with `endpointConsumers`.

This recipe assumes you have an existing asynchronous route, such as the following:

```
<from uri="seda:in"/>
<delay>
  <constant>200</constant> <!-- slow running service -->
</delay>
<log message="Processing ${body}:${threadName}"/>
<to uri="mock:out"/>
```

This route introduces a 200 ms delay in order to simulate a more complex, and therefore time-consuming processing step.

How to do it...

Use the `concurrentConsumers` option to increase the number of threads available to consume messages:

In the XML DSL, this is written as:

```
<from uri="seda:in?concurrentConsumers=10"/>
<delay>
  <constant>200</constant> <!-- slow running service -->
</delay>
<log message="Processing ${body}:${threadName}"/>
<to Uri="mock:out"/>
```

In the Java DSL, the same route is expressed as:

```
from("seda:in?concurrentConsumers=10")
  .delay(200)
  .log("Processing ${body}:${threadName}")
  .to("mock:out");
```

How it works...

The SEDA Component's default behavior is to use only a single thread for consuming incoming messages. This means that when our delay of 200 ms per message is taken into account, at most five messages per second will be processed. To increase this, we can allocate more consumers (threads) to this endpoint by using the `concurrentConsumers` option on the `seda:` endpoint.

When we run a set of messages through the route, we can see from our logging that different threads pick up each message:

```
Processing Message[8]:Camel (camel-1) thread #8 - seda://in
Processing Message[0]:Camel (camel-1) thread #0 - seda://in
Processing Message[4]:Camel (camel-1) thread #3 - seda://in
Processing Message[2]:Camel (camel-1) thread #2 - seda://in
```

With 10 concurrent consumers, we should now expect about 50 exchanges to be processed per second versus the original single threaded version, which only processes five per second.

The threads compete with each other when polling the SEDA Component's in-memory queue. This means that there is no guarantee that they will process the messages in the same order that they are sent to the SEDA endpoint. That is why `Message[8]` is processed before `Message[0]` in the preceding output.

The support for concurrent consumption from an endpoint depends on the component. The `concurrentConsumers` property is part of the `org.apache.camel.component.seda.SedaEndpoint` class (see the *Using Camel components* recipe in *Chapter 1, Structuring Routes*, for a discussion of endpoint properties)—it is not a standard attribute that applies to all components.

There's more...

Not all components allow for concurrent consumption, as the underlying technology for some may be fundamentally sequential. For example, the JPA Component selects rows from a database table when consuming and potentially processing batches of selected rows at a time. If multiple threads were executing the same `select` statement at the same time, the same rows would be processed multiple times.

The following components allow you to have more than one thread consuming from them:

Component	Endpoint attributes
SEDA, VM	`concurrentConsumers` defines the size of a fixed thread pool
JMS, ActiveMQ	`concurrentConsumers` defines the minimum size of a thread pool—more threads will be created if required; `maxConcurrentConsumers` defines the upper bound of that pool
Jetty	`minThreads` defines a minimum number of threads servicing HTTP requests; `maxThreads` defines an upper bound

To check whether concurrent consumption is configurable, you should refer back to the Camel documentation for the component that you are using.

See also

- Camel SEDA Component: `http://camel.apache.org/seda.html`
- The *Using Camel components* recipe in *Chapter 1, Structuring Routes*
- The *Asynchronously connecting routes* recipe in *Chapter 1, Structuring Routes*

Spreading the load within a route using a set of threads

Not all Camel components support specifying multiple consumers (threads) processing messages concurrently (see the *Increased message consumption through multiple endpoint consumers* recipe). Routes that use consuming endpoints, such as `direct:` or `file:`, default to using a single thread to process the message. This recipe will show you how to get around this constraint, by using the `threads` DSL to pass messages that were originally consumed sequentially, for example using `direct:`, to a thread pool so that they can now be processed in parallel.

Getting ready

The Java code for this recipe is located in the `org.camelcookbook.parallelprocessing.threadsdsl` package. The Spring XML files are located under `src/main/resources/META-INF/spring` and prefixed with `threadsDsl`.

This recipe assumes you are starting with a route that starts on a single thread, such as when consuming using the Direct Component, and you want to use a pool of threads for some of the processing steps. The following route is such an example:

```
<from uri="direct:in"/>
<log message="Received ${body}:${threadName}"/>
<delay>
  <constant>200</constant> <!-- simulate slow routing step -->
</delay>
<to Uri="mock: out"/>
```

How to do it...

Using the `threads` DSL allows you to define a portion of your route where messages will be processed by set of threads distinct from the original consuming thread.

In the XML DSL, this logic is written as:

```
<from uri="direct:in"/>
<log message="Received ${body}:${threadName}"/>
<threads>
  <log message="Processing ${body}:${threadName}"/>
  <delay>
    <constant>200</constant> <!-- simulate slow routing step -->
  </delay>
  <to Uri="mock:out"/>
</threads>
```

In the Java DSL, the same route is expressed as:

```
from("direct:in")
  .log("Received ${body}:${threadName}")
  .threads()
  .delay(200)
  .log("Processing ${body}:${threadName}")
  .to("mock:out");
```

How it works...

Within the `threads` block, Camel creates a thread pool that is assigned to consume messages from an in-memory queue. When a thread processes a message through a route up to the `threads` block, it places the exchange onto that queue, from which it is picked up by one of the threads from the pool for further processing.

Using this approach you can consume messages from a single-threaded endpoint, and have multiple threads process the message later in the route, leaving the consuming thread to fetch the next message.

In the preceding example, when we send messages through the route, we can see that different threads process the messages before and after the `threads` block; the `Received` logging statements are also interleaved with the `Processing` statements:

```
Received Message[40]:Camel (camel-1) thread #3 - ProducerTemplate
Processing Message[31]:Camel (camel-1) thread #12 - Threads
Received Message[41]:Camel (camel-1) thread #5 - ProducerTemplate
Processing Message[33]:Camel (camel-1) thread #14 - Threads
Received Message[42]:Camel (camel-1) thread #9 - ProducerTemplate
Processing Message[34]:Camel (camel-1) thread #16 - Threads
...
Processing Message[40]:Camel (camel-1) thread #15 - Threads
Processing Message[41]:Camel (camel-1) thread #10 - Threads
Processing Message[42]:Camel (camel-1) thread #12 - Threads
```

> You may have noticed that there are multiple threads logging `Received` statements. This is because the test requests have been fired into the route asynchronously. The reasons behind this are explained in the *Routing a request asynchronously* recipe.

This technique is very similar to using a SEDA endpoint as described in the *Asynchronously connecting routes* recipe in *Chapter 1, Structuring Routes*. Both techniques use an in-memory queue to pass messages to a consuming thread pool, and can be used with `InOut` as well as `InOnly` exchanges if the consuming endpoint supports asynchronous routing. An example of this is Jetty, which supports accepting an HTTP request with one thread and responding with another through its continuation support.

> This technique should be used carefully if you intend on using it along with transactions. The underlying transactional resources may not support being accessed concurrently from different threads. If you intend on combining these two features, make sure that you test the behavior thoroughly.

There's more...

It is possible to configure a number of options around the `threads` DSL through its attributes. These are the same as that of the `threadPool`, and are described in the *Using custom thread pools* recipe.

As an alternative to setting up the behavior of a thread pool directly within the DSL, a `threads` block may be referenced to re-use an existing `java.util.concurrent.ExecutorService`. See the *Using custom thread pools* recipe for further details.

See also

▸ Camel Async API: `http://camel.apache.org/async.html`

▸ Camel Jetty: `http://camel.apache.org/jetty.html`

▸ The *Increased message consumption through multiple endpoint consumers* recipe

▸ The *Using custom thread pools* recipe

▸ The *Asynchronously connecting routes* recipe in *Chapter 1, Structuring Routes*

▸ Jetty Continuations: `http://wiki.eclipse.org/Jetty/Feature/Continuations`

Routing a request asynchronously

When you send a message using the `ProducerTemplate.sendBody()` method into a Camel endpoint, you may find that even though it contains asynchronous processing, such as through the `threads` DSL (see the *Spreading the load within a route using a set of threads* recipe), your original thread is blocked until the request is fully processed. This is by design, as Camel will not return unless the message was fully processed—keeping track of whether an exchange was fully processed is one of the roles of Camel's **Asynchronous Routing Engine**.

This recipe will explain how to interact with Camel asynchronously through a `ProducerTemplate` instance, so that you can continue doing other work while a message submitted to Camel is being processed.

Getting ready

Java code for this recipe is located in the `org.camelcookbook.parallelprocessing.asyncrequest` package.

This recipe assumes that you have an existing route that will process a message synchronously, and may take a significant amount of time to complete. The following is an example of such a route:

```
from("direct:processInOut")
  .log("Received ${body}")
  .delay(1000) // simulate slow processing
  .log("Processing ${body}")
  .transform(simple("Processed ${body}"));
```

We know upfront that processing a message through this route will take some time, so we would like to send a message into it asynchronously, and get on with doing other work until a response is returned to us.

How to do it...

Use the `ProducerTemplate` interface's `asyncSend()` or `asyncRequest()` variant methods to allow you to send a message asynchronously to a Camel endpoint, and still have the ability to know when the message processing is complete.

1. Send a message into the Camel route using one of the `ProducerTemplate` interface's `asyncSend()` or `asyncRequest()` methods depending on whether you require the exchange to be passed as `InOnly` or `InOut` respectively.

   Here we use `asyncRequestBody()` to initiate an `InOut` conversation from which we expect a response:

   ```
   Future<Object> future = producerTemplate.asyncRequestBody(
       "direct:processInOut", "SomePayload");
   ```

   The `async...()` methods return a `java.util.concurrent.Future` that we can use to check whether the processing of the exchange was completed, that is, whether the request was processed:

   ```
   while(!future.isDone()) {
     log.info("Doing something else while processing...");
     Thread.sleep(200);
   }
   ```

2. Use the `future.get()` method to obtain the response from the route if successful. Calling this method will block the current thread until a response is received.

   ```
   String response = (String) future.get();
   log.info("Received a response");
   assertEquals("Processed SomePayload", response);
   ```

   If an exception was thrown while processing the exchange, `future.get()` will throw a `java.util.concurrent.ExecutionException` interface that wraps the exception raised from within Camel.

   Running this code shows the following output:

   ```
   Doing something else while processing...
   Received SomePayload
   Doing something else while processing...
   Doing something else while processing...
   Doing something else while processing...
   Doing something else while processing...
   Doing something else while processing...
   Processing SomePayload
   Received a response
   ```

How it works...

Internally, a thread pool based upon the default settings (10 threads) is used to process any exchanges sent using the `ProducerTemplate` interface's `async...()` methods. The calling thread submits the message into an in-memory queue for processing by one of the threads in this pool, and continues processing as usual.

There's more...

It is also possible to use a callback, and deal with the return status of the exchange asynchronously by providing `org.apache.camel.spi.Synchronization` implementation to one of the `ProducerTemplate` interface's `asyncCallback...()` methods:

```
Future<Object> future = template.asyncCallbackRequestBody(
    "direct:processInOut",
    "AnotherPayload",
    new Synchronization() {
      @Override
      public void onComplete(Exchange exchange) {
        assertEquals("Processed AnotherPayload",
                    exchange.getOut().getBody());
      }

      @Override
      public void onFailure(Exchange exchange) {
        fail();
      }
    });
```

See also

▶ Camel Async API: `http://camel.apache.org/async.html`

▶ The `ProducerTemplate` interface: `http://camel.apache.org/maven/current/camel-core/apidocs/org/apache/camel/ProducerTemplate.html`

▶ The `Synchronization` interface: `http://camel.apache.org/maven/current/camel-core/apidocs/org/apache/camel/spi/Synchronization.html`

Using custom thread pools

Usually when dealing with an EIP such as Splitter, Multicast, or Aggregator, the default pool of 10 threads that is created for the EIP is sufficient. However, each of these patterns allow you to provide a customized pool if this default pool is inadequate for your needs.

This recipe will outline how to define a custom thread pool in Camel.

Getting ready

The Java code for this recipe is located in the `org.camelcookbook.` `parallelprocessing.threadpools` package. The Spring XML files are located under `src/main/resources/META-INF/spring` and prefixed with `threadPools`.

How to do it...

To define a custom thread pool using the XML DSL, add a `threadPool` definition before any routes in the `camelContext` element:

```
<camelContext xmlns="http://camel.apache.org/schema/spring">
  <threadPool id="customThreadPool"
              poolSize="5"
              thread Name="CustomThreadPool"/>

  <route>
    <!-- ... -->
  </route>
</camelContext>
```

The `id` attribute of the `threadPool` can be used within the `executorServiceRef` attribute of any EIP that supports parallel processing. The following XML DSL fragment inserts our `customThreadPool` into a `threads` block as described in the *Spreading the load within a route using a set of threads* recipe:

```
<threads executorServiceRef="customThreadPool">
```

The Java DSL can also use thread pools defined in this manner:

```
.threads().executorServiceRef("customThreadPool")
```

How it works...

When a `threadPool` is defined in the XML DSL, an `ExecutorService` object is instantiated with the attributes specified, and registered in the Camel Registry with the given `id`.

 The same thread pool can be re-used by a number of different routes, or EIP elements, although care should be taken so as not to starve any individual routes of worker threads.

This is most commonly seen where Java `RouteBuilder` implementations are used in conjunction with the XML DSL, as in a Spring or OSGi Blueprint application. In these cases, the `routeBuilder` references should be defined before the `threadPool`:

```xml
<bean id="routeBuilderUsingRef"
      class="org.camelcookbook.parallelprocessing.threadpools
             .CustomThreadPoolRefRouteBuilder"/>


<camelContext xmlns="http://camel.apache.org/schema/spring">
  <routeBuilder ref="routeBuilderUsingRef"/>
  <threadPool id="customThreadPool"
              poolSize="5"
              maxQueueSize="100"
              thread Name="CustomThreadPool"/>
</camelContext>
```

We can see the custom pool being used through the log output:

```
Processing Message[3]:Camel (camel-1) thread #12 - CustomThreadPool
```

If you are not using the XML DSL, it is possible to define an instance of the `java.util.concurrent.ExecutorService` interface alongside your route using an `org.apache.camel.builder.ThreadPoolBuilder` class.

```java
ExecutorService executorService =
    new ThreadPoolBuilder(context).poolSize(5)
        .maxQueueSize(100).build("CustomThreadPool");
```

The value passed to the `build()` method is the pattern that will be assigned to thread names.

The builder takes the Camel context as an argument, and registers itself as a pool whose lifecycle can be managed by the context.

You can then refer to the pool instance through the `executorService()` DSL statement in any EIP that supports parallel processing:

```
.threads().executorService(customExecutorService)
```

There's more...

You can customize a number of settings when defining pools, including:

Setting	Description
poolSize	The core thread pool size used (mandatory).
maxPoolSize	The maximum number of threads that the pool should contain.
keepAliveTime	How long inactive threads should be kept alive for.
timeUnit	A java.util.concurrent.TimeUnit interface used in conjunction with keepAliveTime (for example, MILLISECONDS, SECONDS, MINUTES).
maxQueueSize	The maximum number of exchanges to hold in the queue for servicing; a value of -1 indicates an unbounded queue.
rejectedPolicy	How to handle messages that arrive in the queue when its maxQueueSize has been reached. Can be either Abort (throw an exception), CallerRuns, Discard, or DiscardOldest.

The last two options govern the behavior of the in-memory queue that feeds the thread pool.

You also have to define a custom thread name for the threads in the pool via the threadNamePattern attribute. The name may contain a limited set of placeholders:

```
threadNamePattern="#camelId#:CustomThreadPool[#counter#]"
```

The following placeholders can be used as a part of the pattern:

Placeholder	Description
camelId	The name of the Camel context
counter	An incrementing counter
name	The original thread name
longName	An automatically generated long name that includes some additional information from Camel

See also

▸ Camel Threading Model: http://camel.apache.org/threading-model.html

Using thread pool profiles

In the *Using custom thread pools* recipe we saw how thread pools could be defined. These can be re-used across multiple EIPs and routes.

This recipe will take that idea to the next level by guiding you through defining **thread pool profiles,** which act as templates for thread pool creation. By referring to a thread pool profile, an EIP will have a thread pool created for its own exclusive use with the characteristics defined in the profile.

Getting ready

The Java code for this recipe is located in the `org.camelcookbook.parallelprocessing.threadpoolprofiles` package. The Spring XML files are located under `src/main/resources/META-INF/spring` and prefixed with `threadPoolProfiles`.

How to do it...

Configure a `threadPoolProfile` class that acts as a template for any thread pools created within your routes.

1. In the XML DSL, define a `threadPoolProfile` block before any `threadPool` and `route` definitions:

```
<camelContext
    xmlns="http://camel.apache.org/schema/spring">
  <threadPoolProfile id="customThreadPoolProfile"
                     poolSize="5"/>
  <threadPool ../>

  <route>
    <!-- ... -->
  <route/>
</camelContext>
```

To instantiate a profile in Java, you use the `org.apache.camel.builder.ThreadPoolProfileBuilder` class:

```
ThreadPoolProfile customThreadPoolProfile =
    new ThreadPoolProfileBuilder(
        "customThreadPoolProfile")
      .poolSize(5).maxQueueSize(100).build();
```

The first argument is the name that the profile will be registered with. You then register the profile into the Camel context:

```
context.getExecutorServiceManager()
    .registerThreadPoolProfile(customThreadPoolProfile);
```

2. Use the `id` attribute of the `threadPoolProfile` class within the `executorServiceRef` attribute of any EIPs that support parallel processing.

    The following XML DSL fragment initializes a `threads` block based on our `customThreadPoolProfile`:

    ```
    <threads executorServiceRef="customThreadPoolProfile">
    ```

    The Java DSL can also use thread pool profiles defined in this manner:

    ```
    .threads().executorServiceRef("customThreadPoolProfile")
    ```

How it works...

When the Camel context starts up, it attempts to satisfy any EIPs that requested an `ExecutorService` instance by name. If an `ExecutorService` instance is available with that name in the Camel Registry, it will be used. If none is found, Camel will check with its internal `ExecutorServiceManager` to see whether a thread pool profile exists that matches that name.

 A thread pool reference that resolves to a profile will have its own unique `ExecutorService` instance created for it by Camel. Therefore, if two EIPs both ask for the same profile, two thread pools will be created, one for each EIP instance.

Setting an `executorServiceRef` name that does not resolve to either an `ExecutorService` instance or a thread pool profile will cause an error to be thrown on Camel context startup.

There's more...

There are a number of options that can be customized within a `threadPoolProfile` definition—these correspond to the equivalent `threadPool` options (see the *Using custom thread pools* recipe). The only exception is that you cannot define the thread names.

See also

▶   Camel Threading Model: `http://camel.apache.org/threading-model.html`

Working with asynchronous APIs

Very occasionally you will want to interact with a third-party API that is asynchronous in nature (that is, one that uses callbacks to return a response) within a Camel Processor.

The most straightforward way to do this is to register a listener with that API, place a request, and block the current thread until a response is received using a `java.util.concurrent.CountDownLatch` instance or similar. This has the downside of using one more thread than you strictly need to, and potentially slows down the rate of consumption from the route's consumer endpoint.

This recipe provides you with an alternative that allows you to truly interact asynchronously with this type of API through an **Asynchronous Processor**. Using this mechanism, the original thread is released to take on more work once the request has been placed, and the response is routed using the thread that triggers the callback.

 This is an advanced recipe that should only be used by developers leveraging a native third-party asynchronous API.

Getting ready

The Java code for this recipe is located in the `org.camelcookbook.parallelprocessing.asyncprocessor` package. The Spring XML files are located under `src/main/resources/META-INF/spring` and prefixed with `asyncProcessor`.

How to do it...

Implement the `org.apache.camel.AsyncProcessor` interface. This allows you to create code with fine-grained control over whether messages are processed synchronously or asynchronously.

1. Define a class that implements the `AsyncProcessor` interface:

    ```
    public class BackgroundThreadAsyncProcessor
        implements AsyncProcessor {
      //...
    }
    ```

The `AsyncProcessor` interface defines a single method in addition to that of its parent interface, `Processor`:

```
public interface AsyncProcessor
    extends org.apache.camel.Processor {
  boolean process(org.apache.camel.Exchange exchange,
      org.apache.camel.AsyncCallback asyncCallback);
}
```

This is the only method that we will be interested in implementing. The regular `process(Exchange)` method can be left empty, or an exception thrown to indicate to other developers that it will never be used:

```
@Override
public void process(Exchange exchange) throws Exception {
  throw new IllegalStateException(
      "this should never be called");
}
```

2. Implement the `process(Exchange, AsyncCallback)` method.

   Rather than introducing a third-party API, we are going to demonstrate asynchronous behavior by submitting a `Runnable` implementation to a `java.util.concurrent.ExecutorService` instance.

   ```
   private final ExecutorService executorService =
       Executors.newSingleThreadExecutor();
   ```

   The `AsyncCallback` is an object passed in from the Camel runtime that we will invoke in our simulated response handler (the `Runnable`) to invoke to indicate that this processor is done.

   The method returns a `boolean` value to indicate whether it is completing synchronously (`true`), or asynchronously (`false`). The `AsyncCallback.done(boolean)` method must always be invoked with the same value that is returned.

   ```
   @Override
   public boolean process(Exchange exchange,
       final AsyncCallback asyncCallback) {
     final Message in = exchange.getIn();
     final boolean completesSynchronously = false;
     backgroundExecutor.submit(new Runnable() {
       @Override
       public void run() {
         in.setBody("Handled async: "
                   + in.getBody(String.class));
         // the current thread will continue to process
         // the exchange through the
         // remainder of the route
   ```

```
        asyncCallback.done(completesSynchronously);
      }
    });
    return completesSynchronously;
}
```

3. Include the processor as part of the route.

   In the XML DSL, first define the processor as a bean:

   ```
   <bean id="slowOperationProcessor"
         class="org.camelcookbook.parallelprocessing
                .asyncprocessor.SlowOperationProcessor"/>
   ```

   Then use the bean reference in a `process` statement:

   ```
   <from Uri="direct:in"/>
   <process ref="slowOperationProcessor"/>
   <to Uri="mock:out"/>
   ```

   In the Java DSL, that same thing is expressed as:

   ```
   from("direct:in")
       .process(new SlowOperationProcessor())
       .to("mock:out");
   ```

How it works...

In the preceding example, background processing by a thread pool is used to demonstrate an asynchronous interaction. Asynchronous libraries work by triggering your code when an interesting event occurs by invoking an event listener. The listener in this instance is `Runnable`.

The `process(Exchange, AsyncCallback)` method is responsible for interacting with the asynchronous API, and returning whether the request was processed synchronously. If it returns `true`, the current thread proceeds to process the exchange as usual. If the method returns `false`, then the current thread will take no further part in processing the exchange, and will be freed up by Camel to process another request from the route's consumer endpoint.

The call to `asyncCallback.done()` indicates to the routing engine whether the exchange was processed synchronously. If `true`, then it gives the engine the opportunity to clean up any reserved resources. If `false`, then the invoking thread will be used to process the exchange through the remainder of the route.

The value returned from `process()` and the argument to `asyncCallback.done()` must be the same.

The technique demonstrated here might also be useful if you know that a certain processing step is always going to take a long time. Handing the processing over to an `ExecutorService` through `Runnable` frees up your consuming thread to handle the next request.

It is generally recommended that you implement your processing using the standard `Processor` interface, unless you identify a good reason why `AsyncProcessor` should be used.

There's more...

An `AsyncProcessor` interface does not need to process every exchange asynchronously, which is why the `process(Exchange, AsyncCallback)` method returns whether or not the invocation was completed synchronously.

Here is an example of conditionally processing a message either synchronously or asynchronously depending on its contents, in this case by inspecting a header that we set:

```
@Override
public boolean process(final Exchange exchange,
    final AsyncCallback asyncCallback) {
  final Message in = exchange.getIn();
  if (in.getHeader("processAsync", Boolean.class)) {
    // process asynchronously
    executorService.submit(new Runnable() {
      @Override
      public void run() {
        in.setBody("Processed async: "
                + in.getBody(String.class));
        asyncCallback.done(false);
      }
    });
    return false;
  } else {
    // process synchronously
    in.setBody("Processed sync: " + in.getBody(String.class));
    asyncCallback.done(true);
    return true;
  }
}
```

Note that when returning `true`, indicating synchronous processing, the `asyncCallback.done(true)` method must be invoked beforehand to give the routing engine an opportunity to clean up any reserved resources.

This technique should be used carefully if you intend on using it along with transactions. The underlying transactional resources may not support being accessed concurrently from different threads. If you intend on combining these two features, make sure that you test the behavior thoroughly.

See also

- The `AsyncCallback` interface: `http://camel.apache.org/maven/current/camel-core/apidocs/org/apache/camel/AsyncCallback.html`

- The `AsyncProcessor` interface: `http://camel.apache.org/maven/current/camel-core/apidocs/org/apache/camel/AsyncProcessor.html`

- Camel Asynchronous Routing Engine: `http://camel.apache.org/asynchronous-routing-engine.html`

7
Error Handling and Compensation

In this chapter, we will cover the following topics:

- ▸ Logging errors
- ▸ Dead Letter Channel: handling errors later
- ▸ Retrying an operation
- ▸ Conditional retry
- ▸ Customizing each redelivery attempt
- ▸ Catching exceptions
- ▸ Marking exceptions as Handled
- ▸ Fine-grained error handling using doTry...doCatch
- ▸ Defining completion actions
- ▸ Defining completion actions dynamically

Introduction

In this chapter, we will be looking at the many ways in which Camel can help you with handling errors within your integration routes. Camel's error handling provides many levels of granularity that can be nested, providing a powerful mechanism for dealing appropriately with issues.

We will also look at Camel's ability to register callbacks when a route, or a part of a route, complete their message processing, either successfully, or with an error. This completion callback capability can act as an alternative to some of the other error handling capabilities discussed in this chapter. For example, rather than deeply nesting exception handlers, it might be easier to use these completion callbacks to clean up after executing a set of processing instructions. This is the mechanism some of the Camel components, such as File, use to perform steps based on success or failure of a consuming route, such as moving the file to an error directory on failure of a route to process the complete contents of that file.

Camel provides three core mechanisms for error handling:

▸ **Error Handlers**: Default, Logging, and Dead Letter Channel error handlers provide a generic (that is, will process any error) place to catch, process, and define redelivery policy. These can be defined at both the Camel context (global), or route levels. There is also a *Transactional Error Handler* that will be discussed in *Chapter 8, Transactions and Idempotency*.

▸ **doTry...doCatch...doFinally**: An equivalent to Java's try...catch...finally exception handling capability, which allows you to define handlers for one or more processing steps. Camel provides a sophisticated exception matching algorithm that does a great job of matching nested/wrapped exceptions, which are commonly seen within integration solutions.

▸ **onException**: This allows you to define exception handlers for specific Java Exception types with options for redelivery and conditional processing. An extension point is also available where you can register a `Processor`, which allows you an ability to modify a message before redelivery. These can be defined at both the Camel context (global) and route levels. This mechanism, just like *doTry...doCatch...doFinally*, matches nested exceptions.

It is important to note that the concept of *global* as applied to error handling is slightly different for the XML and Java DSLs.

In the XML DSL, error handlers defined within the `camelContext` element are applicable to all routes defined within that Camel context, including imported route definition in Java and other DSLs.

In the Java DSL, error handlers defined within the `RouteBuilder.configure()` method are applicable to all routes defined within that `RouteBuilder` implementation.

Camel includes a built-in redelivery capability, which allows you to retry sending a message to a given endpoint. This is useful as it is common within integrations for an external system to be temporarily unavailable. Rather than flagging this as an error, you should just resend messages later. This allows you to easily handle common cases such as external system restarts, or upgrades as part of normal maintenance.

Camel uses a concept of *handled* with errors that controls whether an error should be exposed back to the caller. If an exception is marked as handled, using the `handled(true)` statement of the DSL, then the error handler's processing steps are assumed to have addressed the error, and no error is exposed back to the caller. The error handler may update the message to reflect the error. If the error is not handled then the error is returned to the caller who in turn has the opportunity to deal with it.

A number of Camel architectural concepts are used throughout this chapter. There is a broader overview of Camel concepts in the *Preface*. Full details can be found at the Apache Camel website at `http://camel.apache.org`.

The code for this chapter is contained within the `camel-cookbook-error` module of the examples.

Logging errors

Camel makes it easy to ensure that all uncaught exceptions are logged in a specific way using the logging error handler. You can set this mechanism both globally (at the Camel context level), and at the route level, to log all unhandled exceptions using a log name and level.

This recipe will show you how to use the `LoggingErrorHandler` error handler to log errors caught by Camel at runtime.

Getting ready

The Java code for this recipe is located in the `org.camelcookbook.error.logging` package. The Spring XML files are located under `src/main/resources/META-INF/spring` and prefixed with `logging`.

How to do it...

In the XML DSL, define an `errorHandler` element within the `camelContext` element, and reference the error handler's `id` in the `errorHandlerRef` attribute of the `camelContext` element. The `type` attribute of the `errorHandler` element must be set to `"LoggingErrorHandler"`. You can optionally set the `level` (defaults to `ERROR`), and `logName` (defaults to `Logger`) attributes. This will set up the base error handler for all routes defined within this Camel context. Refer to the following code for the same:

```
<camelContext errorHandlerRef="myErrorHandler"
              xmlns="http://camel.apache.org/schema/spring">
  <errorHandler id="myErrorHandler"
              type="LoggingErrorHandler"
              level="ERROR"
```

```
                  logName="MyLoggingErrorHandler"/>

    <route>
      <from uri="direct:start"/>
      <!-- ... -->
    </route>
  </camelContext>
```

In the Java DSL, within the `RouteBuilder.configure()` method, define an `errorHandler` instance that references a `LoggingErrorHandler` instance, configured using the DSL's fluent API. You can set the `level` attribute (defaults to `ERROR`) and `logName` (defaults to `Logger`). This will configure the base error handler for all routes defined within this `RouteBuilder` implementation.

```
public class LoggingRouteBuilder extends RouteBuilder {
  @Override
  public void configure() throws Exception {
    errorHandler(loggingErrorHandler()
      .logName("MyLoggingErrorHandler")
      .level(LoggingLevel.ERROR)
    );

    from("direct:start")
    //...
  }
}
```

How it works...

Camel uses the SLF4J logging library under the covers to configure logging. The SLF4J library allows Camel to work with many different logging implementations. This allows you to configure runtime properties according to the implementation being used, for example, within the `log4j.properties` file, if `Log4j` is used.

Setting the `logName` attribute is equivalent to calling SLF4J's `LoggerFactory.getLogger(logName)`. This allows you to quickly find and automatically filter log messages by using this String, which helps you determine what is happening within your integration.

For example, here is a log entry based on the preceding sample code. Notice how our `logName` setting is accessible within the log:

```
2013-05-28 07:21:36,913 [main            ] ERROR
MyLoggingErrorHandler        - Failed delivery for (MessageId:
ID-grelber-local-56780-1369740096617-0-3 on ExchangeId: ID-
grelber-local-56780-1369740096617-0-4). Exhausted after delivery
attempt: 1 caught: org.camelcookbook.error.logging.FlakyException:
FlakyProcessor has gone Flaky
```

There's more...

It is also possible to set route-specific error handlers.

In the XML DSL, you can set the `errorHandlerRef` attribute of the `route` element using the following code:

```
<camelContext xmlns="http://camel.apache.org/schema/spring">
  <errorHandler id="myRouteSpecificLogging"
                type="LoggingErrorHandler"
                level="ERROR"
                logName="MyRouteLogging"/>

  <route errorHandlerRef="myRouteSpecificLogging">
    <from uri="direct:start"/>
    <!-- ... -->
  </route>
</camelContext>
```

In the Java DSL, you specify the route-specific error handler after the `from` part of the route definition:

```
from("direct:start")
    .errorHandler(loggingErrorHandler()
        .logName("MyRouteLogging")
        .level(LoggingLevel.ERROR)
    )
    .bean(FlakyProcessor.class)
    .to("mock:result");
```

See also

- ▶ Error handling: `http://camel.apache.org/error-handling-in-camel.html`
- ▶ Error handler: `http://camel.apache.org/error-handler.html`
- ▶ SLF4J: `http://www.slf4j.org`

Dead Letter Channel – handling errors later

Camel's Dead Letter Channel error handler helps when you want to send generic errors to a particular endpoint. It can also be useful if you just want to capture the message that caused the error for manual processing later.

This technique allows you to send the `Exchange` instance that caused the error to a specific Camel endpoint (for example, `activemq:queue:somethingBadHappenedQueue`), or to send the message to another route (for example, `seda:error`). Remember that for Camel, an endpoint URI can refer to either another Camel route (the URI within the `from(...)` element), or it can be a producer endpoint (sends a message somewhere), for example `activemq:queue:errorQueue`.

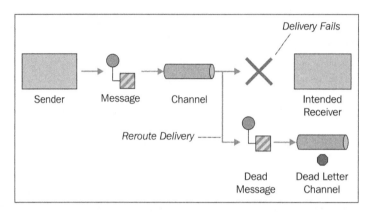

This recipe will show you how to use Camel's Dead Letter Channel error handler to send the exchange to another Camel route for processing.

Getting ready

The Java code for this recipe is located in the `org.camelcookbook.error.dlc` package. The Spring XML files are located under `src/main/resources/META-INF/spring` and prefixed with `dlc`.

How to do it...

In the XML DSL, define an `errorHandler` element within the `camelContext` element and reference its `id` with the `errorHandlerRef` attribute of the `camelContext` element. The `type` attribute of the `errorHandler` element must be set to `"DeadLetterChannel"`. You then set the `deadLetterUri` attribute to the endpoint (or route) you would like to send the message that caused the exception.

The following code will set the base error handler for all routes defined within this Camel context:

```
<camelContext errorHandlerRef="dlcErrorHandler"
              xmlns="http://camel.apache.org/schema/spring">
  <errorHandler
      id="dlcErrorHandler"
      type="DeadLetterChannel"
```

```
        deadLetterUri="seda:error"/>

<route>
  <from uri="direct:start"/>
  <!-- ... -->
  </route>
<route id="myErrorHandlingRoute">
  <from uri="seda:error"/>
  <!-- … -->
</route>
</camelContext>
```

If using the Java DSL, within the `RouteBuilder.configure()` method, define an `errorHandler` instance that references a `deadLetterChannel` instance. The sole argument to `deadLetterChannel` is the endpoint URI to which you want to send the failed messages.

The following code will configure the base error handler for all routes defined within this `RouteBuilder` implementation:

```
public class DlcRouteBuilder extends RouteBuilder {
  @Override
  public void configure() throws Exception {
    errorHandler(deadLetterChannel("seda:error"));

    from("direct:start") //...

    from("seda:error") //...
  }
}
```

How it works...

When an error (Exception) occurs during the processing of a message, and if no exception handling blocks have handled that error (see the *Catching exceptions* section), the Dead Letter Channel error handler will be invoked. It will route the failed exchange to the endpoint whose URI you specified. This is a simple way to capture the message state at the time of failure, so you can have another system (or person) inspect the message and try to address the issue.

Sending the failed message to another route gives you an opportunity to inspect the exchange's headers and properties at the time for failure, to give you more insight into the issue. Camel sets some additional properties that can help you identify the problem, which you may want to keep with the message. For example, Camel sets the `CamelToEndpoint` property to the last endpoint URI that it sent the exchange to; and `CamelFailureEndpoint` to the URI of the endpoint that it thinks caused the failure.

There's more...

The default behavior of the `DeadLetterChannel` is to route the message as it was at the time of the error. However, on occasion you will want to see the original state of the message as it was when it entered a route, to make it easier to reinsert back into the original route. Camel includes a `useOriginalMessage` option that will have the `DeadLetterChannel` route the message as seen when it entered the route that failed, versus the message state at the point of failure. This is useful, as you may have altered the message state as a part of your message processing.

In the XML DSL, you set the `useOriginalMessage` attribute to true on the `errorHandler` element:

```
<camelContext errorHandlerRef="dlcErrorHandler"
              xmlns="http://camel.apache.org/schema/spring">
  <errorHandler id="dlcErrorHandler"
                type="DeadLetterChannel"
                deadLetterUri="seda:error"
                useOriginalMessage="true"/>
  //...
</camelContext>
```

In the Java DSL, the same thing is expressed as:

```
public class DlcRouteBuilder extends RouteBuilder {
  @Override
  public void configure() throws Exception {
    errorHandler(
      deadLetterChannel("seda:error")
        .useOriginalMessage()
    );
    //...
  }
}
```

You can also set route-specific error handlers if you want to handle errors from various routes differently.

In the XML DSL, you set the `errorHandlerRef` attribute on the `route` element:

```
<camelContext xmlns="http://camel.apache.org/schema/spring">
  <errorHandler id="myRouteHandler"
                type="DeadLetterChannel"
```

```
                        deadLetterUri="seda:error"/>

    <route errorHandlerRef="myRouteHandler">
      <from uri="direct:start"/>
      <!-- ... -->
    </route>
</camelContext>
```

In the Java DSL, you specify a route-specific error handler after the `from` part of the route definition:

```
from("direct:start")
  .errorHandler(
    deadLetterChannel("seda:error")
      .useOriginalMessage()
  )
  .bean(FlakyProcessor.class)
  .to("mock:result");
```

See also

> ▶ Error Handling: `http://camel.apache.org/error-handling-in-camel.html`

> ▶ Error Handler: `http://camel.apache.org/error-handler.html`

> ▶ Dead Letter Channel: `http://camel.apache.org/dead-letter-channel.html`

Retrying an operation

Sometimes the best way to fix an error that was triggered when invoking a service is to try sending it again, as the backend infrastructure may be temporarily unavailable. Camel makes it easy to specify policies that automatically retry making calls before flagging a message as an error. This recipe will show some of the ways in which you can control the retry policies for your integration routes.

Getting ready

The Java code for this recipe is located in the `org.camelcookbook.error.retry` package. The Spring XML files are located under `src/main/resources/META-INF/spring` and prefixed with `retry`.

How to do it...

In the XML DSL, define an `errorHandler` element within the `camelContext` element, and reference its `id` with the `camelContext` element's `errorHandlerRef` attribute. Within the `errorHandler` element, create a child `redeliveryPolicy` element, which provides the `maximumRedeliveries` and `redeliveryDelay` attributes, among many other options. This will set the base error handler for all routes defined within this Camel context.

```
<camelContext errorHandlerRef="myErrorHandler"
               xmlns="http://camel.apache.org/schema/spring">
  <errorHandler id="myErrorHandler"
                type="DefaultErrorHandler">
    <redeliveryPolicy maximumRedeliveries="2"/>
  </errorHandler>

  <route>
    <from uri="direct:start"/>
    <!-- ... -->
  </route>
</camelContext>
```

In the Java DSL, you can achieve the same thing within the `RouteBuilder.configure()` method. Here you define an `errorHandler` element that refers to a `DefaultErrorHandler` instance configured using its fluent API. You can set a number of attributes, such as `maximumRedeliveries` (defaults to `0`, which means no redelivery attempts), and the `redeliveryDelay` function (defaults to `1000` ms). The following code will configure the base error handler for all routes defined within this `RouteBuilder` implementation.

```
public class RetryRouteBuilder extends RouteBuilder {
  @Override
  public void configure() throws Exception {
    errorHandler(defaultErrorHandler()
        .maximumRedeliveries(2)
    );

    from("direct:start") //...
  }
}
```

How it works...

Camel's redelivery error handling policy is quite powerful. When an error (Exception) is detected, Camel will automatically attempt to redeliver the same message to the endpoint that failed up to `maximumRedeliveries` times. The value of `maximumRedeliveries` affects redeliveries as follows:

- ▸ `0` (its default value) means do not try to redeliver
- ▸ A negative number, such as `-1`, means retry delivery forever
- ▸ A positive number means that Camel will try to redeliver up to that many times. That is, it will make the initial delivery attempt plus `maximumRedeliveries` redelivery attempts (`1` + `maximumRedeliveries`).

The error handler can also introduce a delay of `redeliveryDelay` milliseconds between each redelivery attempt to allow time for the called service to become available again.

There are many other options within the redelivery policy such as `useExponentialBackOff` delay that increases the `redeliveryDelay` element value by some `backOffMultiplier` for each redelivery attempt up to a specified `maximumRedeliveryDelay`. The Camel Error Handling documentation gives you a lot more detail on the many powerful redelivery options available to you.

If the redelivery policy does eventually become exhausted by exceeding `maximumRedeliveries` attempts, Camel will revert to throwing the exception caused by the last redelivery failure.

There's more...

You can also set route-specific error handlers.

In the XML DSL, you set the `route` elements's `errorHandlerRef` attribute:

```
<camelContext xmlns="http://camel.apache.org/schema/spring">
  <errorHandler id="myRouteSpecificErrorHandler"
                type="DefaultErrorHandler">
    <redeliveryPolicy maximumRedeliveries="2"/>
  </errorHandler>

  <route errorHandlerRef="myRouteSpecificLogging">
    <from uri="direct:start"/>
    //...
  </route>
</camelContext>
```

In the Java DSL, you specify the route-specific error handler after the `from` part of the route definition:

```
from("direct:start")
    .errorHandler(defaultErrorHandler()
        .maximumRedeliveries(2)
    )
    .bean(FlakyProcessor.class)
    .to("mock:result");
```

See also

▶ Error Handling: `http://camel.apache.org/error-handling-in-camel.html`

▶ Error Handler: `http://camel.apache.org/error-handler.html`

Conditional retry

If your error retry logic requires more sophistication than can be expressed by number of retries with delays, then conditional retry can help. It allows you to associate a predicate (expression that evaluates to a `boolean`) with an error handler, or `onException` block, that is used to decide how long to continue retrying. This gives you much finer control over the number of retry attempts by using any of Camel's Expression Languages, including calling out to a Java method, to decide if it should keep retrying delivery of the message.

This recipe will show you how to use the Simple Expression Language to make a redelivery decision based on the content of the message.

Getting ready

The Java code for this recipe is located in the `org.camelcookbook.error.retryconditional` package. The Spring XML files are located under `src/main/resources/META-INF/spring` and prefixed with `retryconditional`.

How to do it...

This example demonstrates the use of the Simple Expression Language to decide if it should continue to redeliver a message based on a message header value (`CamelRedeliveryCounter`), and on a factor external to the message—that is keep redelivering if today is Tuesday (`${date:now:EEE}` evaluates to today's day name of the week).

In the XML DSL, define an errorHandler element either within the camelContext element or within a route element (see the *Dead Letter Channel – handle errors later* recipe). The XML DSL conditional retry requires the setting of the retryWhileRef attribute, which refers to a bean or Predicate within the Camel Registry (typically set as a Spring bean).

```
<camelContext errorHandlerRef="myErrorHandler"
              xmlns="http://camel.apache.org/schema/spring">
  <errorHandler id="myErrorHandler"
                type="DefaultErrorHandler"
                retryWhileRef="myRetryPredicate"/>
  <!-- ... -->
</camelContext>
```

The referenced bean must contain a single method that returns a boolean value. Camel will work out the method to be called through its *Bean Binding* mechanism. In this example, we are using a bean that also has a property setter, so a Simple Expression Language predicate can also be defined within the Spring XML file.

```
import org.apache.camel.Exchange;
import org.apache.camel.Predicate;
import org.apache.camel.builder.SimpleBuilder;

public class SimplePredicateWrapper {
  private Predicate predicate;

  public void setSimplePredicate(String expression) {
    this.predicate = SimpleBuilder.simple(expression,
                                          Boolean.class);
  }

  public boolean matches(Exchange exchange) {
      return predicate.matches(exchange);
  }
}
```

The bean is instantiated as follows:

```
<bean id="myRetryPredicate"
      class="org...retryconditional.SimplePredicateWrapper">
  <property name="simplePredicate"
            value="${header.CamelRedeliveryCounter} &lt; 2
                   or ${date:now:EEE} contains 'Tue'"/>
</bean>
```

Using `retryWhile` in Java is much simpler due to the expressiveness of the DSL. In `RouteBuilder.configure()` method, define an `errorHandler` instance, and use its fluent API to set `retryWhile` to a `Predicate` using any of the Camel Expression Languages, including the Bean Expression Language if you wanted to call a specific POJO method.

```java
public class RetryRouteBuilder extends RouteBuilder {
  @Override
  public void configure() throws Exception {
    errorHandler(
      defaultErrorHandler()
        .retryWhile(
            simple("${header.CamelRedeliveryCounter} < 2 "
                + "or ${date:now:EEE} contains 'Tue'")
        )
    );

    from("direct:start") //...
  }
}
```

How it works...

Camel's error or `onException` handler will keep retrying the processor step that failed until the `retryWhile` loop referenced predicate returns `false`. This will work with any `RedeliveryErrorHandler` based error handler including `DefaultErrorHandler` and `DeadLetterChannel`.

There's more...

Any of Camel's Expression Languages can be used as long as the provided expression evaluates to a `boolean` (`true` or `false`).

You can also set route-specific error handlers. See the *Dead Letter Channel – handle errors later* recipe.

See also

▶ Error Handling: `http://camel.apache.org/error-handling-in-camel.html`

▶ Error Handler: `http://camel.apache.org/error-handler.html`

Customizing each redelivery attempt

Camel allows you to register a Processor instance with the redelivery policy that can change any part of the message and its headers before each redelivery attempt. This can help if there are ways you can tweak the message in response to certain errors.

This recipe will show you how to change the contents of the exchange during each redelivery attempt.

Getting ready

The Java code for this recipe is located in the `org.camelcookbook.error.retrycustom` package. The Spring XML files are located under `src/main/resources/META-INF/spring` and prefixed with `retrycustom`.

How to do it...

Configure an error handler for redelivering a message, and set its `onRedelivery` option to reference a Camel processer that you implement.

1. Implement a `org.apache.camel.Processor` that will get called to process the message before each redelivery attempt:

```
import org.apache.camel.Exchange;
import org.apache.camel.Processor;

public class RetryCustomProcessor implements Processor {
  @Override
  public void process(Exchange exchange) {
    exchange.setProperty("optimizeBit", true);
  }
}
```

2. To use the `RetryCustomProcessor` function within the XML DSL, register it using the Spring `bean` element, and refer to its `id` through the `onRedeliveryRef` attribute of an `errorHandler` element, either within the `camelContext` or `route` element (see the *Dead Letter Channel – handle errors later* recipe):

```
<bean id="myRetryProcessor"
      class="org.camelcookbook.error.retrycustom
            .RetryCustomProcessor"/>

<camelContext errorHandlerRef="myErrorHandler"
              xmlns="http://camel.apache.org/schema/spring">
  <errorHandler id="myErrorHandler"
                type="DefaultErrorHandler"
```

```
            onRedeliveryRef="myRetryProcessor">
        <redeliveryPolicy maximumRedeliveries="2"/>
      </errorHandler>
      <!-- ... -->
    </camelContext>
```

In the Java DSL, within `RouteBuilder.configure()` method define an `errorHandler` instance, and using its fluent API, set the `onRedelivery` attribute to an instance of a Processor:

```
public class RetryCustomRouteBuilder extends RouteBuilder {
  @Override
  public void configure() throws Exception {
    errorHandler(
      defaultErrorHandler()
        .onRedelivery(new RetryCustomProcessor())
        .maximumRedeliveries(2)
    );

    from("direct:start") //...
  }
}
```

> If you are using the `DefaultErrorHandler` function, do not forget that, by default, it does not attempt redeliveries. In order for this recipe to work, you need to set `maximumRedeliveries` to a value greater than or equal to 1. See the *Retrying an operation* recipe for more details.

How it works...

Before each redelivery attempt, Camel will call your referenced processor giving you an opportunity to refine the exchange values.

There's more...

You can combine this recipe with the *Conditional retry* recipe, allowing you both to have access to the message before each redelivery attempt, and to control exactly when to stop trying to redeliver.

You can also set route-specific error handlers. See the *Dead Letter Channel – handle errors later* recipe.

See also

▸ Error Handling: `http://camel.apache.org/error-handling-in-camel.html`

▸ Error Handler: `http://camel.apache.org/error-handler.html`

▸ Processor: `http://camel.apache.org/processor.html`

Catching exceptions

Camel allows you to customize the handling of specific exceptions. Camel's exception matching is far more powerful than Java's in many ways, as it allows matching based on the inheritance tree of the exception. It lets you specify retry policies at the global, and more fine-grained route level.

This recipe will show you how to specify exception handlers for your routes.

Getting ready

The Java code for this recipe is located in the `org.camelcookbook.error.exception` package. The Spring XML files are located under `src/main/resources/META-INF/spring` and prefixed with `exception`.

How to do it...

Configure the `onException` DSL statement with a list of one or more exception class types to catch, and the associated processing actions to take in response.

In the XML DSL, define an `onException` element either within the `camelContext` or `route` element. Within the `onException` element, include one or more `exception` elements with the full package name of the exception that you want this handler to catch, and follow that with one or more route steps (for example, `<to uri="direct:handleError"/>`).

```
<camelContext xmlns="http://camel.apache.org/schema/spring">
  <onException>
    <exception>
      org.camelcookbook.error.shared.FlakyException
    </exception>
    <exception>
      org.camelcookbook.error.shared.SporadicException
    </exception>
    <to uri="mock:error"/>
  </onException>
  <!-- ... -->
</camelContext>
```

In the Java DSL, you define an `onException` block within `RouteBuilder.configure()` method, and include a comma separated list of one or more `Exception` class types that you want to handle. Then using the fluent API, define one or more routing steps that the exchange should flow through when that `Exception` type is matched (for example, `to("direct:handleError")`):

```
public class ExceptionRouteBuilder extends RouteBuilder {
  @Override
  public void configure() throws Exception {
    onException(FlakyException.class, SporadicException.class)
      .to("mock:error");

    from("direct:start") //...
  }
}
```

You can define multiple `onException` blocks globally and within routes. Camel will evaluate matches based on the order you specify for the multiple `onException` handlers. That is, if you specify multiple exception handlers, Camel will evaluate them all for the best match. The order in which you specify them will also be considered in such a way that a handler defined first in the list will get preference over the next one in the list, all other things being equal.

How it works...

Camel uses a sophisticated algorithm for determining which exception handler will handle any given thrown exception. More details are available in the Camel Exception Handling documentation (`http://camel.apache.org/exception-clause.html`).

Camel will match based on several factors, some of which are listed in the following bullet list:

- The order in which the exception handlers are specified, first to last, within the route, and *then* globally. Remember you can specify multiple handlers both within the route and globally.

- The most deeply nested exception within the thrown exception is matched first, and then Camel will look for matches in the other wrapping exceptions.

- The `instanceof` tests are performed to find the closest match based on the inheritance hierarchy of the exception. An exact match will always be used, and then the closest match.

This allows you to define some generic exception handlers globally, and then refine handling within a route based on a very specific exception being thrown.

By default, Camel's default exception handler will rethrow the exception to the caller. For route-specific exception handlers, this may mean the calling routes. For global exception handlers, the exception will be thrown to the consumer endpoint (for example, web service (SOAP/HTTP) listener) through which the message first entered the Camel context. The consumer will respond back to the caller in an endpoint-specific fashion. See the *Marking exceptions as handled* recipe, and the *Catching exceptions* recipe for more details on refining this behavior.

There's more...

You can also set route-specific onException handlers.

In the XML DSL, you define an onException handler definition right after the from element of your route:

```xml
<route>
  <from uri="direct:start"/>
  <onException>
    <exception>
      org.camelcookbook.error.shared.FlakyException
    </exception>
    <to uri="mock:error"/>
  </onException>
  <bean ref="flakyProcessor"/>
  <to uri="mock:result"/>
</route>
```

In the Java DSL, you define the route-specific onException handler in the same way as the global one, only you need to close out the handler's routing fragment with an .end() statement before your regular route steps. The route-specific onException handler is defined right after the from(...) statement:

```java
from("direct:start")
    .onException(FlakyException.class)
      .to("mock:error")
    .end()
  .bean(FlakyProcessor.class)
  .to("mock:result");
```

See also

▶ Error handling: http://camel.apache.org/error-handling-in-camel.html

▶ Exception clause: http://camel.apache.org/exception-clause.html

Marking exceptions as handled

The default behavior for Camel is to call your exception (or error) handler, and rethrow the exception to the caller. This recipe will show how to mark that exception as handled, which tells Camel that it should not consider this to be an error and nothing further needs to be done, that is, do not rethrow that particular exception to the consuming endpoint.

Getting ready

The Java code for this recipe is located in the `org.camelcookbook.error.exception` package. The Spring XML files are located under `src/main/resources/META-INF/spring` and prefixed with `exception`.

How to do it...

Within the `onException` DSL statement, specify a `handled` statement with a predicate that will indicate if the exception has been handled (predicate evaluates to `true`) or if it is not handled (predicate evaluates to `false`, so exception should be re-thrown).

In the XML DSL, define an `onException` element within either the `camelContext` or `route` element. Within the `onException` element include one or more `exception` elements with the full package name of the exception you want this handler to catch, follow that with one or more route steps (for example, `<to uri="direct:handleError"/>`). This is common for all exception handlers.

Then, add a `handled` element with a nested predicate (for example, `<constant>true</constant>`):

```
<camelContext xmlns="http://camel.apache.org/schema/spring">
  <onException>
    <exception>
      org.camelcookbook.error.shared.FlakyException
    </exception>
    <handled>
      <constant>true</constant>
    </handled>
    <to uri="mock:error"/>
  </onException>
  <!-- ... -->
</camelContext>
```

In the Java DSL, within the `RouteBuilder.configure()` method, define an `onException` block and include a comma separated list of one or more class types for the `Exception` types that you want to handle. Then using the `onException` fluent API, define one or more route steps (for example, `to("direct:handleError")`). This is common for all exception handlers.

Then, add the `handled(...)` call with either a `boolean` or a predicate:

```
public class ExceptionRouteBuilder extends RouteBuilder {
  @Override
  public void configure() throws Exception {
    onException(FlakyException.class)
      .handled(true)
      .to("mock:error");

    from("direct:start") //...
  }
}
```

 You can define the multiple `onException` blocks globally and within routes. Camel will evaluate matches based on the order in which you specify the multiple `onException` handlers. See the *Catching exceptions* recipe for more details.

How it works...

The `onException` block behaves like any exception handler as described in the *Catching exceptions* recipe, except that if the `handled` expression evaluates to `true` then Camel will not re-throw the exception.

No further processing of this message will occur within the route where the exception was thrown, and the current message state will be returned to the caller. The exception handler can alter the message before it is returned, so it can create a custom error response as part of its normal exception handling.

There's more...

If you want to continue processing the message that caused the exception from the next step within the route, instead of `handled` you can mark the exception as `continued`. Marking an exception as `continued` means that the exception handling steps will be run on the message, and then the message will pick up processing at the step after the one that threw the exception.

In the XML DSL, use the `continued` element with a nested predicate. Refer to the following code for the same:

```
<onException>
  <exception>
    org.camelcookbook.error.shared.FlakyException
  </exception>
  <continued>
    <constant>true</constant>
  </continued>
  <to uri="mock:ignore"/>
</onException>
```

In the Java DSL, call the `continued(...)` statement with a `boolean` or a predicate:

```
onException(FlakyException.class)
  .continued(true)
  .to("mock:ignore")
```

Camel exception handlers also support redelivery policies (see the *Retrying an operation* recipe), the `onRedelivery` processor (see the *Customizing each redelivery attempt* recipe), and conditional processing (see the *Conditional retry* recipe) just like error handlers.

See also

▸ Error handling: `http://camel.apache.org/error-handling-in-camel.html`

▸ Exception clause: `http://camel.apache.org/exception-clause.html`

▸ The *Retrying an operation* recipe

▸ The *Customizing each redelivery attempt* recipe

▸ The *Conditional retry* recipe

Fine-grained error handling using doTry... doCatch

Camel supports an equivalent to Java's *try...catch...finally* exception handling that provides the finest grained error handling within Camel, in that you can specify exception handling specific to one or more route processing steps. Camel provides a *doTry...doCatch...doFinally* set of declarations that mirror Java's *try...catch* error handling.

This recipe will show you how to use the `doTry` DSL statement.

Getting ready

The Java code for this recipe is located in the `org.camelcookbook.error.dotry` package. The Spring XML files are located under `src/main/resources/META-INF/spring` and prefixed with `dotry`.

How to do it...

In the XML DSL, there are two mandatory steps and one optional steps needed for using `doTry`, which are as follows:

1. Within a route, define a `doTry` element for wrapping one or more processing steps for which you want to provide specific error handling. This must be after the `from` element as `doTry` cannot handle errors thrown from the consuming endpoint.

2. Within the `doTry` element, you can nest one or more `doCatch` elements. Each `doCatch` element can specify one or more `exception` elements with a value of the fully qualified Java class name of the exceptions you wish for it to handle. After the `exception` elements, you can specify one or more routing steps as part of your handler.

3. After the `doCatch` element(s), and still nested within the `doTry` element, you can optionally define a `doFinally` element, that like the Java equivalent will always be called when either the steps in the `doTry` element successfully complete, or after the steps within any triggered `doCatch` exception handler, or after an uncaught (no matching `doCatch`) exception is thrown.

```xml
<route>
  <from uri="direct:start"/>
  <to uri="mock:before"/>
  <doTry>
    <bean ref="flakyProcessor"/>
    <transform>
      <constant>Made it!</constant>
    </transform>
    <doCatch>
      <exception>
        org.camelcookbook.error.shared.FlakyException
      </exception>
      <to uri="mock:error"/>
      <transform>
        <constant>Something Bad Happened!</constant>
      </transform>
    </doCatch>
    <doFinally>
      <to uri="mock:finally"/>
```

```
        </doFinally>
      </doTry>
      <to uri="mock:after"/>
    </route>
```

To implement the same logic through the Java DSL, perform the following steps within a route at some point after the `from(...)` statement:

1. Specify a `doTry()` element followed by the one or more processing steps you wish to specify an exception handler.

2. After the last processing step you wish to wrap, follow with a `doCatch(<list of exception class types>)` element. After the `doCatch(...)` element, you define the exception processing steps to perform for the list of exceptions you provided in the doCatch(...) call. You can define multiple `doCatch(...)` blocks.

   You can optionally follow your one or more `doCatch(...)` blocks with a `doFinally()` statement, which will be always be called regardless of how the message is leaving the `doTry()` block.

```
from("direct:start")
  .to("mock:before")
  .doTry()
    .bean(FlakyProcessor.class)
    .transform(constant("Made it!"))
  .doCatch(FlakyException.class)
    .to("mock:error")
    .transform(constant("Something Bad Happened!"))
  .doFinally()
    .to("mock:finally")
  .end()
  .to("mock:after");
```

 Remember to always finish your `doTry` exception handler with a call to `end()`, either after your last `doCatch(...)` or after the steps within your `doFinally()` block.

How it works...

The `doTry` exception handler is functionally similar to how Java's *try...catch* construct works. By default, the exception is considered as *handled*, which is different from the default behavior of Camel's `onException` handler (see the *Catching exceptions* recipe).

The `doTry` exception handler overrides other defined `onException` and error handlers, as Camel does its best to mimic Java's behavior.

There's more...

If you want the `doTry` handler not to mark a processed exception as handled (that is re-throw the exception to the caller), you can set the `handled` statement to `false`. This will cause the `doTry` handler to behave in the same way as an `onException` block.

In the XML DSL, after the `exception` element(s) specify a `handled` element with a nested predicate:

```
<doCatch>
  <exception>
    org.camelcookbook.error.shared.FlakyException
  </exception>
  <handled>
    <constant>false</constant>
  </handled>
  <to uri="mock:error"/>
</doCatch>
```

In the Java DSL, after the `doCatch(...)` call, use the `handled(...)` statement with either a `boolean` or a predicate:

```
.doCatch(FlakyException.class)
  .handled(false)
  .to("mock:error")
.end()
```

 Remember that by default `doTry` will consider an exception handled, that is, `handled(true)`, which is different from the error and the `onException` handlers which default to `handled(false)`.

If you want to make your `doTry` handler have conditional `doCatch` blocks, you can specify an `onWhen` block with a predicate just like with the other error and `onException` handlers (see the *Conditional retry* recipe).

See also

- ▸ Error handling: http://camel.apache.org/error-handling-in-camel.html
- ▸ Try...Catch...Finally: http://camel.apache.org/try-catch-finally.html
- ▸ The *Catching exceptions* recipe
- ▸ The *Conditional retry* recipe

Defining completion actions

When developing integrations, you will at some point work with non-transactional resources that maintain some sort of state, such as web service endpoints. As an exchange is processed through your routes, it will trigger calls to these endpoints, modifying that state.

We have already seen how a compensating operation may be triggered when an exception is thrown in the *Fine-grained error handling using doTry...doCatch* recipe. As an example, if the original operation called was *place order*, you may have to call a *cancel order* operation to unwind it.

Camel's DSL contains an `onCompletion` statement, which allows you to define actions taken when a message completes successfully or fails at the level of a route.

This allows multiple levels of failure compensation to be written cleanly without nesting `doTry..doCatch..doFinally` blocks.

This mechanism can also be used to implement a two stage pessimistic transaction process, such as:

1. Call an initial operation that you intend to be part of a larger transaction
2. Send the equivalent of a "commit" instruction to finalize it

This pattern is frequently seen in SOA architectures where non-transactional services, such as those exposed via SOAP or REST, are composed into a pseudo-transaction that is coordinated by the caller.

This recipe will outline how to define completion actions to be performed based on whether an exchange was completed successfully or not, through Camel's `onCompletion` statement.

Getting ready

The Java code for this recipe is located in the `org.camelcookbook.error.oncompletion` package. The Spring XML files are located under `src/main/resources/META-INF/spring` and prefixed with `onCompletion`.

How to do it...

In the XML DSL, define an `onCompletion` block within a route. The block may be defined at any point in a route—though by convention it is usually placed at the beginning. Within the block, define processing steps that ought to be executed when an exchange has been processed through the route.

```
<from uri="direct:in"/>
<onCompletion>
```

```
      <log message="onCompletion triggered: ${threadName}"/>
      <to uri="mock:completed"/>
   </onCompletion>
   <log message="Processing message: ${threadName}"/>
```

In the Java DSL, the equivalent logic is expressed as follows:

```
from("direct:in")
  .onCompletion()
     .log("onCompletion triggered: ${threadName}")
     .to("mock:completed")
  .end()
  .log("Processing message: ${threadName}");
```

How it works...

Once an exchange has been processed through a route, a copy of it will be handed off to a background thread pool that will then process it through the onCompletion block. Any subsequent changes made to this copied exchange will not be visible to the caller of the route. The functionality is analogous to an implicit wireTap statement at the end of a route (see *Wire Tap – sending a copy of the message elsewhere*, in *Chapter 2, Message Routing*). We can confirm this through the logged thread names in the preceding examples:

```
Processing message: Camel (camel-1) thread #0 - ProducerTemplate
onCompletion triggered: Camel (camel-1) thread #1 - OnCompletion
```

The onCompletion block will process both failed and successfully completed exchanges. You can specify which type you would like to handle, by applying the onCompleteOnly or onFailureOnly attributes in the XML DSL as follows:

```
<onCompletion onCompleteOnly="true">
   <!-- ... -->
</onCompletion>
<onCompletion onFailureOnly="true">
   <!-- ... -->
</onCompletion>
```

> A failure is defined in by functionality as an Exception that is not handled by the processing thread within a doTry..doCatch..doFinally block or the onException block, and which propagates to the error handler.

The attributes onCompleteOnly and onFailureOnly affect the regular onCompletion behavior only when set to true, as setting them to false would be ambiguous. They should be considered as markers that narrow the onCompletion functionality.

This intent is expressed more clearly through the equivalent statements in the Java DSL:

```
.onCompletion().onCompleteOnly() // ...
.onCompletion().onFailureOnly() // ...
```

An onCompletion block can be *global*, that is, defined outside a route.

In the XML DSL, it will apply to all routes in the Camel context:

```
<camelContext>
  <onCompletion>
    <log message="global onCompletion thread: ${threadName}"/>
    <to uri="mock:global"/>
  </onCompletion>
  <!-- routes defined here -->
</camelContext>
```

In the Java DSL, the meaning of the term "global" is different—the onCompletion function will only apply to routes defined in the same RouteBuilder implementation:

```
onCompletion()
  .log("global onCompletion thread: ${threadName}")
  .to("mock:global");
```

The following rules apply to onCompletion usage:

- If no onCompletion is defined at the route level, and one is defined at the global level, then the global one is used. The combination of conditions (onCompleteOnly/onFailureOnly) is disregarded.

- If an onCompletion is defined at the route level, then none of onCompletion blocks defined at the global level will ever get triggered as a result of the processing of the exchange.

- Only one onCompletion block defined within a single scope will always be considered for execution. This applies even if one defines a failure action, and the other one for successful completion.

  - If two onCompletion blocks are defined at the global level, only the one defined *first* is used.

  - If two onCompletion blocks are defined in a route, only the one defined *last* is used.

- If a route defines an onCompletion block, and passes the exchange to another route that also defines an onCompletion, both will be executed.

There's more...

You can make the `onCompletion` block conditional through the addition of an `onWhen` statement.

In the XML DSL, this is written as:

```
<onCompletion onFailureOnly="true">
  <onWhen>
    <simple>
      ${exception.class} ==
        'java.lang.IllegalArgumentException'
    </simple>
  </onWhen>
  <!-- ... -->
</onCompletion>
```

In the Java DSL, the equivalent would be written as follows:

```
.onCompletion().onFailureOnly()
  .onWhen(
    simple(
      "${exception.class} ==
        'java.lang.IllegalArgumentException'"
  ))
  //...
```

Since only a single `onCompletion` block can be applied to a route by the Camel runtime, the following Java DSL will result in only the `onCompleteOnly` statement being executed:

```
.onCompletion().onFailureOnly()
  // handle failure
.end()
.onCompletion().onCompleteOnly()
  // handle everything going OK
.end()
```

This is a minor inconvenience that can be worked around using the `choice` block (see *Content-based routing*, in *Chapter 2, Message Routing*) in conjunction with a catch-all `onCompletion` statement.

In the XML DSL, this is written as:

```
<onCompletion>
  <choice>
    <when>
      <simple>${exception} == null</simple>
```

```
        <to uri="mock:completed"/>
      </when>
      <otherwise>
        <to uri="mock:failed"/>
      </otherwise>
    </choice>
</onCompletion>
```

In the Java DSL, due to an internal constraint of the DSL, we have to split out the `choice` block into another route to achieve the same effect using the following code.

```
onCompletion()
    .to("direct:processCompletion")
.end();

from("direct:processCompletion")
    .choice()
      .when(simple("${exception} == null"))
        .to("mock:completed")
      .otherwise()
        .to("mock:failed")
    .endChoice();
```

It is possible to define a custom thread pool to handle the procession of the exchange through the `onCompletion` blocks.

In the XML DSL, this is written as:

```
<onCompletion executorServiceRef="customThreadPool">
    <!-- ... -->
</onCompletion>
```

In the Java DSL, the same thing is expressed as:

```
onCompletion().executorServiceRef("customThreadPool")
```

See *Using custom thread pools* in *Chapter 6, Parallel Processing* for more details.

See also

▸   Camel `onCompletion`: `http://camel.apache.org/oncompletion.html`

Defining completion actions dynamically

We have seen in the previous recipe how confirming and cancelling notifications can be defined at a route or global level, so that they can be triggered when an exchange completes processing. This is useful when that logic is tied to a single route, but how do you handle code called from multiple routes that need to do some sort of cleanup upon route completion?

This recipe will show you how to dynamically apply completion steps to an exchange's processing through the use of a `Synchronization` class.

This mechanism is useful when you manipulate a class of resources that need some form of post-processing in the same way. For example, Camel uses this mechanism as a part of its file consumption to move or delete files after it has finished processing their contents. The fact that post-processing happens is transparent to the developer who uses that resource.

Getting ready

The Java code for this recipe is located in the `org.camelcookbook.error.synchronizations` package.

How to do it...

In order to dynamically define completion actions, perform the following steps:

1. Within a `Processor` implementation, implement an `org.apache.camel.spi.Synchronization` interface. This class will be used as a callback by the Camel runtime when an exchange's processing completes successfully or fails. The interface defines two methods:

    ```
    public interface Synchronization {
      void onComplete(Exchange exchange);
      void onFailure(Exchange exchange);
    }
    ```

    You can either implement this interface, or extend the `org.apache.camel.support.SynchronizationAdapter` class, which allows you to override one or the other of these methods as well as allowing you to handle an exchange regardless of the completion status via `onDone(Exchange exchange)`.

2. Once instantiated, bind the `Synchronization` class to the exchange currently being processed through `Exchange.addOnComplete(Synchronization s)`.

The following `Processor` implementation starts an operation requiring confirmation or cancellation, and then triggers the appropriate operation to finalize the transaction:

```
public class ConfirmCancelProcessor implements Processor {
  @Override
  public void process(Exchange exchange) throws Exception {
    final ProducerTemplate producerTemplate =
        exchange.getContext().createProducerTemplate();
    producerTemplate.send("mock:start", exchange);

    exchange.addOnCompletion(
        new Synchronization() {
          @Override
          public void onComplete(Exchange exchange) {
            producerTemplate.send("mock:confirm",
                                          exchange);
          }

          @Override
          public void onFailure(Exchange exchange) {;
            producerTemplate.send("mock:cancel", exchange);
          }
        }
    );
  }
}
```

This example uses calls to the `mock:` endpoints to simulate completion tasks. Routing logic wrapped in callbacks like this should usually be avoided as it can almost always be expressed better as part of a route. Triggering endpoints like this obscures backend interactions from anyone looking at the route. It also makes the route itself difficult to test, especially when your endpoints refer to a heavyweight component that is not easily stubbed.

No additional work is required to enable this functionality other than using the `Processor` in a route as normal:

```
from("direct:in")
  .process(new ConfirmCancelProcessor())
  .choice()
    .when(simple("${body} contains 'explode'"))
      .throwException(
        new IllegalArgumentException(
          "Exchange caused explosion"))
  .endChoice()
  .log("Processed message");
```

How it works...

Each `Exchange` contains a `UnitOfWork` property that is a conceptual holder for the transactional interactions of the Exchange instance. It holds on to a number of `Synchronization` instances that will be triggered as appropriate given the final state of the exchange's processing—completed or failed.

The thread that processes the exchange through the final step of the route will trigger the `Synchronization` object.

Unlike the `onCompletion` block discussed in the *Defining completion actions* recipe, which was limited to one callback per route, you can bind as many `Synchronization` instances as you like to an exchange. This allows you to have separate instances to handle success and failure, and it allows you to dynamically add cleanup logic if you have resources that are conditionally used based on message content or conditions.

 You should clearly document any code that makes use of a `Sychronization` and explain its intent so that processing steps do not appear to happen "by magic".

There's more...

The `Synchronization` instances are carried with an exchange across thread boundaries, such as when entering a `threads` block or crossing a `seda:` endpoint. This may lead to unexpected behaviors when dealing with resources that are bound to threads using `ThreadLocals`. When the `Synchronization` instance attempts to access the resource once the exchange is completed, you will find that the `ThreadLocal` resource is no longer there!

To get around this issue, you should implement the `SynchronizationVetoable` interface, which extends `Synchronization`. This interface defines one additional method:

```
boolean allowHandover();
```

By implementing this method, and returning `true`, you can instruct the `Synchronization` object to not be copied between exchanges. This will execute the completion logic when the first exchange completes processing.

See also

 ▶ Synchronization: http://camel.apache.org/maven/current/camel-core/apidocs/org/apache/camel/spi/Synchronization.html

 ▶ SynchronizationVetoable: http://camel.apache.org/maven/current/camel-core/apidocs/org/apache/camel/spi/SynchronizationVetoable.html

8
Transactions and Idempotency

In this chapter, we will cover the following recipes:

- ▸ Preventing duplicate invocation of routing logic
- ▸ Transactional file consumption
- ▸ Using transactions with a database
- ▸ Limiting the scope of a transaction
- ▸ Rolling back a transaction
- ▸ Using transactions with messaging
- ▸ Idempotency inside transactions
- ▸ Setting up XA transactions over multiple transactional resources

Introduction

Systems integration is all about coordinating the interaction between multiple systems in order for them to interact as a larger whole. This interaction forms a **distributed system**, although people working on integrations tend not to think about what they are building in those terms. Part of the complexity of distributed systems is that they are typically written by different people at different times, using different technologies, doing things in parallel, and yet they need to coordinate on shared tasks. They also need to handle errors in a predictable fashion when that coordination breaks down. All of these factors make work on integrations very challenging, and very interesting.

A **Transaction** is an implementation concept that allows distributed stateful nodes in a system, such as databases and message brokers, to coordinate changes to their state. Updates to state are either committed when a unit of work has been completed successfully, or rolled back when an error occurs. This concept is especially helpful when you start thinking about all of the corner cases where things could go wrong, such as a network cable being tripped over, or a server having coffee spilled on it (it happens).

Your integrations need to maintain the overall integrity of the data travelling through the system at all times. This includes any of the messages that happen to be in-flight through your integration logic when your application process is unexpectedly terminated.

When developing integrations, you need to consider two primary issues, which are stated as follows:

▸ Partner systems will go down. When a customer is placing an order online, it is not satisfactory for them to be billed and then not to have the items sent because the warehouse system was unavailable.

▸ The process running your integration logic will also go down. If a client is billed for an order, and your integration shuts down before you are able to send the order to the warehouse, you need to be able to recover. This needs to happen in such a way that they are not billed twice and eventually get their order, or that the payment is unwound.

In this chapter, we will look at Camel's support for handling failures in your routing logic through the following mechanisms:

▸ Transactions

▸ Idempotency: It executes an operation once and once only

For the purpose of executing transactions, Camel makes use of the Spring framework's `PlatformTransactionManager`. This abstraction unifies the API for dealing with transactional resources. Use of the Spring transaction abstractions happens regardless of whether your application code directly uses Spring.

To use JDBC transactions in your projects, you will need a `JdbcTransactionManager` connection. This can be imported through a dependency on the `spring-jdbc` library in your Maven POM:

```
<dependency>
  <groupId>org.springframework</groupId>
  <artifactId>spring-jdbc</artifactId>
  <version>${spring-version}</version>
</dependency>
```

To use JMS transactions in your projects, you will need a `JmsTransactionManager` connection. This can be imported through a dependency on the `spring-jms` library in your Maven POM:

```
<dependency>
  <groupId>org.springframework</groupId>
  <artifactId>spring-jms</artifactId>
  <version>${spring-version}</version>
</dependency>
```

In both cases, `${spring-version}` is a property that you define in the `properties` section of your POM that states which version of Spring you are using.

Where database access is required in these examples, the Camel SQL Component is used. This component provides the simplest method of demonstrating transactional database access in Camel. Other components that abstract relational database access, such as Camel JPA (Java Persistence Architecture), Camel Hibernate, or Camel Mybatis, will require slightly different configuration, though the general approach shown here will still be valid.

A number of Camel architectural concepts are used throughout this chapter. There is a broader overview of Camel concepts in the *Preface*. Full details can be found on the Apache Camel website at `http://camel.apache.org`.

The code for this chapter is contained within the `camel-cookbook-transactions` module of the examples.

Preventing duplicate invocation of routing logic

When dealing with external systems, it is often necessary to ensure that the same request is not sent multiple times—a process often called deduplication.

Camel implements the **Idempotent Consumer** EIP, which allows you to mark a segment of a route as callable only once for each unique message. This is useful if it is possible for your route to receive duplicate messages, either from an upstream system or from the underlying infrastructure (for example, through a message queue configured for redelivery on failure), and you want to protect routing logic that is intolerant of duplicates.

This recipe explains how to make portions of your route idempotent in Camel.

Getting ready

The Java code for this recipe is located in the `org.camelcookbook.transactions.`
`idempotentconsumer` package. The Spring XML files are located under `src/main/`
`resources/META-INF/spring` and prefixed with `idempotentConsumer`.

How to do it...

In order to use an Idempotent consumer in the XML DSL, perform the following steps:

1. Instantiate an `org.apache.camel.spi.IdempotentRepository`
    implementation class as a regular Spring/Blueprint bean. Implementations of this
    class are responsible for storing keys that represent previously seen messages. Here
    we will use a memory-based `IdempotentRepository`, using the following code:

    ```
    <bean id="wsIdempotentRepository"
          class="org.apache.camel.processor.idempotent
                 .MemoryIdempotentRepository"/>
    ```

2. Wrap the routing logic that you want to only trigger once in an
    `idempotentConsumer` block. An `idempotentConsumer` block determines a
    message's uniqueness through checking the result of an expression against the set
    of previously seen messages in the `IdempotentRepository`. The following XML
    DSL fragment shows this in action:

    ```
    <from uri="direct:in"/>
    <idempotentConsumer
        messageIdRepositoryRef="wsIdempotentRepository">
      <header>messageId</header> <!-- unique key -->
      <to uri="mock:ws"/>
    </idempotentConsumer>
    <to uri="mock:out"/>
    ```

In the Java DSL, the complete setup above can be expressed in a single step as follows:

```
from("direct:in")
  .idempotentConsumer(
      header("messageId"), // unique key
      new MemoryIdempotentRepository())
    .to("mock:ws")
  .end()
  .to("mock:out");
```

When two messages with the same `messageId` header are pushed through either of these
routes, the first will invoke the `mock:ws` and `mock:out` endpoints, while the second message
will trigger `mock:out` only.

How it works...

When an exchange reaches an `idempotentConsumer` statement, the provided expression is evaluated to determine a unique key for that message. In the preceding example, this expression involves a lookup of a header value, but it could have been the result of any of Camel's Expression Languages, including the result of a Java method or XPath query.

The key is checked against all previously seen keys in the `IdempotentRepository` instance. If this value has previously been seen, the routing logic contained within the block is skipped; otherwise the key is inserted into the repository and the routing logic within the block is executed.

The reason behind this behavior is that internally the pattern registers a `Synchronization` instance with the exchange as described in *Defining completion actions dynamically* of *Chapter 7, Error Handling and Compensation*. This callback commits the change to the `IdempotentRepository` when the exchange completes processing, or rolls it back if it fails.

In order to ensure that the changes to the repository are isolated, and subsequent routing logic does not remove the key when an exception is thrown, we need to use a separate Exchange instance with its own `UnitOfWork` for the `idempotentConsumer` logic. This is easier than it might seem.

> If an exception is thrown at any point in the route after entering the `idempotentConsumer` block, *including routing logic defined after the block*, the key is removed from the repository. This will result in a replayed message once again being processed through the block.
>
> In the preceding example, if `mock:out` endpoint threw an exception, the next request with the same `messageId` header would execute both `mock:ws` and `mock:out` endpoints.
>
> This is not usually what you want, as you would expect that only an exception thrown within the `idempotentConsumer` block would have this effect.

To commit the update to the `IdempotentRepository` immediately after the `idempotentConsumer` block, we split out the idempotent logic into its own route, and trigger that route through the `enrich` statement as seen in *Enriching your content with some help from other endpoints* of *Chapter 4, Transformation*.

In the XML DSL, the enrichment logic is expressed as follows:

```
<route>
  <from uri="direct:in"/>
  <enrich uri="direct:invokeWs"/>
  <to uri="mock:out"/>
```

```
    </route>

    <route>
      <from uri="direct:invokeWs"/>
      <idempotentConsumer
          messageIdRepositoryRef="wsIdempotentRepository">
        <header>messageId</header>
        <to uri="mock:ws"/>
      </idempotentConsumer>
    </route>
```

In the Java DSL, this same logic is written as follows:

```
from("direct:in")
  .enrich("direct:invokeWs")
  .to("mock:out");

from("direct:invokeWs")
  .idempotentConsumer(
      header("messageId"),
      new MemoryIdempotentRepository())
  .to("mock:ws");
```

The enricher creates a copy of the original exchange that is then passed through this second route. This second Exchange instance contains a distinct `UnitOfWork` that is completed when that instance has worked its way through the route. It is at that point that the movement of the message through the `idempotentConsumer` block is committed to the `IdempotentRepository` instance. On return from the enricher, the contents of the exchange are made available to the calling route.

If we merely invoked a route through a regular `to` statement, instead of `enrich`, any exceptions thrown after the `idempotentConsumer` block in the main route would cause the message key to be removed from the `IdempotentRepository` instance. This would lead to incorrect behavior, as the routing logic protected by the block would be executed again if the message were to be replayed.

There's more...

It is possible for the `idemponentConsumer` instance to mark exchanges as having been previously seen instead of bypassing their processing. This allows you to route previously seen messages differently from new ones.

To do this, set the `skipDuplicate` attribute on the `idempotentConsumer` block to `false`. When a duplicate message is seen, the CamelDuplicateMessage (Exchange. DUPLICATE_MESSAGE) property will be set on the exchange. You can then use this property to make routing decisions.

In the XML DSL, this is expressed as:

```
<from uri="direct:in"/>
<idempotentConsumer
    messageIdRepositoryRef="wsIdempotentRepository"
    skipDuplicate="false">
  <header>messageId</header>
  <choice>
    <when>
      <property>CamelDuplicateMessage</property>
      <to uri="mock:duplicate"/>
    </when>
    <otherwise>
      <to uri="mock:ws"/>
    </otherwise>
  </choice>
</idempotentConsumer>
```

In the Java DSL, the same routing logic is written as follows:

```
from("direct:in")
  .idempotentConsumer(header("messageId"),
                      new MemoryIdempotentRepository())
      .skipDuplicate(false)
  .choice()
    .when(property(Exchange.DUPLICATE_MESSAGE))
      .to("mock:duplicate")
    .otherwise()
      .to("mock:ws")
  .endChoice()
.end();
```

There are a number of `IdempotentRepository` implementations to choose from depending on the **Quality of Service** (**QoS**) that you would like your route to provide. If none of these provide the sort of QoS that you require, it is possible to write your own.

The following table lists some of the commonly used `IdempotentRepository` implementations, along with tips on their usage:

`MemoryIdempotentRepository`	A fast, non-persistent store that uses a `Map` to store all keys. All data contained within will be lost when the JVM is stopped.
	No support for clustering.
	This class is available in Camel Core and therefore requires no additional dependencies.
`FileIdempotentRepository`	A basic persistent store that uses a map as a cache for looking up keys, and a file that persists the current view of that `Map`.
	All operations that access the file are synchronized, which means that it could be a bottleneck in a high-throughput scenario. Additions append to the file; a removal causes the entire file to be rewritten. It is possible that the cache could be corrupted if a rewrite is taking place when the JVM shuts down.
	As only one JVM should write to a file, it is not suitable for an *Active/Active* (*Hot-Hot*) cluster. An Active/Active deployment is one where two or more processing nodes are working on the same set of data at the same time and appear to act as a single instance to the outside world. Failure of one node means that any others that remain process the request load.
	This repository is OK for use in Active/Passive (Hot-Cold) setups. These are clusters where only one node out of two or more is running at a time, and where a standby is started in the event of the running node's failure.
	This class is available in Camel Core and therefore requires no additional dependencies.
`JdbcMessageIdRepository`	Uses any of the usual standard SQL databases to persist stored messages. Each consumer requires it's own repository, which can all use the same underlying database table to store keys.
	High volume of interaction with the database may be a performance problem as each check, write or delete triggers a SQL query.
	Suitable for Active/Active clustering.

`HazelcastIdempotentRepository`	Uses the open source Hazelcast in-memory data grid / distributed cache to share a map of keys between a number of JVM instances.
	Hazelcast can be configured to persist its caches to a shared database synchronously when the key is written to the cache (write-through, slower), or asynchronously in the background (write-behind, faster, but less reliable as messages could be lost if the JVM shuts down before writing). As the cache is used to do key lookups rather than a store, it is much faster than the `JdbcMessageIdRepository`.
	Suitable for Active/Active clustering.

Additional `IdempotentRepository` implementations are provided by the Camel HBase and Camel Redis Components.

Cache eviction strategies vary depending on the `IdempotentRepository` implementation used. Both the `MemoryIdempotentRepository` and `FileIdempotentRepository` use a fixed-size **least recently used** (**LRU**) Map, while the `JdbcMessageIdRepository` class requires that you set up an external script to periodically delete unwanted records. You should refer to the appropriate API documentation for full details.

By default, the message key is written, but not committed, into the `IdempotentRepository` instance as soon as the exchange enters the idempotent block. This prevents two duplicate messages that reach the block in quick succession from triggering the same logic. By setting the `eager` attribute on the `idempotentConsumer` block to `false`, you can delay this write until the exchange's processing is completed.

In the XML DSL, this is written as:

```
<idempotentConsumer
    messageIdRepositoryRef="wsIdempotentRepository"
    eager="false">
  <!-- ... -->
</idempotentConsumer>
```

In the Java DSL, the same thing is expressed as:

```
.idempotentConsumer(header("messageId"),
                new MemoryIdempotentRepository())
    .eager(false)
```

A `removeOnFailure` attribute is available that can be set to `false` (default is `true`). This comes in useful, for example, if you want to remove keys from the `IdempotentRepository` instance manually through an `onException` block only if a certain type of `Exception` is thrown.

See also

- ▸ Camel Idempotent Consumer: `http://camel.apache.org/idempotent-consumer.html`
- ▸ Camel SQL Component (`JdbcMessageIdRepository`): `http://camel.apache.org/sql-component.html`
- ▸ Camel Hazelcast Component (`HazelcastIdempotentRepository`): `http://camel.apache.org/hazelcast-component.html`
- ▸ Camel HBase Component: `http://camel.apache.org/hbase.html`
- ▸ Camel Redis Component: `http://camel.apache.org/redis.html`

Transactional file consumption

The consumption of files is not something that immediately comes to mind when talking about transactions. Camel provides you with a way to do just this, through the use of the File Component.

This recipe will show you how to perform file consumption, and explain how Camel does its best to guarantee an all-or-nothing process, isolated from other threads and optionally processes, that leaves the consumed file in a state consistent with the overall operation.

Getting ready

The Java code for this recipe is located in the `org.camelcookbook.transactions.fileconsumption` package. The Spring XML files are located under `src/main/resources/META-INF/spring` and prefixed with `fileConsumption`.

How to do it...

The File Component in Camel is part of the `camel-core` library. To consume files from a specific directory, define a `file:` endpoint URI within a consumer endpoint, that is within a `from` statement as per the following pattern:

```
file:///path/to/source
```

When a file is successfully processed, it is moved into the `.camel` subdirectory under the source directory, by default. This can be overridden through the `move` attribute, which takes a relative or absolute path:

```
file:///path/to/source?move=///path/to/completed
```

It is also possible to instruct the component to delete completed files rather than moving them:

```
file:///path/to/source?delete=true
```

How it works...

The component scans the directory referenced in the URI, and processes each file as an individual exchange through the route. Exceptions raised while processing the file are handled gracefully, by reattempting the consumption of the entire file.

It is possible to move any failed files to another directory, by providing the failure location in the `moveFailed` attribute. For example, in the following route, a failed file will be moved to an error directory, where it can be manually inspected; otherwise, on success, its contents will be sent to an output directory:

```
from("file:" + inputDirectory + "?moveFailed=" + errorDirectory)
  .log("Consumed file ${header[CamelFileName]}: ${body}")
  .convertBodyTo(String.class)
  .choice()
    .when(simple("${body} contains 'explode'"))
      .throwException(
          new IllegalArgumentException("File caused explosion"))
    .otherwise()
      .to("file:" + outputDirectory)
  .endChoice();
```

 In this example, the directories are provided as variables when the route is instantiated. See *Reusing routing logic through template routes* of *Chapter 1, Structuring Routes*, for an overview of this approach.

File consumption is performed as kind of *best-effort* transaction. Underneath the covers, the File Component binds a `org.apache.camel.spi.Synchronization` instance to the exchange as described in the *Defining completion actions dynamically* recipe in *Chapter 7, Error Handling and Compensation*. This callback will be invoked by the Camel runtime when that exchange has completed processing.

The File Component provides the logic for moving or deleting, the file if its processing was successful, and either leaving it where it was or moving it to another directory if the file failed. This behavior is configurable through the endpoint URI.

There's more...

The File Component makes use of the technique covered in the *Preventing duplicate invocation of routing logic* recipe to ensure that the same files are not reprocessed. Idempotent consumption is disabled by default, but can be enabled by providing a reference to an `IdempotentRepository` instance in the consumer URI with the `idempotentRepository` attribute. It is useful in the following situations:

- The file consumer has been set to not move files after processing–when the `noop` attribute is set to `true`. Here, an in-memory idempotent repository will be used by default, unless overridden by the `idempotentRepository` attribute.

- The same files will be uploaded into the source directory repeatedly, for example, the last seven days' worth of transactions.

- There will be more than one Camel runtime scanning the same directory. This is often seen in clusters of servers that are running in an Active/Active configuration, where all of the servers are active and executing the same Camel routes. To implement this use case, you would provide an instance of an `IdempotentRepository` implementation whose state is visible to both runtimes. This usually means providing a reference to a `JDBCIdempotentRepository` that refers to a shared database.

There are a large number of other options around consuming files that include the ability to define file name patterns for consumption, ordering, read locking, recursive directory traversals, and others. It is also possible to use the File Component as a producer endpoint in order to write messages into a directory. See the Camel File Component documentation for full details.

See also

- Camel File Component: `http://camel.apache.org/file2.html`

Using transactions with a database

This recipe will show you how to set up transaction management over a database used from a Camel route. It will also detail the transaction propagation behaviors that you can use to combine both transactional and non-transactional database interactions.

Getting ready

The Java code for this recipe is located in the `org.camelcookbook.transactions.databasetransaction` package. The Spring XML files are located under `src/main/resources/META-INF/spring` and prefixed with `databaseTransaction`.

As discussed in the *Introduction* section, Camel's transaction handling relies on Spring's `PlatformTransactionManager` abstraction. Therefore, it is necessary to include the appropriate dependency in your application regardless of whether you are basing it on Spring or not—this includes regular Java as well as OSGi Blueprint applications.

To use Spring-managed JDBC transactions, you will need the following Maven dependencies:

```
<dependency>
  <groupId>org.apache.camel</groupId>
  <artifactId>camel-spring</artifactId>
  <version>${camel-version}</version>
</dependency>
<dependency>
  <groupId>org.springframework</groupId>
  <artifactId>spring-jdbc</artifactId>
  <version>${spring-version}</version>
</dependency>
```

How to do it...

In order to use database transactions, we first need to wire together a number of classes as follows:

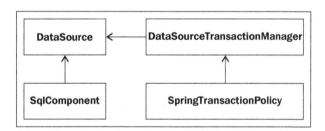

The `javax.sql.DataSource` interface is the main entry point to your database. The actual implementation class used here may come directly from your database vendor, or may be a database connection pool, such as c3p0 (`http://www.mchange.com/projects/c3p0/`).

In this example, a `DataSource` is instantiated to point to a database used for audit records. This instance is referred to as the `auditDataSource`.

The steps required to set up transactional access to a database are as follows:

1. Wire the classes together in Spring.

```
<bean id="sql"
      class="org.apache.camel.component.sql.SqlComponent">
  <property name="dataSource"
            ref="auditDataSource"/>
```

```
    </bean>

    <bean id="transactionManager"
          class="org.springframework.jdbc.datasource
                 .DataSourceTransactionManager">
      <property name="dataSource"
                ref="auditDataSource"/>
    </bean>

    <bean id="PROPAGATION_REQUIRED"
          class="org.apache.camel.spring.spi
                 .SpringTransactionPolicy">
      <property name="transactionManager"
                ref="transactionManager"/>
      <property name="propagationBehaviorName"
                value="PROPAGATION_REQUIRED"/>
    </bean>
```

The `SpringTransactionPolicy` instance defines a transaction propagation behavior, which is interpreted by the Spring framework. A `propagationBehaviorName` value of `PROPAGATION_REQUIRED` indicates that a transaction should be started if one is not already in progress, otherwise the transaction in progress should be used.

By convention, transaction policies are typically given IDs that are the same as the value of their `propagationBehaviorName`. This convention is used by Camel to provide a sensible default configuration for transactions when the beans are not explicitly wired together.

In Java, the same objects can be wired into a standalone Camel context as follows:

```
SimpleRegistry registry = new SimpleRegistry();
DataSource auditDataSource = ...; // defined by you

DataSourceTransactionManager transactionManager =
    new DataSourceTransactionManager(auditDataSource);
registry.put("transactionManager", transactionManager);

SpringTransactionPolicy propagationRequired =
    new SpringTransactionPolicy();
propagationRequired.setTransactionManager(
    transactionManager);
propagationRequired.setPropagationBehaviorName(
    "PROPAGATION_REQUIRED");
```

```
registry.put("PROPAGATION_REQUIRED", propagationRequired);

CamelContext camelContext =
    new DefaultCamelContext(registry);
SqlComponent sqlComponent = new SqlComponent();
sqlComponent.setDataSource(auditDataSource);
camelContext.addComponent("sql", sqlComponent);
```

> In Java, both the `PlatformTransactionManager` and `SpringTransactionPolicy` must be registered in Camel's object registry explicitly, as the transaction mechanism needs to obtain a reference to them. When using Spring, any bean defined in the `ApplicationContext` is visible to Camel.

2. To access the database transaction manner in Camel, define a `transacted` block before accessing the SQL Component:

```
<from uri="direct:transacted"/>
<transacted/>
<setHeader headerName="message">
  <simple>${body}</simple>
</setHeader>
<to uri="sql:insert into audit_log (message) values
        (:#message)"/>
<to uri="mock:out"/>
```

The `transacted` block will start a transaction that is committed at the end of the route.

In the Java DSL, the same route can be represented as:

```
from("direct:transacted")
  .transacted()
  .setHeader("message", body())
  .to("sql:insert into audit_log (message) values
      (:#message)")
  .to("mock:out");
```

Both of the preceding routes will insert the body of a message into the `audit_log` table. If the `mock:out` endpoint throws an exception, the database insert will be rolled back.

How it works...

The `transacted` statement uses conventions to provide sensible transaction behavior. Its processor will fetch a `SpringTransactionPolicy` named PROPAGATION_REQUIRED from Camel's registry. If none is defined, it will fetch a `PlatformTransactionManager` object and implicitly use the PROGAGATION_REQUIRED behavior.

In the preceding code, the `transacted` statement will start a transaction using the `DataSourceTransactionManager` instance. Under the covers, this means it will fetch a database connection from the `DataSource` and set it to manual commit. Any interaction with the `DataSource` object for the remainder of the route by this thread will be through this transaction.

The processor will then set up Camel's `TransactionErrorHandler` to roll back transactions when an exception is thrown and not handled by another error handler.

If the exchange is completed without any problems, the transaction will commit at the end of the route. If an exception is thrown, all database changes made will be rolled back.

There's more...

If you have multiple `PlatformTransactionManager` or `SpringTransactionPolicy` objects defined, or if you just want to be explicit about your configuration, you can define exactly which `SpringTransactionPolicy` object from the registry is to be used by the `transacted` statement.

In the XML DSL, this is written as:

```
<transacted ref="PROPAGATION_REQUIRED"/>
```

In the Java DSL, the same thing is expressed as:

```
.transacted("PROPAGATION_REQUIRED")
```

The following table describes the various Spring-supported transaction propagation behaviors that may be used with the `transacted` DSL statement.

PROPAGATION_REQUIRED	Start a transaction if none is already in progress; otherwise join the existing one. This is the most commonly used option.
PROPAGATION_REQUIRES_NEW	Start a transaction regardless of whether another transaction is already in progress. If a transaction is in progress, it will be suspended, and resumed when this one completes.
PROPAGATION_MANDATORY	A transaction must be in progress by the time this block is reached, if not, an exception will be thrown.
PROPAGATION_SUPPORTS	If a transaction is in progress, it will be used. Otherwise the logic will be non-transactional.
PROPAGATION_NOT_SUPPORTED	If a transaction is in progress when this block is reached, it will be suspended. The logic within will be executed outside of a transaction.

PROPAGATION_NEVER	A transaction must not be in progress when this block is reached, otherwise an exception will be thrown.
PROPAGATION_NESTED	Starts a new transaction whose outcome is tied to any transaction that was already in progress.

See also

> ▸ Camel Transactional Client: `http://camel.apache.org/transactional-client.html`

Limiting the scope of a transaction

The technique shown in the *Using transactions with a database* recipe used the `transacted` DSL statement to initiate a transaction. Using this approach, the transaction is committed when the exchange's processing completes. This recipe will show you how you can control the scope of transactions in a much more granular fashion using the `policy` statement.

Getting ready

The Java code for this recipe is located in the `org.camelcookbook.transactions.transactionpolicies` package. The Spring XML files are located under `src/main/resources/META-INF/spring` and prefixed with `transactionPolicies`.

How to do it...

Set up a `SpringTransactionPolicy` associated with a transaction manager as shown in the *Using transactions with a database* recipe.

 The type of transaction manager is not relevant, as this approach applies to JDBC, JMS, and XA transactions.

Using the `policy` DSL statement, wrap the individual processing steps that you want to enclose in a transaction, referring to the `SpringTransactionPolicy` by name (in this example, we refer to a bean with the id "PROPAGATION_REQUIRED").

In the XML DSL, this is expressed as follows:

```
<from uri="direct:policies"/>
<setHeader headerName="message">
  <simple>${body}</simple>
</setHeader>
<policy ref="PROPAGATION_REQUIRED">
  <!-- Transaction 1 -->
```

```
    <to uri="sql:insert into audit_log (message) values
            (:#message)"/>
    <to uri="mock:out1"/>
</policy>
<policy ref="PROPAGATION_REQUIRED">
  <!-- Transaction 2 -->
  <to uri="sql:insert into messages (message) values
            (:#message)"/>
  <to uri="mock:out2"/>
</policy>
```

In the Java DSL, the same routing logic can be expressed as:

```
from("direct:policies")
  .setHeader("message", body())
  .policy("PROPAGATION_REQUIRED") // Transaction 1
    .to("sql:insert into audit_log (message) values (:#message)")
    .to("mock:out1")
  .end()
  .policy("PROPAGATION_REQUIRED") // Transaction 2
    .to("sql:insert into messages (message) values (:#message)")
    .to("mock:out2")
  .end();
```

How it works...

In the preceding example, the route defines two separate transactions. When the end of the first `policy` block is reached, `Transaction 1` will be committed. When the exchange reaches the second `policy` block, a new transaction will be started. If an exception is thrown by the `mock:out2` endpoint, only `Transaction 2` will be rolled back.

The `policy` block defines a boundary around a series of processing steps with a "before" and "after" processing step being performed by an implementation of the `org.apache.camel.spi.Policy` interface. `SpringTransactionPolicy` implements this interface.

When referring to a `SpringTransactionPolicy` instance, a transaction will be initialized according to the propagation behavior that you have specified (see the *Using transactions with a database* recipe for an outline of the available options). When the `policy` block completes, the transaction will be completed as per the logic defined by that propagation behavior.

There's more...

The `policy` block is a general-purpose mechanism for scoping "before" and "after" behavior. Aside from transactions, it is also used by the Camel Shiro and Camel Spring Security Components (see *Authentication and authorization using Spring Security* in *Chapter 11, Security*) to allow you to define security constrains around processing steps.

Transactions may be *nested* using this mechanism by referring to different `SpringTransactionPolicy` objects. In the following example, we embed a non-transacted SQL insert into an `audit_log` table inside a wider transaction. An exception thrown by the `mock:out1` endpoint would remove the entry from the `messages` table, but not the `audit_log` table.

In the XML DSL, this is written as:

```
<route>
  <from uri="direct:policies"/>
  <setHeader headerName="message">
    <simple>${body}</simple>
  </setHeader>
  <policy ref="PROPAGATION_REQUIRED">
    <to uri="sql:insert into messages (message) values
            (:#message)"/>
    <to uri="direct:nestedPolicy"/>
    <to uri="mock:out1"/>
  </policy>
</route>

<route>
  <from uri="direct:nestedPolicy"/>
  <policy ref="PROPAGATION_NOT_SUPPORTED">
    <to uri="sql:insert into audit_log (message) values
            (:#message)"/>
    <to uri="mock:out2"/>
  </policy>
</route>
```

In the Java DSL, the same routing logic is expressed as:

```
from("direct:policies")
  .setHeader("message", simple("${body}"))
  .policy("PROPAGATION_REQUIRED")
    .to("sql:insert into messages (message) values (:#message)")
    .to("direct:nestedPolicy")
    .to("mock:out1")
```

```
      .end();

  from("direct:nestedPolicy")
    .policy("PROPAGATION_NOT_SUPPORTED")
      .to("sql:insert into audit_log (message) values (:#message)")
      .to("mock:out2")
    .end();
```

If nesting two transactions with the PROPAGATION_REQUIRES_NEW behavior, both `policy` blocks should refer to different `SpringTransactionPolicy` objects with the same behavior otherwise the second `policy` will have no impact:

```
  <bean id="PROPAGATION_REQUIRES_NEW"
        class="org.apache.camel.spring.spi.SpringTransactionPolicy">
    <property name="transactionManager"
              ref="transactionManager"/>
    <property name="propagationBehaviorName"
              value="PROPAGATION_REQUIRES_NEW"/>
  </bean>

  <bean id="PROPAGATION_REQUIRES_NEW-2"
        class="org.apache.camel.spring.spi.SpringTransactionPolicy">
    <property name="transactionManager"
              ref="transactionManager"/>
    <property name="propagationBehaviorName"
              value="PROPAGATION_REQUIRES_NEW"/>
  </bean>
```

The preceding two `policy` blocks are identical except for their `id` attributes. The following code example shows how you could reference the preceding `policy` definitions:

```
  <route>
    <from uri="direct:policies"/>
    <setHeader headerName="message">
      <simple>${body}</simple>
    </setHeader>
    <policy ref="PROPAGATION_REQUIRES_NEW">
      <to uri="sql:insert into messages (message) values
               (:#message)"/>
      <to uri="direct:nestedPolicy"/>
      <to uri="mock:out1"/>
    </policy>
  </route>

  <route>
    <from uri="direct:nestedPolicy"/>
```

```
<policy ref="PROPAGATION_REQUIRES_NEW-2">
  <to uri="sql:insert into audit_log (message) values
          (:#message)"/>
  <to uri="mock:out2"/>
</policy>
</route>
```

 If you intend to wrap all of the DSL statements in a route within a single `policy` block, it is much clearer to use a `transacted` statement instead.

Rolling back a transaction

So far we have seen transaction success or failure determined naturally—that is, by whether an exchange was successfully processed, or if an exception was thrown during its processing. This recipe will provide you with a number of additional options around controlling transaction rollback.

Getting ready

The Java code for this recipe is located in the `org.camelcookbook.transactions.` `rollback` package. The Spring XML files are located under `src/main/resources/META-INF/spring` and prefixed with `rollback`.

How to do it...

You can use the `rollback` DSL statement to throw an exception with an optional message.

In the XML DSL, we use the following code:

```
<from uri="direct:transacted"/>
<transacted/>
<setHeader headerName="message">
  <simple>${body}</simple>
</setHeader>
<to uri="sql:insert into audit_log (message) values (:#message)"/>
<choice>
  <when>
    <simple>${body} contains 'explode'</simple>
    <rollback message="Message contained word 'explode'"/>
  </when>
</choice>
```

In the Java DSL, the same thing is expressed as follows:

```
from("direct:transacted")
  .transacted()
  .setHeader("message", body())
  .to("sql:insert into audit_log (message) values (:#message)")
  .choice()
    .when(simple("${body} contains 'explode'"))
    .rollback("Message contained word 'explode'")
  .endChoice();
```

How it works...

When an exchange triggers a rollback, a `org.apache.camel.RollbackExchangeException` object is thrown with the message specified. This will cause the transaction error handler to rollback any transactions currently in progress for this exchange. The exception itself will be wrapped in an `org.apache.camel.CamelExecutionException` instance before being returned to the consuming endpoint.

Being a regular exception, a rollback may be caught by an `onException` block, such as:

```
.onException(RollbackExchangeException.class)
  .log("Caught rollback signal")
.end()
```

There's more...

You can trigger rollback behavior without an exception being thrown through the use of the `markRollbackOnly` statement. This will cause the exchange to stop being processed immediately, and any transactions currently in progress to be rolled back. Camel will consider the exchange's processing to have been successfully completed.

In the XML DSL, `markRollbackOnly` is an attribute of the `rollback` element:

```
<choice>
  <when>
    <simple>${body} contains 'explode'</simple>
    <rollback markRollbackOnly="true"/>
  </when>
</choice>
```

In the Java DSL, it is a DSL statement in its own right:

```
.choice()
  .when(simple("${body} contains 'explode'"))
    .markRollbackOnly()
.endChoice()
```

If you are nesting transactions, it is possible to roll back the current, or deepest, transaction only by using markRollbackOnlyLast. In the following example, a message that contains the word "explode" will cause the inner transaction, tx2, to be rolled back. No further processing will take place in route2, and so the exchange will not reach the mock:out2 endpoint. The exchange will, however, continue to be processed by route1, and will therefore be sent to the mock:out1 endpoint. The transaction tx1 will be committed successfully:

```xml
<route id="route1">
  <from uri="direct:route1"/>
  <setHeader headerName="message">
    <simple>${body}</simple>
  </setHeader>
  <policy ref="PROPAGATION_REQUIRES_NEW" id="tx1">
    <to uri="sql:insert into messages (message) values
            (:#message)"/>
    <to uri="direct:route2"/>
    <to uri="mock:out1"/>
  </policy>
</route>

<route id="route2">
  <from uri="direct:route2"/>
  <policy ref="PROPAGATION_REQUIRES_NEW-2" id="tx2">
    <to uri="sql:insert into audit_log (message) values
            (:#message)"/>
    <choice>
      <when>
        <simple>${body} contains 'explode'</simple>
        <rollback markRollbackOnlyLast="true"/>
      </when>
    </choice>
    <to uri="mock:out2"/>
  </policy>
</route>
```

In the Java DSL, the equivalent logic is expressed as:

```java
from("direct:route1").id("route1")
  .setHeader("message", simple("${body}"))
  .policy("PROPAGATION_REQUIRES_NEW").id("tx1")
    .to("sql:insert into messages (message) values (:#message)")
    .to("direct:route2")
    .to("mock:out1")
```

```
      .end();

from("direct:route2").id("route2")
  .policy("PROPAGATION_REQUIRES_NEW-2").id("tx2")
    .to("sql:insert into audit_log (message) values (:#message)")
    .choice()
      .when(simple("${body} contains 'explode'"))
        .markRollbackOnlyLast()
    .endChoice()
    .to("mock:out2")
  .end();
```

Using transactions with messaging

This recipe will show you how to set up transaction management over JMS for use within a Camel route, both for consuming and sending messages. This recipe will also detail the corner-case behaviors that you can expect from Camel when dealing with JMS transactions.

Getting ready

The Java code for this recipe is located in the `org.camelcookbook.transactions.` `jmstransaction` package. The Spring XML files are located under `src/main/resources/` `META-INF/spring` and prefixed with `jmsTransaction`.

As discussed in the *Introduction* section, Camel's transaction handling relies on the Spring's `PlatformTransactionManager` abstraction. Therefore, it is necessary to include the appropriate dependency in your application regardless of whether you are basing it on Spring or not—this includes regular Java as well as OSGi Blueprint applications.

To use Spring-managed JMS transactions you will require the following Maven dependencies:

```xml
<dependency>
  <groupId>org.apache.camel</groupId>
  <artifactId>camel-spring</artifactId>
  <version>${camel-version}</version>
</dependency>
<dependency>
  <groupId>org.springframework</groupId>
  <artifactId>spring-jms</artifactId>
  <version>${spring-version}</version>
</dependency>
```

How to do it...

There are two ways to do transactions with the JMS component: set the `transacted` option on the JMS Component, or configure the connection factory of the JMS client library to be transactional and use Camel's `transacted` DSL statement.

When we consume from JMS, we add the `transacted=true` attribute to the endpoint. Both the consumption of the message, and any subsequent sends using that component instance for the remainder of this route, will be transacted:

```
<from uri="jms:inbound?transacted=true"/>
<to uri="jms:outbound"/>
<to uri="mock:out"/>
```

A JMS message will not be sent to the `outbound` queue until after `mock:out` endpoint has been invoked and the exchange's processing completed.

The same route using the Java DSL is expressed as:

```
from("jms:inbound?transacted=true")
  .to("jms:outbound")
  .to("mock:out");
```

This is a quick, but limited mechanism, in that it does not allow us to vary transactional behavior within the route as discussed in the *Limiting the scope of a transaction* recipe.

To get more flexibility around transactional behavior, we need to wire up our classes as shown in the following figure:

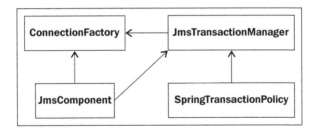

The `javax.jms.ConnectionFactory` class is the main point of entry to communicate with the message broker. Your broker vendor provides the actual class that you should use here.

The ActiveMQ Component is used to access an embedded message broker in these examples. It is a specialized type of JMS Component that is optimized for dealing specifically with ActiveMQ. It should be used in place of the JMS Component when dealing with an ActiveMQ broker.

The plain JMS Component is set up in the same way, except that the class used is `org.apache.camel.component.jms.JmsComponent`.

The steps to be performed for using transactions with JMS messaging are as follows:

1. Wire up your beans, in Spring, as follows:

```
<bean id="connectionFactory" class="...">
  <!-- specific to your broker -->
</bean>

<bean id="jmsTransactionManager"
      class="org.springframework.jms.connection
             .JmsTransactionManager">
  <property name="connectionFactory"
            ref="connectionFactory"/>
</bean>

<bean id="jms"
      class="org.apache.activemq.camel.component
             .ActiveMQComponent">
  <property name="connectionFactory"
            ref="connectionFactory"/>
  <property name="transactionManager"
            ref="jmsTransactionManager"/>
</bean>

<bean id="PROPAGATION_REQUIRED"
      class="org.apache.camel.spring.spi
             .SpringTransactionPolicy">
  <property name="transactionManager"
            ref="jmsTransactionManager"/>
  <property name="propagationBehaviorName"
            value="PROPAGATION_REQUIRED"/>
</bean>
```

The `SpringTransactionPolicy` instance contains on it a transaction propagation behavior, which is interpreted by the Spring framework. The `PROPAGATION_REQUIRED` value indicates that a transaction should be started if one is not already in progress, otherwise the transaction in progress should be used.

By convention, transaction policies are named after their propagation behavior. This convention is used by Camel to provide a sensible default configuration for transactions.

In Java, the same objects can be wired into a standalone Camel context as follows:

```
SimpleRegistry registry = new SimpleRegistry();
ConnectionFactory connectionFactory = ...;
registry.put("connectionFactory", connectionFactory);

JmsTransactionManager jmsTransactionManager =
    new JmsTransactionManager();
jmsTransactionManager.setConnectionFactory(
    connectionFactory);
registry.put("jmsTransactionManager",
            jmsTransactionManager);

SpringTransactionPolicy policy = new SpringTransactionPolicy();
policy.setTransactionManager(jmsTransactionManager);
policy.setPropagationBehaviorName("PROPAGATION_REQUIRED");
registry.put("PROPAGATION_REQUIRED", policy);

CamelContext camelContext = new DefaultCamelContext(registry);
ActiveMQComponent activeMQComponent =
    new ActiveMQComponent();
activeMQComponent.setConnectionFactory(connectionFactory);
activeMQComponent.setTransactionManager(
    jmsTransactionManager);
camelContext.addComponent("jms", activeMQComponent);
```

2. To engage the transaction manager that we have just wired up, instead of the `transacted=true` URI attribute, use the `transacted` DSL statement in your route.

   In the XML DSL, this is defined as follows:

```
<from uri="jms:inbound"/>
<transacted/>
<to uri="jms:outbound"/>
<to uri="mock:out"/>
```

   In the Java DSL, the same routing logic is expressed as follows:

```
from("jms:inbound")
  .transacted()
  .to("jms:outbound")
  .to("mock:out");
```

How it works...

The `transacted` statement uses conventions to provide sensible transaction behavior. Its processor will fetch a `SpringTransactionPolicy` named `PROPAGATION_REQUIRED` from Camel's registry. If none is defined, it will fetch a `PlatformTransactionManager` object and implicitly use `PROGAGATION_REQUIRED` behavior.

In the preceding code, the transacted processor will start a transaction using the `JmsTransactionManager`. Under the covers, it will fetch a JMS `Session` from the `ConnectionFactory` and set its JMS acknowledgement mode to `SESSION_TRANSACTED`. Any interaction with that endpoint for the remainder of the route, by this thread, will be through this transaction.

The processor will then set up Camel's `TransactionErrorHandler` to roll back transactions when an exception is thrown and not handled by another error handler.

If the exchange's processing is completed without any problems, the transaction will commit at the end of the route.

If an exception is thrown at any time in the route, the JMS consumer endpoint involved in a transaction will send a **negative acknowledgement**, or **NACK**, back to the message broker. This will either place the message into a **dead-letter queue** (**DLQ**), or mark the message for redelivery to this or another message consumer, depending on your broker's configuration.

 By default, the ActiveMQ broker, used in the JMS code examples, will send the message to a DLQ after attempting to redeliver the message 6 times.

Sending a message to a JMS producer endpoint engaged in a transaction will open a JMS `Session` in transactional mode, and issue a `send` operation via a JMS `MessageProducer` interface. The `Session` will not be committed, and therefore the message will not actually be sent, until the exchange has completed processing.

It is also possible to define a transaction as only spanning a portion of a route, or to change the transaction policy being used through the policy DSL statement. See the *Limiting the scope of a transaction* recipe for more details.

By and large, it is almost too easy for a JMS endpoint to become engaged in a transaction. This is due to the number of possible combinations in which transactional behavior can be switched on. The following section outlines the combinations that result in transactional behavior.

Consumption from a JMS endpoint will be transacted if:

- ▸ The endpoint contains the `transacted=true` attribute, OR
- ▸ The route defines a `policy` DSL block that refers to a `SpringTransactionPolicy` instance, which uses a `JmsTransactionManager` object that wraps the `ConnectionFactory` instance used by the endpoint, OR
- ▸ The route uses the `transacted` DSL statement, AND
  - ❑ No transaction manager is defined in the Camel context, OR
  - ❑ A `JmsTransactionManager` is defined in the Camel context and it wraps the `ConnectionFactory` being used by the endpoint

A send through a JMS producer endpoint will be transacted if:

- ▸ The route consumes messages using the same JMS endpoint and the endpoint uses the `transacted=true` attribute, OR
- ▸ A `JmsTransactionManager` is defined that wraps the `ConnectionFactory` being used by its endpoint, AND:
  - ❑ It is the only transaction manager defined in the Camel context and the route contains a `transacted` statement, OR
  - ❑ A `SpringTransactionPolicy` is defined that wraps the transaction manager, and it is referenced by a `policy` block that wraps the send, or a `transacted` DSL statement that precedes the send.

 To be truly satisfied that your transactional behavior works as expected, you should unit test it thoroughly.

There's more...

Sending an exchange using the `InOut` MEP to a JMS endpoint triggers *request-reply over messaging*. This is a mechanism that implements a remote service invocation using JMS as a transport. The mechanism is as follows:

1. A temporary queue is created by the JMS endpoint, on which the current thread will wait for a reply. The message broker automatically assigns the name of this queue. The endpoint may cache these queues between requests, which gives a considerable performance boost (the caching level is set via the `replyToCacheLevelName` endpoint attribute).

2. The contents of the exchange are then sent as the body of a JMS Message on the queue named in the endpoint (`outbound`). The name of the temporary queue (assigned by the message broker) is set in the `JMSReplyTo` header.

3. An external service picks up messages from the request queue (outbound) and processes them. If it has been specifically written to deal with request-response, it will send a new message to the temporary queue named in the request's JMSReplyTo header.

4. The message listener receives the response from the temporary queue and places its contents onto exchange, at which point it continues to be processed by the original thread.

 Any messages sent using the InOut MEP over a JMS endpoint do not participate in any transactions running with that component instance.

See also

▸ Camel JMS Component: http://camel.apache.org/jms.html

▸ ActiveMQ Camel Component: http://camel.apache.org/activemq.html

▸ Request reply: http://camel.apache.org/request-reply.html

Idempotency inside transactions

This recipe will show you how to wire up an idempotent consumer that uses a database as its repository for previously seen messages, within a route that uses transaction management with that same database.

This setup is used so that the persistence of message IDs by an idempotent consumer is not affected by the results of any database transactions in progress within the same route.

The net effect is a combination of the behaviors that we have already seen in the *Using transactions with a database* and *Preventing duplicate invocation of routing logic* recipes.

Getting ready

The Java code for this recipe is located in the org.camelcookbook.transactions. idempotentconsumerintransaction package. The Spring XML files are located under src/main/resources/META-INF/spring and prefixed with idempotentConsumerInTransaction.

How to do it...

To get idempotency inside transactions working, you need to perform the following high-level steps:

1. Set up transactional access over a `DataSource` as described in the *Using transactions with a database* recipe.

2. Set up a `JDBCIdempotentRepository` referencing the same `DataSource` with a `TransactionTemplate` that will manage its interaction independently of any other transactions that are in use.

3. Separate the idempotent consumer logic into its own route so that its transaction will be committed once that logic is performed.

In order to use this strategy, you need to wire together a number of classes as follows:

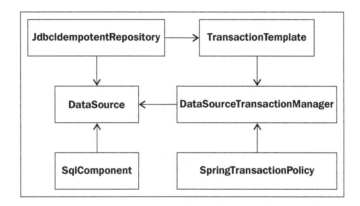

In detail, this is done as follows:

1. Set up a `DataSource` instance for transactional access. The `javax.sql.DataSource` class is the main entry point to your database—the actual class used here may come directly from your database vendor, or may be a database connection pool such as c3p0 (`http://www.mchange.com/projects/c3p0/`).

   In this example, a `DataSource` object will be instantiated that references the database used for audit records. This will be referred to as the `auditDataSource`.

   The following configuration wires up the necessary objects in Spring:

   ```
   <bean id="sql"
         class="org.apache.camel.component.sql.SqlComponent">
     <property name="dataSource"
               ref="auditDataSource"/>
   </bean>

   <bean id="transactionManager"
   ```

```
        class="org.springframework.jdbc.datasource
                .DataSourceTransactionManager">
    <property name="dataSource"
                ref="auditDataSource"/>
</bean>

<bean id="PROPAGATION_REQUIRED"
        class="org.apache.camel.spring.spi
                .SpringTransactionPolicy">
    <property name="transactionManager"
                ref="transactionManager"/>
    <property name="propagationBehaviorName"
                value="PROPAGATION_REQUIRED"/>
</bean>
```

If you are working in a Java environment, without Spring, this is done as follows:

```
SimpleRegistry registry =
    new SimpleRegistry(); // instantiate a registry
DataSource auditDataSource = ...; // defined by you

DataSourceTransactionManager transactionManager =
    new DataSourceTransactionManager(auditDataSource);
registry.put("transactionManager", transactionManager);

SpringTransactionPolicy propagationRequired =
    new SpringTransactionPolicy();
propagationRequired.setTransactionManager(
    transactionManager);
propagationRequired.setPropagationBehaviorName(
    "PROPAGATION_REQUIRED");
registry.put("PROPAGATION_REQUIRED", propagationRequired);
```

In Java, both `DataSourceTransactionManager` and `SpringTransactionPolicy` instances must be registered in Camel's object registry explicitly, as the transaction mechanism needs to obtain a reference to them. When using Spring, any bean defined in the `ApplicationContext` element is visible to Camel.

See the *Using transactions with a database* recipe for an explanation of propagation behaviors.

2. Instantiate a JDBC-based `IdempotentRepository` instance using the same `DataSource` object. In order to isolate its interactions with the database from any other transactions already in progress, we provide it with a Spring `TransactionTemplate`. This template will manage transactional access to the `DataSource` instance, applying the propagation behavior that we specify on it:

```
<bean id="transactionTemplate"
      class="org.springframework.transaction.support
             .TransactionTemplate">
  <property name="transactionManager"
            ref="transactionManager"/>
  <property name="propagationBehaviorName"
            value="PROPAGATION_REQUIRES_NEW"/>
</bean>
```

The behavior defined by `PROPAGATION_REQUIRES_NEW` is to start a new transaction. In practice, for a `DataSource`, this involves using a new JDBC `Connection`. This means that the template will use a JDBC `Connection` that is separate, and therefore transactionally isolated, from any others being used by this thread.

```
<bean id="jdbcIdempotentRepository"
      class="org.apache.camel.processor.idempotent.jdbc
             .JdbcMessageIdRepository">
  <constructor-arg ref="auditDataSource"/>
  <constructor-arg ref="transactionTemplate"/>
  <constructor-arg value="ws"/> <!-- processor name -->
</bean>
```

 Every `idempotentConsumer` that uses a database as the backing store requires its own instance of a `JdbcMessageIdRepository` with a different processor name. This value is used to distinguish a repository's records from that of others in a shared table.

In Java the same objects are wired into a standalone Camel context as follows:

```
TransactionTemplate transactionTemplate =
    new TransactionTemplate();
transactionTemplate.setTransactionManager(
    transactionManager);
transactionTemplate.setPropagationBehaviorName(
    "PROPAGATION_REQUIRES_NEW");

IdempotentRepository idempotentRepository =
    new JdbcMessageIdRepository(auditDataSource,
```

```
                              transactionTemplate,
                              "ws");
```

```java
CamelContext camelContext = new DefaultCamelContext(registry);
SqlComponent sqlComponent = new SqlComponent();
sqlComponent.setDataSource(auditDataSource);
camelContext.addComponent("sql", sqlComponent);
```

The `idempotentRepository` is not placed into the registry, as it needs to be supplied directly into the route definition in the Java DSL.

3. To ensure that any exceptions that happen after the `idempotentConsumer` block do not roll back the insert of the message key into the database, we must extract its logic into a separate route, which we invoke via an `enrich` statement. This behavior is explained in the *Preventing duplicate invocation of routing logic* recipe.

```xml
<route id="main">
  <from uri="direct:transacted"/>
  <transacted ref="PROPAGATION_REQUIRED"/>
  <setHeader headerName="message">
    <simple>${body}</simple>
  </setHeader>
  <to uri="sql:insert into audit_log (message) values
          (:#message)"/>
  <enrich uri="direct:invokeWs"/>
  <to uri="mock:out"/>
</route>
```

We then define the `idempotentConsumer` block with a reference to the `jdbcIdempotentRepository`. The repository instance has been configured with the transaction template that separates its activities from the outer transaction.

```xml
<route id="idempotentWs">
  <from uri="direct:invokeWs"/>
  <idempotentConsumer
      messageIdRepositoryRef=
        "jdbcIdempotentRepository">
    <header>messageId</header>
    <to uri="mock:ws"/>
  </idempotentConsumer>
</route>
```

 Only the work of the `idempotentConsumer` itself (that is, the insertion and removal of previously seen message keys), not any database access wrapped by it, operates in an independent transaction.

In the Java DSL, the same routing logic is written as follows:

```
from("direct:transacted").id("main")
  .transacted("PROPAGATION_REQUIRED")
  .setHeader("message", body())
  .to("sql:insert into audit_log (message) "
      + "values (:#message)")
  .enrich("direct:invokeWs")
  .to("mock:out");

from("direct:invokeWs").id("idempotentWs")
  .idempotentConsumer(header("messageId"),
                      idempotentRepository)
    .to("mock:ws")
  .end();
```

Both of the preceding sets of routing logic will insert the body of a message into an audit log table, and call a mock web service.

- If the `mock:out` endpoint throws an exception, the database insert will be rolled back, while the idempotent repository will maintain a record that the web service was invoked.

- If the call to the web service itself fails, both the database insert and the insert into the idempotent repository will be rolled back.

How it works...

In the preceding code, the `transacted` statement will start a transaction on a new JDBC `Connection` (`C1`) from the `DataSource` using the referenced `DataSourceTransactionManager` instance. Any interaction with the `DataSource` for the remainder of the main routing flow by this thread will be through this connection/transaction.

The processor will set up Camel's `TransactionErrorHandler` to roll back transactions when an exception is thrown and not handled by another error handler. This means that a commit/rollback will be performed on your behalf depending on the outcome of the exchange's processing.

When the message is handed to the `idempotentConsumer` block, this built-in Camel processor will fetch a new database connection (`C2`), and start a new transaction on it using the Spring `TransactionTemplate` provided on the `jdbcIdempotentRepository`. Interactions with the idempotent repository take place through this connection.

If there were any additional database interactions within the routing logic wrapped by the `idempotentConsumer` block in place of the send to `mock:ws` endpoint, these would be executed as part of the original transaction on `C1`.

The transaction used in dealing with the idempotent repository will be committed once the exchange is returned to the `enrich` processor from the `idempotentWs` route.

If the exchange's processing is completed without any problems, the original transaction will commit at the end of the `main` route.

There's more...

If you would like to wrap any database logic contained within the `idempotentConsumer` block within its own transaction, you should initiate a new transaction within the block as described in the *Limiting the scope of a transaction* recipe.

See also

- ▶ Camel Transactional Client: `http://camel.apache.org/transactional-client.html`
- ▶ The *Using transactions with a database* recipe
- ▶ The *Preventing duplicate invocation of routing logic* recipe
- ▶ The *Limiting the scope of a transaction* recipe

Setting up XA transactions over multiple transactional resources

Using the recipes discussed previously in this chapter, it is possible to set up multiple transactions in one route with many `transacted/policy` blocks each referring to a different transaction manager, each managing a different transactional resource. When an exchange's processing is completed, the various transaction managers are instructed to commit one-by-one. If one of them fails to commit, perhaps due to an inconveniently-timed outage, that failure may leave the other backends in an inconsistent state overall, with some already having been committed, and now unable to roll back.

To get around this, you can employ a single over-arching transaction manager to coordinate multiple backends through a standards-based scheme known as *XA transactions*. **eXtended Architecture** (**XA**) transaction are supported in Java through the **Java Transaction API** (**JTA**). To enable this, the resources being managed, databases or message brokers, must be able to have their interactions managed through XA's two-phase commit (2PC) protocol.

This recipe will show you how to set up an XA transaction manager to manage a single transaction across two resources—a database and a JMS message broker. The concepts discussed here can be built on to enable coordinated transactions between whatever combination of brokers and databases you require.

Getting ready

The Java code for this recipe is located in the `org.camelcookbook.transactions.xatransaction` package. The Spring XML files are located under `src/main/resources/META-INF/spring` and prefixed with `xaTransaction`.

The example shown here is based on Spring and the Camel XML DSL. A Java-only version that replicates the same steps described here is provided in the sample code in the `XATransactionTest` class.

> This example uses the Atomikos TransactionsEssentials® open source XA transaction manager due to its popularity, and abundance of documentation. The specifics of setting up other XA transaction managers, such as JOTM, will be quite different, although the end behavior in your Camel route should be the same.
>
> Servers based on the Java EE specification provide JTA/XA out of the box.

To use the Atomikos transaction manager, with support for JMS and JDBC, you will need the following Maven dependencies:

```
<dependency>
  <groupId>com.atomikos</groupId>
  <artifactId>transactions</artifactId>
  <version>${atomikos-version}</version>
</dependency>
<dependency>
  <groupId>com.atomikos</groupId>
  <artifactId>transactions-jdbc</artifactId>
  <version>${atomikos-version}</version>
</dependency>
<dependency>
  <groupId>com.atomikos</groupId>
  <artifactId>transactions-jms</artifactId>
  <version>${atomikos-version}</version>
</dependency>
```

The `${atomikos-version}` used here is `3.9.1`.

To use the Atomikos classes from your Camel application, you will additionally require the following Maven dependencies:

```
<dependency>
    <groupId>org.apache.camel</groupId>
    <artifactId>camel-spring</artifactId>
    <version>${camel-version}</version>
</dependency>
<dependency>
    <groupId>org.springframework</groupId>
    <artifactId>spring-tx</artifactId>
    <version>${spring-version}</version>
</dependency>
```

How to do it...

To get Atomikos-managed XA transactions working across a database and a JMS provider, we need to perform the following high-level steps:

1. Set up an XA-capable `DataSource`, and wrap it with an Atomikos bean that ties it into the XA transaction.

2. Set up an XA-capable `ConnectionFactory`, and wrap it with an Atomikos bean that ties it into the XA transaction.

3. Instantiate the Atomikos transaction classes, and wrap them with a Spring `PlatformTransactionManager` that will be used from Camel through a transaction policy.

4. Use the transaction policy from within a Camel route.

Due to the complexity of XA setups, it is *strongly recommended* that you unit test your configuration.

In order to use XA transactions that span a database and a message broker, we need to wire together a number of classes as follows:

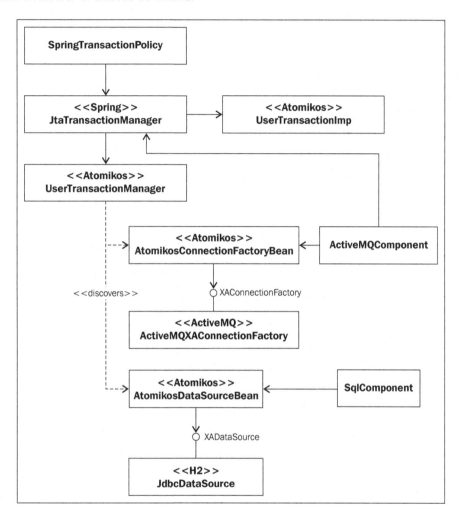

In detail, the wiring is performed as follows:

1. A `javax.sql.DataSource` class is the main entry point to your database. Your database vendor provides the actual class used here. In order for a database to participate in an XA transaction, the `DataSource` implementation needs to also implement the `javax.sql.XADataSource` interface.

   Here we use the H2 in-memory database:

   ```
   <bean id="xa.h2DataSource"
         class="org.h2.jdbcx.JdbcDataSource">
     <property name="URL"
               value="jdbc:h2:mem:db1;DB_CLOSE_DELAY=-1"/>
     <property name="user"
               value="sa"/>
     <property name="password"
               value=""/>
   </bean>
   ```

    If using a database connection pool, make sure that the size of the pool is at least that of the number of concurrent XA transactions that you expect to support. The reason for this is that each active database transaction makes use of a separate connection.

2. Each `XADataSource` resource that you want to engage in an XA transaction needs to be wrapped by an `AtomikosDataSourceBean` object. This bean is a delegate to the underlying `auditDataSource`, and will *automatically register* itself with the XA transaction manager:

   ```
   <bean id="atomikos.dataSource"
         class="com.atomikos.jdbc.AtomikosDataSourceBean">
     <property name="uniqueResourceName"
               value="xa.h2"/>
     <property name="xaDataSource"
               ref="xa.h2DataSource"/>
   </bean>
   ```

    If you would like to use multiple databases from within your route in an XA transaction, you would repeat this configuration step for each database's `DataSource`, assigning unique ids to each database's `DataSource` and each wrapping `AtomikosDataSource`.

   This bean will be the `DataSource` instance that you use from your SQL Component.

   ```
   <bean id="sql"
         class="org.apache.camel.component.sql.SqlComponent">
     <property name="dataSource"
               ref="atomikos.dataSource"/>
   </bean>
   ```

3. A `javax.jms.ConnectionFactory` class is the main entry point to using a JMS-based message broker. In order for a broker to be able to take part in an XA transaction, its `ConnectionFactory` implementation class needs to also implement the `javax.jms.XAConnectionFactory` interface.

   Here we use an embedded ActiveMQ broker:

> Note that for the purposes of XA transactions with ActiveMQ, we need to use a completely different `ConnectionFactory` implementation, instead of the usual `ActiveMQConnectionFactory`.

```xml
<bean id="xa.amqConnectionFactory"
    class="org.apache.activemq
            .ActiveMQXAConnectionFactory">
  <property name="brokerURL"
            value="vm://myEmbeddedBroker"/>
</bean>
```

4. Wrap the `ActiveMQXAConnectionFactory` object with an Atomikos-specific bean that also supports the `ConnectionFactory` interface. This step is required to make the factory visible to the transaction manager:

```xml
<bean id="atomikos.connectionFactory"
      class="com.atomikos.jms
              .AtomikosConnectionFactoryBean"
      init-method="init"
      destroy-method="close">
  <property name="uniqueResourceName"
            value="xa.activemq"/>
  <property name="xaConnectionFactory"
            ref="xa.amqConnectionFactory"/>
  <property name="maxPoolSize"
            value="10"/>
  <property name="ignoreSessionTransactedFlag"
            value="false"/>
</bean>
```

> If you would like to use multiple message brokers from within your route in an XA transaction, you would repeat this configuration step for each broker's `ConnectionFactory`, assigning unique IDs to each `ActiveMQXAConnectionFactory`, and to each wrapping `AtomikosConnectionFactory`.

This bean is the `ConnectionFactory` instance that should be used from your JMS/ActiveMQ Component:

```
<bean id="jms"
      class="org.apache.activemq.camel.component
             .ActiveMQComponent">
  <property name="connectionFactory"
            ref="atomikos.connectionFactory"/>
  <property name="transactionManager"
            ref="jta.transactionManager"/>
</bean>
```

The `jta.transactionManager` bean will be defined shortly.

5. Set up the Atomikos JTA transaction classes as follows:

```
<!-- javax.transaction.UserTransaction -->
<bean id="atomikos.userTransaction"
      class="com.atomikos.icatch.jta.UserTransactionImp">
  <property name="transactionTimeout"
            value="300" />
</bean>

<!-- javax.transaction.TransactionManager -->
<bean id="atomikos.transactionManager"
      class="com.atomikos.icatch.jta.UserTransactionManager"
      init-method="init"
      destroy-method="close"
      depends-on="atomikos.connectionFactory,
                  atomikos.dataSource">
  <property name="forceShutdown"
            value="false"/>
</bean>
```

While the transactional resources `atomikos.dataSource` and `atomikos.connectionFactory` are not explicitly registered with the `atomikos.transactionManager` bean, they do need to be added to the `depends-on attribute` of the transaction manager's Spring bean tag.

This ensures that any XA transactions that are in-flight are allowed to complete before Spring attempts to clean up the underlying resources on `ApplicationContext` shutdown.

6. Wrap these in a Spring JTA-aware `PlatformTransactionManager`. Camel uses the Spring transaction management abstractions as discussed in the *Introduction* section:

```
<bean id="spring.transactionManager"
      class="org.springframework.transaction.jta
            .JtaTransactionManager">
  <property name="transactionManager"
            ref="atomikos.transactionManager"/>
  <property name="userTransaction"
            ref="atomikos.userTransaction"/>
</bean>
```

7. Wrap the transaction manager in a `SpringTransactionPolicy` element, for use within the route:

```
<bean id="PROPAGATION_REQUIRED"
      class="org.apache.camel.spring.spi
            .SpringTransactionPolicy">
  <property name="transactionManager"
            ref="spring.transactionManager"/>
  <property name="propagationBehaviorName"
            value="PROPAGATION_REQUIRED"/>
</bean>
```

8. Use this policy (the `PROPAGATION_REQUIRED` bean id from step 7) in a route that consumes from one JMS queue (`inbound`), and inserts to a database and another JMS queue (`outbound`). Note that for the consumption to be transacted, we need to use the `transacted=true` attribute in the `from` endpoint's URI—Atomikos will very helpfully complain if you fail to do so.

```
<from uri="jms:inbound?transacted=true"/>
<transacted ref="PROPAGATION_REQUIRED"/>
<log message="Processing message: ${body}"/>
<setHeader headerName="message">
  <simple>${body}</simple>
</setHeader>
<to uri="sql:insert into audit_log (message) values
        (:#message)"/>
<to uri="jms:outbound"/>
<to uri="mock:out"/>
```

If an exception is thrown from the `mock:out` endpoint, the send to the outbound queue, and the insert into the database, will be rolled back. The message consumed from the inbound queue will be returned to ActiveMQ, which will attempt to redeliver it up to six times before sending it to a dead-letter queue, by default.

How it works...

The Atomikos XA transaction manager keeps a local log (journal) of transaction operations on disk for rollback purposes (this is not a strict requirement of all XA transaction managers). The transaction manager instructs any XA-aware resources (the database and the message broker) that they need to execute their operations within an externally-coordinated transaction. Both the broker and the database keep their own view of the transaction written to disk.

The database insert and the message send are performed but not yet committed.

Once all of the processing steps are complete, the transaction manager asks each resource whether it is capable of proceeding, that is, committing the transaction successfully. This is known as the prepare phase. During this phase, any responses received from the resources are written to disk by the Atomikos transaction manager.

If all the resources agree they are ready to commit, the transaction manager issues this instruction during the `commit` phase, persisting the fact that it did so, as well as any subsequent success or failure responses that it receives.

If the transaction fails at any time during this process, for example due to a resource outage, the transaction manager will tell all the resources to rollback to their previous state. If the transaction manager's process goes down, there is a recovery process defined by the XA standard that will followed by the Atomikos transaction manager based on the state that it has written to its journal on disk. This recovery process will again attempt to perform the transaction, or tell the resources to rollback.

The XA standard tries to provide a predicable set of outcomes for these various failure scenarios.

The communication involved in coordinating the various resources, and the logging of each step to a journal (disk forcing), take additional time over that of the actual routing logic. In the majority of cases, this is an acceptable trade-off to guarantee consistency. Information around tuning options can be found in the Atomikos documentation.

There's more...

An in-depth discussion of JTA/XA transactions, and the vast number of corner cases and failure scenarios, is beyond the scope this book. If you would like to find out more, refer to the XA Exposed article link given in the *See also* section for an excellent primer.

See also

▸ Atomikos TransactionsEssentials®: `http://www.atomikos.com/Main/TransactionsEssentials`

▸ Java Open Transaction Manager (JOTM), another JTA transaction manager implementation: `http://jotm.ow2.org`

▸ XA Exposed: `http://jroller.com/pyrasun/category/XA`

9
Testing

In this chapter, we will cover:

- ► Testing routes defined in Java
- ► Using mock endpoints to verify routing logic
- ► Replying from mock endpoints
- ► Testing routes defined in Spring
- ► Testing routes defined in OSGi Blueprint
- ► Auto-mocking of endpoints
- ► Validating route behavior under heavy load
- ► Unit testing processors and Bean Bindings
- ► Testing routes with fixed endpoints using AOP
- ► Testing routes with fixed endpoints using conditional events

Introduction

System integrations are traditionally a very difficult thing to test. Most commercial products, as well as home-cooked integrations, have no built-in support for automated testing. This usually results in verifying integration behavior through a manual approach involving triggering events/messages/requests from one window, and watching the end results in the affected systems. This approach has the following drawbacks:

- ► It is extremely time consuming, and inevitably leads to poor test coverage
- ► It is very difficult to test error conditions such as a system outage at just the wrong part of your integration flow

- ▸ It is complicated to verify the performance of integration code in isolation, as well as performing similar non-functional tests such as saturation testing

- ▸ It leaves no artifacts that can be used to detect regressions

Another fundamental problem with testing integrations using live backend systems is that it relies on the availability of those systems. This leaves your development workflow highly exposed to environment instability.

In most companies, the systems being integrated during development are often the test systems of other development teams. This means that they are likely to regularly be unavailable due to maintenance or code upgrades. The higher the number of systems being integrated, the greater the likelihood of any one of them is unavailable and prevents you from testing. This all-too-common scenario leaves teams scrambling for windows of opportunity when all their backends are up as the project deadline approaches.

Wouldn't it be nice if you could merely treat other systems as interfaces and test against those, rather than worrying about the physical implementations?

Camel comes with a built-in test kit that allows you to consider an integration to be just another set of code, in which backends are merely components that can be switched out for test versions.

This chapter covers the core elements of Camel that allow you to test your integrations, as well as providing some tips and techniques that should be applied given a set of circumstances.

If you have been looking at the example code from this book, you will have seen that the majority of the code is driven out of unit tests, and may have worked out which methods do what. This chapter and supporting samples focus exclusively on the JUnit framework, due to its overwhelming popularity among Java developers, being the de facto standard for unit testing. We will drill into the details of what is going on within Camel's support for JUnit so that you can then take that knowledge, and apply it to your testing framework of choice, regardless of whether Camel has explicit support for it or not.

The code for this chapter is contained within the `camel-cookbook-testing` module of the examples.

Testing routes defined in Java

This recipe will introduce you to the main parts of Camel's test support by showing you how to unit test a route defined within a `RouteBuilder` implementation. You will do this without relying on external systems to verify the interactions.

You will see how:

- ▸ The Camel framework gets set up and torn down

- ▶ Mock endpoints can be used to verify the message flow, through an **expect-run-verify** cycle, which should be familiar to those who have worked with mocking frameworks such as **EasyMock** (`http://www.easymock.org`) in the past

- ▶ Messages can be sent to endpoints from outside of Camel, allowing us to trigger routes with a range of payloads in order to verify the edge cases

Getting ready

To use Camel's core test support, you need to add a dependency for the `camel-test` library, which provides the support classes for JUnit testing as well as a transitive dependency on JUnit itself.

Add the following code to the dependencies section of your Maven POM:

```
<dependency>
  <groupId>org.apache.camel</groupId>
  <artifactId>camel-test</artifactId>
  <version>${camel-version}</version>
  <scope>test</scope>
</dependency>
```

The Java code for this recipe is located in the `org.camelcookbook.examples.testing.java` package.

How to do it...

Let us test a simple route defined as follows:

```
public class SimpleTransformRouteBuilder extends RouteBuilder {
  @Override
  public void configure() throws Exception {
    from("direct:in")
      .transform(simple("Modified: ${body}"))
      .to("mock:out");
  }
}
```

The route consumes messages from an in-memory `direct:` endpoint, prepends the message body with the string `Modified:` and sends the result to a `mock:` endpoint.

To test this class, perform the following steps:

1. Create a test class that extends `org.apache.camel.test.junit4.`
   `CamelTestSupport`:

   ```
   public class SimpleTransformRouteBuilderTest
       extends CamelTestSupport {
     //...
   }
   ```

   The `CamelTestSupport` class is an abstract class that is responsible for
   instantiating the Camel context for the routes under test, creating utility
   objects, and injecting annotated properties into the test.

2. Override the `createRouteBuilder()` method, and instantiate your
   `RouteBuilder` implementation to be tested:

   ```
   @Override
   protected RouteBuilder createRouteBuilder()
       throws Exception {
     return new SimpleTransformRouteBuilder();
   }
   ```

3. Define the body of the test. Here, the `MockEndpoint` testing DSL is used to
   outline the messages that you expect an endpoint to receive. A test message is
   sent into the route via a `ProducerTemplate` instance provided for you by the
   `CamelTestSupport` base class. Finally, you assert that the expectations set
   on the mock endpoints in the Camel context were satisfied:

   ```
   @Test
   public void testPayloadIsTransformed()
       throws InterruptedException {
     MockEndpoint mockOut = getMockEndpoint("mock:out");
     mockOut.setExpectedMessageCount(1);
     mockOut.message(0).body().isEqualTo("Modified: Cheese");

     template.sendBody("direct:in", "Cheese");

     assertMockEndpointsSatisfied();
   }
   ```

   The `assertMockEndpointsSatisfied()` method is a catch-all helper method
   that checks that all mock endpoints within your route(s) are satisfied. You can verify
   that the expectations of individual mock endpoints have been met with `mockOut.`
   `assertIsSatisfied()`, where `mockOut` is replaced with a variable referencing
   your mock endpoint.

 If an assertion on a `MockEndpoint` fails, it will throw a
`java.lang.AssertionError` in your test code when
you check to see if it is satisfied.

As an alternative to explicitly fetching mocks, and referring to endpoints in each unit test, you can request an autoinjected `MockEndpoint` and `ProducerTemplate` by defining them as bean properties, and annotating them as follows:

```
@EndpointInject(uri = "mock:out")
private MockEndpoint mockOut;

@Produce(uri = "direct:in")
private ProducerTemplate in;
```

How it works...

The `CamelTestSupport` class is a convenience base class that prepares a Camel environment for your JUnit tests, without requiring that you repeatedly perform a number of repetitive steps every time you want to test a route.

As you can see from the preceding example, all that you need to do in order to set up a test is to override a base method `createRouteBuilder()`, and specify which properties you would like injected. Fundamentally, the base support class will perform the following:

 ▸ Start a Camel context before each test, adding any routes that you have specified through `createRouteBuilder()`, or `createRouteBuilders()` when testing multiple `RouteBuilder` implementations as part of a single test
 ▸ Inject any properties that you have annotated with `@Produce` and `@EndpointInject`
 ▸ Stop the Camel context after each test

If you want to reproduce the preceding behavior from **first principles**, that is without the support class, you first define a `CamelContext` variable as a private member of your test:

```
private CamelContext camelContext;
```

Before each test, instantiate the context, and initialize it with the `RouteBuilder` class under test:

```
@Before
public void setUpContext() throws Exception {
  this.camelContext = new DefaultCamelContext();
  camelContext.addRoutes(new SimpleTransformRouteBuilder());
  camelContext.start();
}
```

After each test method, shut down the Camel context:

```
@After
public void cleanUpContext() throws Exception {
  camelContext.stop();
}
```

You then need to access the Camel context directly, through your private variable, in order to obtain handles on mock endpoints and producer template:

```
MockEndpoint out =
    camelContext.getEndpoint("mock:out", MockEndpoint.class);
ProducerTemplate producerTemplate =
    camelContext.createProducerTemplate();
```

This first principles approach is useful when you are testing from a framework other than JUnit or TestNG (both of which are supported by Camel), or if for some reason you need to extend a base class that itself does not extend CamelTestSupport. This approach is not used that often, as extending Camel's test support classes has proven easier and has become a best practice.

There's more...

Testing routes that consume from a direct: endpoint and produce messages to mock: endpoints is easy. In real life though, your routes will be consuming from, and producing to, endpoint technologies such as CXF for SOAP services (see *Chapter 12, Web Services*), and ActiveMQ for messaging. How then do you go about testing that type of route?

The *Reusing routing logic through template routes* recipe in *Chapter 1, Structuring Routes* describes a technique for externalizing endpoints. This allows you to inject *real* endpoints when your route is deployed, and use direct: and mock: for testing when you instantiate your RouteBuilder in createRouteBuilder() method.

To do this, the previous RouteBuilder implementation should be modified as follows:

```
public class SimpleTransformDIRouteBuilder extends RouteBuilder {
  private String sourceUri;
  private String targetUri;

  // setters omitted

  @Override
  public void configure() throws Exception {
    from(sourceUri)
      .transform(simple("Modified: ${body}"))
      .to(targetUri);
  }
}
```

Then, all that is required to test the route is to inject the `direct:` and `mock:` endpoints inside the test class:

```
@Override
protected RouteBuilder createRouteBuilder() throws Exception {
  SimpleTransformDIRouteBuilder routeBuilder =
    new SimpleTransformDIRouteBuilder();
  routeBuilder.setSourceUri("direct:in");
  routeBuilder.setTargetUri("mock:out");
  return routeBuilder;
}
```

> Be careful when substituting endpoint technologies in this manner. Components may send in object types within exchanges that are different from those that you expected when writing your route. The unit testing of integrations should always be complemented with some integration testing using actual backend systems and their corresponding Camel Components.

There are further base methods within `CamelTestSupport` that you can override to define the details of how the Camel context will be set up. These are all prefixed with `create..()`.

You can override the `createCamelContext()` method to set up the Camel context in such a way that you can test with components that are not embedded in Camel's core library (`activemq:`, `cxf:`, `twitter:`, `leveldb:`, and so on). The following example configures the ActiveMQ Component for use in your tests:

```
@Override
public CamelContext createCamelContext() {
  CamelContext context = new DefaultCamelContext();

  ActiveMQComponent activeMQComponent = new ActiveMQComponent();
  activeMQComponent.setBrokerURL("vm:embeddedBroker");

  context.addComponent("activemq", activeMQComponent);

  return context;
}
```

See also

- Camel Test: http://camel.apache.org/camel-test.html
- Camel Mock Component: http://camel.apache.org/mock.html
- JUnit: http://junit.org/

Using mock endpoints to verify routing logic

The ability to verify message flow using mock endpoints was built into the Camel framework from its inception. The Mock Component in the `camel-core` library provides you with a testing DSL that allows you to verify which messages have reached various named `mock:` endpoints defined in your route. This recipe will describe how to make use of this mock DSL.

Getting ready

To use this recipe you should first have a route test set up as described in the *Testing routes defined in Java* recipe.

The Java code for this recipe is located in the `org.camelcookbook.examples.testing.mockreply` package.

How to do it...

To use mock endpoints, perform the following steps:

1. Within your route, use a `mock:` endpoint URI in any Camel DSL statement that produces a message to an endpoint, such as `to(..)` or `wireTap(..)`:

   ```
   from("direct:start")
     .choice()
       .when().simple("${body} contains 'Camel'")
         .setHeader("verified").constant(true)
         .to("mock:camel")
       .otherwise()
         .to("mock:other")
     .end();
   ```

2. Load the route into a Camel context, by overriding the `CamelTestSupport` class's `createRouteBuilder()` method, and start it as described in the *Testing routes defined in Java* recipe.

3. Obtain a `MockEndpoint` from the Camel context that corresponds to the `mock:` endpoint URI you want to verify against.

   If you are extending `CamelTestSupport`, you can obtain the endpoint as follows:

   ```
   MockEndpoint mockCamel = getMockEndpoint("mock:camel");
   ```

   If you are working from first principles, do the following:

   ```
   MockEndpoint mockCamel =
       camelContext.getEndpoint(
           "mock:camel", MockEndpoint.class);
   ```

4. Use the `MockEndpoint` to define the number and content of the messages that you expect to reach the endpoint once you exercise the route:

    ```
    mockCamel.expectedMessageCount(1);
    mockCamel.message(0).body().isEqualTo("Camel Rocks");
    mockCamel.message(0).header("verified").isEqualTo(true);
    ```

5. Send messages into the route through a `ProducerTemplate`:

    ```
    template.sendBody("direct:start", "Camel Rocks");
    ```

6. Verify that the expectations that you set on the mocks were met:

    ```
    mockCamel.assertIsSatisfied();
    ```

 This general pattern of setting expectations on an injected mock object (endpoint in this case), testing the code, and checking the results is known as an **expect-run-verify** cycle.

How it works...

A `MockEndpoint` is instantiated once when the Camel context is started, and collects all of the exchanges sent to it until the mock is destroyed. Any expectations defined on it are verified against that state.

 As `MockEndpoint` instances are stateful, it is essential that the Camel context be recreated between tests. If the Camel context is not recreated, then assertions against these mock endpoints may fail, as they still contain state from the previous test runs. For example, your number of messages expected assertion will fail as the mock will have gathered all of the messages from the last test run as well as the current run.

The methods on a `MockEndpoint` can broadly be categorized as **expectations** or **assertions**:

▶ **Expectations** are defined *before* a mock is used (that is, before messages are sent to the route containing those mocks), and outline the expected state that the mock should accumulate by the end of the test.

▶ **Assertions** are evaluated *after* the mock has been used, and are used to verify that the expectations have been met. They are also used to evaluate conditions against the total set of the mock's accumulated state.

Expectation method names begin with `expect..()`, and aside from the examples already shown, include methods such as the following:

```
expectedBodiesReceived(Object...)
expectedBodiesReceivedInAnyOrder(Object...)
expectedFileExists(String)
expectedMessageMatches(Predicate)
expectedMinimumMessageCount(int)
```

The `message(int)` statement allows you to define expectations on individual messages, including evaluating expressions on any part of the exchange, as well as answering timing questions:

```
mock.message(0).simple("${header[verified]} == true");
mock.message(0).arrives().noLaterThan(50).millis().beforeNext();
```

Assertions allow you to verify that the expectations were met, as well as assessing the entire set of messages sent to an endpoint during a test. These methods are prefixed by `assert..()`, and include the following:

```
assertIsSatisfied()
assertIsSatisfied(int timeoutForEmptyEndpoints)
assertIsNotSafisfied()
assertMessagesAscending(Expression)
assertMessagesDescending(Expression)
assertNoDuplicates(Expression)
```

There are many more `assert` and `expect` methods available to you other than those covered here. Take a look at the `MockEndpoint` JavaDocs for more information.

There's more...

A `MockEndpoint` instance grants you access to the set of exchanges it received during a test run. This is useful when you want to compare `Exchange` objects received by the endpoint, or verify the mechanical behavior of a route by inspecting the internal state of an individual exchange.

The following code tests whether a particular header is the same for two `Exchange` objects:

```
List<Exchange> receivedExchanges = mock.getReceivedExchanges();
Exchange exchange0 = receivedExchanges.get(0);
Exchange exchange1 = receivedExchanges.get(1);
// JUnit assertion
assertEquals(exchange0.getIn().getHeader("verified"),
             exchange1.getIn().getHeader("verified"));
```

This mechanism is useful for testing such things as exchange equality, or inspecting graphs of objects associated with the message.

 You should only access received exchanges after calling `endpoint.assertIsSatisfied()`.

You can also combine the fetching of an individual exchange with the assertion that it was received through use of the `assertExchangeReceived(int)` helper method. The preceding code could be rewritten as:

```
Exchange exchange0 = mock.assertExchangeReceived(0);
Exchange exchange1 = mock.assertExchangeReceived(1);
assertEquals(exchange0.getIn().getHeader("verified"),
             exchange1.getIn().getHeader("verified"));
```

See also

▸ Camel Mock Component: `http://camel.apache.org/mock.html`

▸ The `ProducerTemplate` interface: `http://camel.apache.org/producertemplate.html`

▸ The `MockEndpoint` interface: `http://camel.apache.org/maven/current/camel-core/apidocs/org/apache/camel/component/mock/MockEndpoint.html`

Replying from mock endpoints

It is common that many of your integrations will call out to endpoints from which you will expect a reply, such as when invoking a web service. We saw how mock endpoints could be used to assess message content in a test in the *Using mock endpoints to verify routing logic* recipe. We will now use those same endpoints to define the test responses.

Getting ready

To use this recipe you should first have a route test set up as described in the *Testing routes defined in Java* recipe.

The Java code for this recipe is located in the `org.camelcookbook.examples.testing.mockreply` package.

How to do it...

In the following route, we have a mock endpoint from which we would like a response:

```
from("direct:in")
  .inOut("mock:replying")
  .to("mock:out");
```

To test this, get a handle to the mock endpoint that you want to simulate a reply from, as described in the *Testing routes defined in Java* recipe. Before a message is sent into the route, define how you want the endpoint to respond through the `whenAnyExchangeReceived(Processor)` method:

```
mockReplying.whenAnyExchangeReceived(new Processor() {
  @Override
  public void process(Exchange exchange) throws Exception {
    Message in = exchange.getIn();
    in.setBody("Hey " + in.getBody());
  }
});
```

How it works...

The `Processor` instance that you have provided to the mock endpoint will be called for every exchange that reaches that mock endpoint. This can be thought of as the default reply. On top of this, you can specify that you want a different processor to be engaged for a particular message. In the following example, we specify a different processor to be used for the first message received; all other messages received will use the processor provided in the previous call to `whenExchangeReceived`:

```
mockReplying.whenExchangeReceived(1, new Processor() {
  @Override
  public void process(Exchange exchange) throws Exception {
    Message in = exchange.getIn();
    in.setBody("Czesc " + in.getBody()); // Polish
  }
});
```

 The number here is 1-indexed, where 1 indicates the first message to flow through the route. This can easily trip you up, as most people are in the habit of thinking of 0 as the first item.

Using a processor gives you maximum flexibility with what you can do when manipulating responses. It may be, however, that what you want to do can be described with a Camel Expression. In this case, the following approach might be more straightforward:

```
mockReplying.returnReplyBody(
    SimpleBuilder.simple("Hello ${body}"));
```

You can also set a header as the reply from an endpoint.

```
mockReplying.returnReplyHeader("someHeader",
    ConstantLanguage.constant("Hello"));
```

You cannot use the two `returnReply..()` methods on the same endpoint in the same test, as the second one will override the first. If you want to set a header *and* body, use the processor approach instead.

> You may be used to having Expression Languages at your fingertips when writing a `RouteBuilder` implementations. Since test classes do not usually extend this base class, you have to use the static methods defined on the individual expression language classes directly. For example:
>
> ```
> import static org.apache.camel.language.simple.
> SimpleLanguage.simple;
> ```

See also

▸ Processor: `http://camel.apache.org/processor.html`
▸ Camel Mock Component: `http://camel.apache.org/mock.html`

Testing routes defined in Spring

This recipe expands on the core testing capabilities described so far by detailing the steps needed to test Camel routes defined using the XML DSL in a Spring application. You will learn how to assemble a test harness that replaces parts of the application in order to test your routes outside a deployment environment, including the substitution of Spring `${..}` placeholders with test values.

Getting ready

The Java code for this recipe is located in the `org.camelcookbook.examples.testing.spring` package. The Spring XML files are located under `src/main/resources/META-INF/spring`.

To use Camel's Spring test support, you need to add a dependency for the `camel-test-spring` library that provides the support classes for JUnit testing of Spring as well as a transitive dependency on JUnit itself.

Add the following to the `dependencies` section of your Maven POM:

```xml
<dependency>
  <groupId>org.apache.camel</groupId>
  <artifactId>camel-test-spring</artifactId>
  <version>${camel-version}</version>
  <scope>test</scope>
</dependency>
```

How to do it...

Consider the following route, defined in the file located in `/META-INF/spring/simpleTransform-context.xml`:

```xml
<route>
  <from uri="direct:in"/>
  <transform>
    <simple>Modified: ${body}</simple>
  </transform>
  <log message="Set message to ${body}"/>
  <to uri="mock:out"/>
</route>
```

To test this route, perform the following steps:

1. Create a test class that extends `org.apache.camel.test.spring.CamelSpringTestSupport`:

   ```java
   public class SimpleTransformSpringTest
       extends CamelSpringTestSupport {
     //...
   }
   ```

   The `CamelSpringTestSupport` class is an abstract class that is responsible for instantiating the Camel context with the routes under test, creating utility objects, and injecting annotated properties into the test.

2. Override the `createApplicationContext()` method from `CamelSpringTestSupport` and instantiate a Spring application context that loads the files containing the Camel routes under test:

```
@Override
protected AbstractApplicationContext
    createApplicationContext() {
  return new ClassPathXmlApplicationContext(
      "/META-INF/spring/simpleTransform-context.xml");
}
```

3. Define the body of the test. Use the `MockEndpoint` testing DSL to set expectations about the message you plan to receive during testing. A message is sent into the route via a `ProducerTemplate` instance provided for you by the `CamelTestSupport` class. Finally, assert that the expectations set on the mock endpoint were satisfied:

```
@Test
public void testPayloadIsTransformed()
    throws InterruptedException {
  MockEndpoint mockOut = getMockEndpoint("mock:out");
  mockOut.setExpectedMessageCount(1);
  mockOut.message(0).body().isEqualTo("Modified: Cheese");

  template.sendBody("direct:in", "Cheese");

  assertMockEndpointsSatisfied();
}
```

As an alternative to explicitly fetching mocks, and referring to endpoints in each unit test, you can request an autowired `MockEndpoint` and `ProducerTemplate`. These are defined as bean properties, and annotated as follows:

```
@EndpointInject(uri = "mock:out")
private MockEndpoint mockOut;

@Produce(uri = "direct:in")
private ProducerTemplate in;
```

How it works...

The `CamelSpringTestSupport` class is a convenience class that provides *feature-parity* with the `CamelTestSupport` class described in the *Testing routes defined in Java* recipe. It is responsible for performing the boilerplate work required to test Camel routes defined within Spring configuration files. At its most basic, the class will do the following:

- Start a Spring application defined by the context returned from `createApplicationContext()` *before each test*.

- Inject any properties that you have annotated with `@Produce`, `@EndpointInject`, or Spring's `@Autowired`. The last one allows your test code to get a handle on any object defined within the Spring application.

- Shut down the Spring application at the end of each test.

Feature-parity with `CamelTestSupport` means that aside from the implementation of a different base method to the Java testing example (`createApplicationContext()` versus `createRouteBuilder()` or `createRouteBuilders()`), `CamelSpringTestSupport` allows the test methods themselves to be written in exactly the same manner as their Java DSL equivalents. Both classes provide access to the same protected variables (`context` and `template`), and honor the same test lifecycle.

The testing method described has a drawback—it requires that a Camel base class is extended. This may not be something that you would like if you want to use another class as the base for your tests. To cater for this, Camel provides what is known as the **Enhanced Spring Test** option.

To make use of this, your test uses the JUnit 4 Runner functionality that allows a custom class to manage the lifecycle of a test. The rewritten test class appears as follows:

```
@RunWith(CamelSpringJUnit4ClassRunner.class)
@ContextConfiguration({
    "/META-INF/spring/simpleTransform-context.xml"})
public class SimpleTransformSpringRunnerTest {
  //...
}
```

As no base class is extended, your tests no longer have access to the protected variables, or utility methods such as `assertMockEndpointsSatisfied()` that are provided by `CamelSpringTestSupport`. The workaround for this is fairly straightforward. The Camel context is injected via the `@Autowired` annotation, just as any other Spring object:

```
@Autowired
private CamelContext camelContext;
```

When using Enhanced Spring Tests you invoke the static `MockEndpoint.`
`assertIsSatisfied()` utility method to assert that all the mock endpoints
in the Camel context interface were satisfied:

```
@Test
public void testPayloadIsTransformed()
    throws InterruptedException {
  mockOut.setExpectedMessageCount(1);
  mockOut.message(0).body().isEqualTo("Modified: Cheese");

  producerTemplate.sendBody("Cheese");

  MockEndpoint.assertIsSatisfied(camelContext);
}
```

One thing to watch out for is that the Enhanced Spring Tests have a
different test lifecycle than those extending `CamelSpringTestSupport`.
Instead of setting up and tearing down the entire Spring application
between tests, *by default, the Spring application is set up once only at the
start of the test class*. This impacts the mock endpoints in classes with
more than one test method, as these are not reset to their initial state
between tests.

To get around this, add the following class annotation to the test:

```
@DirtiesContext(
    classMode=ClassMode.AFTER_EACH_TEST_METHOD)
```

There's more...

Spring applications are usually broken up into multiple context files that address a particular
fragment of an application each—you would generally see one file per horizontal application
tier, or per vertical stack, of functionality. By making use of this approach, you can substitute
alternative Spring configuration files when assembling your tests to replace portions of an
application. This allows you to stub out objects used in your routes that may be difficult to wire
up in a test environment.

It is usually a good idea to keep your `PropertyPlaceholderConfigurer` configuration in
a different Spring XML file from your routes. This allows you to plug in a test version of those
properties for testing.

We can use this particular mechanism to fully externalize our route endpoints, and use dependency injection to make the route more easily testable. Consider the following example:

```
<camelContext xmlns="http://camel.apache.org/schema/spring">
  <propertyPlaceholder id="properties"
                       location="ref:ctx.properties"/>
  <route>
    <from uri="{{start.endpoint}}"/>
    <transform>
      <simple>Modified: ${body}</simple>
    </transform>
    <log message="Set message to ${body}"/>
    <to uri="{{end.endpoint}}"/>
  </route>
</camelContext>
```

By providing an alternative `PropertyPlaceholderConfigurer` instance–defined as a bean with an `id` of `ctx.properties`–in a test file in a test file, we can exercise the route using `direct:` and `mock:` endpoints, while referring to the actual technology endpoints in the production configuration.

Using this approach of substituting in test endpoints, you are validating the logic of the route, and not the behavior of the route with the actual components. This may give you a false sense of security, as the routing logic may not work in the same way when the real endpoints are in use. For example, a consumer endpoint may use a different type of object in the exchange body than what your substituted test endpoint provides, and this will subtlety change your logic.

This sort of testing should always be used in conjunction with an integration test that exercises the real endpoints.

The following example uses the Spring `util` and `context` namespaces for brevity to substitute test endpoints into the preceding route:

```
<util:properties id="ctx.properties"
                 location="classpath:spring/test.properties"/>
<context:property-placeholder properties-ref="ctx.properties" />
```

The `test.properties` file contains the test versions of the properties:

```
start.endpoint=direct:in
end.endpoint=mock:out
```

Splitting out the `PropertyPlaceholderConfigurer` configuration into a different file is particularly useful if the file containing your Camel context definition also contains other beans that need properties injected.

It is a good practice to place any beans that have complex dependencies, or could be considered services, in a separate configuration file to your routes. This makes it easy to provide an alternative version of those beans in your test by providing a different version of that file to the test runtime.

You can alternatively feed properties directly into the context through the `Properties` component by overriding the following method from `CamelTestSupport`:

```
@Override
protected Properties
    useOverridePropertiesWithPropertiesComponent() {
  Properties properties = new Properties();
  properties.setProperty("start.endpoint", "direct:in");
  properties.setProperty("end.endpoint", "mock:out");
  return properties;
}
```

If your `propertyPlaceholder` refers to properties files that are not discoverable at test time, you can instruct the framework to ignore the error instead of throwing an exception that would prevent the Camel context from starting up. You do this by overriding the following method in your test:

```
@Override
protected Boolean ignoreMissingLocationWithPropertiesComponent() {
  return true;

}
```

See also

▸ Spring Testing: `http://camel.apache.org/spring-testing.html`

▸ Properties Component: `http://camel.apache.org/properties.html`

▸ JUnit: `http://junit.org/`

▸ The *Auto-mocking of endpoints* recipe

▸ The *Testing routes with fixed endpoints using AOP* recipe

▸ The *Testing routes with fixed endpoints using conditional events* recipe

Testing routes defined in OSGi Blueprint

This recipe expands on the core testing capabilities described so far by detailing the steps needed to test Camel routes defined using the XML DSL in an OSGi Blueprint application. You will learn how to assemble a test harness that replaces parts of the application in order to test your routes outside an OSGi deployment environment, including the substitution of OSGI Configuration Admin service ${..} placeholders with test values. Camel allows Blueprint-based routes to be tested outside of an OSGI container, through a project called PojoSR that makes it possible to test the code without deploying it.

Getting ready

To use Camel's Blueprint test support, you need to add a dependency for the `camel-test-blueprint` library that provides the support classes for JUnit testing of Blueprint as well as a transitive dependency on JUnit itself.

Add the following to the `dependencies` section of your Maven POM:

```
<dependency>
  <groupId>org.apache.camel</groupId>
  <artifactId>camel-test-blueprint</artifactId>
  <version>${camel-version}</version>
  <scope>test</scope>
</dependency>
```

The Java code for this recipe is located in the `org.camelcookbook.examples.testing.blueprint` package. The Blueprint XML files are located under `src/main/resources/OSGI-INF/blueprint`.

How to do it...

Consider the following route, defined in `simpleTransform-context.xml`:

```
<blueprint
    xmlns="http://www.osgi.org/xmlns/blueprint/v1.0.0"
    xmlns:xsi="http://www.w3.org/2001/XMLSchema-instance"
    xsi:schemaLocation="
      http://www.osgi.org/xmlns/blueprint/v1.0.0
        http://www.osgi.org/xmlns/blueprint/v1.0.0/blueprint.xsd
      http://camel.apache.org/schema/blueprint
        http://camel.apache.org/schema/blueprint/
        camel-blueprint.xsd">
  <camelContext xmlns="http://camel.apache.org/schema/blueprint">
    <route>
```

```
    <from uri="direct:in"/>
    <transform>
      <simple>{{transform.message}}: ${body}</simple>
    </transform>
    <to uri="mock:out"/>
  </route>
</camelContext>
</blueprint>
```

Here, we use a placeholder to fetch the transform message. We define an OSGi Configuration Admin property placeholder in a file alongside it, located in `simpleTransform-properties-context.xml` (namespace declarations partially shown):

```
<blueprint ...
    xmlns:cm="http://aries.apache.org/blueprint/xmlns/
              blueprint-cm/v1.0.0"
    xsi:schemaLocation="...
      http://aries.apache.org/blueprint/xmlns/blueprint-cm/v1.0.0
        http://aries.apache.org/schemas/blueprint-cm/
        blueprint-cm-1.0.0.xsd">
  <cm:property-placeholder
      persistent-id="org.camelcookbook.testing">
    <cm:default-properties>
      <cm:property name="transform.message"
                   value="Modified"/>
    </cm:default-properties>
  </cm:property-placeholder>
</blueprint>
```

> It is a good practice to place any beans that have complex dependencies, or could be considered services, in a separate configuration file from your routes. This makes it easy to provide an alternative version of those beans in your test by providing a different version of that file to the test runtime.

To test this route, perform the following steps:

1. Create a test class that extends `org.apache.camel.test.blueprint.CamelBlueprintTestSupport`:

```
public class SimpleTransformBlueprintTest
    extends CamelBlueprintTestSupport {
  //...
}
```

The `CamelBlueprintTestSupport` class is an abstract class that is responsible for instantiating the Camel context with the routes under test, creating utility objects, and setting up a simulated OSGi environment. To test a route, override the `getBlueprintDescriptor()` method, and return the Blueprint configuration files that contain the Camel routes under test, as well as any support beans, as a *comma-separated string*:

```
@Override
protected String getBlueprintDescriptor() {
    return "/OSGI-INF/blueprint/simpleTransform-context.xml,"
        + "/OSGI-INF/blueprint/simpleTransform-props-context.xml";
}
```

2. Define the body of the test. Here, the `MockEndpoint` testing DSL is used to establish the messages that you expect an endpoint to receive. A message is sent into the route via the `ProducerTemplate` instance provided for you by the `CamelTestSupport` base class. Finally, you assert that the expectations set on the mock endpoint were satisfied:

```
@Test
public void testPayloadIsTransformed()
    throws InterruptedException {
  MockEndpoint mockOut = getMockEndpoint("mock:out");
  mockOut.setExpectedMessageCount(1);
  mockOut.message(0).body().isEqualTo("Modified: Cheese");

  template.sendBody("Cheese");

  assertMockEndpointsSatisfied();
}
```

As an alternative to explicitly fetching mocks, and referring to endpoints in each unit test, you can request an injected `MockEndpoint` and `ProducerTemplate` by defining them as fields and annotating them as follows:

```
@EndpointInject(uri = "mock:out")
private MockEndpoint mockOut;

@Produce(uri = "direct:in")
private ProducerTemplate in;
```

How it works...

Camel's Blueprint test support avoids the need for an OSGi runtime by instantiating the Blueprint context files using the PojoSR library. This library provides a container that supports an OSGi-style service registry without a full-blown OSGi framework. This leads to the container starting and stopping faster, which is more appropriate for unit testing.

The `CamelBlueprintTestSupport` class is a convenience class that provides *feature-parity* with the `CamelTestSupport` class described in the *Testing routes defined in Java* recipe. It is responsible for performing the boilerplate work required to test Camel routes defined within Blueprint configuration files. At its most basic, the class will do the following:

- ▶ Start a Blueprint application defined by the Blueprint descriptors returned from `getBlueprintDescriptor()` *before each test*
- ▶ Inject any properties that you have annotated with `@Produce` and `@EndpointInject`
- ▶ Shut down the Blueprint application at the end of each test

Feature-parity with `CamelTestSupport` means that aside from the implementation of different base methods to the Java testing example (`getBlueprintDescriptor()` versus `createRouteBuilder()` or `createRouteBuilders()`), `CamelBlueprintTestSupport` allows the test methods themselves to be written in exactly the same manner to their Java DSL equivalents. Both classes provide access to the same protected variables (`context` and `template`), and honor the same test lifecycle.

At the time of writing this book the `camel-test-blueprint` library is not as functionally mature as `camel-test-spring`. The only test framework that is supported is JUnit 4. There is also no alternative that would enable you to work with other test frameworks as per the Extended Spring Test mechanism described in the *Testing routes defined in Spring* recipe.

There's more...

The Blueprint Configuration Admin support allows you to define default values for properties. These values are associated with a **Persistent ID (pid)** that corresponds to a named map, which is typically overridden inside an OSGi environment. When testing, you will typically want to override these values with something more suited to your needs.

A simple solution, if your `<cm:property-placeholder/>` block is defined in a separate file from your routes, might be to define a test version of that file and return it from `getBlueprintDescriptor()`.

A better approach is to override the properties individually by overriding the following method in your test class:

```
@Override
protected String useOverridePropertiesWithConfigAdmin(
    Dictionary props) throws Exception {
  props.put("transform.message", "Overridden");
  return "org.camelcookbook.testing"; // Persistent ID
}
```

If you have a lot of properties that require overriding, or a lot of tests that would require you to repeat this code block, you can provide the location of a properties file (ending in `.properties` or `.cfg`) and the Persistent ID to override as follows:

```
@Override
protected String[] loadConfigAdminConfigurationFile() {
  return new String[] {
    "src/test/resources/blueprint/testProperties.cfg",
    "org.camelcookbook.testing" // Persistent ID
  };
}
```

 The Blueprint test mechanism has been written with Maven in mind, and loads the properties file relative to the project root. The test as specified previously will most likely not run from within your IDE, as the PojoSR container will execute within a different absolute directory.

When this mechanism is combined with `useOverridePropertiesWithConfigAdmin()`, the properties file will override the default properties provided in the `<cm:property-placeholder/>` block, and the manually set properties will in turn override the values in the file.

We can use this particular mechanism to make testing easier. Consider the following example:

```
<camelContext xmlns="http://camel.apache.org/schema/blueprint">
  <route>
    <from uri="{{in.endpoint}}"/>
    <transform>
      <simple>{{transform.message}}: ${body}</simple>
    </transform>
    <to uri="{{out.endpoint}}"/>
  </route>
</camelContext>
```

By externalizing the endpoints we can now exercise the route in a test using `direct:` and `mock:`, while referring to the actual technology endpoints in the production configuration.

See also

- ▸ Blueprint Testing: `http://camel.apache.org/blueprint-testing.html`
- ▸ Properties Component: `http://camel.apache.org/properties.html`
- ▸ PojoSR: `http://code.google.com/p/pojosr/`
- ▸ The *Auto-mocking of endpoints* recipe
- ▸ The *Testing routes with fixed endpoints using AOP* recipe
- ▸ The *Testing routes with fixed endpoints using conditional events* recipe

Auto-mocking of endpoints

In the recipes that have involved mock testing so far, it has been necessary to provide a `mock:` endpoint URI directly into a route, either explicitly or through dependency injection. Camel's test support classes provide a mechanism for automatically mocking endpoints that allow you to more easily test routes with embedded URIs. This recipe will show you how to exercise this functionality.

Getting ready

The Java code for this recipe is located in the `org.camelcookbook.examples.testing.automocking` package. The Spring route used here is located under `src/main/resources/META-INF/spring/fixedEndpoints-context.xml`.

How to do it...

Consider the following route, with fixed endpoints:

```
<from uri="activemq:in"/>
<transform>
  <simple>Modified: ${body}</simple>
</transform>
<log message="Set message to ${body}"/>
<to uri="activemq:out"/>
```

In order to set up a mock endpoint on the `to(..)` node without changing the route, perform the following steps:

1. Create a test that extends `CamelSpringTestSupport` as described in the *Testing routes defined in Spring* recipe, loading the preceding XML configuration. Then, override the `isMockEndpoints()` method, returning the name (endpoint URI) of the endpoint(s) that you would like to override:

    ```
    @Override
    public String isMockEndpoints() {
      return "activemq:out";
    }
    ```

    If using Enhanced Spring Testing, your test class should be annotated with:

    ```
    @MockEndpoints("activemq:out")
    ```

2. A mock endpoint can now be fetched from the Camel context, through the mocked endpoint URI, prefixed with `mock:`

    ```
    @EndpointInject(uri="mock:activemq:out")
    MockEndpoint mockOut;
    ```

    It is now possible to test the route as usual, by sending in a message to the start endpoint, and asserting expectations on the `MockEndpoint` interface.

How it works...

Camel will create a mock endpoint for the URIs that you have specified, and use the full name of the original URI, including the scheme (`activemq` in the preceding example), as the name portion of the `mock:` endpoint URI.

As such, `activemq:out` becomes `mock:activemq:out`.

Auto-mocking does not replace the existing endpoints. A message will still be sent to `activemq:out` in the previous example, as well as `mock:activemq:out`. To skip sending to the original endpoint, you should override the `isMockEndpointsAndSkip()` method instead of `isMockEndpoints()`.

The String describing which endpoints to mock may be a full endpoint URI, a wildcard (`*`), or a regular expression. It may also contain `{{..}}` property placeholders, which will be resolved first, before the remainder of the expression is processed.

One thing to note is that if the endpoint URI to be mocked contains attributes, then the matching String used in `isMockEndpoints()` or `@MockEndpoints` needs to use a wildcard in order for the framework to identify a match against the URI:

Considering the original endpoint URI:

```
activemq:out?timeToLive=10000
```

The following wildcard will match that as an endpoint to be mocked:

```
activemq:out?*
```

The URI that is then used to fetch the mock endpoint from the Camel context will not contain any of the original endpoint URI attributes

```
mock:activemq:out
```

There's more...

If you want to mock multiple endpoints within your route, you can specify the list as a regular expression:

```
(activemq:first|activemq:second)
```

You will then be able to access these as usual:

```
@EndpointInject(uri="mock:activemq:first")
@EndpointInject(uri="mock:activemq:second")
```

The approach of overriding `isMockEndpoints()` applies to not only to testing Spring-based routes, but those defined in OSGi Blueprint, and Java `RouteBuilder` implementations as well. The method is defined on `CamelTestSupport`, which both `CamelSpringTestSupport` and `CamelBlueprintTestSupport` extend.

Validating route behavior under heavy load

Every so often you will find yourself developing routes that you need to validate for performance under load, as well as their general correctness. The mocking techniques that have been discussed so far will only help you determine whether a test message correctly exercises the route.

This recipe will show how you can use the `DataSet` Component to generate a set of test data and play it through your route. It will then demonstrate how this same component can be used as a bulk mocking mechanism to validate your route logic under load. This technique is not a replacement for proper system integration load testing. It provides a means to more easily unit test scenarios involving larger numbers of messages.

Consider the following routing logic, which is defined in a `RouteBuilder` implementation that includes property setters allowing us to inject start and end URIs:

```
public class SlowlyTransformingRouteBuilder
    extends RouteBuilder {
  private String sourceUri; // setters omitted...
  private String targetUri;

  @Override
  public void configure() throws Exception {
    from(sourceUri)
      .to("seda:transformBody");

    from("seda:transformBody?concurrentConsumers=15")
      .transform(simple("Modified: ${body}"))
      .delay(100) // pretend this is a slow transformation
      .to("seda:sendTransformed");

    from("seda:sendTransformed") // one thread used here
      .resequence().simple("${header.mySequenceId}").stream()
      .to(targetUri);
  }
}
```

This `RouteBuilder` implementation uses the SEDA Component to allow multiple threads to execute a slow transformation on a number of incoming messages in parallel. When the messages are successfully transformed, they are handed to another route that uses the **Resequencer** EIP. The Resequencer is a pattern built into Camel that sorts exchanges flowing through a route. In this instance, exchanges are sorted according to a header that identifies the original order that they were sent in (`mySequenceId`). This header is set on the incoming messages before they enter the first route.

We would like to verify that the messages are sent out in the order that they came in, and also that we have enough `concurrentConsumers` set on the second route to deal with 100 messages a second.

Getting ready

The Java code for this recipe is located in the `org.camelcookbook.examples.testing.dataset` package.

How to do it...

To apply the DataSet Component for bulk testing, perform the following steps:

1. To generate a set of inbound test messages, extend the `DataSetSupport` class, overriding the abstract `createMessageBody()` method, as well as the `applyHeaders()` template method:

```
public class InputDataSet extends DataSetSupport {
  @Override
  protected Object createMessageBody(long messageIndex) {
    return "message " + messageIndex;
  }

  protected void applyHeaders(Exchange exchange,
                              long messageIndex) {
    exchange.getIn()
        .setHeader("mySequenceId", messageIndex);
  }
}
```

The `DataSetSupport` class is an abstract implementation of the `DataSet` interface, which is used by the `DataSet` Component to generate messages.

2. To generate the messages that will be expected at the end of the route, repeat by extending `DataSetSupport` again, this time skipping the setting of headers:

```
public class ExpectedOutputDataSet extends DataSetSupport {
  @Override
  protected Object createMessageBody(long messageIndex) {
    return "Modified: message " + messageIndex;
  }
}
```

3. In your `CamelTestSupport` test class, register the two beans with the Camel context:

```
@Override
protected CamelContext createCamelContext()
    throws Exception {
  final int testBatchSize = 1000;
  InputDataSet inputDataSet = new InputDataSet();
  inputDataSet.setSize(testBatchSize);

  ExpectedOutputDataSet expectedOutputDataSet =
```

```
            new ExpectedOutputDataSet();
        expectedOutputDataSet.setSize(testBatchSize);

        SimpleRegistry registry = new SimpleRegistry();
        registry.put("input", inputDataSet);
        registry.put("expectedOutput", expectedOutputDataSet);

        return new DefaultCamelContext(registry);
    }
```

If using this style of testing with Spring, the two `DataSet` implementations should be registered as beans in the Spring context.

4. Instantiate your `RouteBuilder` and set two `dataset:` endpoints: the `startURI` endpoint pointing to the `InputDataSet` bean, and the `targetUri` endpoint pointing to the `ExpectedOutputDataSet`:

```
@Override
protected RouteBuilder createRouteBuilder()
    throws Exception {
  SlowlyTransformingRouteBuilder routeBuilder =
      new SlowlyTransformingRouteBuilder();
  routeBuilder.setSourceUri(
      "dataset:input?produceDelay=-1");
  routeBuilder.setTargetUri("dataset:expectedOutput");
  return routeBuilder;
}
```

 The `produceDelay` option is set to `-1` in the source URI so as to start sending messages immediately.

In your test method, fetch the `dataset:expectedOutput` mock endpoint, set the maximum time that it should wait to receive its expected 1,000 messages, and assert that it was satisfied:

```
@Test
public void testPayloadsTransformedInExpectedTime()
    throws InterruptedException {
  MockEndpoint expectedOutput =
      getMockEndpoint("dataset:expectedOutput");
  expectedOutput.setResultWaitTime(10000); // 10 seconds
  expectedOutput.assertIsSatisfied();
}
```

How it works...

The DataSet Component is used here both as a consumer endpoint to generate test messages, and as a producer endpoint to act as a bulk mock testing mechanism.

When the Camel context starts the route, a single thread will be created by the `dataset:input` endpoint. This thread will perform the following steps in a loop:

- Generate the message body by calling `createMessageBody()` on the `input` bean
- Set the message headers through `applyHeaders()`
- Process the resulting exchange through the route

Each time a message is constructed, a `messageIndex` parameter is passed in that allows your code to vary the message.

A `produceDelay` attribute on the URI allows you to set how long the thread should sleep between having finished the routing of the message and generating the next message; `-1` indicates no delay.

When used as a producer in a `to(..)` block statement, a `DataSetEndpoint` interface acts as a bulk mock endpoint that automatically sets its own expectations.

At the other end of our routes, `dataset:expectedOutput` waits to receive 1,000 messages. If the time set in your test by `setResultWaitTime()` expires, the assertion will fail. If the messages were received, the endpoint will generate that same number of exchanges through its own implementation class. It does this in order to compare the received messages against the expected ones.

The two sets of `Exchange` objects are compared to each other *in order*. The ordering is determined by matching the `CamelDataSetIndex` attributes that are set by the consumer and producer `dataset:` endpoints. The two message bodies are then compared for equality. Other headers and attributes are not considered. A mismatch of either the index attributes, or the bodies will result in the assertion failing.

There's more...

It is possible to generate a default set of message headers by overriding `DataSetSupport.populateDefaultHeaders(Map<String, Object>)`. These will be overwritten on a per-message basis in `applyHeaders()`.

There is a `consumeDelay` attribute that can also be used as part of the producer URI to simulate a slow consumer.

See also

- ▶ DataSet Component: `http://camel.apache.org/dataset.html`
- ▶ Resequencer: `http://camel.apache.org/resequencer.html`

Unit testing processors and Bean Bindings

When developing complex `Processor` implementations, it is useful to test them in isolation to ensure that they are fully exercised—something that may not necessarily be straightforward in a production route. Likewise, when developing Java classes marked with Camel annotations for bean binding, you want to check the binding logic as well as logic contained within the class. This recipe presents an approach for testing these types of scenarios.

Getting ready

The Java code for this recipe is located in the `org.camelcookbook.examples.testing.exchange` package.

How to do it...

Processors are typically used for composite actions that involve modifying the body of an exchange as well as a number of headers. Here is a `Processor` implementations `process()` method that we would like to test:

```java
@Override
public void process(Exchange exchange) throws Exception {
    final String something = "SOMETHING";
    Message in = exchange.getIn();
    String action = in.getHeader("action", String.class);
    if ((action == null) || (action.isEmpty())) {
        in.setHeader("actionTaken", false);
    } else {
        in.setHeader("actionTaken", true);
        String body = in.getBody(String.class);
        if (action.equals("append")) {
        in.setBody(body + " " + something);
        } else if (action.equals("prepend")) {
            in.setBody(something + " " + body);
        } else {
            throw new IllegalArgumentException(
                "Unrecognized action requested: [" + action + "]");
        }
    }
}
```

In order to test this processor with an Exchange instance, perform the following steps:

1. Extend `CamelTestSupport` and define an inline route through a `RouteBuilder` implementation that contains only that processor:

```
@Override
protected RouteBuilder createRouteBuilder()
    throws Exception {
  return new RouteBuilder() {
    @Override
    public void configure() throws Exception {
      from("direct:in")
        .process(new ComplicatedProcessor())
        .to("mock:out");
    }
  };
}
```

2. Test the route as usual:

```
@Test
public void testPrepend() throws Exception {
  MockEndpoint mockOut = getMockEndpoint("mock:out");
  mockOut.message(0).body().isEqualTo("SOMETHING text");
  mockOut.message(0).header("actionTaken").isEqualTo(true);

  Map<String, Object> headers =
      new HashMap<String, Object>();
  headers.put("action", "prepend");

  template.sendBodyAndHeaders("direct:in",
                                 "text", headers);

  assertMockEndpointsSatisfied();
}
```

How it works...

By developing a throwaway route, we have enabled the processor under test to be executed inside an actual Camel context. This allows us to feed sample messages to the processor inside the route using a `ProducerTemplate` instance, and check the results using a mock endpoint. This approach distances us from the details of constructing an Exchange object by hand, and instead uses Camel to do it for us.

There's more...

Camel allows you to invoke bean methods directly from your route via a `bean(..)` statement, without needing that you refer to any Camel APIs in the method being invoked. A mechanism called **Bean Binding** is used to map the contents of the exchange to your method parameters (see the *Routing messages directly to a Java method* recipe in *Chapter 3, Routing to Your Code*). Using this mechanism you can access any part of the exchange without relying on the Camel API directly by using Camel's runtime annotations on the method arguments. While the resulting POJO can be tested like any other object, in order to test the bindings, you need to instantiate the bean inside a route and test as done before.

See also

- ▶ Processor: `http://camel.apache.org/processor.html`
- ▶ Bean Binding: `http://camel.apache.org/bean-binding.html`
- ▶ The *Routing messages directly to a Java method* recipe in *Chapter 3, Routing to Your Code*

Testing routes with fixed endpoints using AOP

When working with Camel you may at some point need to test a route that has endpoint URIs hardcoded into it. This tends to be more typical when testing Spring or Blueprint routes.

Consider the following route defined in `/META-INF/spring/fixedEndpoints-context.xml`:

```xml
<route id="modifyPayloadBetweenQueues">
  <from uri="activemq:in"/>
  <transform>
    <simple>Modified: ${body}</simple>
  </transform>
  <to uri="activemq:out"/>
</route>
```

The route endpoints here make use of the ActiveMQ Component to consume from one queue and publish to another. We would like to test this logic as described in the *Testing routes defined in Spring* recipe, in a pure unit test without making any changes to the route.

Camel provides you with a built-in form of **Aspect-Oriented Programming (AOP)** in the form of the adviceWith(..) Java DSL. This feature allows you to modify routing logic, once it has been loaded into the Camel context, to replace the route endpoints with direct: and mock: in order to make it easier to test. This recipe will show you how to use this approach to modify an existing route with fixed endpoints.

Getting ready

The Java code for this recipe is located in the org.camelcookbook.examples.testing. advicewith package.

How to do it...

In order to apply AOP to your tests, perform the following steps:

1. In a test class that extends CamelSpringTestSupport, override the following method:

```
@Override
public boolean isUseAdviceWith() {
  return true;
}
```

This tells the base class to not start the Camel context before running each test method, as it would otherwise do.

2. In your test method, fetch the route by its id (modifyPayloadBetweenQueues), and use the adviceWith(..) block to apply a new set of routing instructions over it using an AdviceWithRouteBuilder:

```
context.getRouteDefinition("modifyPayloadBetweenQueues")
    .adviceWith(context, new AdviceWithRouteBuilder() () {
  @Override
  public void configure() throws Exception {
    replaceFromWith("direct:in");

    interceptSendToEndpoint("activemq:out")
      .skipSendToOriginalEndpoint()
      .to("mock:out");
  }
});
```

3. Start the Camel context manually, and proceed to test the route as you would otherwise do with `direct:` and `mock:` endpoints:

```
context.start();

MockEndpoint out = getMockEndpoint("mock:out");
out.setExpectedMessageCount(1);
out.message(0).body().isEqualTo("Modified: Cheese");

template.sendBody("direct:in", "Cheese");

assertMockEndpointsSatisfied();
```

How it works...

The `adviceWith(..)` statement allows us to provide a set of instructions to lay over the top of a route in order to modify its behavior. We define these instructions through a specialized DSL provided to us by overriding the `AdviceWithRouteBuilder` abstract class.

The `isUseAdviceWith()` method is defined in `CamelTestSupport`, which both `CamelSpringTestSupport` and `CamelBlueprintTestSupport` extend. This means that it can be used regardless of whether you are testing Java, Spring, or OSGi Blueprint routes. To achieve the same behavior in an Extended Spring Test, apply the `org.apache.camel.test.spring.UseAdviceWith` annotation to the test class to indicate the same thing.

There's more...

The `adviceWith(..)` mechanism can be used for a lot more than replacing the consumer and producer endpoints on a route. Using a technique called **weaving**, you can manipulate the route itself to remove or replace individual nodes. This can be handy if one step of your route is responsible for substantial processing that you want to skip for the purposes of testing, as in the following route:

```
from("direct:in").id("slowRoute")
  .process(new ReallySlowProcessor()).id("reallySlowProcessor")
  .to("mock:out");
```

To bypass the long-running process for testing, you can use the following to replace it with a much faster substitute:

```
context.getRouteDefinition("slowRoute")
  .adviceWith(context, new AdviceWithRouteBuilder() {
    @Override
    public void configure() throws Exception {
      weaveById("reallySlowProcessor").replace()
```

```
        .transform().simple("Fast reply to: ${body}");
    }
});
```

In the preceding example, the node is fetched through `weaveById(String)`, where the `id` attribute is one that you have assigned to the `process` DSL statement. You can also fetch nodes by a regular expression that matches the `toString()` representation of the node via `weaveByToString(String)`, or by the internal Camel type of the node (for example, `ToDefinition.class`) through `weaveByType(class)`.

Once a node has been selected via a `weave..()` method, the DSL gives you the following additional modification options:

- `before()`: Add the nodes that follow immediately before the selected node
- `after()`: Add the nodes that follow after the selected node, but before the next one in the original route
- `replace()`: Replace the selected node with the following node(s)
- `remove()`: Eliminate the selected node from the route
- The methods `weaveAddFirst()` and `weaveAddLast()` can be used to add nodes to the start or end of a route that can be useful when you want to validate inputs or outputs, especially in routes used from other routes

See also

- AdviceWith: `http://camel.apache.org/advicewith.html`

Testing routes with fixed endpoints using conditional events

When working with Camel, you may at some point need to test a route that has endpoint URIs hardcoded into it. This tends to be more typical when testing Spring or Blueprint routes.

Consider the following route defined in `/META-INF/spring/fixedEndpoints-context.xml`:

```
<route id="modifyPayloadBetweenQueues">
  <from uri="activemq:in"/>
  <transform>
    <simple>Modified: ${body}</simple>
  </transform>
  <to uri="activemq:out"/>
</route>
```

The route endpoints here make use of the ActiveMQ Component to consume from one queue and publish to another. We would like to test this logic as described in the *Testing routes defined in Spring* recipe, in a pure unit test without making any changes to the route.

Camel provides you with a notification-based DSL for testing this type of route via the `NotifyBuilder`. Unlike the `adviceWith(..)` DSL described in the *Testing routes with fixed endpoints using AOP* recipe, this approach does not rely on modifying the running route in any way. This is useful when you want to engage the actual endpoint technologies in the test, for example when validating performance, while still validating the routing logic.

As such, `NotifyBuilder` can be considered as a form of **black-box** testing where you validate that the outputs match the given inputs without needing to know anything about the internals of the routing. This is in contrast to the testing approaches that we have seen previously that adopt a **white-box** approach where the internals of the routing logic are implicitly visible to the author of the test.

Getting ready

The Java code for this recipe is located in the `org.camelcookbook.examples.testing.notifybuilder` package.

How to do it...

In order to do event-based testing in Camel, perform the following steps:

1. In a test method, instantiate a `NotifyBuilder` instance associated with the Camel context that you would like to test:

```
NotifyBuilder notify = new NotifyBuilder(camelContext)
  .from("activemq:in")
  .whenDone(1)
  .whenBodiesDone("Modified: testMessage")
  .create();
```

2. Send a message into the route using the endpoint technology. This is quite different to the approach that we have used so far where we used a Camel `ProducerTemplate` instance. Now we want to exercise the endpoint's consuming capabilities, whereas the `ProducerTemplate` approach skips that. In our test, we use a Spring `JmsTemplate` that is connected to same ActiveMQ broker used by the route:

```
jmsTemplate.send("in", new MessageCreator() {
    @Override
    public Message createMessage(Session session)
        throws JMSException {
      TextMessage textMessage =
```

```
              session.createTextMessage("testMessage");
          return textMessage;
        }
    });
```

3. Use a standard JUnit `assert` statement to determine whether the `NotifyBuilder` instance raises an event within a specified period of time:

```
assertTrue(notify.matches(10, TimeUnit.SECONDS));
```

How it works...

The `NotifyBuilder` DSL `from()` statement locates a route by its starting endpoint. The `when..()` statements tell the builder to send an event when the conditions described have been matched. The `create()` method completes the construction of the builder, putting it into a state prepared to send events.

The builder's `matches()` method returns a `boolean` value that indicates whether the conditions as outlined were satisfied exchanges flowing through the route in the time specified. If the specified time expires without the conditions having been met, `matches()` will return `false`; otherwise `true` will be returned as soon as the conditions are met.

The `from(startingEndpoint)` syntax can be confusing to maintainers of your code, so a `fromRoute(id)` method is also provided that makes the intent of the builder somewhat clearer.

The `whenDone(number)` method requests that an event be raised when *at least* the specified number of exchanges have been successfully processed through the route. Other alternatives include `whenFailed(int)`, which expects at least the specified number of exceptions to have been thrown, and `whenComplete(int)`, which includes both succeeded and failed exchanges processed. All of these apply to result conditions once the message has fully been processed through a route. The `whenReceived(int)` method matches messages at the start of the route.

The `Done/Failed/Complete/Received` terminology is used in other condition methods, here checking whether an exact number of messages have been processed:

```
whenExactlyComplete(int)
whenExactlyDone(int)
whenExactlyFailed(int)
```

You can also check whether a particular message flowing through the route was successful. The index refers to the sequence of the message assigned as it is processed from the starting endpoint:

```
whenDoneByIndex(int)
```

There's more...

The `NotifyBuilder` can be set up to test more complex scenarios, such as checking whether certain messages reached an endpoint within a route:

```
new NotifyBuilder(camelContext)
  .from("activemq:in")
  .whenDone(1)
  .wereSentTo("activemq:out")
  .create();
```

Here, the `whenDone()` and `wereSentTo()` conditions are considered as being cumulative. You can use the Boolean `and()`, `or()`, and `not()` operators within the DSL to build up more complex checks. For example, here we check whether one message failed, and another succeeded:

```
new NotifyBuilder(camelContext)
  .from("activemq:in")
  .whenDone(1).wereSentTo("activemq:out")
  .and().whenFailed(1)
  .create();
```

Predicates, using Camel Expression Languages such as Simple and XPath, can also be used in your expressions:

```
whenAllDoneMatches(predicate)
whenAnyDoneMatches(predicate)
whenAllReceivedMatches(predicate)
whenAnyReceivedMatches(predicate)
```

You can use the `filter()` method to perform checks against certain messages only:

```
new NotifyBuilder(camelContext)
  .from("activemq:in")
  .whenExactlyDone(1).filter().simple("${body} contains 'test'")
  .create();
```

It is also possible to use the `NotifyBuilder` in conjunction with the `MockEndpoint` DSL to get a finer granularity of assertions over the message content:

```
MockEndpoint mock = camelContext.getEndpoint(
    "mock:nameDoesNotMatter", MockEndpoint.class);
mock.message(0).inMessage().contains(messageText);
mock.message(0).header("count").isNull();

NotifyBuilder notify = new NotifyBuilder(camelContext)
```

```
.from("activemq:in")
.whenDone(1).wereSentTo("activemq:out")
.whenDoneSatisfied(mock)
.create();
```

Here, the expectations set on the mock endpoint will be tested against the exchange state at the end of the route's processing.

 Note that the name of mock endpoint interface does not correspond to an actual endpoint within the route. It is simply used to get a handle on the DSL for the `NotifyBuilder`.

See also

▶ NotifyBuilder: `http://camel.apache.org/notifybuilder.html`

10
Monitoring and Debugging

In this chapter, we will cover:

- ▶ Logging meaningful steps within your route
- ▶ Debugging using logging
- ▶ Throughput logging
- ▶ Enabling step-by-step tracing in code
- ▶ Disabling JMX
- ▶ Configuring JMX
- ▶ Naming your routes to make it easier to monitor
- ▶ Adding JMX attributes and operations
- ▶ Monitoring other systems using the Camel JMX Component
- ▶ Setting breakpoints in your routes

Introduction

In this chapter, we will explore a number of capabilities that Camel includes to make it easier to monitor and debug your Camel integration routes. A number of the logging recipes can be used to help with both debugging your routes, and to track significant events or data within your routes. Many of this chapter's recipes will explore Camel's JMX integration.

Java Management Extensions (**JMX**) is a Java standard technology, included within the default Java runtime, for managing and monitoring applications and systems. JMX allows a runtime environment to remotely expose instrumented resources (MBeans) that have metrics (read/write properties) and operations. This allows remote consoles to do the following:

▶ Collect runtime statistics about system by reading those MBean properties

▶ Make updates to the running system by changing those MBean properties such as updating the number of threads in a pool

▶ Perform actions using MBean operations, such as purging a Queue of messages by calling the Queue MBean's purge operation

A full description of JMX is beyond the scope of this book. You can read more at the Java SE documentation site for JMX at `http://docs.oracle.com/javase/7/docs/technotes/guides/jmx/index.html`.

Camel includes deep JMX integration that provides very fine-grained metrics and operations, which can help to keep your integrations working well in production environments. This integration provides you with the ability to enable, disable, and change configurations that impact runtime behavior of Camel. This includes turning debugging information on or off, and changing configurations that directly impact the routing and processing of messages. Camel, as always, includes meaningful defaults that allow you to use these capabilities with minimal configuration, and allows you to fine-tune, override, and extend as needed.

This chapter includes screenshots of an open source web console called **hawtio** (`http://hawt.io`) which was started by the creator of Apache Camel, James Strachan. This console includes a number of capabilities that you can use with your Camel-based integrations, including: visualizing and editing routes, graphical debugging and message tracing, interacting with JMX, and searching your log entries. This chapter could not do justice to all of the cool features within the hawtio console. However, we have included some screenshots to help you better understand how debugging and monitoring work in Camel, and maybe to encourage you into trying hawtio yourself.

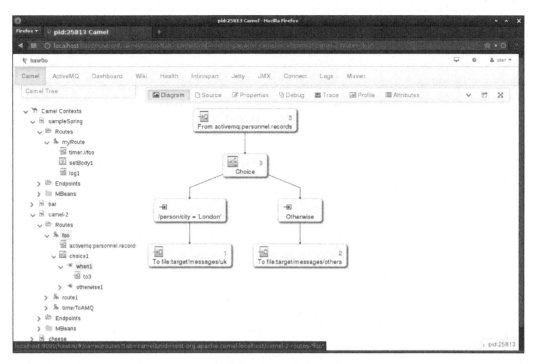

A number of Camel architectural concepts are used throughout this chapter. There is a broader overview of Camel concepts in the *Preface*. Full details can be found at the Apache Camel website at `http://camel.apache.org`.

The code for this chapter is contained within the `camel-cookbook-monitoring` module of the examples.

Logging meaningful steps within your route

Camel includes a Log EIP that is intended for logging interesting milestones within your integration routes. This is different from logging an error (see the *Logging errors* recipe in *Chapter 7, Error Handling and Compensation*) or logging most of the contents of the exchange (see the *Debugging using logging* recipe). This Log pattern gives you the ability to log a message intended for a human being in order to indicate that something meaningful has occurred within your route. This can include a message being routed a specific way, or that the message contains a value of particular interest.

This recipe will show you how to include explicit steps within your route to externally log significant milestones and data from your integrations.

Getting ready

The Java code for this recipe is located in the `org.camelcookbook.monitoring.logeip` package. The Spring XML files are located under `src/main/resources/META-INF/spring` and prefixed with `logeip`.

How to do it...

In the XML DSL, set the `message` attribute to a Simple Expression that will be evaluated and its result logged:

```
<route>
  <from uri="direct:start"/>
  <log message="Something happened - ${body}"/>
  <to uri="mock:result"/>
</route>
```

In the Java DSL, pass in as the single parameter a Simple Expression that will be evaluated and its result logged:

```
from("direct:start")
  .log("Something happened - ${body}")
  .to("mock:result");
```

When a message with a body of "Hello Camel" is passed in, the resulting log should look something like this:

```
INFO   route3              - Something happened - Hello Camel
```

How it works...

The Log EIP, by default, will evaluate the provided Simple Expression, and log the results using a logging level of `INFO`, and using the route ID as the log name. You can override those values, if you wish.

In the XML DSL, this is written as:

```
<route>
  <from uri="direct:start"/>
  <log loggingLevel="INFO"
       logName="MyLogName"
       message="Something happened - ${body}"/>
  <to uri="mock:result"/>
</route>
```

In the Java DSL, the same logic is expressed as:

```
from("direct:start")
  .log(LoggingLevel.INFO,
      "MyLogName",
      "Something happened - ${body}")
  .to("mock:result");
```

This should result in a log entry that looks like the following:

```
INFO  MyLogName                    - Something happened - Hello Camel
```

Here is what the log looks like in hawtio. Notice that you can filter log entries by log name:

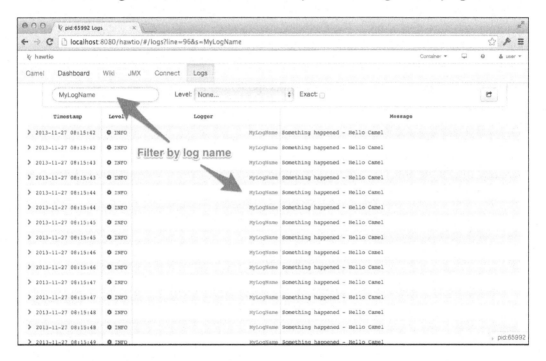

There's more...

Be careful if you are streaming messages and you try to log the body of the message as this will consume the message stream, and the downstream steps will see an empty message. If you need to access the body of a streamed message multiple times, then look to enable *stream caching*.

See also

- Log EIP: `http://camel.apache.org/logeip.html`
- FAQ: `http://camel.apache.org/why-is-my-message-body-empty.html`
- Stream Caching: `http://camel.apache.org/stream-caching.html`

Debugging using logging

Camel includes a Log Component that is useful for debug logging in that it makes it easy to log most, or all of the contents of the messages flowing through your routes. Typically this component is only used temporarily within your routes to help you debug, and is expected to be removed before deployment. The *Enabling step-by-step tracing in code* recipe will cover how you can enable a similar level of logging at runtime. To log significant events within your routes, see the Log EIP (the *Logging meaningful steps within your route* recipe).

This recipe will show you how to use the Log Component to help debug your integrations.

Getting ready

The Java code for this recipe is located in the `org.camelcookbook.monitoring.log` package. The Spring XML files are located under `src/main/resources/META-INF/spring` and prefixed with `log`.

How to do it...

The format for the Log Component URI is as follows:

```
log:<log name>[?<query options>]
```

In the XML DSL, this is written as:

```
<route>
  <from uri="direct:start"/>
  <to uri="log:myLog"/>
  <to uri="mock:result"/>
</route>
```

In the Java DSL, the same route is expressed as:

```
from("direct:start")
  .to("log:myLog")
  .to("mock:result");
```

The resulting log should look something like the following, assuming a message with the body of "Hello Camel" is passed in:

```
INFO  myLog   - Exchange[ExchangePattern:InOnly, BodyType:String,
Body:Hello Camel]
```

How it works...

The Log Component, by default, will log at the INFO logging level, and output the following information to the log system: the MEP (Message Exchange Pattern), the message body data type, and the contents of the message body.

There's more...

There are a number of formatting options within the Log Component that allow you to output more information. For example, to show the full contents of the message, and nicely format it on multiple log lines (versus one very long line), you could configure the endpoint as follows in the XML DSL:

```
<route>
  <from uri="direct:start"/>
  <to uri="log:myLog?showAll=true&amp;multiline=true"/>
  <to uri="mock:result"/>
</route>
```

In the Java DSL, the same configuration is applied as follows:

```
from("direct:start")
  .to("log:myLog?showAll=true&multiline=true")
  .to("mock:result");
```

Here is a sample of the type of output you would see from the preceding configuration. Notice how the log entry is broken up across multiple lines by category (properties, headers, body, and so on):

```
INFO  myLog                          - Exchange[
, Id:ID-grelber-local-65355-1374412338126-1-2
, ExchangePattern:InOnly
, Properties:{CamelToEndpoint=log://myLog?multiline=true
  &showAll=true, CamelCreatedTimestamp=Sun Jul 21 09:12:18
  EDT 2013}
, Headers:{breadcrumbId=ID-grelber-local-65355-1374412338126
  -1-1}
, BodyType:String
, Body:Hello Camel
, Out: null
]
```

Be careful if you are streaming messages and you try to log the body of the message as this will consume the message stream, and the downstream steps will see an empty message. If you need to access the body of a streamed message multiple times, then look to enable *stream caching*.

See also

▸ Log Component: `http://camel.apache.org/log.html`

▸ FAQ: `http://camel.apache.org/why-is-my-message-body-empty.html`

▸ Stream Caching: `http://camel.apache.org/stream-caching.html`

Throughput logging

Camel's Log Component includes the ability to see the average throughput of messages flowing through your route. It is not a perfect measure, though it will help you tune your route to reach the throughput you are hoping for. It can also help you to validate that any Throttle EIPs (see the *Throttler – restricting the number of messages flowing to an endpoint* recipe in *Chapter 2, Message Routing*) you put in place are doing the right thing.

This recipe will show you how to use the Log Component to report (log) the average message flow throughput of your integration route.

Getting ready

The Java code for this recipe is located in the `org.camelcookbook.monitoring.logthroughput` package. The Spring XML files are located under `src/main/resources/META-INF/spring` and prefixed with `logthroughput`.

How to do it...

Use the `groupSize` attribute as a part of the `log:` endpoint URI.

In the XML DSL, this is written as:

```
<route>
  <from uri="direct:start"/>
  <to uri="log:throughput?groupSize=10"/>
  <to uri="mock:result"/>
</route>
```

In the Java DSL, the same route is expressed as:

```
from("direct:start")
  .to("log:throughput?groupSize=10")
  .to("mock:result");
```

The resulting log entry should look something like the following:

```
INFO  throughput  - Received: 10 messages so far. Last group took: 913
millis which is: 10.953 messages per second. average: 10.953
```

How it works...

The Log Component will log a message every time it sees the specified number of messages flow past (`groupSize`), and it will report the amount of time since the last group of messages as well as the average throughput (messages per second).

Analyzing the performance and throughput of any system using tools such as the Log Component's throughput reporting is a bit of an art form. You will need to mentally factor into the reported numbers aspects such as how your route started, how and when the first message was sent to it, what else is running on your test system that may be impacting your test, and so on. This tool provides you with one more measurement that can help you better understand your system.

There's more...

You can also have the Log Component report average throughput during regular time intervals using the `groupInterval` option specified in milliseconds. The `groupDelay` option allows you to say how many milliseconds to wait before starting to track the first group—allowing you to "warm up" your routes.

In the XML DSL, this is written as:

```
<route>
  <from uri="direct:start"/>
  <to uri="log:a?groupInterval=1000&amp;groupDelay=500"/>
  <to uri="mock:result"/>
</route>
```

In the Java DSL, the same route is expressed as:

```
from("direct:start")
  .to("log:a?groupInterval=1000&groupDelay=500")
  .to("mock:result");
```

Here is a sample of the type of output you would see from the preceding configuration:

```
INFO  a  - Received: 10 new messages, with total 15 so far. Last group
took: 1000 millis which is: 10 messages per second. average: 10.128
```

The log entry will report several pieces of information:

- How many new messages this endpoint has received since its last report in the log, and a running total count of messages seen since the log endpoint was started

- How long in milliseconds since the last report, and the window average throughput—number of new messages divided by time since last report

- Average throughput for all messages since the log endpoint was started—in other words, since you started your route

See also

- Log Component: `http://camel.apache.org/log.html`

Enabling step-by-step tracing in code

Camel includes a Tracer interceptor that makes it very easy to enable step-by-step logging of the message. This interceptor will log the current state of the message, and information about the processing step within your route in which the message is located.

This recipe will show you how to enable and configure Camel's Tracer.

Getting ready

The Java code for this recipe is located in the `org.camelcookbook.monitoring.trace` package. The Spring XML files are located under `src/main/resources/META-INF/spring` and prefixed with `trace`.

How to do it...

In the XML DSL, set the `trace` attribute of the `camelContext` element to `true`:

```
<camelContext trace="true"
              xmlns="http://camel.apache.org/schema/spring">
```

In the Java DSL, fetch the associated Camel context, and set its `tracing` property to `true`:

```
public class TraceRouteBuilder extends RouteBuilder {
  @Override
  public void configure() throws Exception {
    getContext().setTracing(true);

    // Route here
  }
}
```

The resulting log entries should look something like the following:

```
INFO  Tracer  - ID-grelber-local-52891-1374579218343-0-2 >>>
(route1) from(direct://start) --> setBody[Simple: Tracing
${body}] <<< Pattern:InOnly, Headers:{breadcrumbId=ID-grelber-
local-52891-1374579218343-0-1}, BodyType:String, Body:Hello Camel
INFO  Tracer  - ID-grelber-local-52891-1374579218343-0-2 >>> (route1)
setBody[Simple: Tracing ${body}] --> mock://result <<< Pattern:InOnly,
Headers:{breadcrumbId=ID-grelber-local-52891-1374579218343-0-1},
BodyType:String, Body:Tracing Hello Camel
```

Notice how, by default, the log output shows the `breadcrumbId` header associated with this message, the step within the route the message is at, and details about the message.

> The `breadcrumb` is a unique ID that allows you to trace the progress of a message within your log files.

How it works...

The Tracer is implemented as an *interceptor strategy*, meaning that it gets injected between each step of every route within the Camel context. The Tracer will log the contents of the message at each step.

There's more...

You can enable Tracing at runtime by setting the JMX attribute tracing on the Camel context's MBean. See the *Configuring JMX* recipe for how to enable JMX in your Camel integrations.

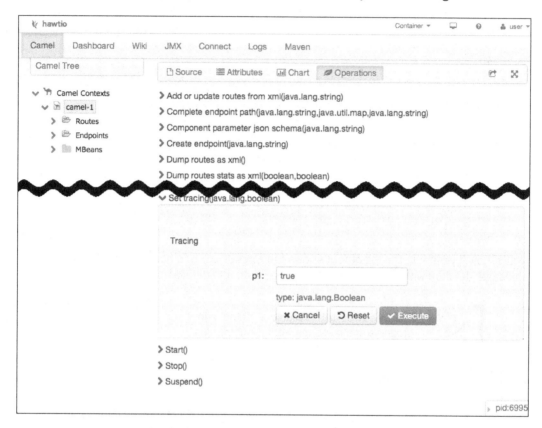

You can change the default configuration used by the Tracer, including the log name and level, as well as message formatting details.

In the XML DSL, define a bean of type `org.apache.camel.processor.interceptor.Tracer` (the `id` does not matter), and set the properties that you would like to change. You can also define a bean of type `org.apache.camel.processor.interceptor.DefaultTraceFormatter` (again, the `id` does not matter), and set its formatting properties as you like. Camel uses Spring's registry to find these beans based on their type, which is why you do not see any code explicitly linking the tracer and formatter with the Camel context.

You still need to set the `trace` attribute of the `camelContext` element to `true`:

```xml
<beans xmlns="http://www.springframework.org/schema/beans"
       xmlns:camel="http://camel.apache.org/schema/spring"
       xmlns:xsi="http://www.w3.org/2001/XMLSchema-instance"
       xsi:schemaLocation="…">
  <bean id="camelTracer"
        class="org.apache.camel.processor.interceptor
               .Tracer">
    <property name="logName"
              value="MyTracerLog"/>
  </bean>

  <bean id="traceFormatter"
        class="org.apache.camel.processor.interceptor
               .DefaultTraceFormatter">
    <property name="showHeaders"
              value="false"/>
    <property name="showProperties"
              value="true"/>
  </bean>

  <camelContext trace="true"
                xmlns="http://camel.apache.org/schema/spring">
    <!-- ... -->
  </camelContext>
</beans>
```

In the Java DSL, create an `org.apache.camel.processor.interceptor.Tracer` instance, customize its properties as desired, and add it as an intercept strategy to the associated Camel context:

```java
public void configure() throws Exception {
  getContext().setTracing(true);

  Tracer tracer = new Tracer();
  tracer.setLogName("MyTracerLog");

  tracer.getDefaultTraceFormatter().setShowProperties(true);
  tracer.getDefaultTraceFormatter().setShowHeaders(false);

  getContext().addInterceptStrategy(tracer);
  // Define route(s) after tracer
}
```

Here is a sample of the type of output that you would see from the preceding configuration:

```
INFO  MyTracerLog  - ID-grelber-local-52917-1374580245804-0-2 >>>
(route1) from(direct://start) --> setBody[Simple: Tracing ${body}]
<<< Pattern:InOnly, Properties:{CamelToEndpoint=direct://start,
CamelCreatedTimestamp=Tue Jul 23 07:50:46 EDT 2013}, BodyType:String,
Body:Hello Camel
INFO  MyTracerLog  - ID-grelber-local-52917-1374580245804-0-2
>>> (route1) setBody[Simple: Tracing ${body}] --> mock://result
<<< Pattern:InOnly, Properties:{CamelToEndpoint=direct://start,
CamelCreatedTimestamp=Tue Jul 23 07:50:46 EDT 2013}, BodyType:String,
Body:Tracing Hello Camel
```

See also

▸ Tracer: `http://camel.apache.org/tracer.html`

Disabling JMX

Camel, by default, enables JMX for all routes and endpoints it creates by default. Sometimes, such as when you are performance testing Camel, you do not want any of the JMX metric-gathering to add any extra overhead, so you may want to disable JMX. In general, it is a good idea to leave JMX enabled, as you will find it useful to help diagnose any runtime issues.

This recipe shows you how to disable JMX.

Getting ready

The Java code for this recipe is located in the `org.camelcookbook.monitoring.jmxdisable` package. The Spring XML files are located under `src/main/resources/META-INF/spring` and prefixed with `jmx-disable`.

How to do it...

In the XML DSL, create a `jmxAgent` element within the `camelContext` element, and set `disabled` to `true`:

```
<camelContext xmlns="http://camel.apache.org/schema/spring">
  <jmxAgent id="agent" disabled="true"/>
  <!-- route definitions here -->
</camelContext>
```

You must set the id attribute in the `jmxAgent` element otherwise you will get a validation error at startup. It does not matter what value you assign.

If you are not using Spring, Blueprint, or other dependency injection frameworks to configure your Camel context, then you need to call `disableJMX()` on your created context *before* you start it. See the *Using Camel in a Java application* recipe in *Chapter 1, Structuring Routes* for more details on bootstrapping Camel from your Java application.

```
public static void main(String[] args) throws Exception {
    final CamelContext context = new DefaultCamelContext();

    // disable JMX - call before context.start()
    context.disableJMX();

    // add routes here...

    // start the context
    context.start();

    // do stuff

}
```

It is important that you call `disableJMX` as soon as possible after you create your Camel context, as Camel will internally setup JMX lifecycle and other settings as a part of its default setup.

How it works...

Camel by default will set up internal lifecycle listeners that will create JMX MBeans as endpoints, routes, and so on get created. Setting JMX as disabled will remove these listeners, disabling the creation of Camel specific MBeans.

Your application, into which Camel is embedded, can still use JMX. The preceding steps only stop Camel from instantiating JMX MBeans.

There's more...

You can also disable Camel's JMX usage by setting a system property at startup time as follows:

```
# java -jar -Dorg.apache.camel.jmx.disabled=true MyCamelApp.jar
```

See also

▸ Camel JMX: `http://camel.apache.org/camel-jmx`

Configuring JMX

Camel, by default, enables JMX for all routes and endpoints it creates by default. This recipe shows you how to configure Camel's interaction with JMX.

Getting ready

The Java code for this recipe is located in the `org.camelcookbook.monitoring.jmx` package. The Spring XML files are located under `src/main/resources/META-INF/spring` and prefixed with `jmx`.

How to do it...

In the XML DSL, create a `jmxAgent` element within the `camelContext` element, and configure the Camel JMX options:

```
<camelContext xmlns="http://camel.apache.org/schema/spring">
  <jmxAgent id="agent"
            connectorPort="1099"
            createConnector="false"
            usePlatformMBeanServer="true"
            serviceUrlPath="/jmxrmi/camel"
            loadStatisticsEnabled="true"
            statisticsLevel="All"/>
  <!-- route definitions here -->
</camelContext>
```

 You must set the `id` attribute in the `jmxAgent` element otherwise you will get a validation error at startup. It does not matter what value you assign.

If you are not using Spring, Blueprint, or other dependency injection frameworks to configure your Camel context, then you need to configure JMX on your created context *before* you start it. See the *Using Camel in a Java application* recipe in *Chapter 1*, *Structuring Routes* for more details on bootstrapping Camel from your Java application.

```
public static void main(String[] args) throws Exception {
  final CamelContext context = new DefaultCamelContext();

  // configure JMX settings
  final ManagementStrategy managementStrategy =
    context.getManagementStrategy();
  managementStrategy.setStatisticsLevel(
    ManagementStatisticsLevel.All);
  managementStrategy.setLoadStatisticsEnabled(true);

  final ManagementAgent managementAgent =
    managementStrategy.getManagementAgent();
  managementAgent.setConnectorPort(1099);
  managementAgent.setServiceUrlPath("/jmxrmi/camel");
  managementAgent.setCreateConnector(false);
  managementAgent.setUsePlatformMBeanServer(true);

  // add Routes here...

  // start the context
  context.start();

  // do stuff
}
```

 You should configure Camel's JMX interaction before creating any routes or endpoints so that all of your JMX settings are consistently applied to all of your Camel MBeans.

Do not configure JMX within your `RouteBuilder` implementations as you will not be able to guarantee the order or timing of that code getting called, which will cause unexpected behavior within you application.

How it works...

Camel, by default, will set up internal lifecycle listeners that will create JMX MBeans as endpoints, routes, and so on. The Camel JMX configuration settings influence how Camel internally creates and configures JMX MBeans for routes and endpoints it creates.

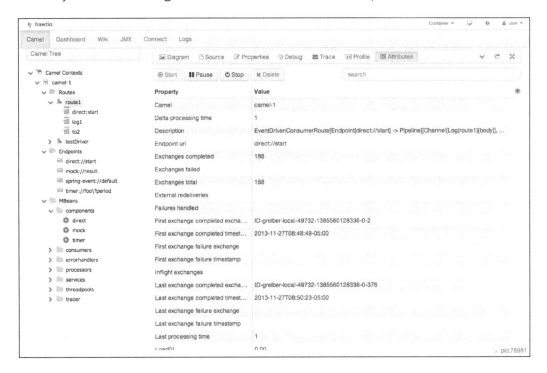

There's more...

The majority of the Camel JMX settings can be configured from system properties provided at application startup, that is, on the command line. These Camel JMX system properties are prefixed with `org.apache.camel.jmx`. See the Camel JMX documentation for details on system property names and values.

See also

▸ Camel JMX: `http://camel.apache.org/camel-jmx`

Naming your routes to make it easier to monitor

Camel, by default, enables JMX on order to allow you to monitor in fine detail your Camel integration routes. Setting meaningful names for your Camel context, and individual routes makes it easier to identify them in your monitoring environment. This recipe will show you how to set specific names for those elements.

Getting ready

The Java code for this recipe is located in the `org.camelcookbook.monitoring.naming` package. The Spring XML files are located under `src/main/resources/META-INF/spring` and prefixed with `naming`.

How to do it...

In the XML DSL, specify `id` attributes for the `camelContext` and `route` elements, as these values will be used as the JMX names. You can optionally add the `jmxAgent` element if you need to customize the JMX configuration for Camel; see the *Configuring JMX* recipe for more details.

```
<camelContext id="myCamelContextName"
              xmlns="http://camel.apache.org/schema/spring">
  <jmxAgent id="agent"/>

  <route id="first-route">
    <from uri="direct:start"/>
    <log message="${body}"/>
    <to uri="mock:result"/>
  </route>
</camelContext>
```

If you are not using Spring, Blueprint, or other dependency injection frameworks to configure your Camel context, then you need to configure JMX on your created context *before* you start it. See the *Using Camel in a Java application* recipe in *Chapter 1, Structuring Routes* for more details on bootstrapping Camel from your Java application.

In the Java DSL, to set the name of the `CamelContext` instance, set its `NameStrategy` to an instance of an `ExplicitCamelContextNameStrategy`. The `DefaultCamelContext` interface includes a helper method, `setName(...)`, that does the same thing:

```
public static void main(String[] args) throws Exception {
  final CamelContext context = new DefaultCamelContext();

  context.setNameStrategy(
      new ExplicitCamelContextNameStrategy("myName"));

  // add routes here…

  // start the context
  context.start();

  // do stuff
}
```

> You should configure Camel JMX before creating any routes or endpoints so that all of your JMX settings are consistently applied to all of your Camel MBeans.
>
> *Do not* configure JMX within your `RouteBuilder` implementations as you will not be able to guarantee the order or timing of that code getting called, which will cause unexpected behavior within you application.

To set the route name within the Java DSL, use `.routeId("<name>")` within your route definition:

```
from("direct:start")
    .routeId("first-route")
  .log("${body}")
  .to("mock:result");
```

How it works...

Camel's default naming strategy for the Camel context is to use its name (that is, `context.getName()`) as the JMX name. This will appear in JMX as an `ObjectName` as per the following, where `contextName` is the Camel context name:

```
org.apache.camel:context=localhost/contextName,type=context,
name=contextName
```

Camel routes work in a similar fashion where the route's `id`, evaluated through, `route.getId()`, is used as the JMX name:

```
org.apache.camel:context=localhost/contextName,type=routes,
name=routeId
```

Notice that the routes are contained, or nested, underneath the Camel context's name. By grouping related integration routes within a named Camel context, it makes it much easier to monitor them via JMX, as all the MBeans will be prefixed with that Camel context name.

If you do not specify an explicit name, Camel will default to "`camel`" for the Camel context name, and "`route`" for the route names. It will append a counter for each additional route, for example, `route-2`.

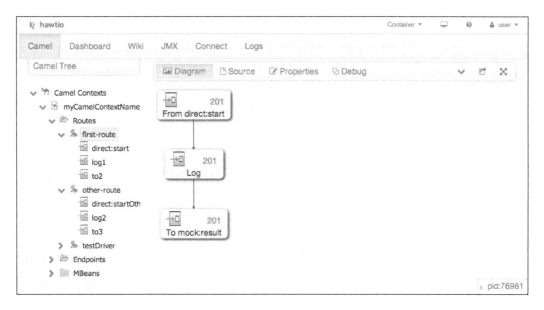

There's more...

The Camel context has an associated `ManagementNamingStrategy` that controls how element names will map to JMX. The default behavior is as described previously, to map the name to the JMX MBean name.

If your Camel routes are deployed within an OSGI container that could have multiple versions of your routes deployed at the same time, Camel defaults to prefixing your Camel context name with the OSGi Bundle ID to differentiate it from other deployed versions.

To change the naming pattern Camel will use for your Camel context, in the XML DSL set the `camelContext` element's `managementNamePattern` attribute. See the Camel JMX documentation (`http://camel.apache.org/camel-jmx`) for a full list of available tokens.

```
<camelContext id="myCamelContextName"
              managementNamePattern="CustomName-#name#"
              xmlns="http://camel.apache.org/schema/spring">
```

In Java, you use the `setNamePattern` method:

```
context.getManagementNameStrategy()
    .setNamePattern("CustomName-#name#");
```

This will cause the Camel context to show up in JMX as follows:

```
org.apache.camel:context=localhost/CustomName-myCamelContextName,
type=context,name=MyCamelContextName
```

Notice how the initial context name includes the naming pattern you specified, `CustomName-MyCamelContextName`, and the name of the MBean is just the name of the Camel context, `MyCamelContextName`.

There is a helper method on the `CamelContext` interface called `getManagementName()` that will return the JMX context value that will be in the prefix of all MBeans within that Camel context.

See also

▸ Camel JMX: `http://camel.apache.org/camel-jmx`

Adding JMX attributes and operations

Camel provides a lot of JMX information for internal constructs (routes, endpoints, and so on) as well as for Java classes invoked from Camel. For example, when you include a call to a custom Java method as a part of a route, Camel will expose that through JMX as a Camel Processor and associate many JMX attributes with it. These include how many messages were sent to that processor, number of redelivery attempts, timestamps for initial and last messages processed, and so on.

There are times when you want to provide custom, or additional, JMX attributes and operations, such as code-specific metrics, and you want the ability to monitor and interact with these from your operational monitoring tools. This recipe shows how to annotate your Java code to expose custom JMX attributes and operations. These will seamlessly integrate with, and augment, the management information provided by Camel.

Getting ready

The Java code for this recipe is located in the `org.camelcookbook.monitoring.` `managed` package. The Spring XML files are located under `src/main/resources/META-` `INF/spring` and prefixed with `managed`.

This recipe's instructions assume you have an existing Java class that you are calling from a Camel route. The following is the base Java code we started adding JMX to:

```java
public class MyManagedBean {
  private int camelsSeenCount;

  public String doSomething(String body) {
    if (body.contains("Camel")) {
      camelsSeenCount++;
    }
    return "Managed " + body;
  }

  public int getCamelsSeenCount() {
    return camelsSeenCount;
  }

  public void resetCamelsSeenCount() {
    camelsSeenCount = 0;
  }
}
```

This recipe assumes that you have JMX enabled and configured within your Camel route. See the *Configuring JMX* recipe for more details.

How to do it...

Use Camel's management annotations—@ManagedResource, @ManagedAttribute, and @ManagedOperation—to decorate the Java classes that you want exposed through JMX along with the rest of Camel's MBeans.

1. Start by annotating your Java class with @ManagedResource, including an optional description for your code that will be associated with the JMX MBean for your code:

```java
import org.apache.camel.api.management.ManagedResource;

@ManagedResource(description="My Bean within Camel")
public class MyManagedBean {
```

2. For each property (for example, `getPropertyName()`) in your code that you want to expose as a JMX attribute, annotate that property together with `@ManagedAttribute`, including an optional description:

```
import org.apache.camel.api.management.ManagedAttribute;

@ManagedAttribute(description = "Number of Camels Seen")
public int getCamelsSeenCount() {
    return camelsSeenCount;
}
```

3. For each method in your code that you want to expose as a JMX operation, annotate that method with `@ManagedOperation`, including an optional description:

```
import org.apache.camel.api.management.ManagedOperation;

@ManagedOperation(description = "Set count to Zero")
public void resetCamelsSeenCount() {
    camelsSeenCount = 0;
}
```

How it works...

When Camel sees you referencing `@ManagedResouce` annotated code, it will include your attributes and operations alongside the standard JMX information that it provides. This will appear in JMX as an `ObjectName` like the following:

```
org.apache.camel:context=localhost/camel-1,type=processors,
name="bean1"
```

Your JMX attributes and operations will be integrated with the ones that Camel provides.

 Camel provides its own management annotations instead of depending on the Spring management framework, as not everyone wants to include dependencies on Spring libraries. If you want to use Spring management annotations, those will work as well.

Camel will automatically categorize how your code is exposed as MBeans based on where your code is referenced within the route. Camel will set the type key in the JMX name based on whether your code is referenced as a processor, endpoint, and so on.

There's more...

Camel will, by default, generically name and number your code within JMX. For example, a `bean()` callout in a Camel route will show up as a JMX MBean `bean1`. If you want to specify your own unique ID, use the `id` DSL after your custom object.

 Naming routes and endpoints using the `id` statement is a great way to help others, including yourself in future, understand what is happening in your routes at runtime. These names will prove most useful in those stressful times, late at night, when something is not working quite right, and you are under pressure to fix it. Seeing meaningful named objects within your JMX console will save you a lot of stress.

In the XML DSL, you can do this by setting the `id` attribute of the `bean` element:

```
<bean id="myManagedBean" ref="myBean"/>
```

In the Java DSL, use the `id` statement:

```
.bean(MyManagedBean.class, "doSomething").id("myManagedBean")
```

This will cause your code to show up in JMX using your provided ID:

```
org.apache.camel:context=localhost/camel-1,type=processors,
name="myManagedBean"
```

See also

▶ Camel JMX: `http://camel.apache.org/camel-jmx`

Monitoring other systems using the Camel JMX Component

Camel includes a JMX Component that can be a JMX consumer for other systems. That is, it can connect to a local or remote JMX MBean server and listen for JMX Notifications that will then flow through the specified Camel route. This component also includes the ability to create and register local JMX Monitor beans that will create JMX Notifications based on changes in other JMX MBeans.

This combination of capabilities—consuming JMX Notifications, and creating local Monitor beans that can generate JMX Notifications—gives you some extra options in terms of monitoring your integration routes. For example, if you have systems deployed remotely across a WAN, you can use this mechanism to aggregate and report on JMX metrics in that remote system onto a channel such as a JMS queue. You can then use this to gather up information within your Data Center.

This recipe will show you how to use the Camel JMX Component to create and register a monitor that watches for changes on an MBean attribute, and then catches those Notifications within a Camel route for processing.

Getting ready

The Java code for this recipe is located in the `org.camelcookbook.monitoring.monitor` package. The Spring XML files are located under `src/main/resources/META-INF/spring` and prefixed with `monitor`.

This recipe's instructions assume that we are monitoring an existing Camel route with an id of "`monitorRoute`". It does not matter which DSL, XML, or Java, that route is written in, or even what that route does since we are monitoring the number of exchanges (messages) that are processed by that route. This will create an MBean with the following name that we will monitor:

```
org.apache.camel:context=localhost/camel-1,type=routes,
name="monitorRoute"
```

The following is the Java DSL version of a route used in the provided example code:

```
from("direct:start")
    .routeId("monitorRoute")
  .transform(simple("Monitoring ${body}"))
  .log("${body}")
  .to("mock:result");
```

This recipe assumes that you have JMX enabled and configured within your Camel route. See the *Configuring JMX* recipe for more details.

How to do it...

Create a Camel route that consumes from the Camel JMX endpoint that is configured with the coordinates for the JMX MBean from which you want to gather data.

> In the Java DSL, use the Camel JMX components provided `JMXUriBuilder` class to make it easier to create the endpoint URI.

1. Create a `HashMap<String, String>` that will contain the `ObjectName` parts for the JMX MBean to be monitored:

```
Map<String, String> map = new HashMap<String, String>();
map.put("context", "localhost/camel-1");
map.put("type", "routes");
map.put("name", "\"monitorRoute\"");
```

Be careful when specifying the "context" portion as that is a combination of the <hostname>/<Camel context management name>, so its value will change depending on the hostname of the server it is running on, as well as the name of the Camel context. In Camel Version 2.13, it is expected that the use of the hostname in the JMX MBean name will become optional, and will be disabled by default.

2. Use the JMXUriBuilder class provided with the Camel JMX Component to make it easier to create the correct URI to specify in the "from" portion of the Camel route. We are specifying the JMX Server ObjectDomain, and ObjectName properties initially; platform indicates local/in-process MBean server. These are followed by the properties that allow the Camel JMX Component to dynamically create a Monitor bean to send JMX Notifications when something interesting happens:

```
JMXUriBuilder jmxUriBuilder = new JMXUriBuilder("platform")
    .withObjectDomain("org.apache.camel")
    .withObjectProperties(map)
    .withMonitorType("counter")
    .withObservedAttribute("ExchangesCompleted")
    .withInitThreshold(0)
    .withGranularityPeriod(500)
    .withOffset(1)
    .withDifferenceMode(false);
```

3. Create a Camel route to process the JMX Notifications:

```
// Resulting URI should be something like
//   jmx:platform?objectDomain=org.apache.camel
//   &key.context=localhost/camel-1&key.type=routes
//   &key.name="monitorRoute"&monitorType=counter
//   &observedAttribute=ExchangesCompleted&initThreshold=0
//   &granularityPeriod=500&offset=1&differenceMode=false
from(jmxUriBuilder.toString())
    .routeId("jmxMonitor")
  .log("${body}")
  .to("mock:monitor");
```

The XML DSL format is similar except that you will either need to manually create the correct URI or call some Java method that will perform the equivalent of preceding steps 1 and 2.

How it works...

The Camel JMX Component is used in this recipe to do two things: create a JMX Notification consumer, and create a Monitor bean to send JMX Notifications.

The URI format to set up the Camel JMX Component to consume JMX Notifications from the in-process platform MBean server is as follows:

```
jmx://platform?options
```

To connect to a remote MBean server, you would specify the URI as follows:

```
jmx:service:jmx:rmi:///jndi/rmi://localhost:1099/jmxrmi?options
```

To specify the `ObjectName` composed of multiple properties, you use the following syntax where the `ObjectName` property name is prefixed with `"key."` and followed by its value. For example, to monitor an MBean with the `ObjectName` property:

```
org.apache.camel:name=simpleBean
```

You specify the following URI:

```
jmx:platform?objectDomain=org.apache.camel
             &key.name=simpleBean
```

The second thing that the Camel JMX Component can do for us is to create a local Monitor bean that will generate JMX Notifications based on change rules we specify.

For example, to generate a Notification every time the value of the `MonitorNumber` JMX attribute changes, we could use the following URI:

```
jmx:platform?objectDomain=org.apache.camel&key.name=simpleBean
&monitorType=counter&observedAttribute=MonitorNumber
&initThreshold=1&granularityPeriod=500
```

Under the covers, the Camel JMX Component will access the JMX API similar to the following example:

```
CounterMonitor monitor =
    new CounterMonitor(); // javax.management.monitor
monitor.addObservedObject(makeObjectName("simpleBean"));
monitor.setObservedAttribute("MonitorNumber");
monitor.setNotify(true);
monitor.setInitThreshold(1);
monitor.setGranularityPeriod(500);
registerBean(monitor, makeObjectName("counter"));
monitor.start();
```

There's more...

In general, you would use the existing JMX aware tools to manage and monitor your Camel routes. The Camel JMX Component is useful in cases where you either can't use a conventional monitoring tool, such as when monitoring systems remotely over constrained network connections, or when you need a more do-it-yourself, custom approach.

The Camel JMX Component generates an XML or Java object that can be processed in subsequent route steps. This allows you to take local action based on the value of the Notification, thereby acting as a lightweight monitoring alert system. It also allows you to aggregate and summarize this data for rebroadcast on other channels, such as summarizing a number of monitored attributes, and periodically publishing on JMS or HTTP to some remote non-JMX listener. This provides you with some extra tools to create a smart agent that can monitor your code, and react to changing conditions—all using Camel.

See also

▸ Camel JMX Component: `http://camel.apache.org/jmx`

▸ Camel JMX: `http://camel.apache.org/camel-jmx`

Setting breakpoints in your routes

Camel's ability to allow you to create route "recipes" (definitions) is very powerful, but it can make traditional debugging difficult. You cannot easily set a breakpoint on a line of Spring XML. Likewise, setting a breakpoint in your `RouteBuilder.configure()` method will not yield the results you want as it only gets called once at startup when your route definition is parsed into a runtime route (other code).

This recipe will show you how, in your unit tests, to define methods that will be called before and after every processor step, giving you a line of Java code where you can set breakpoints to more easily debug your code.

Getting ready

The Java code for this recipe is located in the `org.camelcookbook.monitoring.debug` package. The Spring XML files are located under `src/main/resources/META-INF/spring` and prefixed with `debug`.

This recipe's instructions assume that you have an existing route definition that you are trying to debug. Within this recipe we will debug the following:

```
public class DebugRouteBuilder extends RouteBuilder {
  @Override
  public void configure() throws Exception {
```

```
        from("direct:start")
          .transform(simple("Debug ${body}"))
          .log("${body}")
          .to("mock:result");
    }
}
```

The steps detailed in this recipe are identical regardless of whether your route is defined using the Java or XML DSLs. It does assume you are using Camel's test support, in that your unit tests extend `CamelTestSupport`. For Spring testing, `CamelSpringTestSupport` extends `CamelTestSupport`.

How to do it...

In order to debug messages as they flow through your routes, perform the following steps:

1. In your `CamelTestSupport` extended unit test, override the `isUseDebugger()` method and have it return `true`:

```
public class DebugTest extends CamelTestSupport {
  @Override
  public boolean isUseDebugger() {
    return true;
  }
}
```

2. To enable the setting of breakpoints before each processor step, override the `debugBefore` method from the base `CamelTestSupport` class:

```
@Override
protected void debugBefore(Exchange exchange,
    Processor processor, ProcessorDefinition<?> definition,
    String id, String label) {
  // This method is called before each processor step.
  // Set your breakpoint here
  log.info("Before {} with body {}", definition,
      exchange.getIn().getBody());
}
```

3. To enable the setting of breakpoints after each processor step, override the `debugAfter` method from the base `CamelTestSupport` class:

```
@Override
protected void debugAfter(Exchange exchange,
    Processor processor, ProcessorDefinition<?> definition,
    String id, String label, long timeTaken) {
  // This method is called after each processor step
  // Set your breakpoint here
  log.info("After {} with body {}", definition,
      exchange.getIn().getBody());
}
```

How it works...

An instance of a Camel `Debugger` can be associated with a Camel context. This leverages Camel's `InterceptStrategy` to call Camel `Breakpoint` instances before and/or after each processor step in a route. The `CamelTestSupport` class will enable two simple callback methods that you can override—`debugBefore` and `debugAfter`—if the `isUseDebugger()` method returns `true`. This provides an easy way for you to set breakpoints in your route definitions without needing to learn the full `Debugger` API.

There's more...

The Camel `Debugger` allows you to associate one or more `Breakpoint` instances with your Camel context. Each `Breakpoint` allows you to have code called before and after route processor steps, and on exchange events. The `Breakpoint` instances can also be suspended and resumed. You can also create conditional `Breakpoint` instances that will only be called if its associated `Condition` match, meaning it has rules to say to define which processor steps it should break on. All the things that you would expect to enable full debugging capabilities.

The hawtio console uses the Camel Debugger to allow you to set breakpoints on its visualization of the Camel route.

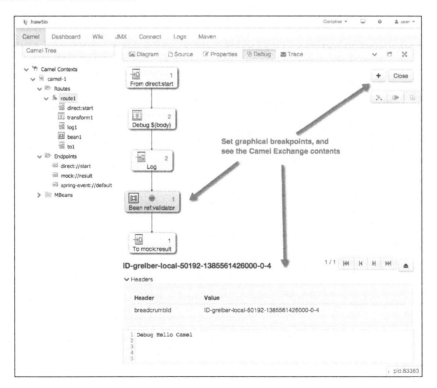

The hawtio console also includes a **Logs** tab that can show you stack traces as shown in the following screenshot:

This allows you to jump directly to the line of code, assuming you have generated a source jar for your Camel Maven project.

```
385
386   root  org  apache  camel  component  bean  MethodInfo              JavaDoc
387
388
389      public boolean isStaticMethod() {
390          return Modifier.isStatic(method.getModifiers());
391      }
392
393      /**
394       * Returns true if this method is covariant with the specified method
395       * (this method may above or below the specified method in the class hierarchy)
396       * @param method
397       * @return
398       */
399      public boolean isCovariantWith(MethodInfo method) {
400          return
401              method.getMethod().getName().equals(this.getMethod().getName())
402              && (method.getMethod().getReturnType().isAssignableFrom(this.getMethod().getReturnType())
403              || this.getMethod().getReturnType().isAssignableFrom(method.getMethod().getReturnType()))
404              && Arrays.deepEquals(method.getMethod().getParameterTypes(), this.getMethod().getParameterTypes());
405      }
406
407      protected Object invoke(Method mth, Object pojo, Object[] arguments, Exchange exchange) throws
      InvocationTargetException {
408          try {
409              return mth.invoke(pojo, arguments);
410          } catch (IllegalAccessException e) {
411              throw new RuntimeExchangeException("IllegalAccessException occurred invoking method: " + mth + " using
      arguments: " + Arrays.asList(arguments), exchange, e);
412          } catch (IllegalArgumentException e) {
413              throw new RuntimeExchangeException("IllegalArgumentException occurred invoking method: " + mth + "
      using arguments: " + Arrays.asList(arguments), exchange, e);
414          }
415      }
416
417      protected Expression createParametersExpression() {
418          final int size = parameters.size();
419          LOG.trace("Creating parameters expression for {} parameters", size);
420
421          final Expression[] expressions = new Expression[size];
422          for (int i = 0; i < size; i++) {
423              Expression parameterExpression = parameters.get(i).getExpression();
424              expressions[i] = parameterExpression;
425              LOG.trace("Parameter #{} has expression: {}", i, parameterExpression);
426          }
427          return new Expression() {
428              @SuppressWarnings("unchecked")
429              public <T> T evaluate(Exchange exchange, Class<T> type) {
430                  Object[] answer = new Object[size];
431                  Object body = exchange.getIn().getBody();
432                  boolean multiParameterArray = false;
433                  if (exchange.getIn().getHeader(Exchange.BEAN_MULTI_PARAMETER_ARRAY) != null) {
434                      multiParameterArray = exchange.getIn().getHeader(Exchange.BEAN_MULTI_PARAMETER_ARRAY,
      Boolean.class);
435                  }
436
```
pid:9256

See also

▸ Camel Debugger: http://camel.apache.org/debugger.html

11
Security

In this chapter, we will cover the following recipes:

- ▸ Encrypting configuration properties
- ▸ Digitally signing and verifying messages
- ▸ Encrypting and decrypting a message
- ▸ Encrypting all or parts of an XML message
- ▸ Authentication and authorization using Spring Security

Introduction

In this chapter we will take an in-depth look at adding a level of security to your routing logic through a number of security-related Camel components. We will focus on making it difficult for an unauthorized party to gain access to sensitive information while messages are in-flight, to manipulate sensitive payloads, and to trigger operations to which that party is not authorized.

Beyond the topics discussed in this chapter, in order to secure your integrations you will also need to consider factors such as:

- ▸ Restricting access to the operating system on which the application runs.
- ▸ Password protecting JMX access so that an unauthorized party cannot change the route at runtime to wiretap or log message contents.
- ▸ Not storing passwords or keys in plain text on the filesystem.
- ▸ Locking down the transport mechanism. For example, applying SSL to message broker connections, or WS-Security and WS-SecurityPolicy with SOAP-based web services.

Security, after all, is a process that is broader than how a single application protects itself.

A number of Camel architectural concepts are used throughout this chapter. There is a broader overview of Camel concepts in the *Preface*. Full details can be found on the Apache Camel website at `http://camel.apache.org`.

The code for this chapter is contained within the `camel-cookbook-security` module of the examples.

Encrypting configuration properties

In real-world applications, we typically store an environment-specific configuration outside of the application, and access it through the properties mechanism described in the *Using external properties in Camel routes* recipe in *Chapter 1*, *Structuring Routes*. This enables us to move an application between development, test, and production environments with no code changes required to repoint it to different databases, message brokers, and so on.

To access these resources we often need to store sensitive information such as passwords. It is considered bad practice to keep these in plain text, as that would allow the reader to freely access those resources. To address this, we need to overlay another mechanism that allows us to hide passwords through encryption.

This recipe will show you how to use the Camel Jasypt Component to manage encrypted configuration values within Camel.

Getting ready

The Java code for this recipe is located in the `org.camelcookbook.security.encryptedproperties` package. The Spring XML files are located under `src/main/resources/META-INF/spring` and prefixed with `encryptedProperties`.

To use the Camel Jasypt Component, add the following to the `dependencies` section of your Maven POM:

```
<dependency>
  <groupId>org.apache.camel</groupId>
  <artifactId>camel-jasypt</artifactId>
  <version>${camel-version}</version>
</dependency>
```

To encrypt passwords you will also require access to the `camel-jasypt` JAR file. This file can be found in the binary download of the Camel distribution in the `lib` directory.

How to do it...

To encrypt configuration properties, perform the following steps:

1. Download the Camel binary distribution from the Apache Camel website (`http://camel.apache.org/download.html`) and extract it into a working directory.

2. Run the following command in the `lib` directory of the location that you just extracted Camel into:

   ```
   # java -jar camel-jasypt-2.12.2.jar -c encrypt
   -p encryptionPassword -i myDatabasePassword
   ```

    The version in the name of the `.jar` file corresponds to the Camel version you downloaded.

   The `-c` flag denotes the task to be performed (encrypt/decrypt). The `-p` argument is the password used to encrypt the property that you wish to hide. The `-i` argument is the input that is to be encrypted. The encrypted version of the database password is printed out:

   ```
   Encrypted text: hRR5B31qPMJpxk078rXmwllpzQNPpR5kXdnNQrOmIfs=
   ```

3. Copy this password and add it to a properties file that provides placeholders to your Camel routes (see the *Using external properties in Camel routes* recipe in *Chapter 1, Structuring Routes*). The encrypted text must be surrounded by an `ENC(..)` string to denote encryption:

   ```
   start.endpoint=direct:in
   log.message=The database password is {{database.password}}
   database.password=
   ENC(hRR5B31qPMJpxk078rXmwllpzQNPpR5kXdnNQrOmIfs=)
   end.endpoint=mock:out
   ```

    Properties can be embedded within each other, and you can mix encrypted and regular content.

4. Enable the Jasypt properties parser within the properties component. If using Spring or OSGi Blueprint, instantiate the parser as a regular `bean`:

   ```xml
   <bean id="jasypt"
         class="org.apache.camel.component.jasypt
               .JasyptPropertiesParser">
     <property name="password" value="encryptionPassword"/>
   </bean>
   ```

The password used here is the same as that provided to the -p argument during the encryption phase in the command line.

Inside the camelContext element, define a propertyPlaceholder element that refers to the properties file to be picked up and the parser bean:

```
<propertyPlaceholder id="properties"
                     location=
                       "classpath:placeholder.properties"
                     propertiesParserRef="jasypt"/>
```

If using Java only, you need to instantiate the parser and PropertiesComponent, and set the component on the Camel context before it is started:

```
JasyptPropertiesParser propParser =
    new JasyptPropertiesParser();
propParser.setPassword("encryptionPassword");

PropertiesComponent propComponent =
    new PropertiesComponent();
propComponent.setLocation(
    "classpath:placeholder.properties");
propComponent.setPropertiesParser(propParser);

CamelContext camelContext = new DefaultCamelContext();
camelContext.addComponent("properties", propComponent);
```

5. Inside your route you can now use encrypted properties as usual; encrypted properties will be decrypted at runtime.

The following XML DSL demonstrates this usage:

```
<from uri="{{start.endpoint}}"/>
<setHeader headerName="dbPassword">
  <constant>{{database.password}}</constant>
</setHeader>
<log message="{{log.message}}"/>
<to uri="{{end.endpoint}}"/>
```

The same route is expressed in the Java DSL as:

```
from("{{start.endpoint}}")
  .setHeader("dbPassword",
             simple("{{database.password}}"))
  .log("{{log.message}}")
  .to("{{end.endpoint}}");
```

In the Java DSL, a `constant(..)` expression does not resolve properties, so we use `simple(..)` instead.

In both cases, the route will print out the decrypted string when a message is passed through it:

```
The database password is myDatabasePassword
```

How it works...

The Jasypt Component uses the password that it has been provided with to decrypt any properties that contain the string pattern `ENC(..)` using the default algorithm `PBEWithMD5AndDES`.

If you want to use a different algorithm, you run the encryption command from the command line, and pass in the algorithm name through its `-a` argument. The same algorithm name needs to be passed to the `JasyptPropertiesParser` through its `algorithm` property.

Algorithm names are defined in the JCE Standard Algorithm Names Documentation. The algorithm used has to be supported by the JCE providers on both the system that you encrypt the password on, and the one that decrypts it. Not all algorithms are available on all JVMs due to export restrictions. For most purposes, the default algorithm is perfectly adequate.

There's more...

Leaving your master password unencrypted in your code is rarely a good idea. The `JasyptPropertiesParser` allows you to pass in the name of a Java system variable, or an environment variable, and resolves the password from that for decryption purposes. To use this mechanism, you prefix the password property as follows:

- **sys:**`jasyptMasterPassword` - This resolves a Java system property, set through `java -DjasyptMasterPassword=...` when starting the JVM that runs the routes

- **sysenv:**`JASYPT_MASTER_PASSWORD` - This resolves to a system variable, set through the shell before the process is started

The choice of the variable name is up to you; it is only the prefix (`sys:` or `sysenv:`) that is important.

You often want to use encryption of properties beyond just those used by Camel (for example, passwords for `DataSource` objects that are instantiated in Spring). For instructions on how to do this, refer to the Jasypt documentation.

- Camel Jasypt Component: `http://camel.apache.org/jasypt.html`
- Jasypt (Java Simplified Encryption): `http://jasypt.org/`
- Standard Algorithm Names Documentation: `http://docs.oracle.com/javase/7/docs/technotes/guides/security/StandardNames.html`

Digitally signing and verifying messages

Digital signatures are a mechanism for signing a message payload using public key, also known as asymmetric, cryptography to prove the authenticity of a message. This scheme additionally provides non-repudiation to a message exchange, meaning that a sender will not be able to deny at a future point in time that the message was sent by him/her.

To use this mechanism, a system uses a pair of cryptographic keys that are made up of a private key known only to itself, and a public key that is freely given out to third parties.

Before sending a message, the system uses the private key to generate a message signature (a type of checksum) based on the message contents, and appends it to the message.

The receiving system uses the sender's public key to verify the signature against the message contents. The verification step proves that the message was not changed after being signed and that the originating system was the one who originally signed it.

> The digital signing of a message does not encrypt its content in any way.

This recipe will show you how to sign and verify messages using the Camel Crypto Component.

Getting ready

The Java code for this recipe is located in the `org.camelcookbook.security.signatures` package. The Spring XML files are located under `src/main/resources/META-INF/spring` and prefixed with `signatures`.

To use Camel's Crypto Component, you need to add a dependency on the `camel-crypto` library.

Add the following to the `dependencies` section of your Maven POM:

```
<dependency>
  <groupId>org.apache.camel</groupId>
  <artifactId>camel-crypto</artifactId>
```

```
  <version>${camel-version}</version>
</dependency>
<dependency>
  <groupId>commons-codec</groupId>
  <artifactId>commons-codec</artifactId>
  <version>1.8</version> <!-- Java 6+ -->
</dependency>
```

To make life easier around accessing keystores in the Spring XML DSL, we will use the `spring-crypto-utils` library. This is not strictly required, but otherwise you would need to write some Java factory methods that Spring can call for the purpose of instantiating `KeyStore` objects.

```
<dependency>
  <groupId>com.google.code.spring-crypto-utils</groupId>
  <artifactId>spring-crypto-utils</artifactId>
  <version>1.3.0</version>
</dependency>
```

Before using the cryptographic capabilities available in Camel you will need:

- ▶ **keystore**: This is a repository of public and private keys
- ▶ **truststore**: This is a keystore that holds the public keys of parties that your system trusts to communicate with

In a production environment, you should ensure that access to the keystore and truststore files is restricted through appropriate file access permissions so that an unauthorized party cannot modify them.

For the purposes of this example, we will use the `keytool` utility that is included as part of the Java Development Kit (JDK):

1. Generate a pair of public and private key for the *sending* code/system (in this example, known by the alias `system_a`). This will automatically produce a keystore, as follows:

   ```
   # keytool -genkeypair -v -alias system_a
   -keystore keystore.jks -validity 3650
   -dname 'CN=Scott,O=camelbookbook.org'
   -storepass keystorePassword -keypass keyPasswordA
   ```

2. Export the public key certificate:

   ```
   # keytool -export -alias system_a -keystore keystore.jks
   -storepass keystorePassword -rfc -file selfsignedcert_a.cer
   ```

3. Import the public key into a truststore for use by the *receiving* code/system:

```
# keytool -import -noprompt -alias system_a
-file selfsignedcert_a.cer -keystore truststore.jks
-storepass truststorePassword
```

4. Repeat steps 1-3 for an alias of `system_b` and a certificate file `selfsignedcert_b.cer`.

The steps mentioned in the preceding list will generate keys using the `DSA` algorithm, and hash it using `SHA1`. The full signature algorithm will therefore be `SHA1withDSA`; the same as the default algorithm used by `camel-crypto`.

 Getting keys and certificates set up and working correctly against Java's cryptography extensions (and therefore `camel-crypto`) is complicated due to the number of options—in particular, there is a strong likelihood of misconfiguring the cryptographic algorithms used. See the `keytool` documentation in the *See also* section of this recipe for details of the defaults, and the Standard Algorithm Names Documentation for the strings to use to set up alternatives.

How to do it...

In order to perform message signing and verification, you will need to do the following:

1. Configure the keystores. If using Spring, add the `crypt` namespace to the `beans` definition, as follows:

```
<beans ...
  xmlns:crypt="http://springcryptoutils.com/schema/crypt"
  xsi:schemaLocation="...
    http://springcryptoutils.com/schema/crypt
      http://springcryptoutils.com/schema/crypt.xsd">
```

Then load the keystore and the truststore as Spring beans (your locations will most likely vary):

```
<crypt:keystore id="keyStore"
                location="classpath:keystore.jks"
                password="keystorePassword"/>
<crypt:keystore id="trustStore"
                location="classpath:truststore.jks"
                password="truststorePassword"/>
```

If using Java, load and register the `java.security.KeyStore` instances within the Camel context as follows:

```java
SimpleRegistry registry = new SimpleRegistry();

// here we are loading keystores stored in our JAR
ClassLoader classLoader = getClass().getClassLoader();

KeyStore keyStore = KeyStore.getInstance("JKS");
keyStore.load(
    classLoader.getResourceAsStream("keystore.jks"),
    "keystorePassword".toCharArray());
registry.put("keyStore", keyStore);

KeyStore trustStore = KeyStore.getInstance("JKS");
trustStore.load(
    classLoader.getResourceAsStream("truststore.jks"),
    "truststorePassword".toCharArray());
registry.put("trustStore", trustStore);

CamelContext camelContext =
    new DefaultCamelContext(registry);
```

 JKS is the default keystore type used to hold key pairs.

2. To sign a message within your route, send the message to a `crypto:` endpoint containing details of the key to sign the message with.

   In the XML DSL, you do this through the following statement:

```xml
<to uri="crypto:sign://usingKeystore?keystore=#keyStore
        &amp;alias=system_a&amp;password=keyPasswordA"/>
```

   In the Java DSL, this is expressed as:

```java
.to("crypto:sign://usingKeystore?keystore=#keyStore
    &alias=system_a&password=keyPasswordA")
```

Here we refer to the keystore that contains the private key of our key pair. The alias is used to distinguish between multiple keys in the same keystore. The key pair's password is required to sign the message.

 The key password is shown in plain text so as to not complicate the example. In a real-world scenario, the password should be injected as an encrypted property. See the *Encrypting configuration properties* recipe for a description of how to do this.

3. To verify the message, send the message to a `crypto:` endpoint that defines which public key from the truststore should be used.

   In the XML DSL, this is performed as follows:

   ```
   <to uri="crypto:verify//usingKeystore?keystore=#trustStore
           &amp;alias=system_a"/>
   ```

   In the Java DSL, the same thing is expressed as:

   ```
   .to("crypto:verify//usingKeystore?keystore=#trustStore
       &alias=system_a")
   ```

   In order to verify a signed message, we need to know which public key in the truststore to use; we do this by using the `alias` attribute.

> When using the `crypto:` URI, there is no need to explicitly instantiate and register the `CryptoComponent` class. Camel automatically discovers and registers certain components that require no manual configuration. It does this by scanning its classpath for files included in component JARs containing metadata specifically for this purpose. These files describe which Component class should be instantiated, and the URI scheme that it corresponds to.

How it works...

In the sign phase, the Camel Crypto Component calculates a signature using the password and key specified, and Base64 encodes it before inserting it into the exchange's `CamelDigitalSignature` header.

These digital signature header names are defined as constants in the `org.apache.camel.component.crypto.DigitalSignatureConstants` class. For example, the `CamelDigitalSignature` header is defined in `DigitalSignatureConstants.SIGNATURE`.

It is up to your routing code to take that header value and pass it appropriately via the transport being used to the system you are communicating with. Likewise, if consuming from a transport, you need to take the signature from the transport mechanism and place it into the `CamelDigitalSignature` header for verification.

The verify phase looks up the truststore for the public key of the system it expects the message to have come from (in our case `system_a`), and checks the signature against the public key. If the message was modified after being signed, or the key to check the signature against is missing or is not the correct public key, the verify step will throw a `java.security.SignatureException`.

This ability to verify gives a certainty that the payload is exactly what was sent. It also provides a mechanism for non-repudiation since only a message signed with the private key of the sender can be verified using their public key.

There's more...

You can change the message signature header that is to be written to when signing, or that is used for verification by setting the `signatureHeader` URI attribute to another value:

```
crypto:sign://usingKeystore?keystore=#keyStore
&alias=system_a&password=keyPasswordA
&signatureHeader=mySignature
```

If you are receiving messages from a number of systems, each of which has its own key pair and signs its messages differently, it is possible to dynamically determine the alias to use from the truststore. To do this, set the `CamelSignatureKeyStoreAlias` (`DigitalSignatureConstants.KEYSTORE_ALIAS`) header before invoking the `crypto:` endpoint.

For example, in the following Java DSL fragment the calling routes indicate to the verification route which system signed the message so that the appropriate key can be fetched from the store. The third route (`"direct:verify"`) sets the `CamelSignatureKeyStoreAlias` header, which is then used to verify the signature using the named key from its truststore:

```
from("direct:sign_a")
  .to("crypto:sign://usingKeystore?keystore=#keyStore
      &alias=system_a&password=keyPasswordA")
  .setHeader("sendingSystem", constant("a"))
  .to("direct:verify");

from("direct:sign_b")
  .to("crypto:sign://usingKeystore?keystore=#keyStore
      &alias=system_b&password=keyPasswordB")
  .setHeader("sendingSystem", constant("b"))
  .to("direct:verify");

from("direct:verify")
  .setHeader(DigitalSignatureConstants.KEYSTORE_ALIAS,
      simple("system_${header[sendingSystem]}"))
  .to("crypto:verify//usingKeystore?keystore=#trustStore")
  .to("mock:verified");
```

A `CamelSignatureKeyStorePassword` (`DigitalSignatureConstants.KEYSTORE_PASSWORD`) header is also available for use if you would like to dynamically provide the password for the keystore during the signing phase.

The Camel Crypto Component also supports the use of public and private keys directly without using keystores. For an overview of how to do this, you should refer to the Camel Crypto for Digital Signatures documentation.

See also

▸ Camel Crypto for Digital Signatures: `http://camel.apache.org/crypto-digital-signatures.html`

▸ Spring Crypto Utils: `http://springcryptoutils.com/index.html`

▸ Key and Certificate Management Tool (`keytool`): `http://docs.oracle.com/javase/7/docs/technotes/tools/solaris/keytool.html`

▸ Standard Algorithm Names Documentation: `http://docs.oracle.com/javase/7/docs/technotes/guides/security/StandardNames.html`

Encrypting and decrypting a message

Camel's Crypto Component is used when you need to encrypt and decrypt an entire message. It provides a Camel Data Format that allows you to marshal (encrypt) or unmarshal (decrypt) your data.

The Crypto Component supports both symmetric (using a shared password) and asymmetric (using public key of recipient) encryption—the latter through PGP.

This recipe will show you how to configure basic symmetric encryption. It will show both marshaling (encrypting) and unmarshaling (decrypting) data. These actions would normally be done in different Camel routes on different systems.

Getting ready

The Java code for this recipe is located in the `org.camelcookbook.security.encryption` package. The Spring XML files are located under `src/main/resources/META-INF/spring` and prefixed with `encryption`.

To use Camel's Crypto Component, add the following to the `dependencies` section of your Maven POM:

```
<dependency>
  <groupId>org.apache.camel</groupId>
  <artifactId>camel-crypto</artifactId>
  <version>${camel-version}</version>
</dependency>
```

To make life easier around accessing keystores in Spring, you should use the Spring Crypto Utils library by adding the following dependency:

```
<dependency>
  <groupId>com.google.code.spring-crypto-utils</groupId>
  <artifactId>spring-crypto-utils</artifactId>
  <version>1.3.0</version>
</dependency>
```

Before using the cryptographic capabilities available in Camel to encrypt and decrypt a message you will require a keystore, which is a repository of keys.

For the purposes of this example we will use the `keytool` utility that is included as part of the Java Development Kit (JDK) to generate the keystore.

Generate a key into a new store that will be shared between the encrypting and decrypting systems as follows:

```
# keytool -genseckey -alias shared -keypass sharedKeyPassword
-keystore shared.jceks -storepass sharedKeystorePassword
-v -storetype JCEKS
```

This process will generate a key using the `DES` algorithm.

> The keystore type `JCEKS` is a particular type of store used for storing private keys. It is different from the default `JKS` store that is used in the *Digitally signing and verifying messages* recipe, which only stores key pairs.

Give this keystore to the people maintaining the system that will be the counterparty to the encryption process. Both systems involved in the encryption/decryption process need access to the same key.

How to do it...

To symmetrically encrypt and decrypt an entire message, perform the following steps:

1. If using Spring, add the `crypt` namespace from Spring Crypto Utils to the beans definition:

   ```
   <beans ...
     xmlns:crypt="http://springcryptoutils.com/schema/crypt"
     xsi:schemaLocation="...
       http://springcryptoutils.com/schema/crypt
         http://springcryptoutils.com/schema/crypt.xsd">
   ```

Next, load the keystore from the specified location, and fetch the shared key from it:

```
<crypt:keystore id="keyStore"
                location="classpath:shared.jceks"
                password="sharedKeystorePassword"
                type="JCEKS"/>
<crypt:secretKey id="secretKey"
                keystore-ref="keyStore"
                alias="shared"
                password="sharedKeyPassword"/>
```

If using Java only, load the shared key using a `java.security.Keystore` instance as follows:

```
KeyStore keyStore = KeyStore.getInstance("JCEKS");

// here we are loading a keystore stored in our JAR
ClassLoader classLoader = getClass().getClassLoader();
keyStore.load(
    classLoader.getResourceAsStream("shared.jceks"),
    "sharedKeystorePassword".toCharArray());

Key sharedKey = keyStore.getKey("shared",
    "sharedKeyPassword".toCharArray());
```

2. If using the XML DSL, define the Crypto Data Format within the Camel context, referring to the shared key in use by the `id` set in the previous step:

```
<camelContext
    xmlns="http://camel.apache.org/schema/spring">
  <dataFormats>
    <crypto id="sharedKeyCrypto"
            algorithm="DES"
            keyRef="secretKey"/>
  </dataFormats>
  <!-- ... -->
</camelContext>
```

If using Java, instantiate the `CryptoDataFormat` inside your `RouteBuilder` implementation instead:

```
CryptoDataFormat sharedKeyCrypto =
    new CryptoDataFormat("DES", sharedKey);
```

3. Add a `marshal` step to your route in order to encrypt the body of the message. In the XML DSL, this is done through referring to the data format by its `id`:

```
<marshal ref="sharedKeyCrypto"/>
```

In the Java DSL, you pass in the data format directly:

```
.marshal(sharedKeyCrypto)
```

4. To decrypt the encrypted body of a message, add an `unmarshal` step to your route that refers to the data format.

    In the XML DSL, this is done as follows:

```
<unmarshal ref="sharedKeyCrypto"/>
```

    The same thing is expressed in the Java DSL through:

```
.unmarshal(sharedKeyCrypto)
```

How it works...

The `camel-crypto` library uses the Camel data format mechanism to take an unencrypted representation of the data and marshal it. This produces an encrypted version of the data using the standard `java.security` APIs without exposing you to any of the gory details of that API.

Unmarshaling using a `CryptoDataFormat` initialized with the same key will give you the original message.

There's more...

There are numerous properties available on the `CryptoDataFormat` class that allow you to customize the algorithm used, the buffer size, the initialization vector, the message authentication algorithm (**message authentication code** or **MAC**), and whether or not a digital signature (**keyed-hash message authentication code** or **HMAC**)) should be appended to the encrypted data. As such, none of the flexibility of the Java Cryptography Extensions is abstracted away should you need to make use of it.

 Algorithm names are defined in the JCE Standard Algorithm Names Documentation. The algorithm used has to be supported by the JCE providers on both the system that you encrypt the message on, and the one that decrypts it. Not all algorithms are available on all JVMs due to export restrictions. For most purposes the default algorithm is perfectly adequate.

If you are sending messages to or receiving messages from a number of systems, each of which encrypts its messages differently, it is possible to dynamically determine the key to be used by the data format. To do this, you need to instantiate the `CryptoDataFormat` without referring to a `java.security.Key`:

```
CryptoDataFormat crypto = new CryptoDataFormat("DES", null);
```

In the XML DSL, the instantiation of the data format is performed as follows:

```
<crypto id="sharedKeyCrypto" algorithm="DES"/>
```

Within your route, you then set the `CamelCryptoKey` (`CryptoDataFormat.KEY`) header to a `Key` instance that the data format should use, before invoking the `marshal` or `unmarshal` step.

In the following Java DSL example, the `encrypt` route fetches a `Key` from the Camel Registry and sets it on this header. The `Key` is fetched by name depending on the value of the `system` header, which is set on the message:

```java
from("direct:encrypt").id("encrypt")
  .process(new Processor() {
    @Override
    public void process(Exchange exchange) throws Exception {
      Registry registry = exchange.getContext().getRegistry();
      Message in = exchange.getIn();
      Key key = registry.lookupByNameAndType(
          "shared_" + in.getHeader("system"),
          Key.class);
      in.setHeader(CryptoDataFormat.KEY, key);
    }
  })
  .marshal(crypto)
  .log("Message encrypted: ${body}")
  .to("direct:decrypt");

from("direct:decrypt").id("decrypt")
  .unmarshal(crypto)
  .log("Message decrypted: ${body}")
  .to("mock:decrypted");
```

> The `camel-crypto` library also provides a `PGPDataFormat` for asymmetric (public key) cryptography. This uses the PGP (Pretty Good Privacy) format as implemented by the Bouncy Castle Java Cryptography APIs.

See also

- Camel Crypto: `http://camel.apache.org/crypto.html`
- Camel Data Format: `http://camel.apache.org/data-format.html`
- Spring Crypto Utils: `http://springcryptoutils.com/index.html`
- Key and Certificate Management Tool (`keytool`): `http://docs.oracle.com/javase/7/docs/technotes/tools/solaris/keytool.html`
- Standard Algorithm Names Documentation: `http://docs.oracle.com/javase/7/docs/technotes/guides/security/StandardNames.html`
- Bouncy Castle Java Cryptography API: `http://www.bouncycastle.org/java.html`

Encrypting all or parts of an XML message

Camel's XML Security Component is used when you need to encrypt and decrypt all or parts of an XML message. A Data Format provided by this component handles transformation between an encrypted and decrypted message.

The XML Security Component supports both symmetric and asymmetric encryption of XML messages as outlined by the W3C Recommendation *XML Encryption Syntax and Processing*. In symmetric encryption, a password shared by the sender and receiver is used to encrypt and decrypt a message. Using asymmetric encryption, the public key of the message recipient is used to encrypt the message, thereby only permitting the intended recipient to decrypt it.

This Camel component allows you to provide an XPath that points to a node, or set of nodes, in the document that will be encrypted; if none is provided the entire document will be encrypted.

This recipe will show you how to configure full asymmetric encryption of XML message payloads. It will show you how to encrypt and decrypt a fragment of an XML message by providing an XPath to the node to be encrypted.

Getting ready

The Java code for this recipe is located in the `org.camelcookbook.transformation.` `xmlsecurity` package. The Spring XML files are located under `src/main/resources/` `META-INF/spring` and prefixed with `xmlsecurity`.

To use Camel's XML Security Component, you need to add a dependency on the Camel XML Security Component that provides an implementation for the XML Security Data Format using the Apache XML Security (Santuario) library.

Add the following to the `dependencies` section of your Maven POM:

```
<dependency>
  <groupId>org.apache.camel</groupId>
  <artifactId>camel-xmlsecurity</artifactId>
  <version>${camel-version}</version>
</dependency>
```

Before using the cryptographic capabilities available in Camel to encrypt and decrypt fragments of an XML message you will need:

- A pair of encryption keys (public and private) held in a keystore for use by the *decrypting* party
- A copy of the encrypting party's public encryption key, held in a truststore that is accessible by the *encrypting* party

For the purposes of this example we will use the `keytool` utility that is included as part of the Java Development Kit (JDK) to generate these keys and place them into the appropriate stores:

1. Generate the keystore that contains both public and private key certificates for the receiving system:

```
# keytool -genkeypair -v -keyalg RSA -alias system_a
-keystore xml_keystore.jks -dname 'CN=Scott,O=camelcookbook.org'
-storepass keystorePassword -validity 3650 -keypass keyPasswordA
```

 The `-keyalg` argument specifies the use of the RSA algorithm. This option needs to be set for asymmetric encryption.

2. Export the public key certificate:

```
# keytool -export -alias system_a -keystore xml_keystore.jks
-rfc -file selfsignedcert_xml_a.cer -storepass keystorePassword
```

3. Import the public key into the truststore of the sending system:

```
# keytool -import -noprompt -alias system_a
-file selfsignedcert_xml_a.cer -keystore xml_truststore.jks
-storepass truststorePassword
```

How to do it...

To encrypt, and subsequently decrypt an XML fragment in a document on the exchange, perform the following steps:

1. To perform XML encryption, first define a reference to the truststore that contains the public key of the message recipient.

   If using Spring, define a `keyStoreParameters` tag outside of the `camelContext` element:

```
<beans ...
    xmlns:camel="http://camel.apache.org/schema/spring"
    xsi:schemaLocation="...
      http://camel.apache.org/schema/spring
        http://camel.apache.org/schema/spring/camel-spring.xsd">

  <camel:keyStoreParameters
      id="trustStoreParams"
      resource="xml_truststore.jks"
      password="truststorePassword"/>

  <camelContext ...>
</beans>
```

The `resource` setting is a Camel resource path, so in this example it will look on the classpath for `xml_truststore.jks`. To find a truststore on the filesystem or on an HTTP server, you prefix the location with `file:` or `http:` respectively.

 The key password is shown in plain text so as to not complicate the example. In a real-world scenario, the password should be injected as an encrypted property. See the *Encrypting configuration properties* recipe for a description of how to do this.

If using Java, add the following code inside the `configure()` method of your `RouteBuilder` implementation:

```
KeyStoreParameters trustStoreParameters =
    new KeyStoreParameters();
trustStoreParameters.setResource("xml_truststore.jks");
trustStoreParameters.setPassword("truststorePassword");
```

2. Within your route, use the `secureXML` data format to marshal the unencrypted XML body of the exchange. This will perform the encryption step.

Using the XML DSL, this is done as follows:

```
<from uri="direct:encrypt"/>
<marshal>
  <secureXML
      secureTag="/booksignings/store/address"
      secureTagContents="true"
      recipientKeyAlias="system_a"
      xmlCipherAlgorithm=
        "http://www.w3.org/2001/04/xmlenc#tripledes-cbc"
      keyCipherAlgorithm=
        "http://www.w3.org/2001/04/xmlenc#rsa-1_5"
      keyOrTrustStoreParametersId="trustStoreParams"/>
</marshal>
<to uri="direct:decrypt"/>
```

The `secureTag` attribute contains the XPath of the message fragment to encrypt (use an empty String for the entire document).

The `xmlCipherAlgorithm` is a reference to the algorithm used to encrypt the XML.

The `keyCipherAlgorithm` is the algorithm that was used when the keys were generated in the *Getting ready* section of this recipe (RSA).

The same route is expressed in the Java DSL as follows:

```
from("direct:encrypt")
  .marshal()
    .secureXML(
        "/booksignings/store/address", // secure tag
```

```
        true,                   // secure tag contents
        "system_a",             // recipient key alias
        XMLCipher.TRIPLEDES,    // xml cipher
        XMLCipher.RSA_v1dot5,   // key cipher
        trustStoreParameters)
    .to("mock:marshalResult");
```

 Unlike in the XML DSL where we reference the id
of the `keyStoreParameters` tag through the
`keyOrTrustStoreParametersId` attribute, in the Java
variant we pass in the `KeyStoreParameters` object directly.

3. To decrypt an encrypted XML document, define a reference to the keystore that
   contains the public and private keys of the message recipient.

   If using Spring, again define a `keyStoreParameters` tag outside of the
   `camelContext` element:

```
<beans ...
    xmlns:camel="http://camel.apache.org/schema/spring"
    xsi:schemaLocation="...
      http://camel.apache.org/schema/spring
        http://camel.apache.org/schema/spring/camel-spring.xsd">

  <camel:keyStoreParameters
      id="keyStoreParams"
      resource="xml_keystore.jks"
      password="keystorePassword"/>

  <camelContext ...>
</beans>
```

   If using Java, add the following code inside the `configure()` method of your
   `RouteBuilder` implementation:

```
KeyStoreParameters keyStoreParameters =
    new KeyStoreParameters();
keyStoreParameters.setResource("xml_keystore.jks");
keyStoreParameters.setPassword("keystorePassword");
```

4. Within your route, use the `secureXML` data format to unmarshal the encrypted XML
   body of the exchange. This will perform the decryption step.

   Using the XML DSL this is done as follows:

```
<from uri="direct:decrypt"/>
<unmarshal>
  <secureXML
```

```
            secureTag="/booksignings/store/address"
            secureTagContents="true"
            recipientKeyAlias="system_a"
            xmlCipherAlgorithm=
                "http://www.w3.org/2001/04/xmlenc#tripledes-cbc"
            keyCipherAlgorithm=
                "http://www.w3.org/2001/04/xmlenc#rsa-1_5"
            keyOrTrustStoreParametersId="keyStoreParams"
            keyPassword="keyPasswordA"/>
    </unmarshal>
    <to uri="mock:out"/>
```

The same route is expressed in the Java DSL as follows:

```
from("direct:decrypt")
  .unmarshal()
    .secureXML(
        "/booksignings/store/address", // secure tag
        true,                          // secure tag contents
        "system_a",                    // recipient key alias
        XMLCipher.TRIPLEDES,           // xml cipher
        XMLCipher.RSA_v1dot5,          // key cipher
        keyStoreParameters,
        "keyPasswordA")                // key password
    .to("mock:out");
```

How it works...

The XML Security Component uses the Apache Santuario library to perform the XML encryption operations.

Given the following payload:

```
<booksignings>
  <store>
    <address>
      <street>123 Main St</street>
      <city>Boston</city>
    </address>
    <authors>
      <author>Scott Cranton</author>
    </authors>
  </store>
  <!-- … -->
</booksignings>
```

The encrypted version will appear as:

```
<booksignings>
  <store>
    <address>
      <xenc:EncryptedData
          xmlns:xenc="http://www.w3.org/2001/04/xmlenc#"
          Type="http://www.w3.org/2001/04/xmlenc#Content">
        <xenc:EncryptionMethod
            Algorithm=
              "http://www.w3.org/2001/04/xmlenc#tripledes-cbc"/>
        <ds:KeyInfo xmlns:ds="http://www.w3.org/2000/09/xmldsig#">
          <xenc:EncryptedKey>
            <xenc:EncryptionMethod
                Algorithm=
                  "http://www.w3.org/2001/04/xmlenc#kw-tripledes"/>
            <xenc:CipherData>
              <xenc:CipherValue>
i19aQxl9a5QV7cVym/5gV9Ih67Jklt6oc3Aph2ec6/zpui+0MC8YJw==
              </xenc:CipherValue>
            </xenc:CipherData>
          </xenc:EncryptedKey>
        </ds:KeyInfo>
        <xenc:CipherData>
          <xenc:CipherValue>
RvUlpr8CN51DcUx+Y3C7msQoprtoqc5vx9CplhmBqstZGHj5ThVuvJArFMaVXloXZs6cd7
w4N1bF/9E1Xa85CAB7uYwKwSFjzRgigndEXV4=
          </xenc:CipherValue>
        </xenc:CipherData>
      </xenc:EncryptedData>
    </address>
    <authors>
      <author>Scott Cranton</author>
    </authors>
  </store>
  <!-- ... -->
</booksignings>
```

This use of message encryption allows you to create routes that can encrypt sensitive information early within your message processing. All subsequent downstream message-processing steps will only have access to the encrypted contents. Through the use of partial message encryption, you can ensure that the most sensitive parts are hidden while still allowing content based routing and other message processing operations based on the non-sensitive parts of the message.

There's more...

The XML Security Component also easily handles documents containing XML namespaces. Consider the following payload:

```
<?xml version="1.0" encoding="UTF-8"?>
<booksignings
    xmlns="http://camelcookbook.org/schema/booksignings">
  <store>
    <address>
      <street>123 Main St</street>
      <city>Boston</city>
    </address>
    <authors>
      <author>Scott Cranton</author>
    </authors>
  </store>
  <!-- ... -->
</booksignings>
```

To encrypt this message using the XML DSL, you define an XML namespace on the `camelContext` element:

```
<camelContext
    xmlns="http://camel.apache.org/schema/spring"
    xmlns:c="http://camelcookbook.org/schema/booksignings">
```

You can then use the `c:` namespace in your XPath Expression:

```
<secureXML
    secureTag="/c:booksignings/c:store/c:address"
    secureTagContents="true"
    recipientKeyAlias="system_a"
    xmlCipherAlgorithm=
      "http://www.w3.org/2001/04/xmlenc#tripledes-cbc"
    keyCipherAlgorithm="http://www.w3.org/2001/04/xmlenc#rsa-1_5"
    keyOrTrustStoreParametersId="trustStoreParams"/>
```

To encrypt the message using the Java DSL, you define a `Map` of prefixes to namespace URIs inside your `RouteBuilder` implementation:

```
Map<String, String> namespaces = new HashMap<String, String>();
namespaces.put("c",
    "http://camelcookbook.org/schema/booksignings");
```

You then provide `Map` as an additional argument to the `secureXML` DSL statement. This allows you to use the `c:` namespace prefix in your XPath Expression to identify the node to be encrypted.

```
.secureXML(
    "/c:booksignings/c:store/c:address", // prefixed XPath
    namespaces,
    true,                                // secure tag contents
    "system_a",                          // recipient key alias
    XMLCipher.TRIPLEDES,                 // xml cipher
    XMLCipher.RSA_v1dot5,                // key cipher
    trustStoreParameters)
```

See also

▸ Camel XML Security: `http://camel.apache.org/xmlsecurity-dataformat.html`

▸ W3C XML Encryption Syntax and Processing: `http://www.w3.org/TR/2002/REC-xmlenc-core-20021210/Overview.html`

▸ Apache Santuario: `https://santuario.apache.org`

▸ Available Data Formats: `http://camel.apache.org/data-format.html`

Authentication and authorization using Spring Security

This recipe will show how using the Spring Security framework you can authenticate credentials passed into a route on an exchange, and determine whether that user/system (**Principal** in security terms) is authorized to access the route based on their role.

Getting ready

The Java code for this recipe is located in the `org.camelcookbook.security.springsecurity` package. The Spring XML files are located under `src/main/resources/META-INF/spring` and prefixed with `springSecurity`.

To use Camel's Spring Security Component, add the following to the `dependencies` section of your Maven POM:

```
<dependency>
  <groupId>org.apache.camel</groupId>
  <artifactId>camel-spring-security</artifactId>
  <version>${camel-version}</version>
</dependency>
```

In order for your configuration to be parsed correctly, you will also need the appropriate Spring Security JARs without any of their Core Spring dependencies in order to avoid version clashes.

```
<dependency>
  <groupId>org.springframework.security</groupId>
  <artifactId>spring-security-core</artifactId>
  <version>${spring-security-version}</version>
  <exclusions>
    <exclusion>
      <groupId>org.springframework</groupId>
      <artifactId>spring-core</artifactId>
    </exclusion>
    <exclusion>
      <groupId>org.springframework</groupId>
      <artifactId>spring-expression</artifactId>
    </exclusion>
    <exclusion>
      <groupId>org.springframework</groupId>
      <artifactId>spring-beans</artifactId>
    </exclusion>
  </exclusions>
</dependency>
<dependency>
  <groupId>org.springframework.security</groupId>
  <artifactId>spring-security-config</artifactId>
  <version>${spring-security-version}</version>
  <exclusions>
    <exclusion>
      <groupId>org.springframework</groupId>
      <artifactId>spring-core</artifactId>
    </exclusion>
    <exclusion>
      <groupId>org.springframework</groupId>
      <artifactId>spring-beans</artifactId>
    </exclusion>
  </exclusions>
</dependency>
```

The `${spring-security-version}` used here is `3.1.4.RELEASE`. Yours should correspond to the same version used by the `camel-spring-security` library.

At the time of writing this book, Camel primarily uses Spring 3.2, but uses an older version of Spring Security—3.1.4. Double check with the Camel documentation and source to verify that you are referencing consistent versions.

How to do it...

The steps that we need to perform to authenticate and authorize an exchange on a route are as follows:

1. Extract the credentials from the exchange and set them in a place accessed by Spring Security, or its Camel wrapper (there are 2 options).

2. Define an authentication mechanism that Spring Security will use to check those credentials against, and fetch the roles that then correspond to those credentials.

3. Define an authorization mechanism that Spring Security will use to check those roles against in order to work out whether the exchange should be processed.

4. Bridge this mechanism to Camel through a `Policy`, and use it from the route.

To carry out the steps described, you need to perform a series of actions as follows:

1. Register two additional XML namespaces in the Spring configuration; one for Spring Security, and another for the Camel Spring Security bindings:

```
<beans xmlns="http://www.springframework.org/schema/beans"
  xmlns:xsi="http://www.w3.org/2001/XMLSchema-instance"
  xmlns:sec="http://www.springframework.org/schema/security"
  xmlns:camel-sec="http://camel.apache.org/schema/spring-security"
  xsi:schemaLocation="
    http://www.springframework.org/schema/beans
      http://www.springframework.org/schema/beans/spring-beans.xsd
    http://www.springframework.org/schema/security
      http://www.springframework.org/schema/security/
      spring-security-3.1.xsd
    http://camel.apache.org/schema/spring
      http://camel.apache.org/schema/spring/camel-spring.xsd
    http://camel.apache.org/schema/spring-security
      http://camel.apache.org/schema/spring-
      security/camel-spring-security.xsd">
```

2. The mechanism by which you obtain credentials is dependent on the consumer transport. As such you will often have to write this part yourself. This can be done using a `Processor`:

```
public class SecurityContextLoader implements Processor {
  @Override
  public void process(Exchange exchange) throws Exception {
    Message in = exchange.getIn();
    String username = in.getHeader("username", String.class);
    String password = in.getHeader("password", String.class);

    Authentication authenticationToken =
```

```
    new UsernamePasswordAuthenticationToken(username,
        password);
  SecurityContextHolder.getContext()
    .setAuthentication(authenticationToken);
  }
}
```

In this simple instance we expect the credentials to come down the route within the message headers. Credentials are stored in an implementation of `org. springframework.security.core.Authentication`.

 The `org.springframework.security.core.context. SecurityContextHolder` is a `ThreadLocal`-based mechanism that is accessed by Spring Security for authentication and authorization.

3. Register the processor as a regular Spring bean:

```
<bean id="securityContextLoader"
      class="org.camelcookbook.security.springsecurity
            .SecurityContextLoader"/>
```

4. Define a user service that maps credentials to roles. Here, we use a very simple instance where these details are stored in the Spring configuration:

```
<sec:user-service id="userService">
  <sec:user name="jakub"
          password="supersecretpassword1"
          authorities="ROLE_USER, ROLE_ADMIN"/>
  <sec:user name="scott"
          password="supersecretpassword2"
          authorities="ROLE_USER"/>
</sec:user-service>
```

A user service is one which, given a user name, fetches the corresponding details—it does not actually authenticate them. Spring Security provides out of the box implementations for accessing databases and LDAP servers, or you can build your own.

5. Next, define an `AuthenticationManager` that will authenticate the credentials using this user service:

```
<sec:authentication-manager alias="authenticationManager">
  <sec:authentication-provider user-service-ref="userService"/>
</sec:authentication-manager>
```

6. Define an access decision manager that will make a decision on whether to permit the given credentials access to the resource.

   Spring Security's authorization process works on the idea of voters (implementations of `org.springframework.security.access.AccessDecisionVoter`) that each get to decide in turn whether the `Authentication` object has access to the resource. Each voter votes to either grant or deny access, or abstain from the vote.

   The access decision manager pulls together the votes, and makes the final decision. Three decision managers are available, which require that either any one voter votes yes (`AffirmativeBased`), all voters vote yes (`UnanimousBased`), or the majority of voters vote yes (`ConcensusBased`).

```
<bean id="accessDecisionManager"
      class="org.springframework.security.access.vote
            .AffirmativeBased">
  <constructor-arg>
    <list>
      <bean class="org.springframework.security.access.vote
                  .RoleVoter"/>
    </list>
  </constructor-arg>
</bean>
```

   The sole voter used here makes a decision based on roles.

7. Wrap the Spring Security mechanisms in a Camel Policy, which provides the hook into a Camel route. Here, we specify that the authentication pulled from the exchange must be in the ROLE_ADMIN role:

```
<camel-sec:authorizationPolicy
    id="adminAuthPolicy"
    access="ROLE_ADMIN"
    authenticationManager="authenticationManager"
    accessDecisionManager="accessDecisionManager"
    useThreadSecurityContext="true"/>
```

8. In your route, trigger the processor that you have defined to extract the authentication from the exchange, and then use the policy around any sensitive code to which access must be protected:

```
<from uri="direct:in"/>
<process ref="securityContextLoader"/>
<policy ref="adminAuthPolicy">
  <to uri="mock:secure"/>
</policy>
```

How it works...

The process for granting access is to:

1. Extract the credentials from the message.
2. Authenticate the credentials using data from the user service.
3. Determine whether the Principal has access to the specified resources.

If either of the preceding steps 2 or 3 fail, an `org.apache.camel.CamelAuthorizationException` will be thrown detailing the problem. This exception can be caught and handled as usual using the mechanism described in the *Catching exceptions*, and *Fine-grained error handling using doTry...doCatch* recipes in *Chapter 7, Error Handling and Compensation*.

There's more...

The `SecurityContextHolder` used to carry the user credentials relies on a `ThreadLocal` internally. This is a design decision stemming from Spring Security's original use within web applications. In the context of integrations with Camel, it occasionally causes headaches, as the `Authentication` object is lost when the exchange crosses a thread boundary, such as when being passed across a `seda:` endpoint as discussed in the *Asynchronously connecting routes* recipe in *Chapter 1, Structuring Routes*. In general, you should extract the credentials from the transport and verify that they have access to the operation being performed within the same thread.

If this is not possible, you can get around this constraint by wrapping the `Authentication` in a `javax.security.auth.Subject` and setting it in the `CamelAuthentication` header (defined as a constant in `Exchange.AUTHENTICATION`) of the exchange. Camel's Spring Security `policy` will extract it from the header and pass it into the authentication and access decision managers.

To do this, you need only to change your `SecurityContextLoader` implementation to perform the following steps instead of initializing the `SecurityContextHolder`:

```
Subject subject = new Subject();
subject.getPrincipals().add(authenticationToken);
in.setHeader(Exchange.AUTHENTICATION, subject);
```

Spring Security breaks down authentication and authorization into separate processes that are configured independently of each other. There is a substantial number of options available. For full details you should refer to the Spring Security documentation.

The Spring Security mechanisms are easy to use within Spring applications. They are much more difficult to use within OSGi Blueprints and plain Java applications, due to the dependency on Spring lifecycle interfaces and the amount of code that is hidden away from you within the custom Spring namespace handlers.

If you require authentication and authorization in one of these environments, you should consider the Apache Shiro security project as an alternative. This is accessible through the Camel Shiro component.

See also

- ▸ Camel Spring Security: `http://camel.apache.org/spring-security.html`
- ▸ Spring Security: `http://docs.spring.io/spring-security/site/`
- ▸ Camel Shiro Security: `http://camel.apache.org/shiro-security.html`

12

Web Services

In this chapter, we will cover the following recipes:

- ▶ Generating the service stubs from a WSDL
- ▶ Invoking a remote web service from Camel
- ▶ Implementing a web service with a Camel route
- ▶ Providing multiple web service operations within a single route
- ▶ Handling web service faults
- ▶ Web service proxying

Introduction

In this chapter, we will explore Camel's capabilities for interacting with SOAP web services, which are commonly used in integration technology. Camel strongly supports the Apache CXF project (`http://cxf.apache.org/`) as a web services framework. As such it is very easy to use CXF to create Camel routes that can both call external web services and act as web service listeners. This chapter's recipes will show you some of the common scenarios for web service integration with Camel that will provide a starting point for your continued exploration of these capabilities.

The CXF library supports both SOAP through the **Java API for XML Web Services** (**JAX-WS**), and REST through the **Java API for RESTful Web Services** (**JAX-RS**). This chapter will focus on SOAP web services based on service contracts defined using the **Web Service Definition Language** (**WSDL**).

CXF is a very rich library with extensive support for the WS-* set of standards. For details on how to make use of these, you should refer to the CXF website.

There are generally two approaches for building SOAP web services:

1. Define a contract for the service through a WSDL file, and then generate JAX-WS and **JAXB (Java Architecture for XML Binding)** annotated Java classes and interfaces from that WSDL. This will provide you with a foundation upon which the service implementation will be built. This is known as *contract-first* development. In system integration, this style of development tends to be the most common way to develop services, as both the service provider and its clients agree on the service interface up front.

2. Build a regular Java service, then annotate it and its supporting data transfer objects with JAX-WS and JAXB annotations. This is known as *service-first* development. Service-first development tends to be more tactical in nature, allowing you to expose classes that were developed with another interface in mind over SOAP.

This chapter will focus on contract-first web service development.

A number of Camel architectural concepts are used throughout this chapter. There is a broader overview of Camel concepts in the *Preface*. Full details can be found at the Apache Camel website at `http://camel.apache.org`.

The code for this chapter is contained within the `camel-cookbook-web-services` module of the examples.

Generating the service stubs from a WSDL

In order to use the Camel CXF Component to either consume from or produce to SOAP web services, you will first need to generate a set of interfaces that define the web service based on a predefined service contract—the WSDL. To do this, we will use a Maven plugin provided by the Apache CXF project.

These generated interfaces take the form of regular Java classes and interfaces marked up with JAX-WS annotations. These classes, used as arguments and return values from the web service methods, are known as models, and they will be generated from the XML schema contained within the WSDL. These classes will be annotated with JAXB bindings to automate the conversion between the Java objects and their XML representation.

Collectively these JAX-WS artifacts make it possible for Camel to call web services or to act as a web service provider.

This recipe will show you the basics of setting up the `cxf-codegen-plugin` to automate the build-time generation of JAX-WS artifacts from your project's WSDL documents.

Getting ready

The `cxf-codegen-plugin` is referenced within a Maven project's `pom.xml` file. This recipe defines a child project, `ws-payments-api`, within the `camel-cookbook-web-services` module for the sole purpose of generating JAX-WS artifacts from the WSDL files that define a web service contract. This project's JAR artifact will be used as a dependency by the `ws-camel-routes` project that includes the Camel routes.

To generate a class representation of a web service, you will require a WSDL file. This chapter makes use of the samples contained within the `src/main/resources/wsdl` directory.

How to do it...

In the Maven project's `pom.xml` file, add the following plugin definition:

```
<build>
  <plugins>
    <plugin>
      <groupId>org.apache.cxf</groupId>
      <artifactId>cxf-codegen-plugin</artifactId>
      <version>${cxf-version}</version>
      <executions>
        <execution>
          <phase>generate-sources</phase>
          <goals>
            <goal>wsdl2java</goal>
          </goals>
          <configuration>
            <sourceRoot>
              ${project.build.directory}/generated-sources/cxf
            </sourceRoot>
            <wsdlRoot>
              ${project.basedir}/src/main/resources/wsdl
            </wsdlRoot>
            <includes>
              <include>*.wsdl</include>
            </includes>
          </configuration>
        </execution>
      </executions>
    </plugin>
    <!-- other plugins -->
  </plugins>
  <!-- other build configurations -->
</build>
```

The ${cxf-version} used in this example is 2.7.7.

How it works...

The default behavior of the `cxf-codegen-plugin`, as shown configured in the preceding *How to do it...* section, is to parse the WSDL files in your project's `src/main/resources/wsdl` directory (specified in the `wsdlRoot` option), and generate JAX-WS and JAXB artifacts in your project's `target/generated-sources/cxf` (`sourceRoot`) directory.

The code generation happens during the `generate-sources` phase of the build (see the Maven documentation for a description of the build lifecycle). Maven will automatically compile these Java source files and include the resulting classes in the module being built. You can then start referencing these classes in your code, including within your Camel routes.

It is considered best practice to create a separate Maven project for the sole purpose of generating the JAX-WS annotated web service API from your WSDL files. This project is then used as a dependency by modules that define your Camel routes. Aside from enabling reuse of the API between modules, it makes the generated classes easier to work with from within an IDE. That is, after the first build of the API project, you get code completion around the generated classes in dependent modules without needing to do anything special in the IDE. This is preferable to doing everything in the same project, as your IDE otherwise depends on a source directory that appears only during a Maven build.

The primary benefit of generating JAX-WS source code from a WSDL, and using it in your Camel routes, is that the body and headers of the SOAP messages are accessible to your routing logic as Plain Old Java Objects (POJOs). This makes it very easy to create routes that work with messages coming from multiple frontend technologies, including web services, and operate on them in a consistent fashion.

Code is generated into packages named in the reverse order of their namespace URIs. Two namespaces are of particular interest, the `targetNamespace` for the service definition and the schema namespace of the payload elements. Consider this fragment from the example WSDL file `paymentService.wsdl` located in `src/main/resources/wsdl/`:

```
<wsdl:definitions name="wsdl-first"
    xmlns:wsdl="http://schemas.xmlsoap.org/wsdl/"
    xmlns:soap="http://schemas.xmlsoap.org/wsdl/soap/"
    xmlns:xsd="http://www.w3.org/2001/XMLSchema"
    xmlns:tns="http://ws.camelcookbook.org/payment-service"
    xmlns:typens=
      "http://ws.camelcookbook.org/payment-service/types"
    targetNamespace=
      "http://ws.camelcookbook.org/payment-service">

  <wsdl:types>
```

```
<xsd:schema
    targetNamespace=
      "http://ws.camelcookbook.org/payment-service/types"
    elementFormDefault="qualified">
  <!-- ... -->
  </xsd:schema>
</wsdl:types>

<!-- ... -->

<wsdl:service name="PaymentService">
  <wsdl:port binding="tns:PaymentSOAPBinding"
          name="PaymentPort">
    <soap:address
       location="http://localhost:9090/paymentService"/>
  </wsdl:port>
</wsdl:service>
</wsdl:definitions>
```

The service interfaces will be generated from the namespace:

```
http://ws.camelcookbook.org/payment-service
```

The Java package that they will be placed into is as follows:

```
org.camelcookbook.ws.payment-service
```

Likewise, the object representation of the schema will be generated from the following namespace:

```
http://ws.camelcookbook.org/payment-service/types
```

The Java package that they will be placed into is as follows:

```
org.camelcookbook.ws.payment-service.types
```

There's more...

You do not have to use the `cxf-codegen-plugin` to generate the required JAX-WS annotated objects; you can instead handcode the JAX-WS classes directly using annotations if you like. Alternatively, the Apache CXF project also includes a `java2ws` tool that comes with an associated wrapper Maven plugin, which will generate the JAX-WS artifacts from your existing Java interfaces for a service-first approach.

See also

► Apache CXF: `http://cxf.apache.org`

► The `cxf-codegen-plugin` documentation: `http://cxf.apache.org/docs/ maven-cxf-codegen-plugin-wsdl-to-java.html`

► Introduction to the Maven Build Lifecycle: `http://maven.apache.org/guides/ introduction/introduction-to-the-lifecycle.html`

► Web Service Description Language (WSDL): `http://www.w3.org/TR/wsdl`

Invoking a remote web service from Camel

Camel's CXF Component makes calling a web service easy by defaulting to using POJOs for the request and response objects, and storing all of the other SOAP details in exchange headers in case you need them.

With Camel's built-in data type conversion and bean parameter-binding capabilities, you can easily call out to your Java methods that expect the body of the SOAP message as either a parameter or as a return type. Camel will automatically handle the conversions between Java and XML. When calling a web service, additional details, such as which operation name to invoke, are set in the exchange separately from the body of the message.

This recipe will show you the basic structure for calling a web service from a Camel route.

Getting ready

This recipe assumes that you have a project with JAX-WS artifacts created as shown in the *Generating the service stubs from a WSDL* recipe. To use the generated API, you need to include a dependency to that project in your build:

```
<dependency>
  <groupId>org.camelcookbook.examples</groupId>
  <artifactId>ws-payments-api</artifactId>
  <version>1.0-SNAPSHOT</version>
</dependency>
```

All the source files for this recipe are located in the `ws-camel-routes` project in the `camel-cookbook-web-services` module. The Java code for this recipe is located in the `org.camelcookbook.ws.client` package. The Spring XML files are located under `src/main/resources/META-INF/spring` and are prefixed with `client`.

How to do it...

To invoke a web service from Camel using the Camel CXF Component, perform the following steps:

1. Configure the web service endpoint that will be invoked by defining a `cxfEndpoint` element outside the `camelContext` element. This element is found in the Camel CXF namespace (`http://camel.apache.org/schema/cxf`). It defines the address of the remote service (`address`), and the interface class that was generated from the WSDL (`serviceClass`).

```
<beans ...
    xmlns:cxf="http://camel.apache.org/schema/cxf"
    xsi:schemaLocation="...
      http://camel.apache.org/schema/cxf
      http://camel.apache.org/schema/cxf/camel-cxf.xsd">

  <cxf:cxfEndpoint
      id="paymentServiceEndpoint"
      address="http://localhost:1234/paymentService"
      serviceClass=
        "org.camelcookbook.ws.payment_service.Payment"/>
  <!-- ... -->
</beans>
```

The `serviceClass` is the interface generated from the WSDL. The `address` represents the URL of the remote service that CXF will invoke.

In the Java DSL, since we cannot use Spring namespace handlers (that is, `cxfEndpoint`), we simply create an endpoint URI string:

```
final String cxfUri =
  "cxf:http://localhost:1234/paymentService?" +
  "serviceClass=" + Payment.class.getName();
```

2. Invoke the web service.

In the XML DSL, reference the endpoint that you configured in step one using the `cxf:bean:` prefix with the operation name that you want to trigger, as well as any additional options specific to this route step:

```
<camelContext
    xmlns="http://camel.apache.org/schema/spring">
  <route id="wsClient">
    <from uri="direct:start"/>
    <log message="${body}"/>
    <to uri="cxf:bean:paymentServiceEndpoint
            ?defaultOperationName=transferFunds"
    />
  </route>
</camelContext>
```

In the Java DSL, we append any additional options to our endpoint URI:

```
from("direct:start")
    .id("wsClient")
.log("${body}")
.to(cxfUri + "&defaultOperationName=transferFunds");
```

How it works...

This code example assumes that the body of Camel exchange is of the type `TransferRequest`, which is the expected request parameter type specified in the WSDL for the `transferFunds` operations. The Camel CXF Component will automatically wrap the message body with the appropriate SOAP envelope including any other SOAP header information configured by the endpoint for security.

In the case of request-response web service operations, the Camel CXF Component will extract the SOAP body of the response, convert it into a POJO, and place it into the body of exchange for further processing by the route.

A lot happens under the covers within the interaction between the Camel and CXF frameworks to correctly wrap and unwrap the POJO message into a web service invocation. This recipe demonstrates only the most basic structure for invoking a web service from Camel. Please see the Camel and CXF documentation in the *See also* section of this recipe for the full range of options available to you when dealing with SOAP web services.

There's more...

In this example, we configured the endpoint with a `defaultOperationName` that will have the Camel CXF Component invoke that operation. You can also set the `operationName` header on the exchange to the web service operation to call. That header's value will override any default operation name configured on the endpoint.

The Camel CXF Component has a `dataFormat` option that allows you to specify that you want the data in a format other than the default POJO mode. For example, to process the raw SOAP XML message, set `dataFormat=MESSAGE`. See the Camel CXF Component documentation for full details.

See also

- ▶ Camel CXF Component: `http://camel.apache.org/cxf`
- ▶ Apache CXF: `http://cxf.apache.org`
- ▶ The *Generating the service stubs from a WSDL* recipe

Implementing a web service with a Camel route

The Camel CXF Component allows a Camel route to act as a SOAP (or REST) web service listener. This allows you to create web service frontends for other systems, including acting as a web service proxy—something that is discussed in-depth in the *Web service proxying* recipe.

This recipe will show you the basic steps of exposing a Camel route as a web service consumer/listener.

Getting ready

This recipe assumes that you have a project with JAX-WS artifacts created as shown in the *Generating the service stubs from a WSDL* recipe. To use the generated API, you need to include a dependency to that project in your build:

```
<dependency>
    <groupId>org.camelcookbook.examples</groupId>
    <artifactId>ws-payments-api</artifactId>
    <version>1.0-SNAPSHOT</version>
</dependency>
```

This recipe's example is based on `paymentService.wsdl`, whose interface has one operation, `transferFunds`.

```
<wsdl:portType name="Payment">
  <wsdl:operation name="transferFunds">
    <wsdl:input message="tns:TransferRequest"/>
    <wsdl:output message="tns:TransferResponse"/>
    <wsdl:fault name="fault" message="tns:FaultMessage"/>
  </wsdl:operation>
</wsdl:portType>
```

All source files for this recipe are located in the `ws-camel-routes` project in the `camel-cookbook-web-services` module. The Java code for this recipe is located in the `org.camelcookbook.ws.service` package. The Spring XML files are located under `src/main/resources/META-INF/spring` and prefixed with `service`.

How to do it...

There are three primary steps to expose a web service listener (consumer) using Camel:

1. Configure the Camel CXF endpoint.

2. Write some code that does something with the message.

3. Write a route that consumes the message from the endpoint, routes the request to the business logic and returns a response, if applicable.

The preceding steps are performed as follows:

1. Configure the Camel CXF endpoint.

   In the XML DSL, you will want to use the `cxfEndpoint` defined in the Camel CXF schema. This makes it possible for your IDE to autocomplete and validate the endpoint's parameters.

   ```xml
   <beans xmlns="http://www.springframework.org/schema/beans"
          xmlns:camel="http://camel.apache.org/schema/spring"
          xmlns:cxf="http://camel.apache.org/schema/cxf"
          xmlns:xsi=
            "http://www.w3.org/2001/XMLSchema-instance"
          xsi:schemaLocation="
            http://www.springframework.org/schema/beans
       http://www.springframework.org/schema/beans/spring-beans.xsd
            http://camel.apache.org/schema/cxf
   http://camel.apache.org/schema/cxf/camel-cxf.xsd
            http://camel.apache.org/schema/spring
   http://camel.apache.org/schema/spring/camel-spring.xsd
            ">

       <cxf:cxfEndpoint
           id="paymentServiceEndpoint"
           address="http://localhost:1234/paymentService"
           serviceClass="org.camelcookbook.ws
                       .payment_service.Payment"/>

       <!-- other stuff -->
   </beans>
   ```

   In the Java DSL, since we cannot use Spring namespace handlers (that is, `cxfEndpoint`), we will just create an endpoint URI String:

   ```java
   final String cxfUri =
       "cxf:http://localhost:1234/paymentService?"
       + "serviceClass=" + Payment.class.getCanonicalName();
   ```

2. Do something with the request. The easiest way to process a web service message is to create a POJO that takes the request object(s) as parameter(s), and returns the response from the method call. Since you have most likely generated the request and response artifacts from the WSDL, you can just simply use them directly in your Java code:

```java
import org.camelcookbook.ws.payment_service.types
        .TransferRequest;
import org.camelcookbook.ws.payment_service.types
        .TransferResponse;

public class PaymentServiceImpl {
  public TransferResponse
      transfer(TransferRequest request) {
    TransferResponse response = new TransferResponse();
    response.setReply("OK");
    return response;
  }
}
```

3. Route the request and response. Not all web services need to return responses. Whether a response is expected is indicated by the MEP within the exchange being set to InOut, as in this example.

   In the XML DSL, you reference the endpoint you configured in step one using cxf:bean. The endpoint must be referenced within the from statement for it to be a Camel consumer, that is, in order for it to create an HTTP listener to receive the SOAP messages and feed messages into the Camel route:

```xml
<route id="wsRoute">
  <from uri="cxf:bean:paymentServiceEndpoint"/>
  <transform>
    <simple>${in.body[0]}</simple>
  </transform>
  <log message="request = ${body}"/>
  <bean ref="paymentServiceImpl"/>
  <log message="response = ${body}"/>
</route>
```

   In the Java DSL, we concatenate any additional options to our endpoint URI as we saw in step 1:

```java
from(cxfUri)
    .id("wsRoute")
  .transform(simple("${in.body[0]}"))
  .log("request = ${body}")
  .bean(PaymentServiceImpl.class)
  .log("response = ${body}");
```

The Camel CXF Component, when acting as an endpoint consumer, will put an array of objects into the Camel message—specifically an array of the request parameters. For Document-style web services, there will only be a single parameter. The `transform(simple("${in.body[0]}"))` step will extract that single POJO request object and place it into the Camel message body for processing by the rest of the route.

How it works...

The Camel CXF Component, when used as a consumer endpoint (in the `from` part of the route), will start an HTTP listener internally that will receive SOAP messages when the Camel route is started. The endpoint will receive and parse SOAP messages it receives, and map them into the route as Camel exchanges.

The mapping is based on the `dataFormat` option of the Camel CXF Component that defaults to `POJO`, which will map the SOAP headers and other related connection information into exchange headers. The SOAP body will be transformed into a POJO according to the JAX-WS bindings, and placed into the message body of the exchange.

It is also possible to consume the message body as an XML document by setting the `dataFormat` parameter to `PAYLOAD`. This is useful for XPath matching and XSLT transformations.

You can also consume the entire SOAP message as an XML document by setting this parameter to `MESSAGE`.

When using the `POJO` data format, the Camel CXF endpoint consumer will create a `MessageContentList`, which is an array of the request parameters. This is what is placed into the exchange message body. Be aware that you will need to access the request parameters from an array, even if your web service is Document-Literal style, that is, it only contains a single parameter. This is a common source of confusion when using the Camel CXF Component.

The Java bean that processes the request could implement the generated JAX-WS web service Java interface `org.camelcookbook.ws.payment_service.Payment`. This would provide stronger typing to the WSDL, but it also forces you to implement all of the web service operations within a single Java class, which you may not want to do. In general, it is easier to just use the generated request and response types in your method arguments to achieve strong typing.

There's more...

The operation name of the invoked web service will be placed into an exchange header called `operationName`. You can use this header to correctly route and process the request. We will see an example of this in the *Providing multiple web service operations within a single route* recipe.

See also

- ▸ Camel CXF Component: `http://camel.apache.org/cxf`
- ▸ Apache CXF: `http://cxf.apache.org`
- ▸ The *Generating the service stubs from a WSDL* recipe
- ▸ The *Providing multiple web service operations within a single route* recipe

Providing multiple web service operations within a single route

The Camel CXF Component has the ability to allow a Camel route to act as a SOAP (or REST) web service listener as we saw in the *Implementing a web service with a Camel route* recipe. Most web services expose more than one operation as part of their interface. This recipe will show you a strategy for handling multiple web service operations within a single Camel route acting as a web service frontend.

Getting ready

This recipe assumes that you have a project with JAX-WS artifacts created as described in the *Generating the service stubs from a WSDL* recipe. To use the generated API, you need to include a dependency to that project in your build:

```
<dependency>
  <groupId>org.camelcookbook.examples</groupId>
  <artifactId>ws-payments-api</artifactId>
  <version>1.0-SNAPSHOT</version>
</dependency>
```

This recipe's example is based on `paymentService2.wsdl`, whose interface has two operations, `transferFunds` and `checkStatus`.

```
<wsdl:portType name="Payment">
  <wsdl:operation name="transferFunds">
    <wsdl:input message="tns:TransferRequest"/>
    <wsdl:output message="tns:TransferResponse"/>
```

```
          <wsdl:fault name="fault" message="tns:FaultMessage"/>
      </wsdl:operation>
      <wsdl:operation name="checkStatus">
          <wsdl:input message="tns:CheckStatusRequest"/>
          <wsdl:output message="tns:CheckStatusResponse"/>
          <wsdl:fault name="fault" message="tns:FaultMessage"/>
      </wsdl:operation>
  </wsdl:portType>
```

All source files for this recipe are located in the `ws-camel-routes` project in the `camel-cookbook-web-services` module. The Java code for this recipe is located in the `org.camelcookbook.ws.multipleoperations` package. The Spring XML files are located under `src/main/resources/META-INF/spring` and prefixed with `multipleOperations`.

How to do it...

In order to provide multiple web service operations within a single Camel route, perform the following steps:

1. Configure a Camel CXF endpoint as described in step 1 of the *Implementing a web service with a Camel route* recipe.

2. Route the exchange based on the `operationName` header using a Content Based Router.

   In the XML DSL, this is written as:

```xml
<route id="wsRoute">
  <from uri="cxf:bean:paymentServiceEndpoint"/>
  <transform>
    <simple>${in.body[0]}</simple>
  </transform>
  <log message="request = ${body}"/>
  <choice>
    <when>
      <simple>
        ${in.header.operationName} == 'transferFunds'
      </simple>
      <bean ref="paymentServiceImpl"/>
    </when>
    <when>
      <simple>
        ${in.header.operationName} == 'checkStatus'
      </simple>
      <bean ref="checkStatusServiceImpl"/>
    </when>
    <otherwise>
```

```
    <setFaultBody>
      <method ref="faultHandler"
              method="createInvalidOperation"/>
    </setFaultBody>
  </otherwise>
</choice>
<log message="response = ${body}"/>
</route>
```

In the Java DSL, the same route is expressed as:

```
from(cxfUri).id("wsRoute")
  .transform(simple("${in.body[0]}"))
  .log("request = ${body}")
  .choice()
    .when(simple(
        "${in.header.operationName} == 'transferFunds'"
    ))
      .bean(PaymentServiceV2Impl.class)
    .when(simple(
        "${in.header.operationName} == 'checkStatus'"
    ))
      .bean(CheckStatusServiceV2Impl.class)
    .otherwise()
      .setFaultBody(method(FaultHandler.class,
                          "createInvalidOperation"))
  .end()
  .log("response = ${body}");
```

When an invalid operation name is detected in the `otherwise` part of the `choice` block, a SOAP Fault is raised through the `setFaultBody` DSL statement. This mechanism is described in more detail in the *Handling web service faults* recipe.

How it works...

The Camel CXF endpoint consumer will place the web service operation name into the `operationName` header on the exchange. You use Camel's Content Based Router to route the request as appropriate, based on this value.

The consumer also sets an `operationNamespace` header that contains the namespace of the SOAP operation. This can be useful if your WSDL supports multiple versions of a web service through a version number in the namespace. In such a case, you can also use this header to route the exchange to different service methods.

The `otherwise` part of the Content Base Router will catch requests with unknown operation names. In this example, a SOAP Fault is returned. See the *Handling web service faults* recipe for more details on Fault handling in Camel.

There's more...

The Camel CXF Component supports the convention of returning the WSDL for a service endpoint when an HTTP request is made to the service URL that includes the `?wsdl` query parameter.

For example, if your web service is accessible through `http://localhost:8080/paymentServicev2`, the WSDL for the service endpoint is accessible via `http://localhost:8080/paymentServicev2?wsdl`.

The component uses the configured JAX-WS artifacts to allow it to generate that WSDL at runtime based on the annotations of the `serviceClass` defined on the endpoint. There are a number of Camel CXF options that allow you to fine-tune the exposed web service and its generated WSDL contract; see the component documentation for further details.

See also

- ▶ Camel CXF Component: `http://camel.apache.org/cxf`
- ▶ Apache CXF: `http://cxf.apache.org`
- ▶ The *Generating the service stubs from a WSDL* recipe
- ▶ The *Implementing a web service with a Camel route* recipe
- ▶ The *Handling web service faults* recipe

Handling web service faults

Sometimes errors happen during the processing of requests, and you want to return that error as a SOAP Fault message. This recipe will show you how to catch exceptions within your web service routes, and return an appropriate SOAP Fault.

Getting ready

This recipe assumes that you have a project with JAX-WS artifacts created as described in the *Generating the service stubs from a WSDL* recipe. To use the generated API, you need to include a dependency to that project in your build:

```
<dependency>
  <groupId>org.camelcookbook.examples</groupId>
  <artifactId>ws-payments-api</artifactId>
  <version>1.0-SNAPSHOT</version>
</dependency>
```

This recipe's example is based on `paymentService.wsdl`, whose `transferFunds` operation can return a fault of type `FaultMessage`:

```
<wsdl:portType name="Payment">
  <wsdl:operation name="transferFunds">
    <wsdl:input message="tns:TransferRequest"/>
    <wsdl:output message="tns:TransferResponse"/>
    <wsdl:fault name="fault" message="tns:FaultMessage"/>
  </wsdl:operation>
</wsdl:portType>
```

All source files for this recipe are located in the `ws-camel-routes` project in the `camel-cookbook-web-services` module. The Java code for this recipe is located in the `org.camelcookbook.ws.fault` package. The Spring XML files are located under `src/main/resources/META-INF/spring` and prefixed with `fault`.

How to do it...

In order to return a SOAP Fault from within a Camel route, perform the following steps:

1. Configure a web service endpoint, and process messages through a route as described in the *Implementing a web service with a Camel route* recipe.

2. Define a `FaultHandler` POJO that has a method to convert an `Exception` into a fault type, as defined in our WSDL:

```
import org.camelcookbook.ws.payment_service.FaultMessage;

public class FaultHandler {
  public FaultMessage createFault(Exception exception) {
    FaultMessage fault =
        new FaultMessage(exception.getMessage());
    fault.setStackTrace(exception.getStackTrace());
    return fault;
  }
}
```

3. Add an exception handling block that will convert a caught exception into the fault type using the `FaultHandler`.

   In the XML DSL, this is written as:

```
<route id="wsRoute">
  <from uri="cxf:bean:paymentServiceEndpoint"/>
  <onException>
    <exception>
      org.camelcookbook.ws.fault.TransferException
    </exception>
```

```
      <handled>
        <constant>true</constant>
      </handled>
      <setFaultBody>
        <method ref="faultHandler" method="createFault"/>
      </setFaultBody>
    </onException>
    <transform>
      <simple>${in.body[0]}</simple>
    </transform>
    <log message="request = ${body}"/>
  </route>
```

In the Java DSL, this same route is expressed as:

```
from(cxfUri)
    .id("wsRoute")
  .onException(TransferException.class)
    .handled(true)
    .setFaultBody(method(FaultHandler.class,
                      "createFault"))
  .end()
  .transform(simple("${in.body[0]}"))
  .log("response = ${body}");
```

How it works...

Camel has the concept of a **Fault**, or an irrecoverable error, that is expressed as a `boolean` fault flag on an exchange. Setting a fault body, as in the example above, implicitly sets this flag. The consuming component, referenced by `from`, can determine whether a fault has been raised and process it appropriately as part of its response processing at route completion time. In the case of the Camel CXF Component, if it sees that a fault message has been set on the exchange, it will convert and return that as a SOAP fault.

See *Chapter 7, Error Handling and Compensation*, for more details on how this recipe's `onException` block works.

There's more...

The `FaultHandler` method takes advantage of Camel's parameter binding capabilities. Camel will put the caught exception into an exchange property called `CamelExceptionCaught`. Camel's parameter binding will automatically map that property to a method parameter of type exception for any bean or method expression language call-out. Refer to *Chapter 3, Routing to Your Code*, for more details on Camel's parameter binding capabilities.

See also

▸ Camel CXF Component: `http://camel.apache.org/cxf`

▸ Apache CXF: `http://cxf.apache.org`

▸ The *Generating the service stubs from a WSDL* recipe

▸ The *Implementing a web service with a Camel route* recipe

Web service proxying

The proxying of requests through to backend services is a common use case for Camel. Decoupling the web service client from the backend service allows you to more easily move or change the backend, as you only need to update the proxy code, as opposed to all of the client systems that would otherwise use the backend directly. This technique is known as endpoint virtualization.

A proxy may also be used to impose a security or auditing layer, for use cases such as exposing the original service to new types of clients, for example, ones external to your company.

This recipe will show you the basics of creating a simple web service proxy in Camel.

Getting ready

This recipe assumes that you have a project with JAX-WS artifacts created as described in the *Generating the service stubs from a WSDL* recipe. To use the generated API, you need to include a dependency to that project in your build:

```
<dependency>
  <groupId>org.camelcookbook.examples</groupId>
  <artifactId>ws-payments-api</artifactId>
  <version>1.0-SNAPSHOT</version>
</dependency>
```

This recipe's example is based on `paymentService.wsdl`. For this example, we are assuming that the proxy and backend service have identical WSDL interfaces. If they were different, you would need to generate the JAX-WS artifacts for both WSDLs in separate projects.

All source files for this recipe are located in the `ws-camel-routes` project in the `camel-cookbook-web-services` module. The Java code for this recipe is located in the `org.camelcookbook.ws.proxy` package. The Spring XML files are located under `src/main/resources/META-INF/spring` and prefixed with `proxy`.

How to do it...

There are two main steps to this recipe: configure the frontend and backend Camel CXF endpoints, and specify a route from one to the other.

1. Configure the endpoints.

   In the XML DSL, within the Spring `beans` element, configure two `cxfEndpoints`; one for the frontend proxy, and the other for the backend service:

```
<cxf:cxfEndpoint
    id="paymentServiceProxy"
    address="http://host1:port1/paymentService"
    serviceClass="org.camelcookbook.ws.payment_service.Payment"/>

<cxf:cxfEndpoint
    id="paymentServiceBackend"
    address="http://host2:port2/paymentService"
    serviceClass="org.camelcookbook.ws.payment_service.Payment"/>
```

   In the Java DSL, we create endpoint URI strings for each of the endpoints:

```
final String paymentServiceProxyUri =
    "cxf:http://host1:port1/paymentService" +
    "?serviceClass=" +
    Payment.class.getCanonicalName());

final String paymentServiceBackendUri =
    "cxf:http://host2:port2/paymentService" +
    "?serviceClass=" +
    Payment.class.getCanonicalName());
```

2. Create the proxy route.

   In the XML DSL, this is defined as:

```
<route id="wsProxy">
  <from uri=
      "cxf:bean:paymentServiceProxy?dataFormat=PAYLOAD"/>
  <log message="request = ${body}"/>
  <to uri=
      "cxf:bean:paymentServiceBackend?dataFormat=PAYLOAD"/>
  <log message="response = ${body}"/>
</route>
```

In the Java DSL, the same route is expressed as:

```
from(paymentServiceProxyUri + "&dataFormat=PAYLOAD")
    .id("wsProxy")
  .log("request = ${body}")
  .to(paymentServiceBackendUri + "&dataFormat=PAYLOAD")
  .log("response = ${body}");
```

> We have used the dataFormat=PAYLOAD option to process the body of the SOAP message as XML. This isn't strictly necessary, but it can help improve throughput as the Camel CXF Component won't convert the message body from XML to POJO and back to XML.

How it works...

This recipe is effectively combining two previous recipes; the *Invoking a remote web service from Camel* recipe, and the *Implementing a web service with a Camel route* recipe into one with the difference being that the Camel route does not process the message, but rather relays it to the backend service.

Our recipe's example assumes that both frontend and backend services have identical WSDL interfaces. If they are different, you can update the endpoint configuration appropriately, specifically setting the serviceClass option to reference the correct JAX-WS WebService artifact. You can then perform any necessary transformations of the body in your proxy Camel route in order to bridge the two interfaces.

You may also need to remove or modify certain exchange headers, as headers set by Camel CXF from the consuming (from) endpoint may interfere with the behavior of the producing endpoint by overriding the default behavior specified by the endpoint URI. For example, if your backend has a different operation name from that of the proxy web service, you would need to update the operationName header before invoking the backend service.

There's more...

You can explicitly add an Error Handler to allow you to specify redelivery settings. Redelivery can be useful to deal with situations such as your backend service becoming temporarily unavailable due to normal maintenance or an upgrade. Camel can attempt to redeliver the message after a delay providing the appearance of continuous availability.

See also

▸ Camel CXF Component: `http://camel.apache.org/cxf`

▸ Apache CXF: `http://cxf.apache.org`

▸ The *Retrying an operation* recipe in *Chapter 7, Error Handling and Compensation*

▸ The *Generating the service stubs from a WSDL* recipe

▸ The *Invoking a remote web service from Camel* recipe

▸ The *Implementing a web service with a Camel route* recipe

Index

Symbols

@Autowired annotation 286
@Consume annotation 76, 87
@DynamicRouter annotation 76
@ManagedAttribute annotation 335
@ManagedOperation annotation 335
@ManagedResource annotation 335
@Produce annotation 89, 90
@RoutingSlip annotation 83

A

ActiveMQ Camel component
  URL 254
ActiveMQ Component 250
addComponent method 20
aggregated messages
  processing, in parallel 160-162
Aggregation Repository
  about 155
AggregationStrategy interface
  implementing, to Multicast EIP 60
Aggregator EIP 152
Apache Camel
  URL 227
Apache CXF project
  URL 377
applyHeaders() template method 299
assertMockEndpointsSatisfied()
      method 274, 286
asynchronous APIs
  working with 186-188
Asynchronous Processor 186, 189
Asynchronous Routing Engine 178
Atomikos TransactionsEssentials
  URL 269

A uto-mocking
auto-mocking
  endpoints 295

B

Bean Binding
  about 92
  unit testing 302, 303
Bindy Component 127
black-box testing 308
breakpoints
  setting, in routes 341-345

C

c3p0
  URL 237, 255
Camel
  about 16
  components, using 24-27
  embedding, in Spring application 21-23
  libraries 16
  routing logic failures, handling 226
  testing 271, 272
  transformation capabilities 109, 110
  using, in Java application 16-19
  versions 17
CamelBlueprintTestSupport class 292, 293
Camel Context
  URL 20
camelContext element 193
CamelContext interface 19
Camel contexts
  spanning, within single Java process 32-34
camel-cookbook-error module 193
camel-core library 24
Camel DSLs 47

Camel endpoint
  messages, sending to 88
Camel Exception Handling documentation
  URL 208
Camel File Component
  URL 236
Camel Hazelcast Component
  URL 234
Camel HBase Component
  URL 234
Camel Idempotent Consumer
  URL 234
Camel JMS component
  URL 254
Camel Parameter Binding
  about 97, 98
  working 99
Camel Redis Component
  URL 234
Camel Registry
  URL 20
Camel Request reply
  URL 254
Camel routes
  external properties, using 34-37
Camels Filtering 53
Camel SQL Component
  URL 234
camel-test library 273
CamelTestSupport class 274, 275
CamelTestSupport test class 299
Camel Transactional Client
  URL 241, 260
camel-xstream library
  used, for Java to JSON
        transformation 122-124
Cheese class 55
Comma-Separated Values. *See* **CSV**
completion actions
  defining 216-220
  defining, dynamically 221, 223
component scanning 23
Composed Message Processor 163
conditional retry
  about 202
  performing 202-204

configuration properties
  encrypting 348-351
configure() method 19
ConsumeMdb class 87
content
  enriching, with Content Enricher EIP 131-136
Content Based Router
  used, for message routing 48, 49
  working 50, 51
content based routing 48
Content Enricher EIP
  about 130
  used, for enriching content 131-136
copyFrom method 96
createApplicationContext() method 285
createCamelContext() method 277
createMessageBody() method 299
create() method 309
createRouteBuilder() method 274, 275, 278
Crypto Component
  about 358
  used, for decrypting message 358
  used, for encrypting message 358
  using, for signing messages 352
CSV
  parsing 128-130
custom Camel Processor
  about 93
  working 96
  writing 93, 95
custom data marshaller
  writing 100-103
custom data type converter
  writing 104-107
custom load balancing strategy 81
custom thread pools
  using 181, 182
cxf-codegen-plugin 381

D

database
  transaction, using with 236-240
Data Format Marshallers
  URL 104
Data Formats
  about 100, 110

implementing 100, 102
DataSetSupport class 299
Dead Letter Channel error handler
  about 195
  using 196
  working 197, 198
dead-letter queue (DLQ) 252
deep cloning method
  adding 56, 57
distributed system 225
doCatch( ) element 214
doTry doCatch doFinally exception handler
  about 192
  used, for error handling 212, 214
doTry DSL statement
  using 212
doTry() element 214
doTry exception handler
  about 215
  working 214
Dynamic Router
  about 74
  creating 75
  using 74
  working 76

E

EasyMock
  URL 273
endChoice() 51
end() method 145
endpoints
  auto-mocking 295, 296
  reusing 37, 38
Enhanced Spring Test option 286
error handlers
  about 192
  Dead Letter Channel 192
  default 192
  logging 192
error handling
  about 191
  performing, with doTry doCatch doFinally
      exception handler 212, 214
error handling mechanisms
  doTry doCatch doFinally 192

error handlers 192
  onException 192
errors
  handling, later 195-197
  logging 193, 194
exceptions
  catching 207, 208
  marking, as handled 210, 211
ExchangeHelper.isOutCapable() 96
expect-run-verify cycle 273
eXtended Architecture. *See* **XA**
external properties
  using, in Camel routes 34-37

F

failover strategy 79
file component 234, 235
FileIdempotentRepository 232
filter statement 52
fragments
  message, splitting into 144-146
  processing 163
fromRoute(id) method 309
from(startingEndpoint) syntax 309
future.get() method 179

G

getBlueprintDescriptor() method 292

H

HazelcastIdempotentRepository 233

I

idempotency
  within transaction 254-259
Idempotent Consumer EIP 227
inOnly DSL statement 70
InOnly processor 88
InOut processor 88
in-route XML transformation
  performing, with XQuery 112-116
integrations
  debugging, Log component used 318, 319
  developing, issues 226

intervals
   messages, aggregating with 159, 160
isMockEndpointsAndSkip() method 296
isUseAdviceWith() method 306
isUseDebugger() method 343

J

Jasypt Component
   about 348
   using 348
Java
   routes, testing 272-276
Java application
   Camel, using in 16-19
javac command 16
java command 16
Java DSL 19, 192
Java Management Extensions. *See* **JMX**
Java method
   using, as Predicate 91
Java Open Transaction Manager (JOTM)
   URL 269
Java process
   Camel contexts, spanning within 32-34
Java, to JSON tranformation
   performing, camel-xstream library
      used 122-124
Java, to XML tranformation
   performing, JAXB Camel Data Format used
      120, 122
Java Transaction API (JTA) 260
JAXB Camel Data Format
   used, for Java to XML
      transformation 120, 122
JdbcMessageIdRepository 232
JMX
   about 314
   attributes, adding 334-336
   configuring 328, 330
   disabling 326, 327
   monitoring, Camel used 337-340
   operations, adding 334-336
JSON, to Java tranformation
   performing, camel-xstream library
      used 122-124

JSON, to XML transformation
   performing,XML JSON component
      used 124-127

L

least recently used (LRU) 233
Load Balancer EIP
   about 77
   using 77
   working 78-80
Log component
   used, for debugging integrations 318
   used, for reporting throughput 320
Log Enterprise Integration Pattern (EIP) 315
LoggingErrorHandler function
   used, for logging errors 193, 194

M

marshal statement 101
matches() method 309
MemoryIdempotentRepository 232
message
   decrypting, Crypto Component used 358-361
   encrypting, Crypto Component used 358-361
   splitting, into fragments 144-146, 163
message body
   transforming, external XSLT resource used
      116-119
   transforming, Simple Expression Language
      used 110, 111
message consumption
   increasing, through multiple endpoint
      consumers 172-174
message content transformation 110
Message Exchange Pattern (MEP) 55
message flow throughput
   reporting, Log component used 320, 321
message routing
   content based routing 48-50
   dynamic routing 74
   Load Balancer EIP 77
   Multicast EIP 59
   one-way Route 72
   Recipient List EIP 64
   Request-Response route 70

Routing Slip 81
Throttler EIP 67
unwanted messages, filtering 52
Wire Tap EIP 54

messages
aggregating, with intervals 159, 160
aggregating, with timeouts 157, 158
digital signatures, verifying 356, 357
mapping, to method parameters 97-99
normalizing, into common XML
    format 136-141
re-aggregating 166, 168
routing, to Java method 86, 87
sending, to Camel endpoint 88, 89
signing digitally, camel-crypto component.
    used 352-355
splitting 166

Message Translator pattern 109
messaging
transaction, using with 248-254

method parameters
messages, mapping to 97

MockEndpoint
about 279
assertions 279
expectations 279
features 280

**MockEndpoint.assertIsSatisfied() utility
    method 287**
mock endpoints
used, for defining test responses 281-283
used, for verifying routing logic 278-281

multicast DSL statement 59
Multicast EIP
about 59
AggregationStrategy interface,
    implementing 60, 61
exception, dealing with 62, 63
using 59
working 60

multicast().stopOnException() flag 62

N

names
setting, for elements 331-334

negative acknowledgement (NACK) 252

Normalizer EIP
used, for normalizing messages into common
    XML format 136-141

O

onCompletion usage
rules 218

one-way route
response, requesting from endpoint 72, 73

onException exception handler 192
operation
retrying 199, 201

OSGi Blueprint
routes, testing 290-292

P

parallel processing
about 171, 172
asynchronous APIs, working with 186-189
custom thread pools, using 181, 182
load, spreading within route 175-177
message consumption, increasing through
    multiple endpoint consumers 172-174
request, routing asynchronously 178-180
thread pool profiles, using 184, 185

Parameter Binding
about 97
annotations 100

Persistent ID 293
Pipeline 53
Plain Old Java Object (POJO) 302
POJO Consuming 86
POJO Producing
about 88
working 89

PojoSR 290
predicate
about 48
writing, as Java method 91-93

process() method 97
Processor class
implementing 56

Processor interface
using 283

Processors
about 302

unit testing 302, 303
ProducerTemplate 90

Q

Quality of Service (QoS) 231

R

random strategy 78
recipientList DSL statement 64
Recipient List EIP
about 64
used, for routing message 64-66
using 64
redelivery attempt
about 192
customizing 205, 206
redelivery decision
making, Simple Expression
Language used 202
related messages
aggregating 152-157
remote web service
invoking, from Camel 382
Request-Response route
about 70
one-way message, sending 70, 71
Resequencer EIP 298
responses
gathering 163, 164
RetryCustomProcessor function 205
round-robin strategy 78
route behavior
validating 297-301
Route Builder
URL 20
RouteBuilder class 272
RouteBuilder.configure() method 197, 341
RouteBuilder interface 298
route policy 45
routes
connecting, asynchronously 29-31
routes, defined in Java
testing 272-277
routes, defined in OSGi Blueprint
testing 290-293

routes, defined in Spring
testing 283-286
route shutdown
controlling 42-45
route specific error handlers
setting 195
route specific onException handlers
setting 209
route startup
controlling 42-45
routes, with fixed endpoints
testing, AOP used 304, 305
testing, conditional events used 307-310
routing logic
duplicate invocation, preventing 227-233
reusing, by connecting routes 27-29
reusing, through template routes 38-41
verifying, mock endpoints used 278, 279
Routing Slip
about 81
using 82
working 82
routingSlip statement 82

S

sayHello() method 105
security
configuration properties, encrypting 348-351
SEDA 31
service provider interfaces (SPIs) 19
service stubs
generating, from WSDL 378
setResultWaitTime() 301
Simple Expression Language
used, for making redelivery decision 202-204
used, for transforming message
body 110, 111
SLF4J logging library 194
SOAP web services
approaches, for building 378
contract-first web service development 378
interacting with 377
Java service, building 378
split block 145
split messages
processing, in parallel 150-152

split statement 144
Splitter EIP
  about 144
  used, for splitting message into
       fragments 144-146
Spring
  routes, testing 283-287
Spring application
  about 287, 289
  Camel, embedding in 21-23
  PropertyPlaceholderConfigurer
       configuration 287
Spring Security
  used, for authentication 370-374
  used, for authorization 370-374
Staged Event-Driven Architecture. *See* SEDA
steps
  including within route 315, 317
sticky load-balancing strategy 79

T

template routes
  routing logic, reusing through 38-41
thread pool profiles
  using 184, 185
Throttler EIP
  about 67, 69
  messages, restricting 67
  using 67, 68
  working 68
timeouts
  messages, aggregating with 157, 158
topic strategy 80
tracer
  configuring 322
  enabling 322, 324
  working 323
transacted DSL element
  PROPAGATION_MANDATORY 240
  PROPAGATION_NESTED 241
  PROPAGATION_NEVER 241
  PROPAGATION_NOT_SUPPORTED 240
  PROPAGATION_REQUIRED 240
  PROPAGATION_REQUIRES_NEW 240
  PROPAGATION_SUPPORTS 240

transaction
  about 226
  scope, limiting 241-244
  using, with database 236-240
  using, with messaging 248-254
transactional file consumption
  performing 234-236
transaction rollback
  controlling 245-247
transform statement 110
Type Converter 110

U

unmarshal statement 101
unwanted messages
  filtering 52, 53
useOverridePropertiesWithConfigAdmin() 294

V

versions 17

W

weave..() method 307
weaving 306
web service proxy
  creating 395, 396
web services
  faults, handling 392-394
  implementing, with Camel route 385-388
  multiple web service operations, promoting
       within route 389-391
  remote web service, invoking from
       Camel 382, 383
  requests, proxying 395, 397
  service stubs, generating from
       WSDL 378-381
weighted load balancing strategies 80
whenAnyExchangeReceived(Processor)
       method 282
whenDone(number) method 309
whenReceived(int) method 309
white-box approach 308
wireTap DSL statement 55

Wire Tap EIP
about 54
used, for sending copy of message 54
using 54
working 55
wireTap statement 54

X

XA 260
XA Exposed
URL 269
XA transaction
setting up, over multiple transactional
resources 260-268
XML DSL 22, 192
XML encryption operations
performing, Apache Santaurio library used
367-369
XML JSON component
used, for XML to JSON tranformation 124-127

XML message
decrypting 366
encrypting 364, 365
exporting 363, 364
XML messages
splitting 146-149
XML, to Java tranformation
performing, JAXB Camel Data Format
used 120, 122
XML, to JSON transformation
performing, XML JSON component
used 124-127
XQuery Expression
used, for performing in-route XML
transformation 112-116
XSLT resource
used, for transforming message
body 116-119

Thank you for buying
Apache Camel Developer's Cookbook

About Packt Publishing

Packt, pronounced 'packed', published its first book "*Mastering phpMyAdmin for Effective MySQL Management*" in April 2004 and subsequently continued to specialize in publishing highly focused books on specific technologies and solutions.

Our books and publications share the experiences of your fellow IT professionals in adapting and customizing today's systems, applications, and frameworks. Our solution-based books give you the knowledge and power to customize the software and technologies you're using to get the job done. Packt books are more specific and less general than the IT books you have seen in the past. Our unique business model allows us to bring you more focused information, giving you more of what you need to know, and less of what you don't.

Packt is a modern, yet unique publishing company, which focuses on producing quality, cutting-edge books for communities of developers, administrators, and newbies alike. For more information, please visit our website: www.PacktPub.com.

About Packt Enterprise

In 2010, Packt launched two new brands, Packt Enterprise and Packt Open Source, in order to continue its focus on specialization. This book is part of the Packt Enterprise brand, home to books published on enterprise software – software created by major vendors, including (but not limited to) IBM, Microsoft and Oracle, often for use in other corporations. Its titles will offer information relevant to a range of users of this software, including administrators, developers, architects, and end users.

Writing for Packt

We welcome all inquiries from people who are interested in authoring. Book proposals should be sent to author@packtpub.com. If your book idea is still at an early stage and you would like to discuss it first before writing a formal book proposal, contact us; one of our commissioning editors will get in touch with you.

We're not just looking for published authors; if you have strong technical skills but no writing experience, our experienced editors can help you develop a writing career, or simply get some additional reward for your expertise.

Apache Tomcat 7 Essentials

ISBN: 978-1-84951-662-4   Paperback: 294 pages

Learn Apache Tomcat 7 step-by-step through a particular approach, achieving a wide vision of enterprise middleware along with building your own middleware servers, and administrating 24x7x365

1. Readymade solution for web technologies for migration/hosting and supporting environment for Tomcat 7

2. Tips, tricks, and best practices for web hosting solution providers for Tomcat 7

3. Content designed with practical approach and plenty of illustrations

Java EE 7 Developer Handbook

ISBN: 978-1-84968-794-2   Paperback: 634 pages

Develop professional applications in Java EE 7 with this essential reference guide

1. Learn about local and remote service endpoints, containers, architecture, synchronous and asynchronous invocations, and remote communications in a concise reference

2. Understand the architecture of the Java EE platform and then apply the new Java EE 7 enhancements to benefit your own business-critical applications

3. Learn about integration test development on Java EE with Arquillian Framework and the Gradle build system

Please check **www.PacktPub.com** for information on our titles

Java 7 JAX-WS Web Services

ISBN: 978-1-84968-720-1   Paperback: 64 pages

A practical, focused mini book for creating Web Services in Java 7

1. Develop Java 7 JAX-WS web services using the NetBeans IDE and Oracle GlassFish server

2. End-to-end application which makes use of the new clientjar option in JAX-WS wsimport tool

3. Packed with ample screenshots and practical instructions

Apache Solr 4 Cookbook

ISBN: 978-1-78216-132-5   Paperback: 328 pages

Over 100 recipes to make Apache Solr faster, more reliable, and return better results

1. Learn how to make Apache Solr search faster, more complete, and comprehensively scalable

2. Solve performance, setup, configuration, analysis, and query problems in no time

3. Get to grips with, and master, the new exciting features of Apache Solr 4

Please check **www.PacktPub.com** for information on our titles

ation can be obtained
ng.com
5